bauhaus: CRUCIBLE OF MODERNISM

Give me a life, and I will soon make you a culture out of it.

—*Nietzsche*

bauhaus

| CRUCIBLE OF
| MODERNISM

ELAINE S. HOCHMAN
FOREWORD BY DORE ASHTON

Fromm International
New York

to my husband

All rights reserved under International and Pan-American copyright Convention. Published in the United
States by Fromm International Publishing Corporation, New York.

First Edition, 1997
LIBRARY OF CONGRESS CATALOGING-IN-PUBLICATION DATA

Hochman, Elaine S.
    Bauhaus : crucible of modernism / Elaine S. Hochman. — 1st Fromm International ed.
      p. cm.
    Includes bibliographical references and index.
    ISBN 0-88064-175-4
    1. Bauhaus — History.   I. Title.
N332. G33B4455 1997
707' . 1 ' 143155 — dc21

96-37073
CIP

10 9 8 7 6 5 4 3 2 1

Manufactured in the United States of America

Contents

Acknowledgments

A book such as this cannot be written without the help of many persons and institutions. In New York I owe thanks to Philip Johnson and former Bauhaus students Walter Allner and Eva Weininger, who so generously shared their recollections with me. I am also indebted to my former professor the late Henry-Russell Hitchcock, whose conversations, while long preceding my involvement in this book, afforded me benefit of his unique insight and scholarship into early modernism. I am particularly grateful to Rona Roob, archivist at the Museum of Modern Art and its library; the library of the Metropolitan Museum of Art; Avery Library at Columbia University; and the New York Public Library. Catherine Stover at the Archives of American Art and Vivian Barnett at the Guggenheim Museum also provided invaluable assistance.

In Boston my research was greatly facilitated by Joyce Tyler at the Archives of American Art; and at Harvard University by Emmy Dana at the Busch-Reisinger Museum and Rodney Denis at the university's Houghton Library. I am especially grateful to T. Lux Feininger for taking the time to share his reminiscences with me. Kitty Gormley, the archivist at the Architects' Collaborative, also kindly assisted me.

In Berlin Peter Hahn, the director, and Margarete Droste, Sabine Hartmann, Barbara Stolle, and Silvia Krankemann of the Bauhaus-Archiv kindly and generously imparted valuable information to me, as well as granted me access to their unique archive. My appreciation also goes to the late Julius Posener and the librarians at the Zentralarchiv of the Staatliche Museen, the Staatsbibliothek, the Kunstbibliothek, and the Landesarchiv.

In Weimar I am grateful to Christian Schädlich, Klaus-Jürgen Winkler, Konrad Püschel, and Folke Dietsch for sharing their wisdom with me. Gitta Günther at the Stadtarchiv, Volker Wahl at the Thüringisches Hauptstaatsarchiv, and Reiner Krauss at the Kunstsammlungen must also be thanked. So too must the archivists at the city's Hochschule für Architektur und Bauwesen, and Stadtmuseum.

In Dessau I am indebted to Rolf Kuhn, the director, and Lutz Schöbe and Wolfgang Thöner of the Dessau Bauhaus. Ulla Jablonowski of the Stadtarchiv also facilitated my research.

Thanks must be expressed to Karin Frank von Maur at the Oskar Schlemmer–Archiv in the Staatsgalerie in Stuttgart and Evelyn Brockhoff at the Deutsches Architekturmuseum in Frankfurt.

I am grateful to Nancy Shawcross at the Charles Patterson Van Pelt Library, the University of Pennsylvania; Brent Sverdloff at the Getty Center for Art History; and the librarians and archivists at the Fonds Kandinsky, Musée National d'Art Moderne, Centre Georges Pompidou in Paris, and the Niedersächsisches Hauptstaatsarchiv in Hannover.

For help in translating the German documents I thank Simon Srebrny, Vincent Trasov, Stefan Lippert, Ulf Fischbech, Ingeborg von Zitzewitz, Mary Horn, and the late Martha Humphreys.

My further thanks go to my editor at Fromm, Fred Jordan, for his judicious guidance; to Stephanie Golden for her help in pulling together the manuscript; and to my agent, Robin Straus, for her unfailing perseverence and support.

Lastly, I must thank my husband Raymond for his encouragement and endless patience. He has truly made this work possible.

Preface

When the Russian writer Ilya Ehrenburg
recalled his first visit to the Bauhaus in
1923, he reminded his readers that the Bauhaus had a difficult beginning
in very troubled times. "It's destiny was not bound to esthetic theories,"
he wrote in 1927, "but to ballots deposed in urns by the philistine
Thuringians." Eventually, the philistines succeeded in dislodging the
Bauhaus from Weimar, and in 1925, Gropius had to reinvest his institution in Dessau, where once again the philistines swarmed angrily.

It is strange that although Ehrenburg recognized the fundamental
problem of the Bauhaus as early as 1927, very few others, apart from the
author of this book, have considered the rapidly shifting fortunes of the
Bauhaus, and its programs, in light of the turbulent social and political
circumstances. All of Gropius's artful dodges; his repeated attempts to
persuade the legislators that the Bauhauslers were straight arrows and
mostly Aryan; his projections of different sets of ideals year by year in
order to elude the official bloodhounds; and his ambivalent relations
with the captains of industry, were to prove of little ostensible avail.
Eventually the Bauhaus, as an institution, collapsed in dreadful circumstances similar to those in which it was born. But the Bauhaus as a vision
could not be destroyed by historical contingencies. Despite Gropius's
sometimes bewildering feints as director of the volatile school, his edu-

cational instincts prevailed. The broad and radical studio methods developed at the Bauhaus are still with us. Anyone familiar with the hundreds of art departments in American universities that burgeoned after the Second World War will recognize, in the so-called Foundation courses, the imprint of the Bauhaus.

In most accounts of the short life of the Bauhaus—it lasted exactly as long as the imperfect Weimar Republic—there are few attempts to sort out the complex factors that probably influenced Gropius's tremendous swings in his governing educational ideology. What began in 1919 as a romantic "spiritual revolution," with all the vague and Utopian fervor Gropius could muster, shifted rapidly to a practical program. By 1922, Gropius was asking the workshops at the Bauhaus to produce "prototypes for mass production." As Hochman proves, such decisions were not taken solely for internal educational reasons. They were all too often direct responses to pressures emanating from those whom the ballot boxes had authorized to be persecutors. Yet, not even the machinations of the dogged officials can account fully for the Bauhaus's numerous contradictions and shifts in policy. The Bauhaus, like most institutions founded in the quicksands of postwar Europe, was caught up in the competing ideologies epitomized by the Russian revolution. On the one hand there were artists fired by the communal ideal of collectivism, and on the other, there were artists investing the individual with power to transform society. These contrasting ideals could be found all over Europe and even in America, in the interwar period. The Bauhaus merely endowed them with unusual acuity thanks to the exceptional quality of its leaders.

The issues of the individual artist versus the collective were fought over at a high level within the confines of the Bauhaus, and would continue in a greatly muted form in its afterlife. One of the strengths of Hochman's text is its attention to the migration of Bauhaus notables to the United States where the ground had been prepared by Alfred H. Barr, Jr. in his famous 1938 Bauhaus exhibition at the Museum of Modern Art. What had been a roiled mix of social and political, as well as aesthetic, issues was purified into an exclusively formal approach in which historical contingencies played almost no role. In America, which had had its own interwar political and social crises, many institutions were all too ready to evade historical implications. One of America's foremost intellectuals, Meyer Schapiro, had early identified Barr's reluctance to acknowledge any but formal and aesthetic issues in the history of artistic modernism. In a celebrated essay, "The Nature of Abstract Art," published in the January-March issue of *The Marxist Quarterly*, 1937, he had taken Barr to task for his essentially non-historical point of view, and for presenting modern art "as an internal immanent process among the artists." While immanence is certainly an endemic element in the history of art, it is just as certainly threatened or modified by other elements, as this book proves beyond a doubt.

By putting the Bauhaus back into its historical matrix, Hochman has forced us to recognize the fragility of all worthy utopian ideals, and the difficulty in maintaining a radical institution. Gropius was forced by circumstances to change the rules of the game constantly, sometimes to the detriment of the institution. No amount of compromise, however (as the last director of the Bauhaus, Mies van der Rohe discovered), could save the Bauhaus, at least as an institution. The questions subliminally posed in this book are perhaps impossible to find answers for, but are nonetheless of great importance to the interpretation of twentieth century history: What might have happened if Gropius had not gone to the Thuringian authorities and disingenuously defended his institution as pure of "alien" elements? What would have happened if he had not bent to the pressure of local politics and banned all political activity within the Bauhaus? It is obvious that all his special pleading did not placate the enemy. Once again, historical contingency works its wiles. By succumbing to political pressure and purifying itself of social and political ideologies, the Bauhaus helped to create its own image as a formal movement divested of social and political implications. But fatefully, the image and the reality did not coincide, as Hochman demonstrates.

But of course, the story goes on. There are just as many shifts in art history as there are in just plain history, and today, we see another extreme which recounts twentieth-century artistic events purely in terms of social and political forces, leaving out what Schapiro identified as the immanent history of art itself. What is so apparent in the story of the Bauhaus is that individual artists—Klee, Kandinsky, Schlemmer, Feininger, Moholy-Nagy, Albers—managed to subsist intact, or nearly intact, even within the troubled milieu of the Bauhaus, and even when faced with powerful external forces. At the same time, the institution, wracked with dissension both internally and externally, could not maintain itself in a steady state. Gropius's original dream of a communal and harmonious ensemble never really materialized, although in its stead an experimental mini-cosmos emerged in which the vitality of its parts contributed to an ideal that has somehow been sustained for almost eighty years. Hochman's Bauhaus history restores what has been so sedulously avoided in most books on the Bauhaus, and in doing so, keeps alive important questions that must be faced by artists, educators,and historians.

—Dore Ashton

Introduction

To look on this architecture simply as architecture, art for art's sake, so to speak, is to miss its point. . . . It has to be understood as a new way of living, a new assessment of what life is for and how it should be lived.
—*Count Harry Kessler to André Gide about modern German architecture*

The Bauhaus is the most celebrated artistic institution of our time. Little in our lives has not been influenced by it, from what we read and wear to how we live. The artists associated with the Bauhaus comprise a virtual Who's Who of modern art and architecture. Among others, these include Bauhaus founder Walter Gropius; Ludwig Mies van der Rohe, its last director; Wassily Kandinsky; Lyonel Feininger; Johannes Itten; Oskar Schlemmer; Paul Klee; Josef Albers; László Moholy-Nagy; and Marcel Breuer.

Founded in Germany in the tumultuous time following World War I, the Bauhaus was the place where, in microcosm, the ideas that would dominate art in the twentieth century clashed and became defined. The Bauhaus was, so to speak, a crucible of new ideas, an incubator of what has come to be known as modernity.

This is not to say that the Bauhaus "invented" modernism. Already in the nineteenth century, many individuals had come to believe that traditional art no longer satisfied the demands of an increasingly industrialized society. But these feelings were generally disorganized, a mere rumbling of discontent. Only at the turn of the century did this impulse, enhanced by rapid developments in technology and science, crystallize into a radical new approach to art, apparent in the works of such diverse artists as Frank Lloyd Wright, Stravinsky, Picasso, and Adolf Loos, to name only a few.

The collapse of the established world order that followed World War I created a totally new sense of the individual's place in the world. Gropius realized this and set up the Bauhaus in the hope of finding an artistic response to the radically altered situation.

But this drastically new Europe that resulted after World War I also ushered in an age of extremism that sought to replace the now vanished verities of the past with those of its own. This extremism, which has so marked our century, was the other side of the coin, so to speak, of the radical social and political upheavals to which modernism proposed artistic solutions. What resulted was ideological warfare between Left and Right; and in this, too, the Bauhaus was a prominent participant. In fact, ideology determined what the Bauhaus said and what it created. (It also determined its ultimate expulsion by the Nazis in 1933.)

The Bauhaus was at the cultural center of Weimar Germany, itself the hub—both geographically and ideologically—of two conflicting views of human life (socialism/communism versus fascism). These two ideologies confronted each other bitterly and totally in Germany during the Weimar Republic, ending in the victory of Hitler and the subsequent world plunge into cataclysmic war. The battles between these warring ideologies were intensely focused and especially contentious at the Bauhaus. Through the Bauhaus we witness the dreams of a particular country at a particular moment that somehow became part of the century's nightmare. Its drama became ours.

The victory of the Allies at the end of World War II dealt a deathblow to fascism. But political confrontation continued, now between communism and the capitalist West. This too was most dramatically evident in a Germany split into two parts. It was not until 1989 that the division of the world into two warring camps came to an end, and once again it was in Germany where the event was made most dramatically manifest, with the collapse of the Berlin Wall.

The division of Germany into East and West had the effect of placing Weimar and Dessau, the two cities where the Bauhaus had been located during the fourteen years of its existence, behind the Iron Curtain. With the school's archives essentially out-of-bounds to scholars and investigators from the West, the theme of the Bauhaus as crucible of modernism remained largely unexplored. This ideological aspect of the Bauhaus has been especially neglected in America, where the school has most often been viewed as a purely aesthetic enterprise, a paradigm of a universal and technologically inspired modernism whose reductivist principles were applied to everything, from the design of coffeepots to that of skyscrapers. To a large extent this idea came from Alfred H. Barr Jr., who became the first director of New York's Museum of Modern Art in 1929 at the age of twenty-seven.

While the difference between America's perception of the Bauhaus and what the school had been in Germany has long been known, the collapse of the Berlin Wall and the resulting access to previously secluded archives in what once was East Germany has allowed us to more precisely understand its nature and degree. What emerges from these newly examined archives is a far different Bauhaus than the one to which we have become accustomed. For the first time we can see the Bauhaus not through the eyes of its usual apologists, but through those of its contemporaries, who—as the documents make clear—looked at the school less for its art (as we have tended to view it) than for the political and cultural connotations they believed this art represented.

This aspect of the school has long been recognized by the Bauhaus's contemporaries and later observers. The painter Oskar Schlemmer, a member of the school's faculty, referred to the Bauhaus as mirroring "the fragmentation of the German people and of the period." The Swiss architect Hannes Meyer, director of the school after Gropius, spoke of the Bauhaus as being "[a] true child of the German Republic." Even the school's opponents saw it as a "microcosm" of what was happening in the Reich. In 1926 Gropius himself acknowledged the Bauhaus's debt to "the circumstances and means of our time." Nearly fifty years later his wife Ise—who almost always echoed his sentiments—declared that any complete study of the Bauhaus would have to take into account the social, political, and economic pressures that were brought to bear on the school, as well as its relationship to the Weimar Republic's broad cultural scene.

Later critics have noted this link too between the Bauhaus and its times.

The cultural historian Peter Gay specifically cited the Bauhaus in referring to "the continuous and tense" interaction that existed between Weimar culture and its politics. George Baird, a former Bauhaus student, commented about the "curious and persistent" parallels that existed between the school and the Weimar Republic. Art historian Frank Whitford wrote that the Bauhaus was being shaped by the very pressures against which the Weimar Republic also struggled to survive.

What has been missing from general view for more than fifty years is not so much an awareness of the Bauhaus's interaction with its society, but an account of the school's daily affairs that could verify and confirm it. The Bauhaus that emerges from these long-secluded documents—personal and official correspondence, confidential ministerial reports, memoranda, minutes of faculty and legislative meetings, newspaper articles, and diary accounts—is one that has never been seen before in the West. We discover a Bauhaus whose glass walls reflect our art as much as our times.

1.

Youth, War, and Revolution

Gropius is the Bauhaus.

—*Oskar Schlemmer*

Adolph Georg Walter Gropius, founder of the Bauhaus, was born in Berlin on May 18, 1883. He was the third child and first son of Walther and Manon Scharnweber Gropius, and the heir of long and distinguished lineages on both sides of his family.

Two distinct strains—military and architectural—ran through his father's side. Gropius's uncles, upright and conservative East Prussian landowners and soldiers, were fiercely proud of their military tradition. Several members of the family, including his father, had fought in the Franco-Prussian War. His uncle Felix, a veteran of that war, would again serve his country in World War I at the age of seventy-five. Walter's cousin Richard, a member of the military since 1863 and still a member of the armed forces at age seventy-five, kept a much-treasured record book listing the battles, ranks, and military decorations of generations of Gropiuses. To a young, sensitive boy such as Walter, his family's military accomplishments must have seemed formidable. His family's architectural legacy, however, was no less impressive and daunting.

The artistic and architectural line of the family began in the late eighteenth century with Gropius's great-grandfather Johann Carl Christian Gropius and his two brothers, Wilhelm Ernst and Georg Christian. Renowned for its own artistic achievements, the family also prided itself on its long and intimate association with one of Germany's greatest artistic figures, the famed nineteenth-century architect Karl Friedrich Schinkel. The Gropius family helped launch Schinkel's career. Schinkel, a frequent guest in the Gropius home, taught drawing and painting to Wilhelm Ernst's son Carl Wilhelm and inspired Carl's son Martin to become an architect. Although Martin was seventeen years old when Schinkel died, he continued under the master's architectural influence by pursuing his architectural studies with one of Schinkel's disciples and went on to become an internationally famous architect.

In 1865, in collaboration with Heino Schmieden, Martin Gropius opened his own architectural firm—Gropius and Schmieden—which designed, among other buildings, the Leipzig Gewandhaus and the Decorative Arts Museum in Berlin, today known as the Martin Gropius Building. Martin was a prominent member of Berlin's educational and cultural circles. In 1877 he was elected to the prestigious Prussian Academy of Art, a membership later denied to his great-nephew. The liaison between the Gropius family and Schinkel would be treasured and maintained through the generations. Walter was christened in Schinkel's Friedrichswerdersche Kirche, in whose cemetery the great architect was buried, even though it was not the family church.

Such an awesome architectural heritage had apparently overwhelmed Gropius's father, Walther, described as a timid and depressed man. Thirty-six years old when his son was born, he had already abandoned an architectural career, becoming instead a civil servant in the Prussian State Building Department. He died in 1911, one year after his son opened his own architectural office.

Hardly outstanding by any standard, the elder Gropius's architectural career may have contributed to his son's enduring lack of confidence in his designing abilities. "G[ropius] is always dissatisfied with . . . his talent," observed Walter's second wife, Ise. While such artistic doubts are not uncommon among even the greatest artists, Gropius remained convinced that his particular strength lay more in his ability to conceptualize—to see the whole—rather than in his architectural talent, which he considered to be "merely adequate." What he achieved architecturally, Gropius ascribed less to innate ability than to his "iron willpower," as he put it, a trait that would be particularly evident at the Bauhaus.

Gropius's mother, Manon, encouraged her son's enduring faith in the possibility of social and spiritual progress. She was described as tolerant, frank, and liberal, qualities probably derived from her Huguenot background. She descended from French émigrés who had sought refuge in Frederick the Great's liberalized Prussia in the beginning of the eighteenth century. Both her father and grandfather enjoyed distinguished, progressive public careers. Her grandfather Johann Christian Friedrich (1770–1882) was a city counselor and an adviser to Baron Karl vom und zum Stein, a Prussian reformer. Her father, August George, was a district counselor in Berlin. According to those who knew her, Gropius's mother was lively, progressive, culturally alert, and, in Gropius's words, indestructibly kind.

Manon Gropius also provided artistic inspiration and emotional support to her son, acting as an important counterweight to his father's more stolid and conservative line. Another son she bore four years after Gropius, Georg, died in 1904 at the age of seventeen. This left Gropius the focus of family attention, mostly from its female members: his sisters, mother, and paternal grandmother, Luise Hönig Gropius, to whom he was particularly attached. He was, as his grandmother put it in a letter to him on his twenty-second birthday in 1905, "his loved ones' pride and joy."

Young Walter was the particular light of his mother's life. She once characterized herself as having been "battered by a cruel life," not surprising for someone married to a weak, depressive husband who had suffered the loss of a son. She seems to have set her mind on her son Walter succeeding where her husband had failed, sustaining him when his interest flagged in his architectural studies. It was she who called his attention to illustrations of Frank Lloyd Wright's work in American magazines and the important Wasmuth publication produced in Germany in 1910; and accompanied him to the Prussian Academy of Art's exhibition of Wright's drawings in the spring of that year. Her devotion to her son seems to have been reciprocated. In heartfelt letters written to her until her death in 1933, Gropius confided his every aspiration, achievement, and moment of self-doubt.

■

A grammar-school reading of Julius Caesar's *The Conquest of Gaul* first stimulated Gropius's architectural leanings. The incisively described details of how the Roman leader had built a bridge across the Rhine inspired him to draw up plans and build a scale model. An epic technical achievement that utilized the river's current to keep the structure in place, Caesar's creation touched a technological chord in the young Gropius. Yet once he decided to become an architect, Gropius had difficulty pursuing the usual academic path to his chosen profession. He registered as a student at Munich's Technische Hochschule in 1903, but dropped out after one semester. Instead he apprenticed himself to a Berlin architectural firm, Solf and Wichards, known to his family.

In 1904, with an eye perhaps on adding to the family's military luster, Gropius, then twenty-one, chose to fulfill his compulsory military service with the elite Fifteenth Hussars Regiment, a unit dominated by Junker officers and aristocratic cadets. He was one of the few bourgeois sons admitted to the regiment—most probably through his family's military connections—and he felt enormously flattered to be part of this elite corps. But his fellow cadets snubbed him, and Gropius suffered acutely. His only pleasure seemed to come from his fine horsemanship. In letters to his mother he spoke with pride of being able to control difficult horses without stirrups, for which he received his commanding officers' praise.

Apart from Gropius's riding skills, which apparently helped gain him promotion to sergeant in 1905 and sergeant major the following year, he seems to have left little mark on the regiment. Gropius was shocked when his request in 1907 to participate in the officer training program for shorter periods was turned down. Bitterly disappointed, he was convinced he was rejected because of class discrimination. His military service had added little to his family's prized and otherwise impeccable record, and he described himself as feeling "shamefully insulted." Still, he retained the bearing of a Prussian cavalry officer—and his fine horsemanship—throughout his life. Many years later he would be described as "the last Prussian architect, incorruptible, with [a] strong, straight-ahead character, charging forward without deviation."

Disillusioned by his military performance, Gropius turned his full attention to studying architecture at the Königliche Technische Hochschule in

Berlin-Charlottenburg. But here too he encountered impediments, these more serious than the class prejudices he had experienced in the military. To his dismay Gropius discovered he could no longer draw; not even "the simplest thing . . . not even a straight line," he confessed to his mother.

> It seems to be a physical disability because I immediately get a cramp in my hand, break off the pencil points, and have to rest after five minutes. During my darkest hours I hadn't thought it could be so bad.

Gropius did not let this disability deter his architectural studies, as might be expected. For someone to even consider being an architect when they can't draw is like a tone-deaf person attempting composing. Both these arts require one to conjure up an image or tone and transpose it directly onto paper. A composer must write down the sounds he "hears." An architect, involved in creating a three-dimensional work, must sketch out his basic ideas, even in a rudimentary form, working out problems from varying perspectives with his pencil or charcoal as he seeks to evolve a form. An architect does not have to be a master draftsman, although two of Gropius's peers, Le Corbusier and Mies van der Rohe, were. So too were such important architects as Otto Wagner and Theodor Fischer, and those who were also trained as painters, like Joseph Olbrich, Richard Riemerschmid, and Gropius's future boss, Peter Behrens. Of course, so too was Schinkel, who was adept at both painting and architecture.

Gropius's collaborators have confirmed during interviews with Winfried Nerdinger, the architectural historian and Gropius specialist, that he rarely lifted a pencil to sketch. A Gropius design would emerge from verbal exchanges. How close the resulting building would come to Gropius's ideas depended greatly on both his ability to say precisely what he wanted and the talent of his collaborator to translate his words into architectural concepts—a hit-or-miss arrangement that accounts for the uneven quality of Gropius's architectural projects. Collaboration would be the hallmark of Gropius's various careers: with Adolf Meyer in Germany before the war, Carl Fieger during the Bauhaus years in Dessau, Maxwell Fry in England, and subsequently Marcel Breuer in Boston. After that the process continued at the firm Gropius founded at the age of sixty-three, known as the Architects' Collaborative. While ideological currents prevalent at the time conspired to help create the Bauhaus as a collaborative enterprise, Gropius's personal need undeniably played an important role.

Gropius's long and productive architectural career is proof enough that such an impediment, critical as it may be, can be overcome. What is significant about Gropius's disability—perhaps of psychological origin—is how he dealt with it. In an effort to rise above his limitations, Gropius chose to look at drawing as a "support activity" rather than an essential element of architectural conception. He admitted being "discouraged" by his problem and "felt sorry" about his future professional ventures, but he did not allow it to stand in the way of an architectural career as others might reasonably have done. This determination not to knuckle under to impediments that might dissuade less obstinate individuals would become one of Gropius's most notable traits and tremendously important to the Bauhaus. Nerdinger referred to it as Gropius's "lordly posture," a disposition that gave him "the lifelong air of a missionary."

This drive to overcome obstacles transformed Gropius, who was normally passive and self-doubting, into a true leader. He once told a friend that one always had to find challenge to stay dynamic. He often spoke of preparing "for battle," and he measured the value of his idea against the strength of the opposition. "[I am] in the middle of a great battle for my idea," he wrote on another occasion, assuring himself and the letter's recipient that he "measur[ed] up to this struggle." Those who knew him best, like Lyonel Feininger, the painter and Bauhaus faculty member, knew that Gropius courted danger.

This incessant need to prove himself affected Gropius's behavior. Normally unassertive, he became combative when obstacles were thrust in his or the Bauhaus's path. This alternating passive and aggressive behavior made Gropius seem both strong and weak, stubborn and irresolute—a pattern that led the architectural historian Nikolaus Pevsner to describe him as a split personality. Behind Gropius's cool demeanor then boiled a "great inner agitation."

Transformed as he was by difficulties, Gropius approached challenge with unfaltering drive and mesmerizing self-assurance. His enthusiasm and commitment in difficult hours inspired loyalty, often devotion, even among those who disagreed with him. "Gropius's enthusiasm carried us all away," recalled a Bauhaus student. Feininger, who described Gropius as "a true, upright man and a great idealist," declared himself ready to "stand by him in every possible way." The fierce tenaciousness he displayed before seemingly insurmountable obstacles time and again at the Bauhaus was accompanied by a charismatic comportment that made him a formidable protagonist. Dark-haired and slender, with the posture and bearing of a Prussian officer, Gropius was rather phlegmatic and pleasant in appearance. Only his blazing blue eyes betrayed the fire that burned within.

When Gropius was confronted by his drawing disability, he characteristically found a way around it. He simply proceeded through architectural school with a hired draftsman in tow. Such an arrangement made for an unusual student life. "I get up at eight o'clock," he wrote, "eat breakfast, and then work with my draftsman straight through until three-thirty."

While a private draftsman was able to lighten Gropius's drawing load in architecture school, nothing could alleviate the boring studies, which—typical of the day—consisted of applying historical styles to new buildings. Gropius found the program restrictive, irrelevant, and dull, and he pursued his studies in desultory fashion. He was sustained only by his mother, who supplied him with the latest European and American publications and alerted him to interesting lectures in Berlin.

A friend and wealthy art patron, Karl-Ernst Osthaus, introduced Gropius to prominent Berlin architect Peter Behrens. In 1908 Gropius went to work in Behrens's office. He left abruptly in 1910 when an error in the height of an attic in one of the firm's buildings—the Cuno house—on which Gropius was working led to a falling out with Behrens. Whoever was to blame for the miscalculation (Winfried Nerdinger has claimed it was Gropius's fault), Gropius's termination in Behrens's office threatened to destroy the career of a man who soon would be hailed as one of the great architectural innovators of the century. Considering that he had neither a professional degree nor a job, the twenty-eight-year-old Gropius took this blow with the same striking fortitude with which he had handled his drawing deficiency. Writing to Osthaus to explain his premature (and embarrassing) departure, Gropius announced *his* decision to "forgo any further collaboration" with Behrens.

Gropius's budding architectural career was saved by his family. His uncle Erich, a professionally trained agronomist and gentleman farmer, asked him to design housing for his farmworkers. The project proved so successful that several neighbors asked Gropius to do the same. Gropius's enduring fascination with technology was now joined to his social consciousness—what Pevsner has referred to as his "burning sense of social responsibility"—which similarly lasted throughout his life.

In 1910 Gropius's brother-in-law Max Burchard, a district magistrate in Alfeld an der Leine, introduced the young architect to Carl Benscheidt, who had founded his own shoe last company and was building a factory in Alfeld. Although an architect had already been hired, Gropius convinced Benscheidt to let him design the factory facade while retaining the original plan, a commission that allowed Gropius to open his architectural office in Berlin that year. Collaborating with his associate Adolf Meyer, Gropius designed an astonishing facade of glass that appeared to dissolve the wall, heralding the nonstructural curtain wall that would soon come to be a hallmark of modern architecture. While the glass wall was not in fact the curtain wall it appeared to be—Gropius was constrained by the original architect's design—the building's implied abandonment of the centuries-old concept of supporting walls was a bold innovation in 1911, and it secured his place in architectural history.

Gropius was also beginning to make a name for himself within the German Werkbund. Founded in 1907, the Werkbund attempted to bring together art and industry in the hope of improving the design of German manufactured goods and hence promote their export. Gropius's friend Osthaus was an important figure within the Werkbund. In 1909 Osthaus created a museum in Hagen dedicated to the Werkbund's ideal of machine-oriented craft (Deutsches Museum für Kunst in Handel und Gewerbe) that became in fact the Werkbund's museum. Brought by Osthaus into the Werkbund in 1910, Gropius would lecture at the museum, and many of his articles would appear in the Werkbund's yearbook.

Given his awkward departure from Behrens's office and the strain of opening his own office, the spring of 1910 was a period of considerable tension for Gropius. In June he went to a sanatorium in Tobelbad in the Austrian Tyrol to relax and recover his health. There he met the alluring Alma Mahler, then thirty-one—four years older than Gropius—who had come to recuperate from the strains of her marriage to the director of the Vienna Opera, composer Gustav Mahler, and the loss three years earlier of her beloved eldest daughter. A love affair developed, and thus began a turbulent relationship that would subsequently and indelibly imprint itself on Gropius and the Bauhaus.

Alma and Gropius, wishing to exchange love letters without alerting her husband, set up an elaborate system of post-office-box arrangements. To Alma's subsequent horror, however, Gropius sabotaged the plan by addressing one of his love letters directly to her husband. Shortly afterward,

Gropius confronted the ailing composer and announced his desire to marry his wife! Although Mahler was understandably shocked and hurt, he generously allowed Alma to choose—a not-too-difficult decision, he thought, between the young and ardent though unknown Gropius and the world famous maestro. Alma rejected her young lover's bold advance (temporarily, it would turn out), but the episode points out Gropius's propensity for relentlessly pursuing his goals, often imprudently. This character trait served the Bauhaus, although Gropius sometimes antagonized people as much as he helped ensure the school's immortality. In this instance, despite his ardor, Alma decided to stay with Mahler, and she and Gropius for the moment drifted apart.

Thanks, however, to his patron Osthaus and his flourishing association with the Werkbund, Gropius had little time to moon over his lost love. In 1913, after Hans Poelzig resigned from his commission to design a factory and office building for the Werkbund Exhibition to be held in Cologne the following year, Osthaus successfully lobbied for the project to be given to Gropius. Backed once more by Osthaus, Gropius in 1914 was elected to the Werkbund's board of directors, becoming its youngest member. But like everything else in Europe during August of that year, the association was abruptly ruptured by the coming of the Great War.

On August 5, 1914, Gropius, now thirty-one, was called to report to his reserve unit, the Ninth Wandsbeck Hussar Reserve Regiment, entering as a sergeant major. Like most everyone else, Gropius anticipated only a brief mobilization and, one might assume, the chance to redress what had been his up-to-now unimpressive military performance. The opportunity to do so came sooner than he expected. Three days after his induction, his unit departed for France to participate in the war's great opening maneuver on the western front, an attempt to encircle the French troops known as the Schlieffen plan, which anticipated victory within six weeks. One month after the war began, the young architect, called upon to lead patrols to locate enemy troop concentrations in the Vosges mountains near the French town of Senones, came under his first enemy fire. The German advance encountered unanticipated and bitter resistance and was halted at the Marne. With the enemy now a scant two hundred meters away, the soldiers settled into the trenches.

The landscape along France's border with Germany is soft and voluptuous. Its loamy black soil, carefully tended fields, rounded hills, and meandering waterways evoke loving nurture and fertility. Between 1914 and 1918, however, it was a scene of despair and death—a fleeting image for those who mercifully died quickly; an enduring nightmare for those, like Gropius, who survived.

He was a brave soldier, sometimes impulsively so. His many letters to his mother offer moving witness to countless narrow escapes and the testing of his endurance, often to the breaking point. One such instance took place on September 21, 1914, when Gropius was sent on a reconnaissance mission to locate well-hidden and heavily guarded French troops on higher ground. He wrote to his mother of his "hammering heart" as he approached his assignment. One hour into the battle, eighty of his men out of a total of three hundred were dead; Gropius's company had to remain motionless among them until nightfall. For two "dreadful" days and nights, Gropius lay under constant enemy fire. Although he emerged feeling grateful to be alive, his nerves were "absolutely shattered." His feat earned him an Iron Cross, Second Class, the first awarded to his regiment. Commenting that its meaning could only be imagined by "a lousy, dirty field soldier," Gropius was tremendously proud of his medal, which no doubt made its way to Cousin George's record books. But the price of entry to the clan's records was high. Gropius, who became an insomniac after this, would hear the wounded's cries for years.

Meanwhile in Vienna, Alma Mahler was getting bored. Her husband had died, and a love affair with the painter Oskar Kokoschka had cooled down. Now the thirty-five-year-old Alma was angling for a replacement, someone who would "serve" her but disappear "*before* everything [fell] apart," as she confided to her diary on October 6, 1914. Recalling her amorous young Prussian architect, she wrote to Gropius on December 23.

By the end of 1914, realizing the war was going to last much longer than he had anticipated, Gropius—promoted on November 1 to lieutenant—had other matters on his mind. His regiment was regularly sent to bolster the entrenched front-line divisions, and he participated in a terrifying series of actions that further undermined his frayed sensibilities. On December 28 his company was ordered to take a seemingly impregnable trench held by the enemy, once again located on higher ground. Under constant fire for four days and nights, the company—all of whose officers had volunteered for this action—dug itself steadily upward toward the French line. On January 1, a fifteen-centimeter mortar grenade exploded directly in front of Gropius, knocking him unconscious for several minutes. "The shock was terrible," Gropius wrote to his mother. The following day, the company—with Gropius leading one wing—jumped into the enemy trench. Gropius described the terrifying battle to his mother.

> A hellish dance began when we exploded a mine in the enemy trench. Our dear captain was shot through the heart right in front of me. Four different artillery batteries started shooting. There were machine guns on both sides and terrible rifle fire. I cannot describe this horrible night, my heart pounds even when I think of it. There were no reserves, so we had to stand up to this for another day and night . . . beat[ing] the men so they wouldn't go to sleep on their feet.

From 250 men, Gropius's company was reduced to 134. With his nerves already shattered from the grenade of the day before, Gropius passed the night in the throes of his torment. After eight sleepless days under enemy fire, his company emerged from the "horrible mountain" bowed but victorious. "I have seen the war in its most terrible form," he wrote. "The best are dead, our wonderful captain and many comrades all gone. We, the few that are left, sit here, dulled and crying with spent nerves."

Gropius was disabled enough from this action for the regiment's doctor to order him to rest for a few days behind the lines. Declared fit by mid-January 1915, he returned to the front, where his attempt to locate the enemy by deliberately drawing fire upon himself cast doubt on how much he had recovered. Totally unnerved by this experience, he needed several days before he could write about it to his mother. "The bullets truly went around me," he wrote, "one through my fur cap, one into the sole of my shoe, one through the right side of my coat, one through the left. . . . I have almost completely unlearned [how] to sleep." Gropius's action earned him another medal, the Bavarian Military Medal IV Class with Swords.

Gropius seemed more impermeable to enemy bullets than to Alma, and in February 1915 their love affair resumed. On August 18 of that year, to his mother's great displeasure, Gropius and Alma were married in Berlin. After a two-day leave, Gropius returned to his post, and Alma went back to Vienna, a perfect arrangement for a woman who wanted a man who would disappear. For Gropius's mother, who rightly saw in Alma a willful rival, her son's marriage was nothing less than catastrophic. In December, mindful of his mother's devotion to his career, Gropius attempted to assuage her fears by describing how his new wife's "steady longing for perfection" would spur him to great achievements. "If you could only see how she rouses people . . . out of their conventional thinking," he wrote.

Indeed, Alma could be said to have been a professional rouser. Married for nine years to the famed Mahler and, as his wife, a leader in Viennese society, she was distressed over finding herself now just the wife of a junior military officer, and an "unknown" one at that. Although she undoubtedly spurred Gropius's ambitions by impressing on him what she had given up in marrying such a "totally . . . unwritten page," she also inadvertently added to his insecurities. It would be partly to live up to his wife's flaming ambitions that Gropius would so energetically pursue his plans for what soon would become the Bauhaus.

Perhaps if she had been born in another day and another place, Alma Mahler might have been able to direct her talents and seemingly bound- less intensity toward making some artistic contribution of her own. But the constraints of society had forced the beautiful, gifted, and apparently irresistible Alma, born in Vienna in 1879, to subordinate her own talents and sensibilities to those of men. She became a professional muse to male genius. An avid reader of Nietzsche, Alma formed both passionate and platonic—but always intense—friendships with such men as Johannes Itten, Oskar Kokoschka, Gropius, and Franz Werfel, to name only a few of her devoted admirers, lovers, and husbands. She had studied musical composition from the same teacher as Arnold Schoenberg; written *lieder* and an unfinished opera; conducted music; lived in a home designed by Josef Hoffmann; and through her stepfather, the painter Carl Moll, a founding member of the Vienna Secession and one of Vienna's leading avant-garde figures, had come to know virtually everyone of cultural importance in Vienna before she married Gustav Mahler.

Alma was twenty-three years old in 1902 when she married Mahler, the director of the Vienna Opera and her elder by nineteen years. Mahler was an unbending and rigorously disciplined man. He had insisted that she subordinate her interests, indeed her very life, to his needs—a subservient role she had not anticipated. In 1910, the year Freud had diagnosed Mahler as suffering from an Oedipus complex, the sexually repressed maestro had imposed celibacy on himself over Alma's objections. It had been that year, one year before the composer died, that she met Gropius.

In March 1916 Gropius suffered another narrow escape from death. He was assigned by military intelligence to observe enemy positions from the air, and his plane crashed. The pilot was killed; Gropius walked away. In October the birth of his daughter, Manon, briefly lifted Gropius's gloomy spirits and apparently Alma's as well. But by the end of 1917 Gropius described himself as slowly falling apart. Unknown to him, Alma in Vienna was beginning a love affair with the Austrian writer Franz Werfel, eleven years younger than herself.

The situation in Germany was not much better than on the battlefield. Difficulties such as severe food shortages had begun early in the war. By June 1915 bread rationing had been imposed. By October, potatoes were in such short supply that an Imperial Potato Office was established. Its prohibition of the use of potatoes as fodder brought farmers and consumers alike to the streets in a series of food strikes. By January 1917 Berlin was described as a city of "thundering hunger"; people were collapsing and growing desperate. By the end of the year, clothing, fuel, and decent housing (at affordable prices) were also in short supply.

Most of these hardships were borne by the working class. Aware of how much the war effort depended on them, the government—normally unsympathetic to workers' demands—was forced to heed labor's growing demands for political reform and a greater voice in industrial affairs. The government's new attentiveness to the workers distressed the industrialists, the military, and the old guard, whose interests lay in preserving the existing Bismarckian order. To them the government's efforts bore the unmistakable odor of socialism, long a black word in Germany and one whose innuendoes the Bauhaus would be saddled with.

Already in 1870, Bismarck had declared socialism to be a threat to the "monarchical-conservative elements in Europe" and accused it of inciting revolution. The opposition by the German socialists to the forced annexation of Alsace-Lorraine in 1871, not to mention the bloody course of events of the Paris Commune, had further inflamed the conservative public's nearly pathological view of socialism. Socialists had to endure what Gordon Craig has referred to as a "deluge of patriotic abuse" and, in some German states, even persecution. Such denunciation continued throughout the 1870s, when socialism was variously described as "the red menace," "an un-German madness," an "invitation to barbarism," and the equal of bestiality.

The passage in 1891 of the Erfurt Program by the German Socialist parties, which identified socialism with the working class, heightened the perception of socialism as a danger to the state. Kaiser Wilhelm II agreed. "The party that dares to attack the foundations of the state," the Kaiser proclaimed, "that rises against religion and that does not even call a halt before the person of the All-Highest Sovereign . . . must be destroyed." For nearly fifty years the term *socialism* continued to provoke nothing less than a collective fit among Germany's ruling circles. It was in this frame of mind that they nervously watched the government's wartime concessions to labor's demands for workers' rights and political reform. Such reform represented to them nothing less than the country's death knell. For labor, however, it was a necessary outcome of the war.

The absence of a clear goal in the war provided another source of dissension on the home front. By 1916 this issue had splintered and compromised the war effort to such an extent that Hindenburg threatened to refuse responsibility for continuing the war. Different constituencies—even within the German Supreme Command—perceived the war variously as one of conquest, annexation, and defense. German industrialists, the working class, the Prussian Junkers, the military, and the various political parties all saw the war as stepping-stones to their own agendas.

One group's demand was another's outrage. As the war effort crumbled and discussions about possible peace attempts became more frequent, these varying and unresolved goals became more fiercely contested. The Pan-Germans, worried that their country would fail to annex neighboring territory with German-speaking minorities, threatened revolution; at the same time the issue of the war's goals divided the majority Social Democratic Party (Sozialdemokratische Partei Deutschlands, the SPD), a tense coalition of radical Marxists, trade unionists, and liberal parliamentarians. What remained of the moderate SPD wanted to continue the war, while the more radical wing, which included the Marxist Spartacists, set up their own party, the Independent Social Democratic Party (Unabhängige Sozialdemokratische Partei Deutschlands, the USPD), known as the Independents, which sought immediate negotiations to secure a peace without annexations.

But the despair that permeated the home front nearly as much as it stalked the battlefields was not due simply to people's anxieties, suffering, and deprivations. It derived in part from the profound letdown many had felt after their euphoric greeting of the war, a joyous mood that had transcended social class. One newly commissioned officer compared war to Christmas, while Thomas Mann "joyfully" anticipated the emergence of a "stronger, prouder, freer, [and] happier . . . German soul." This nationalistic outpouring had not been confined to Germany. It had taken place all over Europe, propelling a generation of men to march off to war confident that they were participating in one of history's great moments of spiritual regeneration.

The need for spiritual renewal preoccupied Gropius's generation. Indeed, it had become a problem for much of the nineteenth century, when millions of people who had left their family villages to seek jobs in the rapidly industrializing cities had found themselves alone and alienated in strange places that neither understood nor respected their tradition. People were looking for some common spiritual ground—some unifying spirit they could share with others—within their burgeoning new industrial surroundings.

The subject of spiritual renewal had preoccupied Friedrich Nietzsche, the German philosopher, whose writings since 1890 had been indispensable reading in German homes, including Gropius's. Nietzsche's thoughts, which profoundly influenced Gropius and his generation, were as probing as they were dramatically expressed. "Only where there are tombs are there resurrections," he once wrote. People at first believed spiritual rebirth would arrive with the new century. When this did not happen, they looked for it in the joyous nationalistic upsurge that had accompanied the outbreak of the war. But instead of spiritual unity they, like Gropius, found only shellshock, screams in the night, and despair. It would be from this black and despondent mood, and the determination to make all things new—which Gropius felt deeply—that the Bauhaus would soon emerge.

By 1916 the exultation that had accompanied the war's beginning had disappeared, consumed by lice, filth, mutilation, and the utter senselessness of a war that had witnessed the costly campaigns of Verdun in February and the Somme in July. The German poet Rainer Maria Rilke, unable to write his poetry, claimed the war had made him "mute." By then Gropius too had succumbed to bitterness. Like others, Gropius had anticipated the spiritual regeneration universally hailed at the war's beginning. By August 1916, however, Gropius's nerves were shattered and his mind darkened. He described himself as "livid with rage,"

sitting here enchained through this mad war which kills any meaning of life. . . . Defeat is hard to take for a man. The war is going
to ruin people. Its duration is destroying the nerves of the more
sensitive people.

In addition to the nearly incomprehensible numbers of men who died,
the toll among those who survived was horrendous. Some were emotionally disabled for years. The artist Karl Schmidt-Rottluff, haunted by his
memories of the war, was unable to paint fully two years after the war's
end. In the army only one year, the Brücke painter Ernst Ludwig Kirchner,
then thirty-five, suffered a mental and physical collapse from which he
never recovered. Adolf Hitler, evoking the "graves of . . . hundreds of
thousands . . . [of] silent mud- and blood-covered heroes," vowed revenge.
Others, like Gropius, sought redemption and revolt. In August 1916
Gropius referred to the mood of the troops in the front as "dangerous,"
to which he added, "Thank God."

The civilian population in 1916 felt similar anxiety and fear. A nihilis-
tic mood prevailed. "I defend no ideals and no beliefs, only myself," the
painter George Grosz bitterly declared.

Beliefs? Ha! In what? In German heavy industry, the great profi-
teers? In our illustrious generals? Our beloved Fatherland? At least
I had the [guts] to say what so many were thinking. . . . What I
saw filled me with disgust and contempt for people.

The Dadaist Richard Huelsenbeck, blaming German "Kultur" for the
debacle, condemned it all as shit.

By 1917 disillusion and desperation were blighting home and battlefield alike. The writer Carl Zuckmayer, then a young artillery officer
only partially recovered from a bad head wound, recounted how his
regiment's medical officer had declared him healthy enough to return to
the front to get killed. Even the Kaiser—up to recently an untouchable
symbol of Teutonic might and continuity—fell victim to the embittered
mood. Ridiculed as the "hare who roars like a lion," the Kaiser was
scorned by workers and soldiers alike. The troops had become so angry
that they were ordered to unload weapons and turn in their ammuni-
tion and bayonets during royal inspections, an order that was usually
greeted by hoots of laughter. The Kaiser's son, Crown Prince Willy,

made his own bid for Imperial ridicule. Dressed in white flannels, he had saluted an army regiment taking off for the front with a wave of his tennis racquet.

Both at home and in the trenches the scent of revolt filled the air. A cut in the bread-rationing quota brought the first major strikes in 1917. Coming as they did a month after the March revolution in Russia, they filled some Germans with dread. To the starving workers at home and the weary men on the front, condemnation of the past and the search for scapegoats was no longer enough. Prepared by Nietzsche to believe that "chaos . . . gives birth to a dancing star," the people believed something new had to be created. Gropius shared this feeling, seeing in April the need for an intellectual change.

While the desire for revolution had become indisputable, its purpose remained vague. The writer Ernst Toller captured this unclear mood. "We wanted to create a whole new world," he wrote, ". . . to change the existing order . . . [and] the hearts of men."

> Didn't we swear to our friends out there on the field of death, crouched together below the parapet or huddled together in the dugout, in shattered woods and villages, under the hail of shrapnel, and beneath the light of the stars—didn't we swear then by all that was most sacred that one good thing must come out of the war— an uprising of youth? Europe must be rebuilt, its foundations laid anew. Our fathers had betrayed us, and the young who had known war, hard and unsentimental, would begin the business of spring-cleaning. If we had not the right to, who had?

By the end of 1917 the war was increasingly seen as a catastrophe. Gropius, still on the western front, was emotionally shattered. He described himself as "crumbling" and felt as though he was "buried alive." He agonized over a career that seemed lost before it had even begun. Bitterly he bemoaned being "entirely forgotten by the world . . . [and] ruined as an artist."

By early 1918 this sense of doom pervaded Germany. On January 28 workers struck in Berlin, Kiel, Hamburg, Magdeburg, Cologne, and Munich. Antiwar journals proliferated. A postwar revolution now appeared inevitable and Gropius, like other front-line soldiers, thought only of "sav[ing] some strength for the tough peacetime battles" that lay ahead. Less out of ideology than a sense of hopelessness and despair, Gropius had become a revolutionary. Exactly what he was revolting against was initially unclear, although he would later lash out against the Jews, calling them "weaklings and pigs at home [who] will destroy everything we achieved."

> The Jews, . . . poison which I am coming to hate more and more, are destroying us. Social democracy, materialism, capitalism, profiteering—everything is their work and *we* are guilty that we have let them so control our world. They are the villains.

Neither in his despair nor in his search for scapegoats was Gropius alone. A poem by Richard Fischer expressed sentiments similar to those of Gropius.

> On the field of honor
> This Golgotha of murderous demise
> Ploughed and tended by hands
> That stink of money and lies!

Only the mounting of a major German assault against the British front between St. Quentin and Arras on March 21, 1918—known as the Michael Offensive—temporarily eased thoughts of revolt. When the British line held fast at Ypres, General Ludendorff shifted the assault to the area where Gropius was stationed between Soissons and Reims. On May 27, while participating in this offensive, Gropius was wounded and hospitalized for a third time. His body eventually recovered, but his mental state did not. A weeklong medical furlough in June, which he spent with his pregnant wife in Vienna, could not diminish his despair, as he revealed to his mother. "For four years I have given my all for this insane war, and have lost, lost, lost," he wrote on June 11, 1918.

> I rack my brain about what is to become of us. . . . It is clear to me that I am near the poverty line. . . . I worry terribly about the new child. You cannot imagine what it means to put a child into this world right now and look after it. . . . I cannot bear this passivity to which I am condemned.

Two weeks later Gropius returned to the Soissons-Reims front, where the Germans, during the first week in June, succeeded in crossing the Marne. A formidable accomplishment earned at great cost of life, it brought them within sight of the positions they had occupied at the beginning of the war. More travails, however, lay in store for Gropius.

Toward the end of June 1918 a timber and stone French town hall that had been hit by an artillery bombardment collapsed on Gropius, burying him in the rubble. Suffering head, chest, and arm wounds, Gropius lay immobilized near the downed fireplace, surrounded by the corpses of his comrades. In and out of consciousness for two days and nights, Gropius hovered precariously between life and death, sustained by soot-flecked air from the broken flue. He was the only one among his contingent to survive. At dawn on the third morning German troops arrived to search for and bury their comrades. After hearing his weak calls, they pulled Gropius out of the debris.

From a sanatorium where he was recovering, Gropius wrote to Alma. "[E]ven a little taste of life makes me entirely foolish," he wrote, pleading for time to allow "the latest wave of voices of my war-crisis to abate." But in true Nietzschean fashion, the terrifying experience generated a spark that fired him to take stock of his life and plan his future. While deploring the circumstances that had caused his suffering, Gropius evoking Nietzsche's claim that artistic creativity arose out of suffering—declared himself "almost happy to have had this experience. . . . It is . . . a starting point. We . . . nonwinners who have nothing to lose . . . [are] perhaps the appointed precursors of the new world. For now, I . . . perceive [that] . . . I have found a way."

Alma too was creative. Two months after her husband's ordeal and while he was still convalescing, she gave birth to Werfel's son. Gropius thought the boy was his. He learned otherwise after overhearing an intimate telephone conversation between his wife and Werfel. Already unstrung and deeply in love with Alma, he could not bring himself to give her up. For the next four years—critical ones for the Bauhaus—Gropius would remain a deeply shaken man, thanks as much to Alma as to the war.

The publication in the summer of 1918 of the first volume of Oswald Spengler's *The Decline of the West*, a compelling and monumental recasting of Nietzsche's Sturm und Drang, expressed the sense of redemptive gloom that had come to pervade Gropius's and much of his contemporaries' mood. Born in 1880, Spengler was only three years older than Gropius, and his description of fear, death, and the sense of "immense loneliness" found great resonance among his grim and dejected generation. For Spengler, as for Nietzsche, man's sudden glimpse of death—and his reflection on it—constituted one of life's decisive moments, revealing "the secret of the perceivable world" that he believed to be the source of all higher thought, from religion, science, and philosophy to the creation of a new culture. Lying buried under the ruined town hall, Gropius had experienced this.

So too did Germany in the fall of 1918, when the war effort collapsed. At the end of September General Ludendorff realized that Germany could not win the war and advised the government to sue for peace. The government did so on October 3, when it dispatched a bid for peace to U.S. president Woodrow Wilson. Many Germans, unprepared for their country's defeat, were shocked. Unlike France, Germany had neither been devastated by the war nor suffered foreign troops on their soil. In fact, German troops were still in enemy territory on several fronts when the peace bid was made. Barely six months earlier Germany had negotiated a triumphant peace accord with Russia, known as the Treaty of Brest-Litovsk, which had heartened even the most demanding annexationists. That the move toward peace should have been advanced by the military leadership, who had previously been so unswervingly committed to territorial annexation, was even more unexpected.

Many Germans mourned a war that now appeared to be a devastating exercise in futility. "So it was all for nothing," wrote Toller, "the millions of dead, the millions of wounded, the starvation at home. All for nothing." Dead as well was everything for which Germany, indeed Europe itself, had stood. "Our admirable rationality has become madness," wrote Hermann Hesse, "our gold is paper, our machines can only shoot and explode, our art is suicide; we are going under, friends." Seeking blame for this unexpected capitulation became a national obsession. Some pointed the finger at "the Pan-German-militaristic-conservative combine." Others, seeing it as "a stab in the back," blamed the Jews and the socialists, now—thanks to the Russian Revolution—transformed into Bolsheviks. Regardless of whatever or whomever was to blame for the country's disgrace, Germany had to contend with the shock of the calamitous war and the debacle of an equally humiliating peace. The search for blame would become an obsession of the Weimar Republic and would ultimately help lift the resolutely enraged Adolf Hitler to power.

In Germany the call for peace unleashed many long-accumulating, suppressed social and political reactions. As Gropius himself noted, hardly anyone doubted that a revolution was on its way. These expectations were realized on October 22, 1918, when three hundred workers went on strike at the Maybach motor works in Friedrichshafen, Württemberg, chanting "The Kaiser is a scoundrel!" and "Up with the German Republic!" The following day sailors in the port city of Kiel revolted after their officers attempted to put the fleet out to sea rather than submit to what they—like so many others—saw as a dishonorable peace. "Death with honor," the officers declared, "rather than peace with ignominy." Dock workers, who bore their own long-standing grievances, joined the mutinous sailors and stormed the prisons where hundreds of arrested sailors had been taken by the police. The rioting sailors and workers took over the city of Kiel. Soon Munich, Hannover, Hamburg, the Rhineland, and Leipzig were swept by revolt.

Cities throughout Germany erupted in a sea of red. In Berlin tens of thousands of red-flag-waving Berliners marched down the Unter den Linden. Ecstatic mobs surged through the city's other streets, accompanied by soldiers in red armbands with red streamers flowing out of their caps and rifles. Slowly moving military vehicles were jammed with flag-bedecked soldiers and civilians whose placards hailed the revolution.

The euphoria of the moment masked any realistic assessment of what was going on. Guns were fired and barricades erected, but there were hardly any wounded or dead. Leftist newspapers acclaimed spurious Red triumphs. "The Red flag is over Berlin!" effused the *Vorwärts*. "Berlin is in the Hands of the Workers' and Soldiers' Councils!" the newspaper declared, referring to the Soviet-style councils of shop stewards and soldiers that had been set up. It was obvious that the people wanted socialism. What sort of socialism, however, remained obscure. The *Vorwärts* hailed the "Red-ness of the time" while explicitly rejecting "*Socialismus asiaticus,*" otherwise known as Bolshevism.

Only the small Spartacist group—led by the fiery Karl Liebknecht, one of the founders of the Social Democratic Party (Sozialdemokratische Partei Deutschlands, the SPD), and Rosa Luxemburg—was truly committed to Bolshevism. In Munich on November 8, 1918, their colleague Kurt Eisner, the vehemently antiwar leader of the Bavarian Independent Socialist Party (the USPD), established a revolutionary Bavarian People's Republic. Liebknecht and Luxemburg were trying to do the same in Berlin, and their aggressive revolutionary actions, combined with the still-raw memories of the terrible Russian Revolution of the year before, panicked the leadership of the Social Democratic government, who, like their Wilhelminian predecessors, tended to view any opposition as subversive.

Despite the growing unpopularity of the Kaiser and the accelerating clamor for radical change that had accompanied the civil unrest of the war's last years, the SPD's leadership—like everyone else—had been caught short both by the suddenness of the war's end and their unanticipated transformation into a temporary, transitional government until a republic could be established. The Social Democratic leader, Friedrich Ebert, and his frightened party cohorts believed that little separated the Workers' and Soldiers' Councils from Bolshevism. The SPD saw the unfocused and disorganized crumbling of the civic fabric as the first wave of a Bolshevik takeover. With this in mind—and casting fearful glances at Eisner in Munich and Liebknecht in Berlin—the nervous German government expelled all Russian diplomats from the country.

The government's fears were compounded on November 9, when the Kaiser abdicated (and fled to Holland), and Berlin fell to the workers. Only now, with the front pages of the country's newspapers filled with pictures of Red flags flying over the Brandenburger Tor and the Maikäfer Barracks—the outpost of the Kaiser's troops in the heart of Berlin—did the revolution truly sear itself into the nation's consciousness.

Philip Scheidemann, Ebert's party colleague, apparently panicked. Scheidemann, anxious to head off an anticipated declaration by Liebknecht of a German Socialist Republic, abruptly and without any party consultation announced the establishment of such a republic, which infuriated Ebert when he learned of it moments later. The German Socialist Republic, soon to be known as the Weimar Republic, was thus born, almost against its will and more out of fear of socialism than out of any genuine republican enthusiasm. The purportedly socialistic Republic, which never recovered from the comical circumstances of its birth, began its existence with socialist pitted against socialist and a socialist government that bore few socialist convictions.

Such confusion that would take a grave toll on the Weimar Republic as well as on the soon-to-be-born Bauhaus. The Social Democratic leadership, continuing to fear the supposed Bolshevik threat, allied themselves that evening with the equally nervous German Military High Command, a move that mocked the party's promise to create a government of the people. Instead it alienated much of their already divided support. General

Wilhelm Groener, the former head of the War Office who had replaced General Ludendorff in the Supreme Army Command, assured Ebert of the High Command's support. But he could not guarantee the same from its rank-and-file soldiers, many of whom were abandoning their posts to march with striking workers and join the revolutionary "soviets," the Workers' and Soldiers' Councils that were springing up throughout the country.

The taut faces of the returning soldiers reflected their conflicting loyalties. Should they listen to their officers, maintain law and order, protect the fatherland, and confront their rebellious comrades through the sights of their guns, or should they join them? Whatever their stance, the hundreds of thousands of soldiers constituted both a major presence and a threat. Among them was Gropius, released from military service on November 18 and returned to Berlin "to participate in the revolution."

Like so many of the artists and intellectuals streaming into Berlin, Gropius was burning with hope, throttled artistic impulse, and pain. "The mood is tense here," he wrote to Osthaus, "and we artists have to strike while the iron is hot." Convinced that "a new beginning" was needed, and anxious to resume his fledgling professional career, Gropius made plans. "I am working on something entirely different now—a *Bauhütte*," he confided to Osthaus. He was referring to the medieval guildlike associations of artist-craftsmen who, bound by a common religious belief, had built Europe's great cathedrals. To those like Gropius who felt betrayed, alienated, and wasted by their society, the spiritual unity and connectedness these medieval guilds appeared to possess seemed an appealing beacon. Five months before, Gropius had lain crushed and half dead beneath a pile of rubble. Five months from now, seeking to grip salvation's "secret wing beats," he would found the Bauhaus.

2.

The Beauty of Efficient Form: Tyranny, Treason, or Salvation?

Background to the Bauhaus

Behold this gateway, dwarf! . . . It has two faces. Two paths meet here; no one has yet followed either to its end. . . . They contradict each other . . . they offend each other face-to-face; and it is here at this gateway that they come together. The name of the gateway is inscribed above: "Moment."

—Nietzsche

In mid-April 1915, while stationed in Moussey, a French village on the war's western front, Gropius received a letter from the architect Henry van de Velde, a Werkbund colleague (and one of its founding members), asking if he would be interested in taking over his position as director of Weimar's School of Arts and Crafts. Gropius was one of only three Werkbund colleagues to be asked if they wanted the position. The other two were the Jugendstil architects August Endell and Hermann Obrist, both of whom for various reasons eventually dropped out of the running.

The coming of the war that previous August transformed the Belgian-born van de Velde into an alien enemy. Despite having lived and worked in Germany for more than a decade, he was forced to resign his director-ship one month after the war began. He was allowed to remain in Weimar until his contract expired in April 1915, when he wrote to Gropius. Van de Velde had created the School of Arts and Crafts, and certain it would collapse without him, he insisted on having a voice in selecting his successor. Fritz Mackensen, the head of Weimar's other art school, the Art Academy, was handling the actual hiring.

The offer became moot in July 1915, when the closure of van de Velde's school was announced. Unable to offer the directorship of an institution that no longer existed, Mackensen instead asked Gropius to head the Art Academy's craft department, which would be expanded to include architecture. Such a sudden shift characterized the negotiations that would ultimately forge the Bauhaus. The school would never be able to extricate itself from the resulting confusions and misunderstandings. Begun for one reason and pursued for another, the Bauhaus would emerge four years later in a way neither Weimar nor even Gropius himself in 1915 could have foreseen.

Van de Velde had been called to Weimar in 1902 by Grand Duke Alexander, who had acceded to his grandfather's throne the year before at age twenty-five. Anxious to make his own mark in his new duchy and influenced by his mother, the Dowager Grand Duchess Pauline, Alexander wanted to expand Weimar's small, floundering craft-oriented industries by improving their products' design. To do this he turned to the thirty-nine-year-old van de Velde. An imposing and highly polished personality, van de Velde was one of the day's most renowned and articulate advocates of applying industrial principles of utility and efficiency to art, an interest that five years later would lead him to help found the German Werkbund.

To carry out Alexander's wishes, van de Velde set up a series of arts and crafts seminars to advise local manufacturers on how to improve their products and help evaluate new models created by handicraft students. The idea appealed to everyone except the manufacturers, as a demoralized van de Velde confided to Gropius on July 8, 1915. When manufacturers were doing well, van de Velde wrote in a letter, they could not care less about improving the design of their product. They became interested only when sales were down. Then heaven help the design consultant if profits from the newly designed product did not at least double. Another problem was that manufacturers viewed van de Velde's program as competitive with them and therefore feared sharing product information with him. Gropius would encounter both these problems at the Bauhaus.

In 1906 van de Velde tried to reverse this situation—and also provide a constant supply of well-trained young graduates for Weimar's industries—by expanding the seminars into a school. Thus the Saxony Grand Ducal School of Arts and Crafts (Grossherzoglich-Sächsische Kunstgewerbeschule) was born, joining practical workshop training (personally supervised by van de Velde) with a four-year educational program. It had been to head this school that van de Velde initially contacted Gropius and his two Werkbund associates. In 1908 the school officially opened in a van de Velde–designed building that would shortly house the Bauhaus. But aside from institutionalizing the seminars' objectives, the school had done nothing to assuage the local manufacturers' fears.

These local tradesmen's complaints had not bothered Mackensen, the Art Academy's director who was negotiating with Gropius. As director of an art academy that since its establishment in 1860 had prepared young painters for traditional painting careers, he considered himself and his school as being above commercial interests. But like other art-school reformers of the day, Mackensen admired the hands-on workshop program that van de Velde had created. He wanted to incorporate such practical training into the academy's traditional art theory and history curriculum as a way of making it more relevant to the day's needs. The Art Academy had already begun such reform in 1902, when Hans Olde, a German Impressionist painter and Mackensen's predecessor as director of the school, had expanded the school's program for painters to include more practical training in sculpture and crafts. To accomplish this he had appointed himself, the sculptor Adolf Brütt, and the newly arrived van de Velde to head the departments of painting, sculpture, and crafts, respectively.

To reflect its newly broadened scope, the Art Academy in 1910 had been renamed the Saxony Grand Ducal College of Fine Arts (Grossherzoglich-Sächsische Hochschule für bildende Kunst). Mackensen, then a forty-four-year-old painter and sculptor who had been teaching at the Academy for two years, was appointed the school's new head. Mackensen was a reformist like his predecessor and planned to continue Olde's efforts. It had been within this context of retaining and hopefully expanding van de Velde's craft program within the Art Academy—to which he specifically committed himself in his correspondence with Gropius—that he had begun negotiations with the young Berlin architect.

Nearly everyone in the Academy endorsed the idea of practical training, but few could agree on how best to accomplish it. Should an entirely new institution he created that jointly trained both art and craft students? Mackensen had suggested this to the Grand Ducal Interior Minister in December 1914. Such an arrangement would give art students practical workshop training and expose craft students to the school's more intellectually demanding academic studies. However, Mackensen's letter to Gropius of November 22, 1915, indicated that this notion had been dropped. Now the idea was to incorporate an enlarged craft and architecture department *within* the Academy, which would provide assistance to local craft industries (much as van de Velde's seminars had attempted to do).

Few within the Academy, however, could agree on the best way to integrate this practical training program. The subject was endlessly debated. Some felt the Academy was training aesthetic snobs whose art was divorced from reality and whose education—combined with their usually less-than-Rembrandtian talent—doomed them to a lifetime of financial impoverishment. Others looked down at craft-school programs as artistically unenlightened and intellectually undisciplined. For four years administrators argued over whether the Academy should be an art school that taught craft or one school that taught both. At the heart of this debate lay a major preoccupation about the kind of art contemporary artists should produce and how best to train them for this, an issue that was part of a much broader dialogue about the relevancy of art in modern industrial society. Concern over this issue, like that of spiritual renewal, had dominated much of nineteenth-century artistic discussion.

Art traditionally had been patronized by the Church and kings. But long after such patronage had disappeared, art continued to reflect this elevated sponsorship. By the middle of the nineteenth century artists and critics had become concerned about how so lofty an enterprise could remain relevant. The painter Edouard Manet complained that he felt as though he were entering a tomb when he walked into the atelier of his teacher Thomas Couture, the famed French painter of historical epics. More than half a century later, Gropius would feel similarly about architectural training that consisted of learning how to apply historical styles to modern buildings.

This gap between traditional art and modern life was felt everywhere in the industrialized world. In England John Ruskin and later William Morris argued for an architecture based on function rather than empty imitation of the past. Ruskin's comment in 1870 that "[all] the architectural arts begin in the shaping of the cup and the platter, and . . . end in a glorified roof" had been one of the earliest suggestions of functional priorities for architecture, the beginnings of what would popularly come to be known as "less is more." While Ruskin himself was no lover of machinery, his appreciation of utilitarian principles opened the eyes of others to machinery's virtues. Oscar Wilde, for example, in 1883 spoke of the unity between "the line of strength and the line of beauty," a remarkable prophecy of the Bauhaus's own declarations nearly half a century later.

Not everyone admired technology, but most agreed that, for better or worse, it marked the modern world. In 1903 Friedrich Naumann, with a nod to Nietzsche, described the machine as "the human will turned to iron." What better way then to make art relevant than to apply technology's principles of uniformity and utility to its design, as Ruskin and Wilde had intimated? This perceived linkage between art and technology—and the attempt to join the moral force of art with the utilitarian principles of the machine—became one of the central preoccupations of the German Werkbund.

There were other considerations behind the creation of the Werkbund. Kaiser Wilhelm II had been jealous of the preeminence enjoyed by his English cousin Edward VII thanks to England's industrial might. Even though Germany had surpassed England's supremacy during the 1890s, its dominance was tenuous and, some worried, temporary. Anxious to secure Germany's export leadership, the government in 1896, in response to the Kaiser's personal request, had sent Hermann Muthesius, an architect in the Prussian civil service, to England to report on British technological and cultural achievements. Although Muthesius was officially posted as technical attaché to the German embassy in London, some have suggested his real job had been to spy.

In line with his mission, Muthesius had become acquainted with such artistic figures as William Morris, a leader of the English Arts and Crafts movement, and Charles Rennie Mackintosh, both of whom had tried to make art more relevant by relating it to practical craft application. Muthesius was bowled over by the implications of these teachings. Bringing them back to Germany, he called for a radical revision of architectural and craft teaching to emphasize hands-on training. To implement these programs, which were already in use in van de Velde's school in Weimar, the Kaiser invited Muthesius to set up architectural and building-trades schools. Their underlying principles would be continued at the Bauhaus.

Although the English Arts and Crafts movement had ignored the machine, Muthesius recognized the potential of the group's craft mentality for industrial production and wanted to apply their functionalist approach to create mass-produced objects. These objects, Muthesius insisted, should not imitate handmade goods but instead derive their form out of the principles of machine production itself. Van de Velde and Oscar Wilde, to name but two, harbored similar views. Wilde, in fact, predisposed by the English movement, had expressed such notions twenty years earlier.

What Muthesius and these others proposed—a machine-based, industrial aesthetic to produce simple and replicable everyday objects—was essentially a new art, as applicable to architecture as to everyday household goods. With this in mind, and undoubtedly reflecting the pecuniary purpose of his original English mission, Muthesius, along with Peter Behrens and van de Velde among others, founded the German Werkbund. The Werkbund subsequently involved itself in a broad range of issues relating to mass production, from the design of the factory building and the utilization of industrially produced materials such as steel and plate glass, to the workers' environment, from their workplace to their homes.

Aside from enhancing German exports, as the architectural historian Julius Posener has suggested, there was another reason for the Kaiser's support of the Werkbund. Committed as it was to all aspects of the technological process, the Werkbund promoted the creation of factories. In Posener's view, it was hoped that the pleasant environment and a newfound pride in his work would turn the worker away from dreaded socialism to wholeheartedly embrace capitalism.

The Werkbund's aims would eventually create a new German art, as Muthesius had anticipated, but at its core it remained economic and nationalistic—objectives which no one even tried to deny. Kurt Schumacher, speaking at the opening meeting of the Werkbund in Munich in October 1907, declared that art was an aesthetic and moral force that together "ultimately lead to the most important power of all: economic power." The new machine aesthetic then, propelled as it had been by the Kaiser himself, was generally recognized as integral to Germany's official national economic policy. It had been this promise of better design equaling better profits that attracted the support of enlightened German industrialists, such as Walther Rathenau of the AEG (Allgemeine Elektricitäts-

Gesellschaft), who, pursuing this aim, hired Peter Behrens as his company's official designer.

But addicted as Germany was to lofty-sounding ideology, making money hardly seemed an appropriate goal for a traditionally elevated undertaking such as art. Was this then the answer to art's long search for relevance? The new century had pursued this quest with near religious fervor. Money was certainly relevant to a commercial age. But what did it have to do with art? If the new art was to be the art of the machine, of mass production, where would this leave the artist? Because efficiency was prized in the factory, did that mean it was advantageous outside the factory too? What, if anything, did art have to do with efficiency?

For Muthesius and the Werkbund the machine—not the artist—distinctly and uniquely defined the new art and irrevocably separated it from the past. But for craftsmen, artists, and architects, machine art posed a grave threat. What was their role and the place of art in an industrialized society? Was the artist simply the creator of types rather than a unique work of art, as Muthesius argued; or was the uniqueness of a work of art critical, as van de Velde declared? Did the industrialist really need an architect to design a factory shed? If simple utility was the criterion, why not have engineers design everything from a kitchen utensil to a building? Unless some way could be found for the artist to be intrinsically involved in machine art, craftsmen, artists, and architects alike seemed headed for oblivion. Most important, did the factory aesthetic incorporate art's so-called eternal values? Without nobility, truthfulness, and other high-minded principles, would there still be art?

In 1914 these confounding questions boiled to a head in the German Werkbund. One group, headed by Muthesius, argued for typicality, and the other, led by van de Velde, claimed the uniqueness of the work of art. (Not surprisingly, among van de Velde's supporters were Gropius, Endell, and Obrist.) Only the coming of the war in August temporarily halted the agitated dispute that divided Germany's artistic community. The issue would fester and reappear after the war, not in the by then moribund Werkbund, but in the Bauhaus.

The Werkbund played an important role in the creation of a radically new art for a radically new audience—not kings, not organized religion, not wealthy merchants, but ordinary working people—and it was Gropius's involvement in the group that cast him at the forefront of what would soon become known as modernism. In 1907, when the Werkbund was founded and Gropius was twenty-four, the world stood on the cutting edge of a startling new epoch. Radio, movies, railroads, and motor cars were beginning to transform people's lives beyond imagination. People were living longer and better than ever before. William Crawford Gorgas had eradicated yellow fever in the Panama Canal Zone, the electrocardiogram had been invented, and Einstein had formulated his theory of relativity. The first motor buses had begun to run in London; the Wright brothers had successfully flown the first airplane; and, in St. Petersburg, the first workers' soviet (council) had been created. For a ten-dollar steerage fee, immigrants could book passage to America.

Fast, buoyant, and impossibly exciting, modern life seemed full of new experiences and opportunities. Artists, having felt alienated from society for so long, jumped ecstatically into this thrilling adventure, emboldened and inspired by modernity's seemingly endless possibilities. They turned away from such traditionally noble themes as Madonnas and classical myths and found inspiration in what was happening in the streets. The poet Blaise Cendrars wrote of opening the windows of his poetry to Paris's burgeoning boulevards. "Let's go! . . . Friends, away! Let's be off!" declared Marinetti in his Futurist Manifesto of 1909.

> Mythology and the Mystic Ideal are behind us at last. We're about to witness the Centaur's birth and soon we shall see the first flight of Angels! . . . We must shake the gates of life, test the bolts and hinges. Let's go!

In Paris in 1907, the Cubists held their first exhibition, Picasso painted his *Les Demoiselles d'Avignon*, and Matisse completed his *Luxe, calme et volupté*. Instead of palaces being erected for kings, "people" buildings— factories, workers' housing, and office buildings—were going up. In Buffalo, New York, Frank Lloyd Wright had completed his Larkin Building (1904). In Berlin the AEG company commissioned Peter Behrens to design a turbine plant (1909). Railroad trains had begun to crisscross Europe and national barriers seemed on the verge of disappearing. Umberto Boccioni, the Italian Futurist painter, exhibited in Munich and Berlin, and Ezra Pound's comments appeared in an avant-garde journal in St. Petersburg.

Muthesius's declaration in 1902 that modern art not only had to involve the ordinary person in its creation but indeed had to be created for his pleasure and benefit articulated the new century's radically altered priorities. The tool for this physical, social, and cultural transformation would be the machine. But not everyone was overjoyed by the potential of technology. Some found its implications frightening. To accept change—much less welcome it—implied a willingness to question, and perhaps deny, acclaimed verities from social caste to king. It meant opening the door to democratization and social leveling—or that despised word in Germany, *socialism*—and with it the abandonment of the status quo. For what else did such a concept of modernity proclaim but the acceptance of the ordinary?

The supporters of the new machine-based art cast the opponents of technology as philistines and reactionaries, which in many cases they were. But the overall situation was far more complex. There were many thinking individuals who understood the conflict between traditional values and the modern world's need for a competitive commercial position. Spengler, for example, believed that the "dictate of money" crushed all spiritual values. He compared the machine economy to a "mighty tree [whose shadow fell] over everything," turning worker and entrepreneur alike into slaves.

Antipathy to the machine—and the implications of an industrialized society, which the Werkbund would make the crux of a new art—was old as the Industrial Revolution itself. For John Ruskin, technology and the machine represented nothing less than hell. He may have admired the mesmerizing sight of a locomotive—the day's most compelling symbol of technology—as much as his contemporaries. But Ruskin despised its hideous shriek, comparing it to that of "a thousand unanimous vultures . . . [that left him] shuddering in real physical pain." What the Werkbund envisioned as a potential for positive social transformation, Ruskin and others saw as a promise of environmental disaster, of a world engulfed in a "perpetual plague of sulfurous darkness . . . [and] blackened streams . . . thick with curdling scum . . . [that] oozed an unctuous, sooty slime."

Such criticism of industrialization was heard throughout Europe. In 1855 the French poet and art critic Charles Baudelaire, a supporter of the avant-garde, referred to progress as a "gloomy beacon" that, like a scorpion, stings itself with its own terrible tail. The Irish writer George Moore in 1888 called machinery "the great disease . . . the plague which will sweep away and destroy civilization." If Ruskin worried about the defiling of the environment, Moore was concerned about the impact on society of making "the duke, the jockey boy, and the artist . . . exactly alike."

Even those sensitive to the problem of artistic irrelevancy and the need for art to change—such as Eugène Fromentin, the French painter and writer—had not necessarily subscribed to the doctrine of industrial nirvana. "Beware of the modern," Fromentin had declared, ". . . invoke the antique."

In Germany, however, thanks to the country's pursuit of economic might and the Kaiser's openness to emulating British industrial know-how, artistic controversy remained focused more on the fine than the practical arts.

Germany eagerly sought to apply English manufacturing principles to its own goods, but when Germans emulated foreign art (particularly French) they evoked cries of outrage. Pronouncements that German art (unlike German industry) should remain pure and free from foreign influence—usually a reference to the French—had already been heard during the nineteenth century. One need only recall Hans Sach's address ("Latin Nonsense with Latin Trumpery") at the end of Wagner's opera *Die Meistersinger*; or consider two best-selling books, Julius Langbehn's *Rembrandt as Educator (Rembrandt als Erzieher)* of 1890 and Houston Stuart Chamberlain's *Foundations of the Nineteenth Century (Grundlagen des neunzehnten Jahrhunderts)* of 1899, which depicted the history of German art as "a struggle between our innate tendencies and those foreign ones forced on us." One conservative newspaper in 1897 described interest in foreign art as a "ridiculous fad" that corrupted German art and the German art market. In 1911 a group of German artists who believed their livelihoods were threatened by "the great invasion of French art" published a pamphlet declaring French art to be morally corruptive. "Let us repeat it again and again, a people can be raised to its peak only through artists of its own flesh and blood," they proclaimed, as they vigorously denied that envy belied their complaints.

What in France and England had been a spirited but civilized and essentially apolitical debate, in Wilhelminian Germany turned into an embittered struggle with political and racist overtones. Manet's advocacy of a thematically indifferent art had amused French society and critics. But in Germany Max Liebermann's comment that "a well-painted turnip is as beautiful as a well-painted Madonna," which expressed a similar point of view, provoked accusations of slander and treason.

Education and stature had no effect on attitude. Henry Thode, a professor of art history at Heidelberg and one of Germany's most famed art
historians, insisted that German art had to serve German moral and patriotic ideals. "What today might be called international because it can be
found everywhere is, and always will be, French," Thode declared at a
series of highly publicized and well-attended public lectures he had given
in Heidelberg in 1905. Thode, who identified German art with the "great
and genuine," had accused French art of being both unsuitable and unre-
lated to "us Germans." An article published that year carried this argument further, declaring that the nationalistic spirit of German art was necessary for the country's drive toward political hegemony.

True German art was equated with a nationalist ideological force; con-
versely, foreign art was tantamount to treason. This view was reinforced and
symbolized by Kaiser Wilhelm II, Germany's most preeminent cultural
patron and a self-declared art connoisseur (not to mention amateur artist).
The Kaiser's limited artistic sensibility and his unlimited cultural power
produced a "dangerous dilettante," in the view of the eminent critic and
art historian Julian Meier-Graefe. However pragmatic the Kaiser had been
in his support of foreign technology, his views on art were rigidly conservative. The monarch's unwavering certainty on artistic issues undoubtedly
masked both his and his country's cultural insecurity and jittery obsession
with uniqueness. But the parameters the Kaiser articulated and defined—
no matter how preposterous or ridiculed and challenged by artists and
intellectuals—not only helped transform the German aesthetic debate into
one about morality and politics, but they remained virtually intact within
conservative German circles for the next four decades.

The Kaiser had expressed his artistic ideas on December 18, 1901, at the
dedication of the so-called Siegessäule complex, a series of gargantuan
and pretentious sculptural depictions of his Hohenzollern ancestors in
Berlin's Tiergarten. Art, he declared, had to help "guard and perpetuate . . . German ideals," which for him meant Prussian ideals. If it failed
to do this it was not simply bad art, but "a sin against the German people." Like most of his contemporaries, the Kaiser believed art was under-
pinned by eternal, immutable values. Others might struggle to define this
vague underlying morality—Wilhelm harbored no doubts. For him these
values were laws, as unchanging and timeless as nature and the divine
right of kings. To attempt to alter even one of these laws was equivalent,
the Kaiser declared, to threatening "the development of the universe."

Thanks to Wilhelm, the debate for or against progress in art turned into an argument for or against Germany itself. Differing artistic views, regardless of aesthetic or political considerations, became equivalent to heresy.

Such had been the case with the Berlin Secession, even though their demands—such as the right to artistic experimentation, to admire foreign art, and to relax the Kaiser's iron grip on state patronage and official exhibitions—had been modest enough. But the fact that the Berlin Secession had been founded (in 1898) and headed by Max Liebermann, a famed Berlin painter and Jew—and that many of its supporters, such as Walther Rathenau and the Cassirer cousins, Bruno and Paul, were also Jewish— added a racist dimension to an acrimonious issue already seen as endangering the state. "It is characteristic and significant," a Dr. Volker had written in 1903, "that the transmitters of this type of art and its first critical heralds are—I don't want to say Jews, but rather, and this is the essential point—representatives of the specific Jewish spirit residing in the West End of Berlin" (where the Cassirers had their art gallery that featured foreign and Secessionist art).

> That many Germans join and follow them is not surprising. The zeal and activity of these people has suggestive power. . . . They have turned the Jew-infested Berlin West End into an art market of the first magnitude, and they have learned how to take complete control of this market. The Cassirer Gallery, which might as well be called "Liebermann Gallery," is nothing but a miniature version of the Secession, whose affairs rest in clever "cashier" hands.

To those conservatives who agreed with this view, the prominent Jewish participation merely confirmed the "un-Germanness" of modern art. French Impressionism, long seen as un-German, now was burdened with anti-Semitic sentiment, a trait that would remain associated with modern art until the end of Hitler's Third Reich. Others, among them the Expressionists, opposed the Kaiser's rigid creed, claiming—like the Secessionists—an artist's right to create as he pleased. Some used their art to protest Wilhelm's narrow aesthetic dogma. The writer Stefan Zweig lashed out more broadly against the subservient conformity on which the authoritarian regime depended. In 1909, citing Nietzsche's "will . . . to action," Zweig claimed that art must do more than generate ecstasy. Because the artist bore "the rhythm of the new . . . turbulent life" within himself, he was obligated, Zweig declared, to incite passion and arouse the masses.

Many Expressionists attacked the totalitarian ideology that underlay the Kaiser's narrowly prescribed art. To the monarch's mandate for a servile and conforming public they responded with provocative and outrageous behavior. To the Kaiser's promulgation of purportedly immutable and unchanging laws they replied with calls for anarchy. In 1913 the German poet and cabaret performer Erich Mühsam declared the creation of art, tyrannicide, the deposing of a sovereign power, and sex to be equivalent revolutionary acts. The poet Johannes Becher was even more explicit.

> You mongrels, . . . boozers! Clowns! Fops! Onanists! Pederasts!
> Fetishists! Merchants, burghers, aviators, soldiers! Pimps, whores!
> You great harlots! Syphilitics! Burghers, all children of mankind!
> Wake up! Wake up! I summon you to a violent rebellion, to fiery
> anarchy. I inspire you, I provoke you to malevolent battle!
> Revolution! Revolutionaries! Anarchists!

Supported by activist members, a flurry of provocative Expressionist journals were published. *Der Kampf*, appearing in 1904, advocated anarchism. *Der Sturm*, founded in 1910, opposed the complacency and conformity of Wilhelminian culture. "We don't want to entertain [the public]," Rudolf Kurtz wrote. "We want to artfully demolish their comfort." Frank Pfemfert, the politically active editor of *Die Aktion,* specifically committed his journal to cultural battle (*Kulturkampf*), where artists would lead the coming spiritual revolution. While many Expressionists remained apolitical and committed to their art, the deliberately provocative rhetoric of their activist brethren made Expressionism a synonym for anarchy and political upheaval.

From the sober proscriptions of the German Werkbund to the ecstatic yearnings of the Expressionists, a buoyant utopianism—a sense of being on the cusp of something new—gripped the Wilhelminian art world as it had other European centers. In Germany, however, while Gropius was coming of artistic age, this aesthetic turbulence generated fragmentation and particularly vicious controversies with broad political and moral overtones. The debates raged between various groups and even within those supposedly on the same side of the artistic fence, such as the Werkbund, and among the varying Expressionists.

The Kaiser, for example, supported polytechnical schools and the most advanced efforts to join craft and industry. But he simultaneously endorsed the most boring, bombastic, and restrictive art. In 1908 he sacked Hugo von Tschudi, the director of Berlin's National Gallery, for purchasing works by such disapproved of French painters as Daumier and Courbet. Yet if Wilhelm II thought nothing of using artistic terms pejoratively—"Secessionist junk" was one of his favorite phrases—those who themselves had been the object of Kaiserian wrath often behaved similarly. The artist Käthe Kollwitz, denied the award of a gold medal by the Kaiser in 1898 and annoyed over the success enjoyed by Matisse in his first German exhibition, endorsed a movement that protested German support of foreign artists. The Werkbund opposed Impressionism, claiming it was ruining the quality of German draftsmanship.

Gropius plunged into this cantankerous artistic scene on January 29, 1911, with a Werkbund-sponsored lecture at Osthaus's museum in Hagen. It was the first of a series of Werkbund lectures and articles that would bring his name to public attention. Gropius would mark this speech as the beginning of his critical thinking; in truth it revealed little more than standard Werkbund notions, indeed little more than what Muthesius had proposed in 1902 and van de Velde had attempted to put into practice in Weimar that same year. Like them and his Werkbund colleagues, Gropius assumed the machine represented the good and urged the application of its strictly utilitarian principles to design, from mass-produced objects to architecture. Echoing the Werkbund in general, Gropius acknowledged that while the purpose of industrial production was to create goods at lowest cost, the economic advantages of this stripped-down mass-production technique would also benefit the industrialist, the worker, and society at large. Such ideas had been voiced before, but they served to stamp the twenty-eight-year-old Berlin architect if not as an originator then as an advocate and forceful protagonist of the day's new and controversial artistic views.

By mid-December 1915 the negotiations that would result in the founding of the Bauhaus had made some progress. In early December Gropius had visited Weimar during an army leave, and Mackensen was eagerly awaiting his proposal for the new department. The Art Academy still could not make up its mind whether it wanted a new school or simply an enlarged craft department. Gropius seemed more concerned about obtaining some guaranteed building commissions from the state as part of his contract than in resolving the particular nature of the post. He would not "compromise" on the issue of the building commissions, on which his "entire artistic existence depend[ed]," Gropius insisted in correspondence with Mackensen. Such assertiveness bore the unmistakable imprint of Alma, whom he had married in August. "This position is not so great," the new Frau Gropius had written about Weimar's offer. "Only if they give you everything you ask for in *writing* should you enter into it. . . . I know all about that from [Gustav's] experience."

> Before you commit yourself, I would demand to speak to the
> Grand Duke himself since your contact M[ackensen] is not to my
> liking. But the reasons that made me think positively of Weimar
> will be negated if I have to think of you in a subordinate artistic
> position. . . . Would you have enough time . . . to carry out build-
> ing commissions? . . . [M]ake demands. All that can happen is that
> you won't get the job.

However much he may have been goaded by Alma with regard to the issue of building commissions, the fact remained that what he was asking for was no more than what van de Velde had received.

In November 1918 Gropius—depressed and made "desperate" as much by Alma, who three months earlier had born another man's son, as by the war—returned to Berlin to find work and partake in the revolution. He had difficulty finding either. Despite the sounds of machine guns and exploding hand grenades resonating through the city's streets, the revolution was hard to find. What little there was to see, most Berliners preferred to ignore. The theaters were jammed: *Das Süsse Mädel* at the Palast, *The Gypsy Baron*, and *The Merry Widow* all played to packed houses. Neither gunfire, crashing windows, nor screams disturbed the festivities in Friedrichstrasse's crowded cafés and dance halls. Pedestrians calmly crossed busy Potsdamer Platz, ignoring the Red revolutionaries jammed into trucks shouting and brandishing guns at them as they went by. Such a scene prompted one astonished observer to report "[r]evolution in the trucks [and] apathy in the streets." Berlin seemed more like a madhouse than a city in revolt. No single civil authority was in control, and few could figure out what was going on. The confused events Gropius and others saw as a "colossal, world-shaking upheaval" were viewed by much of the bewildered German public as fleeting acts from some absurd crime film.

The only certainty was that the country had changed. So too had Gropius. Like so many of his countrymen, almost by accident he had become a revolutionary, less from knowing what he wanted than from knowing what he did not. Although his rebelliousness had become pronounced early in the year, it was not until November that the extent of his transformation became fully apparent. In a speech he gave at the Leipzig Trade Fair, titled "The Victory over European Manufacturers' Narrowmindedness," Gropius no longer castigated the Jews as much as capitalism itself, its profit-making motive berated not simply as "unimportant . . . [and] usurious mercantile trivia," but as reflecting what he now termed a "calamitous adoration of power."

At the very moment when his Werkbund-based proposal sent from the battlefield in 1916 was being considered by the Weimar authorities, Gropius blamed Germany's industrial interests for having caused the war. Advocating a school based on the Werkbundian attempt to integrate art and industry and at the same time scorning industry's singular purpose of making money evidently did not appear to him to be in conflict; it reflected as much the day's impassioned confusion as his own personal conversion.

But in November 1918 Gropius's thoughts seemed to be less of Weimar than of resuming his architectural career. He had been away four and a half years and, anguished over being forgotten, had confessed to Osthaus that "most of the footprints I had left behind have been wiped away." At the moment, however, his defeated country—its economy collapsed and nervously anticipating heavy war reparations—was neither capable of nor interested in building.

Gropius's only hope was Weimar, and nearly three years after submitting his Bauhaus proposal, that situation still remained unresolved. In spite of his attempt to assuage the concerns of Weimar's craft industries, the city's Craft Guild had rejected Gropius's proposal, claiming—among other objections—that it was more suited to large industries than to the particular handicraft problems of Weimar's small cottage industries. To Mackensen's exasperation, the Grand Duke—without whose approval nothing could be done—had ignored it. "All of my many efforts to induce His Royal Highness the Grand Duke to reach a decision . . . have unfortunately failed," a weary Mackensen wrote to the Minister of the Interior in March 1917, more than a year after Gropius had submitted his proposal.

The Art Academy still could not make up its mind whether to create a new institution or enlarge the architecture and craft department within the existing school. The city's obvious lack of enthusiasm for Gropius's proposal—little more than a reiteration of his prewar Werkbund ideas—along with Gropius's preference for resuming his architectural career made the appointment less than appealing for both interested parties. But as Gropius ruefully admitted to his mother, the Weimar situation was at the moment his only hope, and if it "should materialize, I would prefer it to anything else."

On December 24, 1918, the Academy and Gropius, apparently reconciled, signed a preliminary agreement. In more normal times Gropius might never have considered the Weimar proposal. Above all, he wanted to build, and Weimar was not looking for a builder. Industrial might repelled him; Weimar was seeking to acquire it. He gripped the past to forge a better future; Weimar, the apotheosis of Wilhelminian conservatism, gripped the past to avoid the future. It was a measure of the time's desperation—"beyond imagining," commented Gropius—that he now turned his hopes to Weimar.

3.

A Fragile Moment
Weimar, Gropius, and the Avant-Garde

Weimar culture was the creation of outsiders, propelled by
history into the inside, for a short, dizzying, fragile moment.

—*Peter Gay*

Weimar's meandering cobblestoned streets
and delicately scaled buildings spoke of
a quieter, more assured time. Goethe had lived here; so too had Bach, the
great German painter Lucas Cranach, the poet Schiller, and more recently
Liszt and Nietzsche. Grand Duke Alexander's grandfather, who died in
1901, had sat on Goethe's knee as a child. His frequent recollections of
Weimar's most illustrious resident gave the city's citizens a lingering sense
of their glorious past, whose significance had swollen in their minds as the
town's importance faded. While some considered Weimar a "literary
churchyard," a "Pompeii of the German spirit," its proud citizens believed
their city represented all that was meant by "German ideals." Others
might talk of these—in Weimar they were lived.

This splendid past, however, as Grand Duke Alexander recognized, had failed to keep the city's craft-oriented businesses from falling behind their more industrialized competitors elsewhere. Van de Velde, of course, had been brought in to try to fix the problem. But the Belgian architect had larger ambitions. Like Muthesius, van de Velde recognized the possibilities of creating a new art out of industrial principles. Fancying himself another Colbert (the founder of French industrial production under Louis XIV), van de Velde saw his school as only the first step in the creation of industrialized art. Weimar, according to his plans, would be the new art's trailblazing hub.

To accomplish this, van de Velde came up with a grandiose plan to overhaul Weimar's entire artistic establishment, which included—in addition to his industrial arts program—the area's cottage craft industries, the Art Academy, its theater, and two museums. He intended to have himself appointed the town's director general to coordinate and radicalize these institutions' various, often conflicting programs. Understandably, however, this aspiration did not sit well with the court's ministers. Jealously protective of the control they exerted over the city's cultural institutions, they joined Weimar's craft industries in opposing van de Velde's efforts.

Both in his plan to use his school as a launching pad for a more ambitious program and his propensity to rankle entrenched local interests, van de Velde anticipated Gropius. In one area, however, the Belgian appeared to have been more astute than his successor, and that was in recognizing his need for a strong ally within Weimar's fine arts community. For this, van de Velde turned to Elisabeth Förster-Nietzsche, the philosopher's sister. A driving force in the attempt to make Weimar an artistic and intellectual center, she was the one who had earlier suggested bringing in van de Velde. She was enthusiastic about van de Velde's plans and suggested inviting Count Harry Kessler to head one of Weimar's museums. In 1902, soon after van de Velde had begun his work in Weimar, the Grand Duke—pressed by several of his ministers under Frau Förster-Nietzsche's sway—appointed Kessler as museum director.

Kessler, who was well known within German avant-garde circles, was the perfect partner for van de Velde. A highly cultivated and charming man—and a prominent collector of modern art—Kessler had connections at the highest levels of society and politics. Gropius's patron Osthaus was one of his good friends. Despite Kessler's obvious suitability, van de Velde, a hardened veteran of Berlin's bruising art wars, had harbored no false hopes about their chances of succeeding in conservative Weimar, privately warning Kessler of the "struggles, intrigues, and dangers" that lay ahead. Kessler, however, remained undaunted—indeed, he described himself as "challenged" by the battles he recognized lay ahead. "All we want is to create," Kessler wrote to van de Velde from Paris.

> How can intrigues hinder us in that? You are your own boss in your studios, and I in my museum. We will be able to accomplish what we have in mind: a clear, healthy, advanced and productive teaching. Sour faces behind our backs will make no difference. . . . [T]heir . . . opposition . . . cannot harm us.

Kessler plunged into his task exuberantly, negotiating loans with major Parisian art dealers and putting up his own funds to help pay for the opening exhibit of works by Delacroix and Courbet. He intended to focus the museum's exhibitions on modern French art—practically a declaration of war in Wilhelminian Germany—but also planned an ambitious series of exhibits of modern Dutch, Belgian, Nordic, and German art. The opening exhibition had been a major success, acclaimed by leading critics around the country. Only in Weimar had the exhibit been greeted with undisguised hostility.

Van de Velde was able to harbor his grandiose plans thanks to the backing he had received from the Grand Duke's mother, the Dowager Grand Duchess Pauline. Her steadfast and highly visible public support of van de Velde held the opposition of the city's powerful reactionary forces in frustrated check. Prominently seated next to the formally dressed Belgian architect in her open carriage—complete with lackeys and important officials in full court dress—she accompanied van de Velde on his frequent visits to local factories and workshops. These moments of High Court pageantry impressed even the most doubting of Weimar's citizens. While these demonstrations succeeded in lowering the disapproving mutterings, they also raised van de Velde's hopes. These, however, collapsed with Pauline's death in 1905, when the previously checked antagonism against van de Velde and Weimar's cultural progressives emerged in full force.

The Grand Duke was never as committed as his mother was to the modernist cause. In 1906 Alexander went on a hunting trip to India and some court officials decided to use his absence to unseat Kessler. The occasion was provided by an exhibition of a Rodin nude sculpture that the French artist had dedicated to the Grand Duke. After some vehement (and anonymous) criticism appeared in the local newspaper *Deutschland*, "outraged" court officials founded an association to "protect the Sovereign" from further artistic insult. The campaign proved successful. Kessler resigned after the Grand Duke demonstratively ignored him upon his return to Weimar.

Van de Velde continued to run his school, but he realized his days in Weimar were numbered. In 1914 he learned through a friend that the Grand Duke—newly captivated by the neo-Biedermeier style and wanting to establish it as the official basis of teaching at van de Velde's School of Arts and Crafts—had begun to look for his successor. The approach of the war had aggravated the court's hostile mood, and van de Velde, more isolated and suspect than ever, was forced to concede that his school and plans for an enlightened partnership between industry and art had failed. On July 15, 1914, he submitted his resignation. The following year, their cause strengthened by the chauvinistic sentiments aroused by the war, the anti–van de Velde forces succeeded in convincing the Grand Duke to close the School of Arts and Crafts. In October 1915, with his school turned into a reserve military hospital and he into an "enemy alien," van de Velde left Weimar. His controversial legacy, however, remained behind, to be inherited by his successor: Gropius and the Bauhaus.

Part of this heritage—undoubtedly exacerbated by the war—was the Art Academy's pronounced nationalistic priorities in seeking van de Velde's successor. In July 1916 Mackensen declared himself to be looking for someone who would "follow the German spirit more than van de Velde." Only such an individual, Mackensen insisted, would be able to assure "even more profit to the Grand Duchy's trade in the great new time after the war."

The discord van de Velde had aroused—as well as the difficulty of the art-reform issues themselves—made the Academy hesitant about reopening the former School of Arts and Crafts. Their waffling on this issue of a new school versus an enlarged craft department had been the only constant in the Academy's endless deliberations. On October 10, 1917, they endorsed expanding the handicraft department (to include an architectural division) within the Academy's traditional program. One week later they shifted their position, declaring themselves ready to consider "[a]n entirely different form of art education" that would include greater emphasis on practical crafts training. What had apparently caused this change was the Academy's anticipation of the war's end and their expectation that Weimar would resume its traditional role as the spiritual center of

Germany. With the city "once again called upon to guide the spirituality of the world's peoples," as Mackensen put it, Weimar more than anywhere else in Germany had to lead the way with a reformed art school.

What came to Weimar on Saturday, November 9, 1918, was revolution. Similar to what was happening elsewhere in Germany, a local Weimar Workers' and Soldiers' Council demanded an end to the war and the resignations of the Kaiser and the Grand Duke. As one member of the Thuringian State Assembly proudly declared, the overwhelming majority of Weimar's citizens considered themselves unwavering monarchists, and so they—like most Berliners—simply ignored the council's goings-on. The leaflets, however, floating silently down from the sky over Weimar could not be ignored. Dropped by pilots of the Third Air Force Reserve unit stationed at the nearby bases of Webicht and Nohra, the pamphlets declared that the army was in control of the government and that revolution was on the march. "Weimar's hour of destiny has come," they proclaimed. "Political power will follow. . . . Long live the Socialist Republic!"

The Kaiser abdicated and so too—under pressure and after considerable stalling—did the Grand Duke. Swiftly and with stunning silence, the revolution had come to Weimar. A local newspaper, echoing citizen sentiment, asked how a revolution could take place so quietly. On November 13, 1918, four days after the monarch's resignation, Weimar's mayor, Martin Donndorf, expressing the feelings of most of the town's inhabitants, swore his unswerving loyalty to the former Grand Duke.

Weimar's reaction to the revolution was hardly typical. Most German cities were far more evenly divided between those who resisted the revolution and those who welcomed it. The national Social Democratic government, preoccupied by efforts to keep the revolution from deteriorating into civil war, contributed to the mayhem by ignoring critical issues. How socialistic was the new German Socialist Republic going to be? Would industry be nationalized? What would be the new socialistic state's relationship to Russia? Most important at the moment, however, was the issue of what sort of government would run the country, a Soviet-style proletariat Council government with power in the hands of the workers or a parliamentary democracy with elected representatives. The former, which Eisner had set up in Bavaria on November 8, 1918, was favored by the Independent Social Democratic Party (the USPD) and the radical Left. Parliamentary democracy—which the radical Left viewed as little more than a restoration of the despised old power structure in a new guise—was preferred by conservatives and the Social Democratic Party (the SPD).

The government's and nation's attention to these critical matters was diverted by the announcement, at the end of November 1918, of the British Prime Minister's insistence that Germany pay maximum war reparations, a demand that further stunned the country. The distress and anger this aroused, coming so quickly after the traumas of the defeat and fall of the monarchy, cut through everyone—every German family, group, and institution. From Prussia to Munich, Germany was rent apart. Politicians argued over the type of government to succeed the monarchy and the kind of socialism they wanted. Returning from the trenches, thousands of weary soldiers were forced to decide whether to join their rebellious comrades or shoot them as traitors.

Gropius discovered this split within his own family when he attended the funeral of his uncle Erich in mid-January 1919. He knew the war had profoundly changed him, "from Saulus to Paulus," he wrote. But he was shocked to discover how alienated he had become from his own family. The revolution that Gropius was embracing as an opportunity for change, his family—like so many others—considered a catastrophe. "They see only what is coming down . . . not what is growing up," Gropius wrote to his mother. He described the atmosphere around his relatives as "foreign" and wrote how "totally alone" he had felt among them.

The stumbling, virtually incoherent disorder that was "growing up" was reflected within the avant-garde. The end of the war and the apparently spontaneous uprisings of November that the government—and Gropius's family—were watching so apprehensively were for Gropius and many within the avant-garde a source of hope, a signal that the despised and repressive Wilhelminian regime was finally and irrevocably over and that their appraisal of its malevolence had been correct. They had been disappointed that their millenialist hopes had neither arrived with the new century nor with the coming of the war as they had anticipated. Now, spurred by assertions of "the Red-ness of the times" and the creation of Eisner's Bavarian Socialistic Republic, they saw the revolution as their long-awaited opportunity to remake all things new. Heeding Nietzsche's charge to "overthrow [the] old . . . conceit . . . and its rotting, decaying glory," they moved to involve themselves in the society from which they had so long felt excluded.

But in claiming that the world had to be changed and that they knew how to change it, Gropius and his utopian colleagues unwittingly assumed the role of cultural arbiter previously held by the Kaiser. Instead of the monarch, now *they* sought to define culture. "You do it my way," Wilhelm had earlier said. Now, the avant-garde did the same. The avant-garde's declaration of their own one "true" way continued in an altered form the German tradition of cultural authoritarianism that had been so contentious under the Kaiser and that most of them had opposed. In doing so, the avant-garde—like the Kaiser—propelled complex cultural issues onto the public stage, entangling them with political and moral considerations that had recently proved so disastrous. To this extent Gropius and his colleagues' revolt against Wilhelminian culture—of which the Bauhaus formed a part—continued in many ways in an altered form.

Many previously apolitical (even antipolitical) artists and intellectuals, believing that a revolutionary new age had dawned and that their long-awaited moment of spiritual regeneration was at hand, moved to ally themselves with the political revolution. These attempts to seize the revolution for their own purposes not only burdened them with the role of cultural determiner they declared themselves committed to overthrow, but also pushed them into some of the same quandaries their political brethren were experiencing. For like them, the cultural avant-garde could not agree among themselves what their purposes were, and instead of solutions they found only chaos and disintegration.

The most notable of these politically transformed artistic groups was the Bund zum Ziel. Founded in 1917 by the activist writer Kurt Hiller, the Bund sought to establish a messianic community to provide leadership for the spiritual revolution they believed was necessary to create an ethical world. This Bund, a collaborative enterprise, considered itself socialistic but apolitical and utopian. In Hiller's words, the Bund exemplified "neither the mentality of [the] trade union . . . the crudeness of the expropriating mob, nor the doctrine of any cozy Marxists." For Hiller and the Bund, socialism represented a fraternalistic way of thinking rather than a party doctrine.

Hiller and his contemporaries, including Gropius, described such an apolitical, socially oriented and utopian community and its goals as *geistig*, a German word that has no true equivalent in English. Usually translated as "spiritual" or "intellectual," *geistig* really means something more. Its truest meaning derives from the Cartesian division between body and soul—one (the body) "low," and the other (the soul) "high." *Geistig* relates to the soul and transcends the "lower" values of the body and material things. To be *geistig* is to reach for the highest aspirations of which a human being is capable. Hiller had conceived his Bund zum Ziel as a *geistig* community, and it was as a *geistig* community that Gropius was planning the Bauhaus. Similar to Hiller with his Bund, Gropius sought to bring together a group of talented artists and craftsmen who, working together as equals, would lead the public toward "the foundations of an enlightened society."

Anxious to gain a voice for his group in the new social order, Hiller called a meeting of his Bund zum Ziel on November 7, 1918, to decide how to accommodate the group to the new political situation. The most practical way seemed to be an alliance with a political organization whose aims matched those of the Bund. The USPD with its radical Workers' and Soldiers' Council appeared to be such a group. Like the Bund, the Independents advocated an egalitarian society and overthrow of the old economic and political power structures. Hiller, swept like everyone else by the heady winds of change, moved quickly to ally his up-to-now apolitical Bund with the Independents. The Bund zum Ziel changed its name to Aktivistenbund, to emphasize its new activism, and compiled a list of political aims. What had begun as a theoretical call to arms now became a call for political action.

The fall of the Kaiser on November 9 seemed to confirm the apparent transformation of a hypothetical situation into reality. The revolution seemed truly at hand, and the sudden ability to realize what had earlier only been dreamt about blurred the boundaries between political and spiritual revolution even more. The forces conspiring to terrorize Ebert's Social Democratic government filled Hiller's group with hope.

The following day Hiller, "[i]n a frenzy of optimism" he would later write, changed the name of the Aktivistenbund to the Council of *Geistig* Workers (Politischer Rat geistiger Arbeiter, the RGA) and moved to strengthen the group's solidarity with the Workers' and Soldiers' Councils. Meeting in Berlin's Zirkus Busch, the two allies voted to commit themselves to the radical program of national Council government that Eisner had established in Munich. The sudden shift from theoretical utopia to revolution left many of the RGA's politically inexperienced members reeling. Almost overnight, as Oskar Schlemmer—a future Bauhaus faculty member and one of the RGA's student delegates—commented, *bourgeoisie* became "a dirty word."

Hiller's alliance with the Workers' and Soldiers' Councils, one of the

Left's most radical groups, not only identified the avant-garde with the far Left, but thrust them into the compromising position of seeking political support for what they considered their apolitical goals. The RGA's program advocated a bewildering array of ideas, endorsing among other issues the radical reform of education, workers' rights, the inviolability of life, and sexual freedom. In addition to this confused agenda, the program's ecstatic mood could not disguise the fact that such terms as *brotherhood* and *Geist* were easier to talk about than to act upon. Further, as both the SPD and the USPD would soon demonstrate, shared opposition (to Wilhelminian values) did not assure unity in what they were *for*. Pressed to put these fuzzy ideas into immediate action, the ideological glue that appeared to bind these "enlightened" individuals inevitably disintegrated.

Because the RGA's broad utopian program ignored the specific concerns of its varying artistic constituencies, in mid-November 1918 several left to set up councils that were more responsive to their needs. Among these were the November Group and the Work Council for Art (Arbeitsrat für Kunst, the AfK). Like its parent council, the RGA, these groups often overlapped membership; they shared a propensity for noble-sounding but vague rhetoric and a wish to participate in the political process to promote their particular interests—broad ambitions rarely satisfied in their brief lives.

The AfK was the architects' organization. In December, shortly after the group's founding, Gropius apparently joined. In February 1919 he became its leader. Considerable confusion surrounds the group's origin, but it now appears to have been founded by the visionary Expressionist architect Bruno Taut, a Werkbund colleague who had a profound influence on Gropius. Like Gropius, Taut defined architecture in terms of social responsibility, declaring that the architect's main task was to transform society. As a longtime participant in the anarcho-socialistic movement, Taut's ideology was more developed at the war's end than Gropius's, and he was by nature more outspoken. When asked what the revolution brought to architecture, Taut replied, "Everything." A convinced Nietzschean like so many of his contemporaries, Taut believed the huge gap that existed between the "sad, lonely artist" and society needed to be mended. He described his proposal in architectural terms, referring to a "great cultural construction" that the spiritual architect would naturally lead. "We want to be builders of a new pure culture," Taut asserted.

Taut's desire, and that of the avant-garde Expressionists, to restore the feeling of spiritual oneness between the artist and society had more than a whiff of an exalted religious tone. In a sense they were seeking God, and religious invocations pervaded their statements. Taut referred to the architect as a "priest who serves God" and claimed that there could be neither culture nor art without religion. Others alluded to the quasi-religious nature of art and the *geistig* society. Art must "elevate, transport, and edify souls . . . [becoming] to those who have become free what religion once meant to those who were enslaved," wrote one prominent art critic. The architect Heinrich Tessenow urged architects to "create something that is truly like the kingdom of heaven." Gropius's Leipzig speech reflected this religiosity. He advocated not so much a return to religion as a return to the all-embracing spiritual unity that lay *behind* religion. "We roam in chaos," Gropius declared, "and have no common central issue, no vital religion. . . . In our torn times, we no longer know [a] strong common feeling."

In line with this ecstatic notion of enlightened society, Taut and other visionary Expressionist architects frequently utilized the image of the Gothic cathedral as a symbol of spiritual unity. In an article that appeared in November 1918, Taut described such a cathedral as "a fantastic construction that towers above . . . everyone's soul as it soars to the sky." The building of such a cathedral—at once both real and metaphorical—was a physical *and* moral enterprise, a double meaning of *Erbauung* (building up) that Taut specifically evoked in describing his new light-filled "phoenix" as "a true house of ideas" that would arise from the ashes of the old world. Occasionally Taut interchanged his cathedral imagery with that of the *Volkshaus* (People's House), a building where the "period's genuine artists would unite [a]ll the arts . . . under the wing of a new, crystal-clear architecture," an enterprise symbolizing "everything," including science, religion, and "the unity of the masses." Taut wrote, "Architecture is the age's tangible expression for all of us—all of us who work and dream are builders, builders of a new culture."

Gropius had similarly referred to a "miraculous cathedral" in his Leipzig speech, declaring that the "great spiritual idea [would manifest itself] in . . . a cathedral of the future, whose light [would] be reflected onto the tiniest object of our daily life." Five months later this cathedral image—along with much of Taut's terminology—would reappear in the Bauhaus Manifesto's declaration of "the new structure of the future . . . [rising] toward heaven . . . like the crystal symbol of a new faith," its symbolism resonating in Feininger's famed accompanying woodcut. For Gropius the Bauhaus—like Taut's *Volkshaus*—was both a physical and moral enterprise.

Conceived as a protest against the supposed evils of an oppressive Wilhelminian society, such a *Volks-* or *Bau-haus* by definition had to be egalitarian, a socialist principle Taut particularly emphasized. Art in the future would no longer be merely a "luxury for the rich," nor would distinctions of "rank or class" mar such a unified mankind. Up to now Gropius's revolutionary utterances had betrayed little if any political content. This changed with his Leipzig speech, when Gropius referred to an enlightened society "without the presumptuous class distinctions that seek to erect . . . arrogant wall[s]" between people. This egalitarian notion also appeared in the Bauhaus Manifesto; Gropius claimed the school for "a new guild of creators . . . without . . . presumptuous class distinctions."

It was this advocacy of a new society and the need to produce artists to create and lead it that brought Taut and his colleagues to emphasize art-school reform. For Taut, "teaching, religion, and art form[ed] a complex in the creation of culture." Given this view, the creation of art schools was not simply an accessory to the spiritual revolution, but its very source; and art-school reform such as Gropius was planning for the Bauhaus was not simply *an* issue in the revolution, but *the* issue.

School reform had long been a socialist issue. In 1866 Karl Marx had advocated the creation of work-schools, where students would receive both intellectual and practical training in production techniques. In 1906 the SPD had made the issue of school reform a centerpiece of its program. Gropius's similar raising of art-school reform as the core issue of his aspirations for a better world not only linked him with the Left in the public's mind, but placed him squarely in disputed political territory. This uncomfortable position created all kinds of problems for him in years to come and led to many embittered battles, throughout which Gropius steadfastly sought to maintain a stance above party politics.

In his Leipzig speech Gropius claimed that "the government—and we too are a part of the government—should throw itself totally into [finding solutions]. . . . That's what we are fighting for. We should not waste any time." Gropius's new leftist inclinations were also apparent in his veiled reference to the Soviet revolution of the year before. "We are the forerunners . . . of a new, common view of the world that is being born in these years of reorganizing the world," he had declared. While one must be careful about ascribing a specific political bent from such a vague comment, it is clear that, at the least, Gropius saw the German revolution within the context of a larger universal social upheaval.

Toward the end of December 1918, Taut's AfK agenda appeared in print. Titled "A Program for Architecture," the leaflet asserted architecture's utopian and humanitarian priorities and declared the unity of the various arts "under the wings of a new architecture." The AfK wanted the government to create a national arts agency to coordinate future artistic legislation. It demanded support for radically inclined architects, experimental building sites, and the design of large-scale workers' housing developments. Such sweeping ambitions—if they were realizable at all— were only possible with governmental backing. For this reason the AfK, like its parent RGA Council, envisioned itself as a political lobbying group. "[T]he AfK wished to directly influence the government," Taut acknowledged some months later.

Their initial lobbying efforts were a pronounced failure. Sometime between mid-November and December 27, 1918 (the exact date remains unknown), Taut, Gropius, and Wilhelm Valentiner, an SPD member and former assistant to Wilhelm von Bode, met with government cultural ministers to try to secure political backing for their program, not unlike the RGA's effort some weeks earlier to ally itself with the Workers' and Soldiers' Council. The meeting, however, came to nothing after one of the ministers asked for their specific recommendations and the trio drew a blank. "The revolutionary gentlemen" were dismissed and negotiations terminated.

Despite its unpromising start, the AfK could point to some political success. Without mentioning the AfK by name, articles favoring the group's views appeared in two major leftist newspapers, *Die Freiheit* and *Vorwärts*, along with announcements of its formation and its mid-December program. John Schikowski, *Vorwärts*'s art critic and a founding member of the AfK, wrote frequently about the affinity between the AfK's vision of artistic upheaval and the political insurrection. Is it simply "a purely fortuitous accident," he asked in one article, "that an upheaval in the artistic sphere occurs simultaneously with the social and political revolution?"

This publicized rapport between the cultural avant-garde and the Left highlighted the former's affinity with the political revolution and reaffirmed a long-held public view. Some, though by no means a majority, had viewed this supposed rapport favorably. In 1913 Wilhelm Hausenstein, for example, a prominent art critic, member of the SPD, and one of the founding members of the AfK, had declared Expressionism to be the art of a future socialist society. Most Germans, however, shared Kaiser Wilhelm II's negative view of the cultural avant-garde as synonymous with the anti-German, which within 1918's postwar revolutionary context metamorphosed into the suspect political Left.

Despite the euphoria of the day, a considerable number of Germans—including, some might argue, the "socialist" government itself—continued to fear socialism as a basic threat to Germany's political and social order. Such misgivings were fed by Germany's conservative press. A report by the *Berliner Tageblatt*, for example, of marauding workers storming and looting official buildings on November 11, 1918, and the government's attempt to protect the museums during the revolution, gave the distinct impression that socialists represented some sort of danger to Germany's cultural heritage. The adoption of the word *council* (with its Soviet implications), the anarcho-socialistic background of many within the artistic avant-garde, and the artists' very public attempt to seek political liaison with the more radical (but certainly not the *most* radical) leftist constituency—not to mention the treasonous associations that lingered from the Kaiser's days—made the connection in the public's mind of radical art with radical leftist politics. Although this attempted marriage would never be consummated, memory of the courtship, however tenuous, remained.

Gropius had really been changed—one might say transformed—by his war experiences. Like many of his contemporaries, he was preoccupied now by spiritual issues and revolutionizing society. From this perspective the Werkbund's preoccupations—as important as they may have been in the century's early years in defining some of the issues of modernism in Germany—now seemed dated and obsolete. "I regard the Werkbund as dead," Gropius declared on December 23, 1918. "Nothing more can come out of it." In Weimar, however, Art Academy officials—knowing nothing of Gropius's radically changed sentiments—were preparing to hire him on the basis of his 1916 Werkbund-inspired Bauhaus proposal.

4.

Storming into Weimar
The City as Relic or Harbinger

The hour of the manifesto is past; the slogans have been
coined, the dividing lines drawn.

—Oskar Schlemmer

Weimar spurned the revolution as zealous-
ly as it revered the past. Its working
class—the natural benefactor and potential supporter of Gropius's leftist
ideas—constituted only about 12 percent of Weimar's approximately
forty thousand inhabitants. And even they were relatively conservative.
During the war Weimar's workers had not been particularly active in
demanding political and social reform, nor had they belonged to political
organizations in any significant majority, unlike their cohorts in other
industrialized cities of similar size. Their local leaders lacked the know-
how and resources to organize a Workers' and Soldiers' Council in the
early days of the revolution; Spartacists were sent from Berlin to do so.
Soon after the Berliners left, Weimar's Council crumbled into insignifi-
cance before the organized and aggressive tactics of the more conservative

Social Democratic Party (the SPD).

The city's two major newspapers, *Deutschland* and the extremely reactionary *Deutschnationale Weimarische Zeitung*, reflected Weimar's conservative mood. On November 9, 1918, the latter stopped its presses to protest the revolution. Both newspapers continued to wage relentless opposition to the revolution, mostly through Citizens' Assemblies (Bürgerversammlungen) they helped organize.

Weimar's conservatism, so ideologically distant from Berlin, was shared by its artists and intellectuals. The faculty of Weimar's Art Academy had opposed the creation of a Council government the radical Left was demanding and petitioned the state authorities to urge the creation of a National Assembly. In Berlin, unknown to them, the man they would shortly appoint to their faculty was vigorously advocating the opposite.

The strength of Germany's Independent Social Democratic Party (the USPD) had forced the national Social Democratic government in Berlin to share power with them in the provisional government. In Weimar no such counterforce existed. There the SPD, led by fifty-eight-year-old August Baudert, ruled what had become the Free State of Saxony-Weimar. Baudert—like his national counterpart, Ebert—greatly feared Bolshevism. His reference to it as "dangerous fire" had earned him praise from his conservative opponents. It had been largely due to Baudert's conservative instincts that Weimar had suffered so silent a revolution.

Weimar's inadvertent ascendancy to world attention began in Berlin on December 19, 1918, when the first National Congress of Workers' and Soldiers' Councils voted overwhelmingly to establish the new German Republic as a parliamentary democracy rather than the Soviet-style Council government demanded by its radical USPD wing. Disappointed by these results, the Independents left the provisional national government, with whom it had been sharing power. The Spartacists, hopelessly split from the Independents, were even more despondent. Breaking away from the Independents, they founded the German Communist Party (Kommunistische Partei Deutschland, the KPD) and began a campaign of armed insurrection. By the middle of January 1919 both Spartacist leaders Karl Liebknecht and Rosa Luxemburg would be brutally murdered and Weimar chosen by the newly elected German Constituent Assembly as the site of the new National Assembly. The city, which would eventually bestow its name on the German Socialist Republic, was about to assume the national role that its citizens had long felt to be its due.

Publicly the national government claimed it chose Weimar due to the city's central location and its symbolic stature in German culture. But the real reasons were the town's pronounced political conservatism and its easily defensible location. This was not to say, however, that Weimar was free from political unrest. Like their compatriots elsewhere in Germany, hundreds of Weimar workers demonstrated in mid-January 1919 to protest the killings of Liebknecht and Luxemburg. Again, on January 23, more than a thousand workers and soldiers participated in a funeral service for the slain Spartacists organized by the city's Workers' and Soldiers' Council. As splintered and weak as this Council may have been, the demonstrations were enough to make Baudert worry about a Spartacist putsch. So too did the national government, which sent in a rifle battalion of about one thousand Free Corps troops (a right-wing militia recruited from the mostly demobilized army) led by General Ludwig von Märcker.

Like his national SPD colleagues, Baudert was also suspicious of the USPD because it supported the Workers' and Soldiers' Council. Baudert tried to undermine their authority by allying himself with the rightist military, which thanks to the government's concerns about security was assuming a formidable presence in Weimar. Märcker's Free Corps troops, bolstered by local police and special agents sent from Berlin, rigidly enforced a decree forbidding anyone other than the elected representatives of the National Assembly to come into Weimar, unless they carried a passport issued by Weimar authorities specifically stating the reason for being there. A cordon of troops surrounded the National Theater, where the National Assembly met, while well-armed soldiers fortified thirty-five surrounding communities. A more distant security parameter was set up to secure the railroad line from Erfurt, Apolda, and Jena, Thuringia's other large cities. Not only did Gropius need a passport to get into Weimar (the state of Thuringia's capital city), but he was also required to secure an official letter from the Art Academy simply to buy a railroad ticket from Berlin to Weimar. Troops would remain in Weimar until 1920. Hermetically sealed off from the outside world, the city was under siege as Gropius set up the Bauhaus.

Until July 31, 1919, when the National Assembly would adopt a constitution, Germany's local governments existed on a provisional ad hoc basis, which in Weimar assumed a particularly bewildering cast. The least problematic aspect of this transitional period was the city's change of name, from the Grand Duchy of Saxony to the Free State of Saxony-Weimar. The administration of the former Grand Duchy remained in the hands of the old court bureaucrats, a reflection of Weimar's conservatism. Reluctantly ripping off their gold-braided epaulets, they now set about to run a revolutionary state.

This confused state of affairs hampered the founding of the Bauhaus, because Gropius had no idea who was authorized to approve the agreement he had signed with the Art Academy in December. Moreover, while he was planning to use the Bauhaus to implement his socialistic ideas of "total change" and "radical transformation," he was negotiating to accomplish this with the Grand Ducal Saxon State Ministry, which was responsible for the art schools. Its recognition of the revolution consisted of scratching out the words *Grand Ducal* on its stationery. Aside from its humor, the situation points up the day's absurdities: socialistic governments allying themselves with the Right rather than with their own political confreres; courtiers administering revolutionary governments; and Gropius negotiating with a state that no longer existed.

Based on the understanding he had reached with Art Academy officials on December 24, 1918, Gropius assumed the creation of the Bauhaus to be a fait accompli. His letters of January 1919 referred frequently to the "Weimar Bauhaus." Yet he had heard nothing from Weimar. Understandably concerned, Gropius wrote to his friend Ernst Hardt, the newly appointed director of Weimar's National Theater, asking for his advice. Hardt suggested that he contact Baron von Fritsch, the pre- and postrevolutionary *Hofmarschall* (Lord High Chamberlain). Addressing him as "Your Excellency"—a breach of revolutionary etiquette—Gropius wrote to him on January 31, 1919.

After briefly recapitulating the history of the negotiations, Gropius did not ask if the appointment was still forthcoming—considering the general confusion he might well have asked, the school's opponents would later claim—but simply when and under whose auspices his agreement could be approved. In passing, Gropius mentioned a slight expansion of his plans. "For a long time I have been preoccupied with the idea of reorganizing Weimar's artistic life and have developed specific plans for this, part of which I submitted to the ministry . . . some time ago." Gropius referred to his involvement in the AfK with similar circumspection.

> At present I am engaged here in Berlin in speaking and writing on the subject of freeing the separate arts from their isolation and . . . joining them under the wings of a great architecture. . . . I am determined . . . to dedicate my life to realizing this concept.

Perhaps concerned that these radical-sounding plans might alarm von Fritsch, Gropius assured him he appreciated Weimar's cultural traditions. His new ideas, he declared, were best accomplished in a small town "where the remains of an old tradition [exist] to promote them."

Gropius's reassuring instincts were right on the mark, for Weimar was veering even more rightward. The choice of the city as the seat of the national government, and the heavy troop presence, had bolstered its officials' conservative leanings: the former inflated their view of the town as the center of Germanic ideals and the latter confirmed their Bolshevik fears. Gropius, however, was setting up the Bauhaus in accord with the revolution's urgent spirit and aspirations, which the school's supporting community violently opposed. This disparity was not the only harbinger of trying times ahead.

With its Werkbund principles disavowed, the Bauhaus program of 1916 had been formulated in war days for the government of a hereditary prince that no longer existed and a social system that its author was now dedicated to change. Distracted and suffering emotional stress, Gropius was negotiating with an Imperial Department of State and a provisional government of dubious legality and duration. What's more, he was committing himself to a program that bore little relation to the institute he intended to set up, or to the country in which it had been conceived.

The adoption in December 1918 of the parliamentary system had many ramifications, aside from turning the country and the world's attention to Weimar. It decimated the Council movement, along with the hopes of the USPD, the Workers' and Soldiers' Councils, and the avant-garde, who had so exuberantly allied themselves with the Councils' proponents. The radical Left believed the parliamentary electoral system represented nothing less than a return to power of the old "militaristic-capitalist forces" against which they had rebelled. Yet as betrayed as the radicals may have felt, the Councils' decision on December 19 represented not just the will of most of the delegates at the meeting, but also that of the overwhelming majority of Germans, including many of its most eminent citizens. "I don't want politics," Thomas Mann wrote, "I want impartiality, order, and propriety. If that is philistine, then I want to be a philistine."

On December 23, the day before Gropius signed his agreement with Weimar's Art Academy, the Spartacists responded to the vote by opening guerrilla warfare in Berlin. The reaction of the avant-garde to the Councils' decision, if less savage than that of the Spartacists, was no less embittered. Adolf Behne, an influential art critic of the *Monatshefte* and longtime friend of Taut, wrote how shamed and saddened he felt about the revolution's meager achievements. Indeed, aside from lifting censorship and returning to power the "slightly repainted" old regime, he charged the ten-week-old revolution with having accomplished nothing.

Gropius shared Behne's disappointment. In a letter to Osthaus he described socialism as "sullied . . . totally disgraced . . . [and] need[ing] a long time to salve its honor. Our only option now is to ignore the real world and to build a private, separate world for oneself." Others took the failure of the Council movement even more to heart. Taut, for one, was shattered. He removed himself from the public scene and the Work Council for Art (the AfK)—the latter temporarily, it would turn out—and bitterly denounced politicians. "Let them rule any way they want," he declared.

Most Germans, however, did not feel this way at all about the revolutionary goings-on. Having suffered deprivations and hardships during the war's four long years, they were anxious to renew their normal lives. They abhorred the chaotic and frightening radical Left, a feeling heightened by sensationalistic coverage by the nationalist press of Berliners scurrying to evade bullets and grenades. By comparison, the "order and propriety" of the good old days looked better than ever. Responding to this nostalgic mood and spurred by the elections for National Assembly on January 19, 1919, radical rightist parties sprang up throughout Germany. The new German National People's Party (Deutschnationale Volkspartei, the DNVP) declared the revolution to be the gravest crime (*Verbrechen*) ever committed against the German people and swore "eternal remembrance of what the *Hohenzollerns* have done for our country and our people."

Like the utopian socialists, the Right also spoke of spirit, of wanting a new and better society. They too, as the German National Party (Deutschnationale Partei, the DNP) declared, wanted "to clear away the rubble." Their spirit, however, was not the universalist one of Gropius and his colleagues, but rather the "preservation of our German-ness." "Save our country, our freedom, [and] our German-ness," urged a group of university professors on January 14, 1919. The Union for National and Social Solidarity demanded the country protect itself from Bolshevism. "Whoever follows Liebknecht is abandoning German independence," declared one of their newspaper appeals. "Serving Russian Bolshevism will lead to tyranny and control. Bolshevik troops are approaching the German border." To many Germans these fears applied not just to the Spartacists but to all those associated with the radical Left, including artists and intellectuals like Gropius and organizations like the AfK—and soon the Bauhaus.

With a demoralized Bruno Taut no longer interested in directing the AfK, Gropius took over the group's leadership in February 1919. As the AfK's leader Gropius would consolidate his various postwar preoccupations into a comprehensive vision that would emerge the following month with the Bauhaus. What Gropius said as head of the AfK would influence what the Bauhaus would be. How the school came to be seen by Weimar and much of the German public would be influenced by what the AfK did.

Gropius's leadership of the AfK, however, did more than just help define his ideology. Typically, the challenge catalyzed him and—in true Nietzschean fashion—transformed his war-induced anguish, exhaustion, and doubts into a heady mood of ecstatic creativity. "The AfK gives me real joy," he wrote to his mother.

> All important modern artists, architects, painters, [and] sculptors under one cover. . . . [It] is incredibly beautiful and animating. . . . Really important people visit us. This is the type of life I've always wanted, but I needed the cleansing effect of the war. . . . Now I have the pleasure of seeing what I can accomplish through my own inner strength. I know that this was only possible because I have transformed my innermost self.

Newly empowered and energized, Gropius discovered himself as the AfK's leader. It was in such a fervent, enraptured state, which imbued in him a previously unknown sense of near omnipotence, that Gropius one month later opened the Bauhaus doors.

This resolute, assertive mood was evident in his first speech before the AfK as its leader on March 22, 1919, the day after the Bauhaus opened.

Gropius totally opposed any compromise, describing it as "the beginning of the end." Despite the arrogant edge to his stance, Gropius's tone was more subdued than his Leipzig address of the previous November, a reflection most likely of the dejected mood of those who had supported what they now referred to as the failed revolution.

As deeply as they felt this defeat, Germany's disheartened liberals still believed their country needed "a new spirituality," as Gropius declared three months after the Council's December vote. "The thrones [may] have been toppled," he commented, "but the old spirit remains deeply rooted." What was altered were the means by which they intended to bring it about.

The choice of a National Assembly and the government's involvement in the deaths of the Spartacist leaders had made it painfully clear, Gropius noted, that the government could no longer be counted on to help create the enlightened society. Instead the idea arose of a *spiritual* rather than a political revolution—a so-called second revolution to which Gropius himself specifically alluded. Others believed this as well. Walther Rathenau, for example, referred to Germany's need to be saved by a "second revolution, . . . not that of the Cossacks [i.e. the Soviets], but a revolution in our way of thinking." In fact, Gropius's statement that "a spiritual and not a political revolution [would] liberate us" represented one of the day's most broadly held convictions among Germany's disillusioned liberals. Gropius and his AfK colleagues thus continued to prepare for the enlightened society. Despite his quieter tone, Gropius's vision of the AfK remained as messianic as that of his predecessor, Taut.

Gropius moved to accommodate the AfK to the changed conditions in essentially two ways. With Gropius now referring to the AfK's earlier hopes of approaching the government as "fanciful," he shifted the organization away from Taut's overtly political activism toward the creation of a Bund, which he referred to as a *Bauhütte*, or guild. It would be a messianic artistic community that would enlighten and lead society to renew itself by "sweep[ing] aside the divisions between their various artistic disciplines." Reflecting the day's inward mood—the "private, separate world" of inner reflection to which Gropius referred—he envisioned this artists' collaborative as a secret sect, "a conspiracy" that would lay in wait for the proper moment before "fiercely" springing into public action.

The AfK then—despite the collapse of its political ambitions—still sought to create a new spiritual society. The group continued to refer to the cathedral-like *Volkshaus*, where, as Gropius declared, collaborating artists would live and work together, "supported by all the people . . . like the masters of the Gothic cathedrals in the medieval *Bauhütten*." Gropius explained this idea, similar to what Taut had written earlier, in an article for an AfK-sponsored Exhibition of Unknown Architects that opened in March, almost simultaneously with the Bauhaus.

> Artists . . . [t]ogether, let us want, conceive, create the new building idea. Painters and sculptors, break through the barriers to architec-ture, and become co-builders, co-contenders for the ultimate goal of art: the creative conception of the cathedral of the future, which will unite everything in one form, architecture, sculpture and painting.

Barely two weeks later this text would reappear virtually unchanged in the Bauhaus Manifesto.

The AfK, in lieu of governmental backing, decided to approach the pub-lic directly through publications and exhibitions. After the creation of a *Bauhütte*, this became the AfK's second major objective. Gropius not so much altered Taut's original program for the AfK as shifted its priorities. The organization's radical goal of leading the spiritual transformation of society—and Gropius's total dedication and unswerving will to achieve it—remained the same. It was in this context of a confrontational, uncom-promising, secret, elitist sect—"we *geistig* ones will show you the way"—that the Bauhaus emerged in March. Impelled by the heady challenge of finally being able to *do* something, Gropius moved quickly to make his "radical" changes.

Like Bruno Taut, Gropius believed the "superhuman architect" was the natural leader for the country's spiritual renewal. It was within this titanic, aggrandized, and essentially Nietzschean perspective that Gropius viewed himself as architect-leader of both the AfK and the Bauhaus, the possessor of spirituality, the Promethean molder of worlds (shared as well by Taut and Adolf Behne), the true revolutionary, capable of accomplishing where politicians had failed. From this view the AfK and the Bauhaus moved to break down barriers between the arts; between the arts and the people; between the arts and craft; and between artists of different nations.

"We look to the artists," wrote Behne. "Artists are brothers, however scattered over the earth they may be. . . . In this . . . artists are our hope." This activist perception, which informed Gropius's leadership of the Bauhaus, also moved the AfK to attempt to ally itself with various artistic communities in Germany and beyond its borders. By early 1919 the AfK would be able to list more than a dozen radical groups with whom it had established contact. Their earliest and most aggressively pursued alliance was with their fellow artists in Russia.

The Allied blockade of Russia made communication difficult and such an undertaking formidable. Although sporadic correspondence did exist at the time, German artists knew very little about what was going on in Russia, aside from the fact the country had succeeded in toppling the old order; it was on the verge of setting up a radically new egalitarian society; and important avant-garde artists, such as Wassily Kandinsky and Vladimir Tatlin, were at the forefront of radical artistic organizations. But as little as they may have known, they recognized Russia as a place where "things got started"—as Behne put it—in art as in politics.

German and Russian artists made their first postwar contact through Ludwig Bähr, a painter, ex–German army officer, and member of the German diplomatic mission in Moscow. Sent to fight on the Russian front, Bähr had been captured and held there as a prisoner of war. Fluent in Russian by the war's end, Bähr had been asked by the German government to maintain contacts with the Russian intelligentsia, much as Muthesius had done in England. When Bähr returned to Germany in December 1918, he brought with him an appeal from a newly established Russian artistic organization known as the International Office. This organization, directed by a committee that included Tatlin and Kandinsky, was set up specifically to establish contacts with western artists. Their message to the AfK about "progressive fighters of the new art [working to construct] a new universal artistic culture" electrified the German avant-garde. "News from Russia has finally arrived," wrote an ebullient Schlemmer.

> Moscow is said to be flooded with Expressionism. They say Kandinsky and the moderns are splashing whole quarters with color, using blank walls and the sides of houses as the surfaces on which to paint modern pictures. An artificial spring conjured up,

with giant sunflowers, flower beds in a potpourri of color. . . . The
fallen art of Czarist Russia replaced by Tolstoy, Dostoevsky, Jaurès,
Robespierre. Russia: the youth of Europe.

Gropius, however, was unable to reply to his Russian cohorts. On
January 26, 1919, the AfK sent a wire to Moscow acknowledging their
"great sympathy" and interest in collaborating with their Soviet colleagues. But the Allied blockade of Russia probably prevented it from getting through. Lack of a translator and a Russian typewriter, and the
German government's notably unenthusiastic reception of this idea, further stymied Gropius's and the AfK's efforts.

With Communist-led uprisings erupting all over Germany in protest
against the murders of Liebknecht and Luxemburg, the government's
unsympathetic response was hardly surprising. On January 22, 1919, for
example, strikers at Berlin's power stations succeeded in plunging the capital into darkness and bringing it to a virtual standstill. Not until March
25—four days after the Bauhaus had opened—could Gropius send an AfK
response to the Russian revolutionary artists.

To do this, Gropius seems to have had to resort to clandestine means.
On March 24, according to Harry Kessler, who was present, Gropius met
with a Soviet Government representative by the name of Markovski, who
had secretly remained in Berlin at the Kaiserhof Hotel. While there is no
other confirmation of this meeting, it does not seem far-fetched to assume
that Gropius was trying to get around government obstruction by arrang-
ing hand delivery of the AfK's message, just as the Russians had earlier
done with Bähr.

The AfK enthusiastically returned their Russian colleagues' greetings.
Addressed to "Comrades," the message declared that "we, like you, are
united in our unwavering will to do everything to reclose the cleft that
power politics has wrenched between our peoples." It condemned "with
disgust the criminal deeds of the militarists . . . [and the] era of fraud" and
thanked their "brothers" for their offer of friendship.

> We take it happily and praise you. Whatever else may come, we
> will always seek out only the people, and believe that nations will
> die if they oppress humanity. [Terms such as] *Fatherland, glory,
> honor* are only phrases for a crushed human heart. . . .
>
> Comrades, this, our handshake, is the sign of our unity, our

promise, that we . . . carry our fiery seriousness silently in our
hearts. . . .

We are ready to send representatives to a conference where we
could plan together what we as artists must do to unite with the
people.

The AfK suggested an exchange of art and artists (as teachers) and the
planning of joint exhibitions. "Above all," the AfK asserted, they wanted
their Russian comrades to share in their creation of a new enlightened
society, "the goal of [our] common work . . . the great work of love that
will lead us back to beauty after the days of Europe's ugly hate." The AfK
enclosed a copy of its program, which outlined its "ideal of the future . . .
the collaboration of architects, painters, sculptors, musicians, and poets"
and asserting that its "mission is to be artists," the AfK concluded their
response with "brotherly greetings."

This Russian entanglement seemed to rouse Gropius politically. For
where he had earlier referred to a vague unity of artists and people, he
now uncharacteristically wrote of the "proletariat," a far more politically
charged term. "Capitalism and power politics have made us lethargic in
the creative realm and a broadly enveloping bourgeois philistinism is
choking the life out of art," he wrote in an article entitled "Architecture
in a Free People's State."

> The intellectual bourgeoisie of the old Reich—indifferent . . . intel-
> lectually lazy, arrogant and miseducated—has proven its inability
> to serve as the bearer of German culture. With the unshackling of
> its rigid world . . . [and] its spirit toppled, it is now in the process
> of being remolded. New classes of people, not yet fully formed, are
> pushing their way up from the depths. They are the target of our
> hopes. . . . It is to them that the artist of the future will turn.

The AfK-sponsored Exhibition of Unknown Architects that opened at the
J. B. Neumann Gallery in Berlin on March 25, 1919, four days after the
inauguration of the Bauhaus, specifically sought such proletarian support.
Taut, in fact, urged the "revolutionary proletariat" to visit the exhibition.
The AfK's advocacy of artistic freedom and the breaking down of barriers between the arts, its opposition to the status quo, and the retrogressive
values of the bourgeoisie were similarly evident at the exhibition. Given

such broad and diverse aims, it is not surprising that the exhibition turned out to be a mind-boggling assortment of architectural projects, paintings, sculptures, and some works that defied categorization. Mushroom-shaped towers; erotic, polyplike forms; assemblages of cans, bottles, and tufts of hair; theater decorations; projected new cities; and sober plans for workers' housing projected a confusing mixture of ecstasy, sobriety, fantasy, utopian faith, and confrontation. After the exhibit closed in Berlin it traveled around Germany for several months, including a brief stay in Weimar.

The AfK's propagandizing efforts on behalf of the exhibition revealed a similar intent to shake things up. In a pamphlet that accompanied the exhibition, Taut appealed for proletarian support while Gropius wrote about toppling the boundaries between the arts, a seemingly innocuous subject that despite its low-key tone was no less confrontational and critical of the current state of affairs than the exhibition itself. In it, Gropius derided modern cities as "deserts of ugliness" and their "gray, shallow imitative" buildings as "humiliating evidence . . . of our spiritual downfall into hell (*Höllensturz*)."

Without overt sloganeering or displays of raised fists, the AfK exhibition and its accompanying texts clearly delivered an underlying political message of protest and hope that was—as an otherwise sympathetic critic for the German Werkbund put it—"subversive of all existing values." This exhibition and the critical reactions it aroused, along with Gropius's association with the AfK, reflected on the newly opened Bauhaus.

The AfK's attempt to communicate with the Russian artists, along with its exhibition and publications, reflected the day's mercurial and confused political scene. Many liberals, disgusted with the government's involvement in the murders of Luxemburg and Liebknecht and their use of the heavily armed Free Corps to suppress the rebellion, began to look more favorably at the extreme Left, which now attracted some rather unexpected new admirers. Kessler, for example, described the well-known banker Simon Guttmann as "a complete Spartacist"; and Walther Rathenau, the son of the founder of the giant AEG company, was also making "no bones about his strong attraction to Bolshevism." The latter, in Kessler's words, went so far as to describe Bolshevism as "a splendid system . . . that [in] a century . . . will rule the globe."

Many artists were similarly attracted to Bolshevism at this time. Schlemmer wrote of his "faith in [Russia] and everything that comes from there." It no longer seemed a question of whether or not Bolshevism was coming to Germany. Most assumed it was. Not the Russian kind, as Schlemmer commented, but a specifically German variant. Making his only public advocacy of this sort, Gropius too expressed his sympathy for Bolshevism. "Since we have no culture but only civilization at the moment, I am convinced that Bolshevism, despite all its evil side effects, is the only way within the foreseeable future to create the foundations of a new culture," he commented in response to a poll.

Part of this Bolshevik sympathy was undoubtedly aroused by the government's increasingly reactionary turn. For neither Rathenau, Schlemmer, nor Gropius were Bolshevists. Gropius's moderating instincts, his patrician background, genuine disdain for party politics, and essentially aesthetic priorities restrained him from making any sustained, total commitment to the radical goals he so vociferously championed. Like Taut and Behne, Gropius adhered to the supposed analogy between the abused proletariat and the abused artist and the need for art to ally with the masses. But Gropius never took the next logical step of advocating the violent overthrow of the government to achieve these goals.

Along with many intellectuals of the time who were the sons and daughters of well-to-do families, Gropius never recognized the inherent incongruity of an elitist priesthood advocating egalitarianism or unity with the masses. Despite the AfK's pro-proletariat stance, Gropius pursued (and received) support from wealthy bourgeois patrons—the day's radical chic—whom he rewarded with "deluxe editions" of the AfK's radical program. Gropius's ideological ambiguity was evident elsewhere too. He encouraged the radical Left to participate in the AfK but refused to allow proletariat representatives into the organization's directing council, despite being urged by others to do so.

As reluctant as Gropius may have been to embrace revolutionary action, he never suppressed the publication of politically radical articles in AfK publications, such as those written by Ludwig Meidner, an artist and writer committed to proletarian revolt. A notable discrepancy then existed between the radicalism the AfK preached and what it was actually able—or in Gropius's case, willing—to do. This characteristic, however, cannot be attributed simply to quirks of Gropius's personality, for such a bizarre scenario was repeating itself throughout the newly emerging republic. Much like the Berlin demonstrators who had carefully avoided stepping on the grass as they marched through the Tiergarten during the November

Revolution, Gropius and his AfK associates perambulated through the motions of revolution, venting long-simmering resentments, aspirations, and post-battlefield fatigue. Gropius's propensity for advocating extreme positions he did nothing to carry out created a split between the AfK's (and soon, the Bauhaus's) words and actions and exposed the group to a reactionary backlash. Given the day's hyperpoliticized mood, the AfK's vocal and highly public activities were seen by both its adherents and opponents in a distinctly Bolshevik light.

Whatever Gropius's personal equivocation may have been, his radical public stance in the AfK remained unwavering. Once the AfK displayed "sufficient strength" (that is, created a community of united artists), it would join the masses and demand that the government "enforce our will." Then, with the artistic collective "flourishing and healthy" and the large-scale *Volkshaus* building project begun, the AfK, he declared, "should, in God's name, go to the devil." What would replace the AfK in Gropius's mind was the Bauhaus.

Understandably discreet as Gropius was in revealing his radical intentions to the Weimar authorities, he did discuss them privately. In his letter to Hardt, Gropius referred to his "storming into Weimar . . . [w]ith a real hunger [to] seek enlightened people to create the foundation stone of an enlightened society." Gropius's aim with the Bauhaus, similar to that of the AfK, was nothing less than an upheaval of society through a radically altered art. Passionately convinced of the importance of what he was attempting, Gropius suffered no false modesty. His Weimar idea, he declared to Hardt, was "not a minor one."

Three years earlier, in his initial Bauhaus proposal, Gropius had pinned his hopes on technology bettering workers' and artists' lives and helping industry become more profitable with well-designed products. After the war and revolution, his view had metamorphosed, like his country and himself. Technology, having brought mass destruction, was now discredited. With Germany smashed both morally and physically, technology seemed not only beside the point, but downright immoral, as Gropius noted in his Leipzig address. Spiritual transformation—the creation of a peaceable and nonmaterialistic society—was the cry of the hour; and it was within these new parameters that Gropius now viewed the Bauhaus, as he did the AfK. No longer was Gropius interested in just improving the profitability of Weimar's local industries: The Bauhaus, by providing the model of the collaborative artistic community working hand in hand with the proletariat, would help the country spiritually transform itself.

In line with this lofty ambition, Gropius proposed that the Art Academy (with its newly created Architecture and Craft Department) merge with van de Velde's now defunct School of Arts and Crafts so that the resulting institution would "eventually produce [under one roof] everything related to building: architecture, sculpture, painting, furnishings, and handicrafts." On March 20 Gropius requested that the combined schools be called the Bauhaus, an obvious nod to the medieval *Bauhütten*. The next day the Bauhaus celebrated its opening.

On March 29 the provisional Thuringian government formally approved Gropius's directorship of both Weimar institutions under the single title of the State Bauhaus in Weimar (Staatliches Bauhaus). Backed now by the government support he had so long sought, Gropius joyously confided his expansive plans to his mother. "[The school] can really grow into something now," he wrote. "I believe that even a further political change to the left will not pass by my institute."

What Gropius had planned, however, was not at all what Weimar was expecting. Although Gropius's statements (in his Leipzig address) and AfK activities were all matters of public record, the Weimar authorities seemed unaware of his radical sentiments, which, like those of his colleagues, shifted with the ebb and flow of the revolution. Weimar awaited a modest reform of art training; Gropius and his colleagues wanted to blaze a new cultural path.

The opening of the Bauhaus took place within a tumultuous political milieu that added to the difficulties the school would soon encounter. Germany in the spring of 1919 was hovering on the edge of civil collapse. Outraged by a government that had not only been involved in the murders of their Spartacist leaders but also seemed reluctant to enact the radical social change they had anticipated, the rebels intensified the level of their uprisings in cities throughout Germany. Bremen, Cuxhaven, Mülheim, Düsseldorf, Halle, Braunschweig, Magdeburg, Leipzig, Munich, Dresden, and Berlin, to name only a few, resonated to their fury. The Free Corps, granted a free hand by the fearful and frustrated government, responded with equal savagery. Many German liberals, caught up in the heady promise of a new world of hope and justice, overlooked the brutal actions.

On March 6 Kessler described the vicious battles taking place in Berlin as heralding the beginning of civil war; J. B. Neumann, the owner of the gallery where the AfK exhibition was held, similarly hailed the "beginning world revolution," and Gropius that day made known his intention to "further radicalize" the AfK. Two days later, as Berlin witnessed more bloodshed than at any time since the start of the revolution, Kessler thought Bolshevism had come to Germany.

Following the January 1919 elections for the National Assembly, Thuringia's citizens had gone to the polls on March 10 to elect a new state government to replace the provisional one (with whom Gropius was negotiating). The result, a coalition government between the Social Democrats and the center German Democratic Party (Deutsche Demokratische Partei, the DDP), determined that the Bauhaus would be financed and supervised by a far more conservative administration than the provisional SPD authorities who had established and approved the school. With more than a thousand people dead from the fighting in Germany by the second week of March and the national government's declaration of martial law, Weimar's fears of Bolshevism no longer seemed unwarranted.

Events taking place outside Germany's borders amplified fears. On March 21, 1919, the day the newly named Bauhaus opened its doors, Béla Kun established a Soviet republic in Hungary. With Budapest as close to Munich as Edinburgh is to London, Kun's act mesmerized Germany. A journalist and former war prisoner from Moscow, he moved quickly to nationalize farmland and organize revolutionary tribunals. Among the Hungarian intellectuals who flocked to join Kun's regime were the philosopher György Lukács (appointed Deputy, then full Commissar for Education) and László Moholy-Nagy, a twenty-four-year-old writer, painter, and contributor to the radical journal *Ma* whom Gropius, four years later, would appoint to the faculty of the Bauhaus.

How much Kun's actions had excited Weimar's Bolshevik fears became apparent on March 23, when citizens awarded 66 percent of their votes to rightist parties in the election for the local Weimar City Council, an astonishing figure considering the scant 15 percent the Right had been able to garnish in January's national elections.

Germany's concern about the proximity of Kun's republic to Bavaria proved justified. In early April 1919 the Bavarian People's Republic, its founder Eisner assassinated two months before, collapsed into near anarchy; and on April 6 Ernst Toller formed the First Bavarian Soviet Republic in Munich. Through a series of decrees he established the Bavarian Red Army, disarmed the bourgeoisie, and set up revolutionary tribunals. Toller followed Kun's precedent and invited notable intellectuals into his government. One of them, Gustav Landauer, a German anarchist offered the position of Educational Minister, had particularly influenced Taut. In light of the latter's influence on Gropius, this was a matter of considerable importance to the Bauhaus. Landauer in turn invited Taut and Heinrich Tessenow (it is unclear whether he invited just one or both of them) to become Building Ministers of the new republic.

In turn, Landauer's Bavarian Cultural Program—only the rough notes of which survive—advocated a unified arts under architecture's leadership that was remarkably similar to what Taut and the AfK proposed. "The new era of human history," wrote Landauer,

> should find its expression in the public buildings and monuments which will be built from now on . . . through official commissions. This applies to all the arts: painting and sculpture are, from the outset, to be incorporated into architecture."

Gropius's Bauhaus Manifesto—also influenced by Taut and appearing quite accidentally at the same time—assigned a similarly exalted role to architecture.

The obvious kinship of the Bauhaus program to the new Bavarian Soviet republic alarmed Weimar's citizens, whose reactionary antennae were already quivering. It seemed the radical proposals being espoused in Munich were about to appear in their city as well, in the form of the Bauhaus. While Landauer's plans never saw the light of day, his position in the Bavarian republic and the similarity of the Bauhaus program (not to mention the AfK's) to his own caused many Weimar citizens to look upon the Bauhaus as a Bolshevik enterprise.

But with battles raging between the Free Corps and Spartacist rebels, Bavaria was hardly Germany's only concern that April. Mobs rampaged through Dresden, Magdeburg, and Danzig while twenty thousand workers across the nation went on strike. Berlin looked like a battlefield. Some of the city's most important streets, including Wilhelmstrasse, were jammed with artillery and machine guns. Steel-helmeted Free Corps troops armed with hand grenades roamed the city.

Reaction to what was going on in Germany and beyond ranged widely. Liberals and members of the avant-garde, such as Oskar Schlemmer, continued to rejoice over the turn of events. Believing these events heralded a turning point in human history and marked the beginning of the new spiritual order, Schlemmer and his colleagues viewed them with hope. "Things are happening!" echoed a euphoric Kessler on April 12. "A colossal fermentation of ideas is . . . paving the way for a new . . . revolution . . . [this time] a genuine one." But others, like Weimars residents, were apprehensive. The Allies, too, viewed the goings-on in "Red" Bavaria with grave concern. The French reinforced their troops in Alsace. The Entente, meeting in Paris to formulate the peace terms, left no doubt about its aversion to a Bolshevik Germany. They gravely warned that continuation of the peace process was dependent on a quick end to the "Soviet goings-on" in Munich and Bavaria. On April 12, 1919, the Allies issued a news release declaring "that no final peace can be made with a Germany, large parts of which are in league with Russia." That same day in Weimar— whose citizens, in the local elections three weeks before, had displayed a conservatism strikingly at odds with its own liberal state of Thuringia, as well as the country as a whole—Gropius's appointment as director of the Bauhaus was officially announced.

5.

A Hornet's Nest

Tradition Meets the New, Changed World

Beware of spitting against the wind!

—*Nietzsche*

Weimar residents detested their art school's new name. In November 1918 the revolution and the abdication of the Grand Duke had forced Weimar's unrepentant monarchists to swallow the loss of the princely title the Saxony Grand Ducal College of Applied Arts. Now, five months later and for unexplained reasons, another name—Bauhaus—was being forced down their throats, a name they found distasteful. "Miserable, disastrous" was how Leonhard Schrickel, *Deutschland*'s art critic, described the change. The painter Lyonel Feininger, Gropius's first faculty appointment to the new school, wrote of the town's "enormous bitterness" over the new name. Weimaraners, like most inhabitants of the former princely states, were suspicious of any outsider—none more so than Berliners, whom they found pushy, insolent, and presumptuous. The school's new name reinforced this opinion. Encircled as they were by threats of change and fearing the loss of the "German" values they saw themselves as representing, Weimar's citizens were in a particularly wary and defensive mood when the Bauhaus opened its doors.

Long a source of civic pride, the Art Academy had been very much a part of Weimar's sense of its old glory, a vital testament to the city's continuing cultural preeminence. Weimar was proud of the distinguished figures who had been associated with the school. They included some of the country's most renowned artists, such as Max Liebermann, Max Beckmann, Arnold Böcklin, Theodor Hagen, and Ludwig von Hoffmann. The Academy had always stood at the forefront of school reform, opposing what Weimar, like Gropius, saw as Wilhelminian philistinism. In their view of the Art Academy as both forward-looking and an upholder of tradition, Weimar's citizens saw themselves.

Their pride in their school was not unjustified. In 1902, while Wilhelm II was ranting against Impressionist art in Berlin, Weimar had brought in Hans Olde, one of Germany's leading Impressionist painters, to direct the Academy. The school's expansion the following year (to include more "practical" training in sculpture and crafts) had been made in an attempt to align itself with the day's most progressive trends. To help them in their nearly four-year-long deliberations over Gropius's appointment, the Academy had sought the advice of Wilhelm von Bode, one of the country's most outspoken proponents of art-school reform. The Academy's decision on October 3, 1917, to offer craft classes (applied arts) along with the school's normal program had put the school firmly behind von Bode's reformist views, a stance they defended by referring to the school's reformist tradition. "Right from its beginnings," they declared, "the Weimar Academy has stood in sharp contrast to [the] obsolete academies."

Von Bode was deeply involved in the Academy's decision to bring in Gropius, personally interviewing him in Berlin prior to his appointment. It was only after von Bode's approval that the school's board of directors voted unanimously to bring in the young and relatively unproven architect. They had considered Gropius because of their self-view as progressives, which was why Professors Klemm, Thedy, Engelmann, and Fröhlich remained on the faculty when the Academy became the Bauhaus. Max Thedy, painter, engraver, and—since Fritz Mackensen's retirement in 1918—acting director of the Academy, was the most senior of the three.

Nearly sixty-one years old when the Bauhaus began, the much-beloved Thedy had been a professor at the Weimar Academy since 1883, the year of Gropius's birth. Unfortunately his highly finished, thematically grandiose, and pretentious-looking art, which hung in the collections of major museums throughout Germany, was precisely the traditional art that Gropius's Bauhaus would try to overcome.

As for modern artistic trends, the Academy believed them to be represented within its ranks by Walther Klemm, a painter and graphic artist, and the sculptor Richard Engelmann. Among Germany's most recognized artists, both had been teaching at the Academy since 1913. The thirty-six-year-old Klemm had trained in Vienna with Kolo Moser, a prominent Secessionist. Strongly influenced by Japanese prints, Klemm's woodcuts had been exhibited by the Vienna Secessionists in 1905. Shortly thereafter, Klemm returned to Germany, where his style was influenced by Expressionism. Fifty-one-year-old sculptor Richard Engelmann's claim to modernity was the three years he had spent in Rodin's atelier twenty years earlier, between 1896 and 1899. Returning to Berlin in 1899, he had become a member of the Berlin Secession. Engelmann's memorial to the historical playwright Ernst von Wildenbruch had earned him particular renown in Weimar.

Like most German artists who did not create in the more traditional styles, Klemm and Engelmann were considered Expressionists. So too was Feininger, who found this purported affinity amusing. Sardonically he wrote to his wife, Julia, that "Weimar, under Klemm and Engelmann, already has its Expressionist 'genius.'" The addition of what they considered to be a third Expressionist to the faculty grated on the Academy community; yet to label Klemm and Engelmann "modernists" in 1919 was ludicrous. Both Feininger and Gropius considered them "old, reactionary fumblers" who created mere "wallpaper designs."

Thedy, Klemm, and Engelmann had all been on the board of directors of the old Academy, roles they continued at the new Bauhaus. Three other Academy professors, all "traditionalists," also continued to teach at the new Bauhaus: the painter Otto Fröhlich, sculptor Richard Förster, and Fritz Fleischer, a painter who taught color techniques. (The last two were not fully appointed instructors.) Such a conservative faculty was hardly in keeping with Gropius's plans; he realized that the Bauhaus teaching staff, as Feininger put it, would have to be "renewed and strengthened."

■

Apart from the Academy's desire to associate itself with the day's most progressive trends in art education, the collapse of the German art market in July 1918 had convinced the long-procrastinating professors that their graduates needed to have some way of supporting themselves outside their profession. Practical training in gilding and decorative painting seemed to offer graduates the means of earning a living without demeaning their calling as artists. It was with this in mind that they had approved adding Gropius's craft-oriented training program to their curriculum.

Not until the end of April 1919, when several statements and the school's Manifesto were published in *Deutschland*, did they discover that gilding picture frames was not what Gropius had in mind. As would become his habit, Gropius released slightly differing versions of the Manifesto to various newspapers and journals. On April 25 *Deutschland* published the version that had previously appeared in *Vorwärts*, the Social Democratic Party (the SPD) newspaper, a fact the conservative Weimar newspaper pointedly noted. In this version the phrase "Let us then create a new guild of craftsmen without the class divisions that raise an arrogant barrier between craftsmen and artists!" was modified to read "without the class divisions *that separate them from the masses* and raise an arrogant barrier between craftsmen and artists." The change, indicated by italics, sounded an undeniably political tone, especially in the day's heated political environment. So too did the addition of another word (italics added) in a subsequent passage.

> Let us wish for, conceive, create together the new [way of] building of the future that will . . . rise one day toward heaven out of the hands of millions of craftsmen as the crystal symbol of a *coming* new faith.

Although the more politically provocative references were dropped from later published versions of the Bauhaus Manifesto, the *Vorwärts* version was how Weimar learned about the new school.

The belief that culture could transform society was nothing new; it had been proclaimed by the German Expressionists since 1911. But the political nuances this utopian notion had acquired since the war were accentuated by the day's tumultuous events. The revolution and the toppling of such apparently eternal verities as kings—and, as it now appeared, the privileged class as well—lent the Bauhaus Manifesto a particularly radical if not subversive tone. Its reference to a "crystal symbol of a new faith," whether "coming" or already here, made very clear its societal association and ambitions. As German rebels were attempting to overthrow society's old ways—in Bavaria, this already had been accomplished—Gropius's Bauhaus proclaimed its intentions of similarly seeking to overturn art's time-honored assumptions. No more Titians or Michelangelos creating for kings, popes, and wealthy merchants. Art was to be redirected toward the interests of the common man, creating objects for his daily life and establishing an egalitarian, enlightened community that would point the way to a better world. Clearly influenced by the Work Council for Art (the AfK), Gropius's Bauhaus Manifesto attempted nothing less than to similarly overthrow the principles that had traditionally sustained art.

But the Manifesto challenged more than just the traditional academic art establishment. It questioned the very notion of what art was about and for whom. Indeed, the Manifesto's linking of its artistic ambitions with "a new faith" threatened the status quo in general. The program's disparaging reference to "salon art" reinforced its rebellious tone. By salon art Gropius meant traditional art, such as sculpture and painting, which existed separately and apart rather than united under architecture, as the Bauhaus proposed to create. In an article published earlier that year Gropius berated salon art as a vestige of the despised old order, the "bourgeois philistinism . . . of the old Reich—indifferent . . . intellectually lazy, arrogant, and miseducated—[that had] proven its inability to serve as the bearer of German culture."

The Manifesto's radical spirit was also highlighted by its strong emphasis on craft. While a commitment to combining practical and theoretical training could hardly be considered radical within the context of a reformed art school—which, after all, was what the Bauhaus was supposed to be—the emphasis on craft went far beyond this. The Bauhaus curriculum, the Manifesto declared, would not simply include the learning of a practical trade, but would *begin* with it. Its assertion that "the school is the servant of the workshop, and will one day be absorbed in it" made clear the school's goal.

Architects, sculptors, painters, we must all return to the crafts! . . .

> There is no essential difference between the artist and the crafts-
> man. The artist is an exalted craftsman. . . . [P]roficiency in craft is
> essential to every artist. Therein lies the prime source of creative
> imagination. Let us then create a new guild of craftsmen.

The Manifesto's reference to eliminating "class divisions" flung a further challenge in the face of German tradition, namely the country's preference for a hierarchical and authoritarian school structure. Unlike other
German schools, art or otherwise, the Bauhaus was to be an egalitarian
community of "kindred spirits" (a Bund, so to speak) whose collaborative
efforts would aim to break down the barriers that existed between the arts
and the crafts. To this end Gropius eliminated such traditional, hierarchical, and status-oriented titles as professor and student, substituting
instead the term *master* and, for the varying levels of students, *apprentices*, *journeymen* (those who had passed the first examination set by
Weimar's local guilds), and *junior masters*.

Because the Bauhaus's ultimate aim was to provide a model for an
enlightened society, its program extended beyond the classroom, encour-
aging "friendly relations between masters and students outside of work
[through] plays, lectures, poetry, music, costume parties . . . [and] cheerful
ceremonials." Unheard of for German schools, this notion resulted in the
famed Bauhaus parties, perhaps the only school enterprise that was universally admired by politicians, Right and Left. To further encourage the
sense of community and equality between faculty and students, a student
union was set up, with student representatives elected from each workshop. Two student representatives were to participate in the meetings of the
Masters' Council, the faculty group that determined the school's policies.

Surprising for an institution that declared architecture to be the goal of
all the arts, the Bauhaus had no formal architecture department. Adolf
Meyer, Gropius's associate in his private practice, taught some architecture courses at the Bauhaus. Students audited such technical courses as
engineering principles and practice on an ad hoc basis, either at Weimar's
Building Trades School or at lectures given in the Bauhaus several hours
each week by faculty members from the Building Trades School. Mindful
of his own traditional—and what he considered irrelevant—architectural
training, Gropius remained convinced that architecture was best learned
through hands-on practice. The few architecture students at the Bauhaus
(six in 1919) worked in his private office.

Students graduated from the Bauhaus when they passed their particular vocation's qualifying examination given by Weimar's Chamber of Trade, gaining their certification just like any other craftsmen. Journeymen (the more advanced students) could similarly work toward qualifying for the master's test. These were the only examinations Bauhaus students were required to take. Gropius, who prided himself on not doing "anything by force," felt very strongly that rules and regulations—indeed any imposing of his will on others—represented a particularly odious vestige of Wilhelminian mentality. He also believed that students ultimately learned best by themselves; he worried that too many rules would turn the Bauhaus into just another art academy. Rigidity was to be avoided. Bauhaus students received no grades. No classes were required, nor was attendance taken. Gropius abolished the Academy's highly organized curriculum, leaving Bauhaus students to study what they wanted and behave as they wished.

Yet despite the Manifesto's elevated claims and the new titles for students and professors, the Bauhaus was little more than a conventional academy when it opened its doors to its initial 150 students in March 1919. The workshops from van de Velde's old school, on which the Bauhaus craft training program depended, had been dismantled and sold. The only craft training available during the first semester was printmaking, which had been taught in the former Academy. Eventually the Bauhaus's workshops would include metalworking; wood, ceramic, plaster, and stone carving; mural and glass painting (as well as mosaic work and enameling); cabinetry; the graphic arts (such as etching, engraving, lithography, printing, and typography); and theater. But by fall the only additional workshops were in wall painting, weaving, and bookbinding. The drawing and painting classes taken by the Bauhaus's first students were similar to those offered at the Academy. The Bauhaus's two most valuable contributions to modern-art education, the *Vorkurs* (introductory course)—which sought to help students discover their innate talent—and the joint teaching of each workshop by an artist (form master) and a craftsman (craft master), were not in effect during the school's initial session. Rather, the Bauhaus evolved slowly over the course of several years, depending on the availability of qualified workshop instructors, materials, and funds, and Gropius's constant redefining of the school's principles.

The Manifesto's professed search for utopia ("the crystal symbol of a new faith") and simultaneous advocacy of practical craft training attracted a diversity of students. About half came to the Bauhaus seeking its other-worldly utopianism. These tended to be dreamers and poets yearning for universal brotherhood and worshipping untrammeled soulful expression in countless manifestos and proclamations. Leftists for the most part (without being necessarily political), they—like Gropius—opposed tradition, which they held responsible for the brutal war. Some were attracted by the school's hands-on craft approach and came simply to learn a trade. Their ages, backgrounds, and levels of professional training varied as much as their reasons for being there. Some were mature veterans. Many were genuinely dissatisfied with traditional academic teaching and wanted a more experimental approach.

Still others attending the Bauhaus—some of whom belonged to the aristocracy—were former students from the Academy who had remained. They *wanted* the traditional artistic training and disciplined decorum their classmates (and director) rejected as symptomatic of bourgeois "rigidity and authoritarianism." They deplored the lack of constraints and guidelines of the Bauhaus's open directorship and the cantankerous, self-questioning atmosphere it generated, and felt slighted by Gropius's reference to them as "little Raphaels."

By the end of May 1919 the Bauhaus student body was irreparably split between those who were seeking traditional academy training and those who opposed it. Half wanted to learn technical finish and how to transmit high moral ideals through their art; half berated these, seeking only soulful expression. Half admired the laissez-faire attitude of Gropius's directorship—seeing it, like their director, as necessary for an experimental and self-generating creative atmosphere; half saw it only as a void.

The faculty that had remained from the old school, insulted by Gropius's assertion that their "salon" art was irrelevant, were also grumbling. They *enjoyed* the prestige accorded the artist (and professor) in status-conscious Germany and felt threatened by Gropius's attempt to level the difference between craft and art. Not only did it remove the aura they believed surrounded their profession, but they saw Gropius's attempt to raise craft to the level of the fine arts as demeaning to them as to their art. If their trade was no more "noble" than that of crafts, then they were no better than mere craftsmen, which for many of the faculty represented an even greater degradation in their eyes. The change in the school's name, along with its undeniably greater emphasis on craft, seemed to them to transform what had been a prestigious *Hochschule* (college) into an inferior *Gewerbeschule* (trade school).

To the complaints of the "little Raphaels" and the former Academy professors were added those of the Weimar community, many of whom were put off by the students' bohemian ways, particularly their weird and tattered dress. The students' unconventional garb—home-dyed soldier's uniforms with ripped-off collars and Russian-style smocks—strange looking as it was, stemmed more from poverty than from an attempt to make any ideological statement. The Weimaraners, however, saw the students' style as a deliberate mockery of their city's princely and sedate traditions. Provocative behavior seemed to confirm this. These passionate, radical, unruly students took particular glee in shocking Weimar's staid citizenry in a way extraordinary for its time. They painted bathing trunks on the town's nude statues and exposed their bare feet in sandals. The women cropped their hair and wore short skirts. The men let their hair hang down to their shoulders or shaved it off completely. Even Feininger had to admit that the students' behavior was "totally out of control" (*"ganz ausser Zucht"*).

The arrival of the AfK's Exhibition of Unknown Architects in Weimar gave one of the city's local critics an opportunity to articulate the growing reservations about the Bauhaus. The review, appearing on May 18, 1919, was entitled "The Future of the Fine Arts in Weimar" and focused as much on the Bauhaus as it did on the exhibition. Designed to shock the far more sophisticated Berliner, the exhibit horrified the newspaper's critic, who signed himself only as "n." Claiming words simply failed him, he decried that houses were depicted as dragons. The jocular mood Gropius had intended as a way of removing art from its haughty pedestal struck the critic as a lack of respect for so high a subject as art. "The times are too serious and art too holy for such youthful fantasies," he declared. "Such absurdities have already been dealt with in politics," he added, alluding to the events of May 1, 1919, when the Spartacists had suffered a major defeat with the crushing of the Bavarian Soviet Republic by Gustav Noske's Free Corps troops. A terrifying affair that had left more than six hundred dead, including Landauer, it allowed Weimar—insulated, politically homogeneous to a degree unusual within Germany, and, as Feininger put it, "stuffed full of the military"—to ridicule Spartacist "absurdities" with even greater aplomb than before.

Critic "n" did acknowledge that much of the Bauhaus's program was "challenging and useful." But he objected to what he called the program's condescending tone and intimations that Weimar's artistic ways "need[ed] to be enlightened." Gropius, he complained, seemed to be "put[ting] Weimar in its place," and he asked who he was to advise "the [keepers of the] jewel of authentic German art" on the future.

The following day some members of Weimar's artistic community filed a formal complaint to the State Ministry against what they claimed were Gropius's plans "to strip the Bauhaus more and more of its character as an art institute" and change it into a craft school. The notion that art represents no higher spirit than craft, along with the Manifesto's appeal to the masses, seemed uncomfortably similar to the egalitarianism being preached by the Reds—an undeniable if nebulous link that aligned the fears of the holdover professors with those of the community.

Meanwhile mutiny was rocking the Bauhaus from within. Unable to bear what was happening to their school, some former Academy students moved to oust Gropius and Feininger, his faculty ally. By May 21, less than six weeks after the opening of the Bauhaus, Feininger described the school as "a hornets' nest."

The difficulties increased the following day when the Thuringian State Assembly began to consider the Bauhaus's first budget. On February 28, 1919, Gropius had submitted his initial budget estimate to the provisional legislature (the current Assembly's preceding legislative body), and it had been on the basis of these figures that the legislature had approved the establishment of the Bauhaus. It now appeared that Gropius had seriously underestimated the needed funds; also, the value of the mark had dropped sharply since February. Gropius had to ask for far more money than he had originally requested from a far more conservative Assembly.

In addition to underestimating the school's normal operating expenses, Gropius needed money to rebuild the workshops, which, as he rightly claimed, were indispensable to the school. The delicate situation brought Gropius himself to present the school's budget before the Assembly. Speaking before the legislators, Gropius—like van de Velde before him— emphasized the school's goal of trying to help Weimar's craft industry improve its trade, a message particularly meaningful in light of Germany's collapsed economy and the anticipation of horrendous reparation claims. Gropius assured the legislators that such budgetary demands were only temporary. Once the Bauhaus became profitable, its "annually recurring budget deficit . . . [would] gradually decrease."

The Assembly, however, was unconvinced. They turned down the Bauhaus's budget request, forcing the school to operate on a hand-to-mouth basis thanks to a series of short-term loans issued by the Educational Ministry. Encouraged by the legislative rejection, the school's opponents organized a meeting that evening to launch what Feininger (and undoubtedly Gropius) realized would be a "vicious" campaign against the Bauhaus, what Feininger described as *"ein Kampf aufs Messer angesagt"*—literally, a struggle with knives. Calling themselves the Saviors of the Fatherland and the All-Germans, opposition to the Bauhaus entered the political ring, from which it would never leave.

The Allied announcement of their peace terms on May 7, 1919, had thrust Weimar, indeed all of Germany, into a particularly depressed and vindictive mood. From that date until July 9, when the National Assembly reluctantly and indignantly ratified the treaty—described by Kessler as a "frightful moment of tragic magnitude"—an outraged Germany's search for scapegoats and revenge left no institution unscathed, especially one so unformed, provocative, and powerless as the Bauhaus. Chancellor Philipp Scheidemann, speaking at the University of Berlin on May 12, expressed his nation's sullen mood. He accused the Entente of trying to make Germany a nation of "slaves and helots . . . doing forced labor behind barbed wire and prison bars" and declared that German acceptance of the treaty was incompatible with its national honor. Harry Kessler, normally a compulsive diarist, was so depressed by the situation that he was unable to write anything for more than a month.

Two months before, the Bauhaus had opened to the Bolshevik threat. In May the announcement of what would become the Versailles Treaty and the crisis it provoked in Germany collided head-on with the school's struggle to get on its feet.

Demonstrations against the Versailles Treaty erupted throughout Germany. On May 14 thousands of protesters took to Weimar's streets to protest the signing of the treaty and—not surprisingly for the city—demand the replacement of the National Assembly by a restored monarchy. Nerves were on edge. Local opposition to the Bauhaus ballooned to proportions that even van de Velde's most dedicated opponents could not have imagined. Two days before Gropius's budget address to the state's legislators, *Deutschland* published a blistering denunciation of Expressionism as a form of dementia praecox and an attempt to "poison

our German national soul." The article, written by a local Weimar neurologist and titled "On the Affinity between Expressionism, Bolshevism
and Mental Illness," mentioned neither Gropius nor the Bauhaus by
name. But the association of the school with Expressionism's utopianism
and ecstatic mood had become well recognized in the town by this time.
"[W]e must make it our highest goal," the Weimar doctor wrote, "to keep
our youth, the future of our nation, away from such products of madness."

The Bauhaus was also the object of another disguised assault. A brochure attacking "Bolsheviks in the Arts" was distributed to legislators in
the State Assembly just as it was considering the school's funding. For the
Weimaraners, the Bauhaus was coming to personify all those powerful
and mysterious forces allied against them and dedicated to their ruin, as
embodied by the insulting and terrifyingly punitive Versailles Treaty.

The decision over whether or not to sign the treaty obsessed and divided
the country from the government down. The military, for whom the terms
of the treaty were especially onerous, was unilaterally opposed to signing.
Some military leaders urged resuming the war. Until the army agreed to
the treaty's terms of reducing its forces to one hundred thousand men;
prohibiting airplanes, offensive weapons, and armor; and dissolving its
general staff, war college, and cadet schools, the Rhineland—which was
to be permanently demilitarized—would be occupied by the Entente's
military forces.

Many Germans had expected severe terms. But the treaty, blaming
Germany alone for the war and exacting terrifying reparations, struck
most as unjustified. Germany's request to amend the proposed treaty was
rejected by the Allies on June 16, and the country was given an ultimatum
of five days to accept the terms as offered. From the upper echelon of the
(still existent) Supreme Command to the troops of the reconstituted
Reichswehr, angry rumblings of revolt were heard.

By June 19 the Reichswehr was in near mutiny, and the Cabinet
irreparably split. Chancellor Scheidemann, unable to resolve the breach
within his Cabinet, submitted his government's resignation the following
day. Two days later the new Cabinet, headed by Socialist Gustav Bauer,
proposed signing the treaty under protest and with reservations, especially
with regard to acknowledging Germany's sole guilt for the war (the basis
of the reparation demand) and the Allied insistence on the extradition of
the former Emperor and trying him, along with his generals, for war
crimes. On that date, conforming to the terms of the treaty, the German

navy was scuttled, an event that moved Harry Kessler to write of his inde-scribable depression, "as though the entire sap of life had dried up inside." His reaction reflected the sentiments of his countrymen everywhere.

As the nerve center of Germany, Weimar was especially touched by this disgruntled and anxious mood. Leaflets declaring "Down with the traitors who want to sign!" were dropped by airplanes flying over the city. General von Märcker's troops stationed there protested against the gov-ernment's qualified signing of the treaty. The refusal of some of the troops to protect the national government brought President Ebert himself in front of the Weimar palace to reassure the soldiers. The agonizing pres-sure over whether or not Germany would accept the treaty was felt even within the Bauhaus.

On June 22, as Germany scuttled its fleet and the new Cabinet accepted (with qualifications) the Versailles Treaty, Gropius addressed the students at a student exhibition. The speech's uncompromising stand, along with its dry and edgy tone, was strikingly exceptional for Gropius, a reflection perhaps of his own and the day's distraught mood. One can only surmise what the terrible accusations against his country could have meant to a man who had suffered so grievously defending its honor.

Gropius had decided to speak to the students because of what he referred to as the Bauhaus's "incredibly confused state" ("ungeheuerste Zerrissenheit"), caused, he felt, by the students' incomprehension of what the school was about. The exhibit provided a perfect opportunity to move—as he put it—"sharply and uncompromisingly" to clarify the situation.

One year before, he had lain pinioned beneath the bombed-out rubble of the French town hall. His comments indicated that his experience remained the fulcrum of his artistic views. Art, he declared, was based on intense emotional experience, such as "hardship, privation, shock . . . love, . . . or the strongest experience of all . . . that of one's own death."

> The ones who went through such experiences in the war returned completely changed. They feel that they cannot continue in the old way. . . . Uncertain, . . . [they] fight a hard battle with themselves. One day they will suddenly break out of themselves and know where they have to go.

Gropius declared that this intensely personal (and Nietzschean) view of art would not only "transform man's *entire* life and his whole inner make-up," but it was particularly appropriate to the "enormous catastrophe of world history in which we now find ourselves."

Gropius, who saw "finished" paintings as representing "the old way," complained that there were too many of them in the student exhibition. Given the day's "enormously chaotic" situation, he asked how anyone could possible create art as before. Such perfectly rendered traditional art, he declared, may have suited the "totally different prewar time," but now only the "average petty, lazy, and indifferent bourgeois" who were unprepared to delve deeply into themselves, or those who "merely want to play with their tiny talent," could paint in such a manner. Gropius suggested that these people seek other careers, as an impoverished Germany could no longer afford to pay for their education. Only those who were prepared to expose their innermost suffering, Gropius asserted, should remain at the Bauhaus, where they would "gather together . . . [into] small, secret, self-contained . . . guilds . . . [and] conspiracies . . . [at whose core] is concealed a mystery, a nucleus of faith [that will be given] an artistic form."

Gropius's attempt to be fair and equitable is almost palpable. He struggled to balance his complaints against highly finished, dry academic art and what he called the quest for self-expression at the expense of technique. But he insisted that only a single type of art (Expressionism) was appropriate for the times. Perhaps Gropius was so disappointed that the students failed to comprehend his deeply held vision of a radically new art for a radically changed world that he forgot about letting everyone find their own way. Perhaps it was the anxious temper of the day.

Whatever the reason, Gropius's one-sided and unyielding comments, as heartfelt as they may have been, did little to clear the air at the Bauhaus. If anything, the undercurrent of resentment and tension increased after the speech, especially among the students and professors from the old Academy. By July Feininger was describing the Bauhaus's sullen mood as "tremulous." By month's end a campaign was launched at the Bauhaus to bring back van de Velde, who was visiting Weimar at the time. Accused of insult, deception, Bolshevism, lunacy, and treason; its leadership under broad attack; and its students divided, the four-month-old Bauhaus, still unable to gain critical funding, teetered on the brink of collapse.

6.

"A Plague Bacillus"

The Political Implications of the Bauhaus, Imagined and Real

Opinions about the future of society are political opinions.

—Malcolm Cowley

Expressionism, the style to which Gropius was trying to bind the Bauhaus, was by mid-1919 irrevocably linked with the revolution. The Left praised the style because it believed that a "socially fermenting time demanded [an] equally fermenting art" and that the Expressionists' desire to "form the new . . . through art [represented] the will of society." The Right, on the other hand, denounced Expressionism for these same reasons, as well as condemning its "decadent" internationalism.

Expressionism had been associated with subversive politics since Wilhelminian days. But it was not until the Berlin Art Show during the summer of 1919 that critics specifically connected the style with the Left. Expressionism's attempt to destroy traditional art was linked to the Bolshevik effort to smash social conventions; and Expressionist artists, accused of being "reckless fellow-travelers," were derided for their "false" ideas that art had to imitate the turbulence of "politically crazy times." One particularly outraged member of the Anti-Bolshevik League, who showed up regularly at the exhibition, loudly attacked art that tried to destroy and dishonor the fatherland. Aside from such political censure, critics accused Expressionist art of "bizarre madness" and degeneracy, accusations long attached to modern German art.

Despite its name, the Berlin Art Show was not a single exhibition but a series of separate exhibitions sponsored by several artistic groups held simultaneously in the city's Glass Palace. Opening on July 24, 1919, the exhibition (which closed on September 13) was a gargantuan affair displaying 1,280 works of art by 580 artists in 27 rooms. Most of the Expressionistic art appeared in the November Group's section, which included works by the Russian painter Marc Chagall and the Swiss Paul Klee, the latter invited by Gropius the following year to teach at the Bauhaus.

The exceptionally hostile response to this exhibition reflected the black mood into which Germany had fallen. The humiliating treatment meted to them by the Versailles Treaty confirmed many Germans' long-standing suspicion of things foreign and broadened existing schisms from the military to the art world. As Gordon Craig has observed, the treatment of their country as a pariah by the West drove many Germans to vigorously defend what they believed to be their own unique qualities. At the same time self-respect nearly demanded condemnation of what was perceived as non-German, now metamorphosed into *anti*-German. The despised Versailles Treaty legitimized and reinforced precisely what the Right had been complaining about and imbued their grievances with a moral punch they had lacked before. The Right, emboldened by the national mood of outrage, self-contempt, and the angry search for scapegoats, launched a vigorous assault; to which the Left—its zealousness sparked by the growing strength of the reactionaries—keenly responded. The debate that developed in the art world was certainly nothing new. What was notable was its particular savagery.

The Expressionists' appeal to the proletariat, especially evident within the Work Council for Art (the AfK), along with their view of art as an expression of the proletariat's will and their advocacy of change, sufficed to identify the style with the Left. This connection between Expressionist art and the Left would become even more firmly established toward the end of the year when a debate in the Prussian State Assembly gave various political parties the opportunity to voice their attitude toward Expressionism. Virtually without exception the parties of the Center and the Right—the German National People's Party (the DNVP) and the German People's Party (Deutschen Volkspartei, the DVP)—would more or less condemn Expressionism. On the other hand the Left would praise Expressionism's opposition to the status quo and its identification with the revolutionary aspirations of the working class.

For Gropius Expressionism was the art movement that would sweep away the cobwebs of the past. It would clean the air for the intellectual and spiritual renewal of German society. But for much of the bourgeois public, the critics, and the right-wing politicians, the word *Expressionism* spelled dangerous ideas. What they heard were the antibourgeois proclamations, demands to abolish the gulf between rich and poor, reform the school system, and attacks on the prewar rulers of Germany who had supposedly plunged the country into misery. No matter how fervently Gropius presented the Expressionism of the Bauhaus as an art movement of spiritual and intellectual dimensions for the rejuvenation of German culture, he and the Bauhaus were becoming tarred with the brush of political extremism.

Given the inflammatory context of the day, the word *political* was a volatile and elusive term, to which the German language—far more accommodating than English—differentiated between *Kultur-Politik* (cultural politics) and *Partei-Politik* (party politics). Within this frame of reference, Gropius in 1919 was as assuredly committed to *Kultur-Politik* as he was disinterested in *Partei-Politik*. Those who knew Gropius best have consistently emphasized his indifference to party politics. Attempts to label Gropius otherwise were condemned as "slanderous" by T. Lux Feininger, one of Lyonel Feininger's sons. Yet it is undeniable that Gropius's utopian vision was leftist-oriented and could, in the broadest sense, be called political, no matter how much he shunned party politics.

In terms of its appeal the Bauhaus always provoked more sympathy from the Left than the Right. It would always be from the more radically inclined members of the Social Democratic Party (SPD), the Independent Socialists (USPD), and the Communists (KPD) that Gropius would seek (and obtain) political support for the Bauhaus. In Weimar and later in Dessau the Communists would provide the school's most loyal and consistent political support.

But it was not in Gropius's nature or his upbringing to call for class warfare, and throughout his career he would correctly deny that he had ever done so. But his advocacies, conceived in a *Kultur-Politik* context, hovered a hair's breadth away from the *Partei-Politik* he deplored. In the fervent postwar atmosphere this distinction between artistic identification with the masses and the Bolsheviks' urgings for proletarian revolt was simply lost among the avant-garde and politicians of the Left and Right alike. It was in this sense of using "art for political battle" that both Expressionism and the Bauhaus were now seen.

Gropius, however, did not perceive his activities this way at all. Thus he continued his involvement in the AfK, which had expanded its propaganda efforts. In line with its attempt to win over proletarian enthusiasts the AfK—with the help of J. B. Neumann—planned to publish a propagandistic pamphlet titled *Bauen*. It never saw the light of day, but a prospectus edited by Adolf Behne did appear in June 1919, its antibourgeois tone signaled by the red paper on which it was printed. The AfK published ringing manifestos and continued to seek and establish liaisons with other radical artistic groups. The Bauhaus prospectus was distributed by the AfK; the school in turn distributed the group's brochures among its students.

One of these AfK pamphlets, titled *To All Artists!* (*An Alle Künstler!*) reinforced this apparent linkage between Expressionism, Bolshevism, and—thanks to Gropius's involvement—the Bauhaus. Although a complaint leveled against the Bauhaus would describe the publication as "a strongly Spartacist propaganda leaflet," its various essays reflected more a shared sense of the need for radical social change than any consistent and coherent political ideology, as well as the day's blurring of the lines between political and artistic revolutions.

The pamphlet had been initially published in January 1919 by the German National Publicity Office (Die Werbestelle der deutschen Republik) and distributed free to all artists and art schools. In April, perhaps because the first printing had run out and the by now more conservative government was unwilling to continue financing it, the AfK and the November Group jointly republished it. This new edition was not identical to the original. Articles were added and others were revised. Several clearly differentiated between spiritual and political revolutions; others addressed both. Titles often implied a political extremism that was hardly borne out by the accompanying texts. The brochure's anonymously written opening essay, for example, "Call to Socialism," merely decried the timidity of the revolution. Ludwig Meidner's essay, "There Can Be No More Exploiters and Exploited," referred to artist unity with the proletariat. Max Pechstein's "What We Want" described how a unified art and craft would mirror the future unified society and thus transformed the learning of craft into "a public affair" and social mandate. As nebulous and politically vacuous as these articles may have been, the inclusion of two essays written by political figures—Konrad Hänisch, the Social Democratic Prussian Cultural Minister, and Kurt Eisner, the assassinated former Prime Minister of the Bavarian People's Republic—cast the leaflet in an undeniably political light.

In addition to publishing polemical pamphlets, the AfK planned a proletarian exhibition in association with a well-known Spartacist-led organization, the Free Youth Group for Socialism (Freie Jugend), which was scheduled to open in Berlin on January 1, 1920. Like his conservative counterparts, the leader of this group, the Spartacist (and Expressionist advocate) Ernst Friedrich, frequently equated radical art with radical politics in the many articles he wrote for his organization's journal.

Gropius continued the AfK's efforts to contact other radical groups, both in and outside Germany. A memorandum sent to the AfK's membership in June 1919 specifically referred to efforts to make "international connections . . . with artists in all countries." In October the AfK was invited to found a German chapter of the Paris-based Internationale de la pensée (known as La Clarté), whose goal was "to join the spiritual line of the worldwide international . . . [o]n the basis of international understanding and revolutionary world-renewal." Although the grave financial difficulties that the AfK—like most revolutionary groups—was experiencing in the fall and winter of 1919 prevented the group from taking up La Clarté's offer, the invitation was enthusiastically received and plans made to continue discussions.

In addition to his AfK activities, Gropius worked ceaselessly to curry support from sympathetic leftist legislators in Thuringia's State Assembly, where the Bauhaus budget remained unapproved. He also sought support for establishing the Bauhaus as a prototype for statewide art-school reform, a subject of particular interest to the Left. His lobbying among legislators, however, strengthened the perception of the Bauhaus as a politically involved leftist organization. This moved the school's most vociferous opponents—some disgruntled local Weimar artists, students from the former Art Academy, and local crafts organizations—to ally themselves with the conservative members of the State Legislature, who in turn began to see the Bauhaus as a way to rally political support.

On Wednesday, December 10, 1919, an advertisement in *Deutschland* announced a meeting of the Free Union for Municipal Interests (Freie Vereinigung für städtische Interessen), to be held two days later at the Erholung restaurant in Weimar. Sponsored by various local arts and craft groups, the "extraordinary meeting" would discuss "the new art in Weimar," a euphemism for the Bauhaus, now declared a threat to the "nation's traditional artistic drive."

Many of the charges leveled against the Bauhaus at the meeting were spurious and overblown, similar to those directed against the radical art in the Berlin Art Show. The new art was accused of being "Jew's art"— long a complaint of the Berlin Secessionists—which *Deutschland* claimed was met with applause. The Bauhaus was accused of harboring "representatives of Communist-Spartacist inclinations" who engaged in all kinds of propaganda activities, as well as "foreign elements," the code for Jews. One Bauhaus student, Hans Gross, delivered a stinging nationalistic denunciation of the school and urged that an alternative institution be established where true German "fellows of steel and iron" could dedicate themselves to depicting the *volkisch* (roughly translated as the indigenous people's) soul.

Other complaints, however, like those by Dr. Emil Herfurth, a leader of the German Nationalist Party (Deutschnationale Partei, the DNP) in the Thuringian Assembly, addressed what might be considered more reasonable misgivings, including the school's derision of the city's traditions and artistic preferences. "The purpose of the meeting should not be to exhaust ourselves in hostile attacks on modern art," Herfurth declared, "but rather to express our attachment to the trustworthy old art. We are fond of it and want it to be considered for our school. One should greet the new art cautiously."

Some of Weimar's disgruntled local artists aired their gripes as well. Several of them had anticipated being asked to join the Bauhaus faculty. Not only had they been ignored, but they had found themselves being deprecated for their traditionalist styles, now transformed into "true German values."

Because the Bauhaus, as a state institution, was funded by Thuringia and received little support from the city (aside from a small scholarship fund for local students), Gropius—who was present at the meeting—did not take these charges too seriously. Whether or not his appraisal of the situation was correct, the director's downgrading of the town's complaints stemmed also from his elevated view of the Bauhaus's utopian mission. This frame of mind predisposed him to dismiss the accusations against the school as merely "poisonous propaganda" and his adversaries as "narrow-minded dilettantes . . . caught . . . in a net of the most stupid, furious, and subjective attacks"; or as he wrote one month later, as a "small clique of resident mummies . . . [engaged in] a witch-hunt against me and the Bauhaus."

In the context of the country's inflammatory atmosphere, the Weimar meeting was rather innocuous. Coverage by newspapers across the country, however, elevated what was a rather commonplace local dispute into a national cause célèbre with broad public implications. It was from this national coverage that much of the German public learned about the Bauhaus.

A more ominous note was introduced on December 14, when Leonhard Schrickel, in a *Deutschland* article, raised the touchy issue of the Bauhaus's legitimacy, a subject that was not broached at the meeting. He charged that the Bauhaus had only been authorized by a "provisional government . . . in a moment of rashness . . . after the anarchy of the revolution" and enjoined the current government to correct the situation. The Right would seize upon this issue and turn Gropius's annual legislative request for funds into an endless rehash of the Bauhaus's supposedly questionable legitimacy. Schrickel also berated the school's Expressionistic preferences as childish, indiscrete, and excessive, "a form of puberty . . . a violent reaction . . . that we have all once been through." What Gropius characterized as a yearning for authenticity, for being at the forefront of an effort to recreate human society—the very core of the Bauhaus's art— did not represent a new aesthetic and intellectual reorientation, Schrickel claimed, but an adolescent excrescence, a form of artistic acne—painful, embarrassing, and something that would go away.

The "new art's" attempt to reach beyond German tradition was derided as "internationalism." It was a variant of the old Wilhelminian complaint, recently reinvigorated by the humiliating *Diktat*, as the Versailles Treaty was being called. Given Germany's defensive and shamed mood, to admire anything that lay beyond the nation's borders was to venerate the enemy. "For the Entente nations," Schrickel wrote, "that is not of great significance, but for us trampled-on Germans it is . . . *the* misfortune."

> We must be German in every fiber. . . . The cultivation of an a-national art is [tantamount to] an attempt on the life of the fatherland choking under the enemy's grasp . . . [and] must be rooted out now from root to branch and destroyed like a plague bacillus.

Encouraged by Schrickel's support, the Bauhaus opponents continued their campaign, meeting again on December 18, 1919. New issues emerged at this meeting, such as the number of non-German students at the Bauhaus; its so-called transformation into a craft school; and "expulsion" of Hans Gross, the nationalistic student who had spoken out against the school at the earlier meeting. The departing Gross was accompanied by thirteen other Bauhaus students, presumably from the old Art Academy. The announcement in the *Thüringerische Landeszeitung* that "[f]urther consequences [of Gross's expulsion] will ensue, since nationalist circles refuse to submit to leftist [threats] of terror" added an alarming new tone to the proceedings.

The following day Schrickel, disregarding the fact that Gross had voluntarily resigned, said Gross and his "like-minded companions" had been forced out because of their ideas for a "German" Bauhaus. That same day fifty Weimar citizens addressed a petition against the Bauhaus to the Thuringian Privy Council (Staatsrat). Although the Privy Council unanimously decided in favor of the Bauhaus, Gropius realized the matter was far from over. "[T]he opposition," he wrote, "will continue to scream."

What Gropius did not anticipate was that some of this screaming would come from the Bauhaus's own faculty, most notably the former Academy professors whose students' works the Bauhaus director had so vigorously rebuked in June's student exhibition. The town's obvious hostility to the Bauhaus undoubtedly encouraged the professors. At a Masters' Council meeting on December 18, 1919, they insisted that traditional art-school subjects such as still-life study and easel painting be included in the Bauhaus's curriculum. Gropius had eliminated these traditional academy courses as irrelevant to what the Bauhaus was trying to accomplish. But anxious now to avoid adding the professors' voices to the growing community unrest, he immediately acceded to their request. His move, however, failed to assuage everyone. In a demonstration of the professors' continuing dissatisfaction, Fritz Fleischer, a disgruntled local artist and a part-time faculty member, resigned.

The Bauhaus controversy, known as the Weimar Art Battle (die Weimar Kunstkämpfe), captivated the press. Invectives pro and con filled editorial pages across the country. "From Weimar," declared the *Hamburger Abendblatt*, "it has been reported that a serious conflict has broken out in public between the leadership, most of the student body at the State Bauhaus and the overwhelming majority of intelligent, art-loving bourgeoisie and the old established artistic community." Berlin newspapers trumpeted "The Struggle for the Staatliches Bauhaus." The press divided along political party lines. Leftist newspapers defended the Bauhaus. An article in *Vorwärts* described the affair as a "smear campaign [Die Hetze] . . . concocted to make a political affair out of a stupid Weimar scandal." Rightist newspapers depicted the Bauhaus issue as one of "protecting . . . our *Volk* from disintegration, decline and loss of standing." No one seemed interested in the Bauhaus's art.

Encouraged by the national response and despite their defeat in the Privy Council, the opposition—described by a local newspaper as "Weimar's best artists"—pushed ahead. They accused the Bauhaus of "discarding and treating the Art Academy's entire tradition and every thing of which Weimar has been proud with meticulously displayed contempt"; of giving preference to foreigners and allowing "a strongly Spartacist propaganda leaflet from Berlin to be officially distributed to all the students" (the *To All Artists!* pamphlet); and requested the State Ministry of Saxony-Weimar to begin an "immediate and detailed" official investigation into "the Gross case" and the conditions prevailing at the Bauhaus.

On December 18, the day the opposition met and the professors lodged their complaints at the Masters' Council meeting, an obviously pressed Gropius abandoned his reluctance to impose rules on the students and forbade all political activities in the Bauhaus. Some, like Feininger, thought Gropius had acted too late. But having made such an issue of allowing the students to do what they wanted (regardless of how compromised this may have been by his June address), Gropius's prohibition, however delayed, marked—for him at least—a profound admission of the seriousness of the school's problems. Having given way, as carloads of documents attest, Gropius adamantly opposed any further political involvement for members of the Bauhaus community, himself included. "[W]hatever I do must have no political overtones," Gropius wrote to Adolf Behne, the *Monatshefte* art critic who was helping the Bauhaus director run the AfK. "I personally keep away from getting mixed up in politics," Gropius declared to Walter Müller-Wulckow, an eminent editor and art critic.

By January 1920, in response to actions initiated by Weimar's disgruntled art community, both the Bauhaus and Gropius himself were under official investigation by the state of Thuringia for mismanagement of funds. Each side, seeking to gain support, justified its position in broadly ideological terms. For the nationalists the issue involved the country's honor. Gropius too saw it as "not [just] a Weimar affair, but a German phenomenon . . . not a tempest in a teapot but the start of a dramatic confrontation . . . between the old art education and the growth of a new worldview."

Under attacks that might have broken less committed men, and strained as well by his continuing and ambivalent attempts to gain Alma's consent to a divorce (and shared custody of their child), Gropius responded with characteristic defiance, charged by the crisis with a new sense of energy and determination. "I am in the terrible vortex of dangers," he wrote to Lily Hildebrandt, a woman friend. "The mob agitates against me with the lowest means." Characteristically, he perceived his difficulties in terms of the military confrontations he had so miraculously survived. "I am in the middle of a fight about the Bauhaus idea," he wrote to his mother on December 29, 1919. "[T]he idea is at stake. . . . I am proud of this fight." To a friend, Edwin Redslob, about to leave his directorship of the museum in nearby Erfurt to assume the position of National Arts Commissioner (Reichskunstwart) in the federal government, Gropius commented that he would "painfully miss" him in his "shock troops." "The battle must be fought," he declared to Hans Poelzig. "Nobody leaves me in peace."

Gropius seemed as impelled by the battle's purpose as by its sheer challenge. Adversity emboldened and energized him. It masked his uncertainties and transformed him into an inspired leader. Yet his actions appeared to confirm his opponents' claims. This was certainly the case with the Workers' Art Exhibition, cosponsored by the AfK and the Spartacist-dominated Free Youth. The exhibit opened in a working-class section of East Berlin on January 1, 1920, and included paintings by Feininger as well as works by such well-known artists as Bruno and Max Taut and the Russian painter Marc Chagall. In its effort to reach out to the proletariat, the exhibition also included anonymous art, workers' and children's art, and art created by members of the Free Youth and the Communist and Communist Workers' (KAPD) Parties.

The message of the show was clear: Art could be created by anyone and no longer belonged only to the privileged classes. Lectures by Behne, Bruno Taut, and Ernst Friedrich—one of which was a memorial tribute to Gustav Landauer—were given on Sundays, so that workers could attend. The exhibit was well attended. It collapsed, however, in four weeks, after the building's landlord brought a successful lawsuit charging misuse of the premises (which were not supposed to be used for art shows) and that the exhibition and lectures were a cover for Bolshevik agitation.

Gropius's association with the exhibition, however peripherally, belied his frequent and impassioned avowals of avoiding politics—and played into the hands of his opponents. Still operating without an approved budget, the Bauhaus faced a battle of a new sort in the Thuringian State Assembly at the end of January 1920. The school's opponents no longer confined themselves to the issue of money. ("There is talk of 180,000 [marks] and that in these difficult times," commented *Deutschland* on January 23.) Now, for the first time, they began to challenge the Bauhaus's continued existence in Weimar. Claiming that the school had brought "something alien into our 'little town,'" the newspaper asked if Weimar was "big enough and rich enough to support such an undertaking?"

Gropius's claims to the contrary, the Bauhaus was now perceived in Weimar and throughout Germany as a politicized institution. As such, its fate became linked not to the value of its artistic aims or to some spiritual revolt, as its leader preferred to believe, but to cultural-political developments that he deplored as much as he seemed to pursue them.

7. The Paradox of Bauhaus Politics, 1920

Denial and Pursuit

It is darkening, but we don't know whether it is dawn or dusk.

—*Kurt Tucholsky*

Standing at his window on March 18, 1920, Gropius was deeply moved to see some of his Bauhaus students participating in the funeral procession that unfolded on the street below. The procession, the largest that Weimar had ever seen, was for the workers slain five days before during the Kapp Putsch. The seemingly endless number of posters that displayed slogans such as "Long live Luxemburg!" and "Long live Liebknecht!" left little doubt about the event's politics. Or, for that matter, the Bauhaus's sympathies, considering the presence of its students and the fact that many of the placards had been made in the school's workshops, despite Gropius's ban on political activities.

Gropius had second thoughts about his ban after he noticed several Thuringian ministers participating, and he moved to join the procession himself. But Alma, his estranged wife, who was visiting him at the time, restrained him. She was aware of the difficulties the Bauhaus was going through and thought it best he not get "mixed up in politics." Gropius remained at home. Yet while his sympathies undoubtedly lay with the slain workers (and his students), the school's dependence on the public purse of a conservative constituency required that he ignore his personal leanings and chastise those from the Bauhaus who had taken part in the funeral. Even so, he ignored his own ban on political activities by participating in the competition to design a memorial honoring those who had died.

Alma's fears about the political ramifications of the school's participation would prove correct. The Bauhaus's production of the banners (at taxpayers' expense) gave the outraged Weimar Right an issue to embrace. Two years later it provided the excuse for a Reichswehr raid on the school. More damaging to the school, however, was its involvement in the artistic enterprise that memorialized this event.

The Kapp Putsch marked a turning point in the history of the Weimar Republic. While some saw this event as a slightly ludicrous and failed attempt by a group of disgruntled generals to take over the German government, others viewed it as a brief, heroic, and never-to-be-repeated moment of leftist unity, when German workers rose up as one to save their republic.

The government's continuing use of the antiunion military to repress various workers' movements had convinced German workers that the coalition Social Democratic government was hardly sympathetic to their interests. A strike by two hundred thousand workers across the country on January 3, 1920, expressed their disgruntlement. Its culmination ten days later in a bloody demonstration in front of Berlin's Reichstag left 42 dead and 105 wounded. The government, convinced that the radical Left was behind the worker unrest, shut down various leftist newspapers in response. On January 14, after imposing a state of emergency throughout the Reich, the government brought in military force to suppress the strike, a response that by now had become habitual. Two years after the revolution, the Left was coming to realize that the so-called socialist government was not merely unsympathetic to their interests but an outright threat.

The military, whose resentful grumblings had continued since the announcement of the Entente's peace terms the year before, was not as pleased with the government as the Left supposed. In February 1920 the

unnatural marriage between the rightist military and the putative workers' regime was tested when the government tried to disband certain Free
Corps units and put some of the military commanders on trial for war
crimes, stipulations of the Versailles Treaty that the Entente was impa-
tiently insisting upon. General von Lüttwitz not only flatly refused to dissolve some of the Free Corps troops, but he made his own demands before
a startled President Ebert. On March 11 Ebert responded to Lüttwitz's
insubordination by firing him.

Two days later the military delivered its response when the first-rate
"Ehrhardt" Free Corps Marine brigade, led by General Wolfgang Kapp,
marched into Berlin in an attempt to topple the Republic. Ebert and his colleagues, however, having been warned in advance of the putsch, had
slipped out of Berlin. From Stuttgart they remembered their old friends the
workers, and in a flash of inspiration asked them to mount a general strike
to counter the putsch attempt. Putting aside their complaints against the
government, the workers agreed. More united and organized than they had
been in November 1918, the workers mounted nationwide strikes that
brought the country to the brink of collapse. The government fired the military commanders, who in turn fired the government. German troops had
no idea who was in charge. The rest of the country, observing the ludicrous
goings-on, did not know if they were witnessing history or farce.

In Weimar events had mimicked those in Berlin. The local head of the
Reichswehr, General von Hagenberg, had joined the putschists. In
response, a quickly formed workers' action committee had ordered a general strike that closed all Weimar factories, railroads, power plants, and
stores, as well as the Bauhaus workshops. Unlike most other German
cities, however, Weimar was chock-full of heavily armed troops.
Predictably, the putsch there followed a particularly bloody course.

Weimar's workers, distrusted by the Thuringian government and without firearms to defend themselves before the soldiers, asked Baudert, the
Thuringian State Minister, to release the government's stockpile of guns.
Baudert, who continued to suspect the Left, refused. Slightly later, however, he changed his mind, after von Hagenberg—who had assumed command of the Weimar garrison, the security police, and the local militias—
presented his own ultimatum for Baudert's government to resign.
Deciding that arming workers was better than being out of a job, Baudert
approved the arming of three hundred workers, and gun battles erupted
throughout Weimar.

Von Hagenberg's troops, aided by reinforcements from Naumburg, arrested Baudert, occupied the government building and other strategic places in Weimar, and threatened draconian measures against anyone who participated in a strike action. On Monday, March 15, 1920, thousands of workers defied this order by gathering in front of the Town Hall to protest von Hagenberg's actions. After their orders to disperse were ignored, the military opened fire on the crowd at point-blank range. Eight people were killed immediately—one of them a worker at the Schmidt stove factory where the Bauhaus fired its pottery—and thirty-five were wounded. A ninth worker was killed on a nearby street. By Wednesday, March 17, Germany was virtually paralyzed and the putsch in Weimar—as elsewhere—collapsed.

Perhaps more than any other single artistic work created during the Weimar Republic, the memorial to the fallen workers—known as the Monument to Those Who Fell in March (März-gefallenen)—epitomized the hour's political yearnings and tensions. In 1933 the Nazis would blow it up: thirteen years later the Communists would restore it. From start to finish—from the events it commemorated to its commission, from its destruction to its restoration—this work would never be anything less than a political icon. It was created by Gropius (and several members of the Bauhaus) at the very moment he was vigorously denying his and the Bauhaus's involvement in politics. Similar to the paradoxical situation that existed between Gropius's leftist inclinations and his inability to express them due to the school's financial dependence on conservative Thuringia, so too did his utopian, apolitical goals diverge from the political means needed to achieve them—an essential dilemma at the heart of Gropius's and the Bauhaus's situation in Weimar.

Commonly attributed to Gropius, this monument, referred to at the time as a Bauhaus design, was probably a collaborative effort. Like the event it commemorated, it was surrounded by controversy from the start. "A conflict is brewing in Weimar about the erection of the monument to those who fell in March," *Deutschland* declared about the competition, which in addition to the Bauhaus's bid included entries by the sculptors Joseph Heise and Richard Engelmann. Those who supported the Bauhaus entry received threatening letters, a Weimar "tradition," the newspaper claimed.

Initially the conflict surrounding this project appeared to be more artistic than political. "Two artistic approaches stand opposed," a local Weimar newspaper commented. By the time the competition was awarded to the Bauhaus entry in 1921, however, political connotations once again predominated. According to one of Thuringia's leftist newspapers, the Bauhaus design was chosen by "a large majority of Weimar's working class . . . [who felt that its design] perfectly represented . . . the ideas of the working class . . . and the victorious proletariat." Weimar's bourgeoisie did not take this result well. They threatened to reduce the city's promised financial support. The dedication of the memorial in 1922 would bring the *Thüringische Zeitung* to lambaste the city as a "'center' of socialist art," their comment directed as much to the monument as to the Bauhaus.

Gropius was involved in two other projects in 1920 that, although less conspicuous, would prove to be no less politically contentious than his monument to the fallen workers. Gropius was still unable to gain approval of the Bauhaus's budget from the Thuringian State Assembly. His school, he complained, had become a political "plaything." He decided instead to circumvent rightist-inclined Thuringia by seeking support for the Bauhaus as a prototype for reformed art schools from the more liberal national government, much as von Bode and Muthesius had earlier proposed. To do this, however, he had to present the Bauhaus as a radical art institution with an integrated art and craft teaching program. This in turn depended on his getting rid of the Bauhaus's former Academy professors and replacing them with more radical teachers.

The political machinations in the State Assembly holding up approval of the Bauhaus budget were only part of the school's financial troubles. The former Grand Duke and the state were deadlocked in a battle over a financial settlement, and the Bauhaus, as the legal heir to the former Saxony Grand Ducal College of Arts, was one of the victims of the dispute. Until the issue was resolved, the Bauhaus—even without all the complaints, petitions, inquiries, and legislative obstructions—could not officially receive any funds. The government's sporadic advance of emergency credits on which the school struggled to operate barely paid model fees or wood to heat the building, much less operate workshops and buy needed art materials. The precariousness of this financial arrangement drove Gropius to distraction. "The situation cannot go on this way," he complained to the Thuringian Cultural Minister. "I am very worried about what is going to happen at the Bauhaus."

I can no longer be responsible for consoling the masters and students [by telling them] that tools and raw materials will be coming in the future. We cannot work without materials and tools. If assistance is not provided immediately, the continuing existence of the Bauhaus looks bleak. . . .

Please, Your Excellence, help us. We want to accomplish so many things.

To Gropius's disgust, the annual debate in the State Assembly over the Bauhaus's budget had turned into a vote-getting demonstration by various rightist political factions over who best represented Weimar's "German" values, a situation that had intensified with the ratification of the Versailles Treaty on January 10, 1920. The nearly universal discontent with its terms had vitalized the Right across the country. The rapidly growing German Workers' Party changed its name to the National Socialist German Workers' Party (Nationalsozialistische Deutsche Arbeiterpartei, the NSDAP); while in Weimar the nationalist parties escalated their attack on the Bauhaus. On January 22 the opposition—now known as the "Weimar Citizen's Group" and led by Herfurth, the leader of the German Nationalist Party (the DNP), had held a well-attended gathering at the Armbrust restaurant in Weimar. Out of this meeting a compendium of the community's gripes against the Bauhaus emerged. So did a united political opposition and the idea, as had been published the day after this meeting, that Weimar was neither "big enough [nor] rich enough to support" such an enterprise.

Herfurth's complaints had appeared in *Deutschland* on February 8 and also separately, as a brochure, perhaps to distribute among the legislators of the State Assembly. In a manner the Nazis would soon perfect, Herfurth's arguments compellingly demonstrated how real grievances could be stretched and distorted into fictive ones. Many of the issues Herfurth had raised touched sensitive nerves in Weimar. Disclaiming interest in the Bauhaus's relative merits, Herfurth had asked if the changes wrought by the new school were worth the destruction of Weimar's beloved Art Academy. And why, Herfurth demanded, should the town support an institution whose director viewed their artistic efforts so contemptuously and who dismissed their past accomplishments as "antiquated and [something to be] disposed of"? He called the Bauhaus's advocacy of

Expressionism "one-sided [and] intolerant" (an opinion Feininger apparently shared) and opposed to the Academy's tradition of artistic freedom. Herfurth also claimed that the former Art Academy had not been "fully aware of Gropius's reforms or . . . of the consequences for the school and Weimar."

No argument about art in Germany, especially at this particular moment in time, could escape ideology; in Germany art *stood* for something else. Since this great beyond is invisible, one can attribute to it any quality one wants. The tradition and past that Gropius and the Bauhaus program viewed as materialistic, narrow, and exploitative was for Herfurth healthy, attached to the soil (*bodenständig*), and the people (*volkstümlich*), modest, honest, vigorous, and creative. In other words, as Herfurth put it, "German [art] at its best." These qualities, he declared, were well represented in its old Art Academy. "Its rape," he asserted, "is Weimar's rape." Since Weimar represented German values, its desecration by the Bauhaus was equivalent to the detested Entente's violation of Germany.

Herfurth insisted that the Bauhaus respect Weimar's local traditions, reconcile itself to Thuringia's limited financial means, and tolerate diversity in the art it advocated, if it wished to remain in the city. Claiming that the Bauhaus's ambitions made it an enterprise that Weimar could ill afford, he suggested the school seek support instead from the national government and recommended the reestablishment of the Art Academy, "as master and not as maid."

For his own reasons, Gropius had already come to the same conclusion. In a letter of January 3, 1920, to his friend Edwin Redslob (the newly appointed National Arts Commissioner), Gropius had attempted to place the Bauhaus within a national context by describing the school's battle in Weimar as one of national importance. One week later Gropius was even more specific. Writing to Hans Poelzig, Gropius suggested that "[t]he national government . . . tackle the [Bauhaus] issue on a large scale, and connect it with a unified school for children that mixed handicraft training with an academic high school [*Gymnasium*]."

Aside from the Bauhaus's financial crises and troublesome political fallout, Gropius's ambitions had been spurred by the prestigious Second Congress of the Prussian Art Academy. At its Berlin meeting the previous November the Academy had proposed that a standardized art and craft program (*Einheitskunstschule*) be established for all the country's art academies, modeled after "Mr. Gropius's Bauhaus in Weimar." While this testimonial enhanced Gropius's national standing, he had done nothing about it at the time. By January, however, confronted by the prospect of having to contend with the upcoming meeting of the Weimar Citizens' Group and the debate on the school budget in the State Assembly, Gropius seriously began to pursue his new strategy of bypassing the Thuringian authorities through national funding. On January 17 Gropius released a report of the Congress's recommendation to *Deutschland*. In it he claimed that the accolade had placed the Bauhaus "at the forefront of a national movement to recover German artistic creativity," and he urged that the school's activities not be restrained.

This idea of the Bauhaus as a prototype for radical change in art education was nothing new. Gropius had never thought of the Bauhaus as a local art school. Rather, he had conceived it as the first step toward the creation of a spiritually enlightened society, of which educational reform was a fundamental component. A longtime socialist issue, school reform remained a primary concern of Germany's current Social Democratic government. In July 1919 the Cultural Ministry had organized a series of meetings on educational reform in which Gropius, Taut, and several prominent members of the prewar Werkbund, such as Behrens and Muthesius, had participated. One month later the Social Democrats had adopted educational reform as one of the party's official goals and integrated its principles into the Weimar Constitution. Although the Social Democratic government, as usual, had mouthed more than it would seriously pursue, Gropius—as he had earlier done with the November Revolution—would base his Bauhaus strategy on its anticipation.

The Social Democrats first introduced school reform in a 1911 Reichstag debate, and it had remained a highly controversial and politicized issue ever since. After debating it for several years, the Reichstag finally rejected the bill, which had been opposed by all the rightist parties, some conservatives, and even some liberals who were against any significant educational change. Nearly a decade later, school reform remained a socialist issue, with predictable alignment by the Right and Left.

Gropius's efforts to link the Bauhaus with this controversial issue were not without their strategic intent. His ambitious goals for the school really went beyond Weimar's mandate. The Thuringian authorities were more to the right than their national counterparts, and a stand in favor of school reform was not only more principled in terms of his own convictions, but also promised to garner nationwide support for his efforts and turn his struggle for the Bauhaus into a national issue. Yet as justified as Gropius's endeavors may have been, the controversial history of this issue, as well as the current political unrest, virtually ensured that its pursuit would plunge the Bauhaus into politics.

Gropius's ambitions were also fueled by the appointment, on January 1, 1920, of his Werkbund acquaintance Edwin Redslob as National Arts Commissioner. A longtime Thuringian representative to the Werkbund, Redslob had long supported radical art. He had attended van de Velde's lectures in Weimar as a sixteen-year-old student, and he maintained a close personal association with the Belgian architect. Redslob also had a record of helping his friends. His first action after being appointed director of Erfurt's art collections had been to obtain a commission for van de Velde. From Erfurt, Redslob had moved to Stuttgart, where he had assumed a similar position as museum director. It was from there that he was called to Berlin. In 1920 Redslob seemed well placed to help the Bauhaus, and his appointment must have seemed nothing less than a godsend to the beleaguered Gropius.

Gropius turned to him for governmental support time and time again. Less than two weeks after Redslob's appointment Gropius—desperate for money and confronting the upcoming meetings of the State Assembly and Herfurth's group—had literally begged for "a small advance [from the national government] for the Bauhaus . . . on the strength of [the school's] overall merits." Even a token of government support, Gropius had pleaded, would "keep the ranters quiet."

> It is a critical moment. [We must push with every means at our disposal] to break through the reactionaries. You are the person now who has the say in this direction. Do you want to do something and can you? It has nothing to do with me . . . but [rather] about the idea of how one can create fertile ground for artistic growth again.

Gropius also asked his friends to lean on Redslob with regard to the Bauhaus. On January 29, 1920, for example, Gropius—describing the Bauhaus as the first attempt to "breach . . . the old fossilized state art education"—had asked the architect and fellow AfK member Otto Bartning to speak to Redslob. Despite the gravity of the school's situation, Gropius was not blind to the difficulties of trying to link the Bauhaus with national school reform. Other states, he realized, might also ask for such subsidies. Yet in spite of this potential problem, he believed that the efforts should continue. "All [attempts to help the Bauhaus] should be mobilized . . . in this direction," he wrote.

Unfortunately, Redslob was not as powerful as Gropius thought. While there were many reasons for Redslob's limited influence, not the least was Germany's strong local tradition of cultural support, which few states were willing to cede to the national government. The Werkbund had envisioned the position of National Arts Commissioner linking the artistic community with the highest levels of government. It wanted an independent ministry responsible only to the Chancellor, a sort of "benevolent cultural dictator." The government, however, had established the office as a division within the Ministry of the Interior, an arrangement that imposed tight and unanticipated constraints.

Gropius's efforts, however, were hampered less by Redslob's relative impotence than by the continued presence of the Weimar Academy's traditional professors. Even without Gropius's national ambitions, these professors had become a source of constant friction within the school. Professor Thedy remained embittered over Gropius's bias against "salon" art and his remarks in June at the students' exhibition, most of which were directed against Thedy's students and, indirectly, Thedy's own work. Thedy accused Gropius of not understanding art. Writing to the Bauhaus director, Thedy urged him to go look at paintings by Titian, Rubens, Velázquez, and Rembrandt before claiming that art could not exist "outside of architecture."

Thedy was not the only Bauhaus painter to feel this way. In fact, none of the painting masters—including Feininger and those who would follow Thedy, such as Klee and Kandinsky—agreed with Gropius that painting's significance derived from its association with architecture. Indeed, Gropius's position remained more hypothetical than realized within the Bauhaus. No painter ever associated with the Bauhaus would contradict Thedy's assertion to Gropius that "painting is an end in itself."

Meanwhile, Herfurth's group recognized the benefits of a potential alliance with the angry, disillusioned, and influential professors. They wooed them with the appealing prospect of reestablishing their old art school, an idea that currently corresponded with Gropius's own notions. He had realized that "[t]he cleft between old academia" and what the

Bauhaus was trying to accomplish had become "unbridgeable." What Gropius wanted most of all now was to fill the Academy professors' faculty slots with radical artists, whose presence would strengthen his case for national funding.

But this path too—like his attempt to associate the Bauhaus with the school reform issue—was fraught with hazard. Thuringia could hardly support one school, much less two. The legal basis for the Bauhaus's existence in Weimar lay in its status as the sole heir to the Grand Ducal school. To reestablish the Academy as the heir of the old school would compromise the Bauhaus's legitimacy and endanger national support. It was critical that such a second institution be set up as a subsidiary of the Bauhaus. For this reason Gropius sought to reestablish the old Academy as an affiliated but noncompetitive Old Weimar Painting School (Alte Weimar Malschule). Unfortunately, the Bauhaus opponents, driven by the same economic need to find a source of funding, also recognized the legal situation.

The dual aspects of Gropius's plan—to establish the Bauhaus as a national model, along with a new, potentially competitive art institution in Weimar—had necessitated some fancy footwork on his part. For obvious reasons, Gropius could not let the Thuringian government know that he was planning to override their authority. Gropius could reveal his total commitment to "a divorce . . . [between] the old academics and our new way" only to his friends. To the Thuringian Cultural Minister he declared the Bauhaus's interest in setting up a new school as an attempt to comply with "the wishes of many Weimar artists." It was a risky course, one whose elements of subterfuge, strategic complexities, and political and legal hazards spoke more of a lurid spy tale than the running of a public institution. But it was just the type of situation that energized Gropius. He said he felt "like the overseer of a dike during a big storm, [who is] trying to see that every hole is stuffed so that the dike won't break," aware that his strength was "growing with the task." To Redslob he vowed he would never give up.

The enlargement of the battlefield after the January 22 meeting and his need to seek national support forced Gropius to search out a wider range of allies. He wrote letters to any cultural figure he thought could help rally support: influential critics, architects, and artistic groups across the country. "Please help us," he wrote to the well-known art critic Walter Müller-Wulckow, "as we are in danger of losing this outpost of art." Occasionally the zealousness of his supporters backfired. An exceedingly polemical article written by Behne in response to Gropius's anxious urgings inadvertently riled up Weimar even more, provoking what the Bauhaus leader described as "an unbelievable public demonstration . . . against me and the Bauhaus." Most damaging, Behne's article seemed to have pushed Professor Thedy, the most respected and revered of the former Academy professors, firmly into the enemy camp.

These precarious and politically hazardous maneuvers Gropius had pursued in mid-January and February 1920 were accompanied by impassioned avowals of the need to avoid political entanglement. Nothing he did could have "political overtones," he confided to Behne on January 15, seven days before the Weimar Citizen's Group meeting. "I see it very clearly now," Gropius wrote to Behne subsequently, "that every [political] party is dirt."

> They produce hate and more hate. We must destroy parties. I want to found an apolitical community here, [that is] what we are striving for and what we want. [Such a] community is only possible with people who reject parties, who commit themselves to an idea and fight for it. I felt the same with the AfK. . . . It is gradually becoming unworthy . . . to belong to a political party. . . . [E]ither you are political or you are objective. Both at same time are not possible.

Gropius's rejection of political linkage at the same time as he sought political backing was neither cynical nor dishonest. Indeed, it was necessary, given the paradoxical nature of the Bauhaus's elevated, essentially apolitical ambitions and the political maneuverings needed to achieve them. Gropius—similar to Kessler, Schlemmer, and Neumann—focused on his ultimate goal. His opponents were watching *how* he sought to achieve it.

8.

What Happened to November?

The End of the Revolution and Its Implications for the Bauhaus

"Revolution!" the People howl and cry
"Freedom, that's what we're needing!"
We've needed it for centuries—
　　our arteries are bleeding.
The stage is shaking. The audience rock.
The whole thing is over by nine o'clock.

The day looks gray as I come to.
Where is that People—remember?—
　　that stormed the peaks from down below?
What happened to November?
Silence. All gone. Just that, in fact.
An act. An act.

—*Kurt Tucholsky*

Arriving at the Bauhaus in 1921, Andor Weininger found himself confused and a little astonished. It was Sunday, and he was not expecting to find many people in the school's vestibule; neither was he expecting to hear music—"the kind of song one hears in church"—coming from somewhere upstairs. Following the sound, the twenty-two-year-old Hungarian (of German descent) climbed the two flights of stairs, his skepticism mounting with each step. Perhaps he had misread the program of the Bauhaus with its call for a return to craft and "the creation of a new guild of craftsmen." Locating the source of the singing behind a shut door, Weininger peeped through the keyhole and was even more astonished by what he saw. Young people dressed in brightly colored one-piece outfits—"one in red, another green, another blue or gray"—sat in neat rows singing chorales and praying. Straightening himself quickly when the service was over, Weininger asked the disbanding singers if they had been participating in a religious service. The Bauhaus students, laughing at the newcomer's ignorance, replied that they had participated in a Mazdaznan ceremony, conducted by "a high priest of [the] sect," Johannes Itten.

With his shaved head, round wire-rimmed glasses, and flowing robes, Itten cut an indelible figure around the Bauhaus. "Half schoolmaster, half pastor" was how Paul Klee described him. "Demonic . . . [and] impossible to ignore," asserted Paul Citroen, a Bauhaus student and member of the Mazdaznan group. Itten, he added, was either "ardently admired or . . . hated."

> For those of us who belonged to the Mazdaznan circle—a special community within the student body—Itten exuded a special radiance. One could almost call it holiness. One was inclined to approach him only in whispers; our reverence was overwhelming.

Itten, however, was more than just a particularly flamboyant guru of an esoteric Persian sect, prescribing breathing exercises and vegetarian diets that made the Bauhaus reek of onions and garlic; more even than simply "Gropius's highest-ranking officer," as he was once described. By virtue of his commanding temperament, broad responsibilities, and influence on the Bauhaus curriculum, Itten in 1921 was generally conceded to be the Bauhaus's leading personality. He stood out "brilliantly" among the otherwise generally reserved faculty. Some thought he even dominated Gropius. More than any other Bauhaus member at this time, Itten had an enduring impact on the school. It was with him that many believed the Bauhaus would succeed or fail.

Itten had taught in Vienna since 1916 and was already a well-known pedagogue and art theorist when he came to the Bauhaus. Sometime during 1917 he had met Alma Mahler in Vienna, and by the following year their relationship—which Alma described as "brotherly . . . oddly fraternal and unerotic"—had become close. Itten's diaries revealed their growing intimacy. "I was at Frau Mahler's once again for a long time," Itten wrote on July 6, 1918. "Kauders [his nickname for Alma] came to visit me," he wrote four months later. "We spoke about melody—line—Bach—Franck—harmony—color—Schoenberg—van Gogh."

In the spring of 1919 Alma introduced Gropius to Itten, insisting, in her inimitable way, that if Gropius wanted to carry out his intentions at the Bauhaus, he had to invite Itten to teach there. This Gropius did despite admitting he did not understand Itten's abstract art. Thus with no craft or architectural background—nor with any particular interest in the school's utopian principles—the Bauhaus's most influential teacher, along with fourteen of his Viennese pupils, arrived in Weimar in June 1919.

At that particular moment, however—as his behavior at the student exhibition that month had revealed—Gropius himself was less interested in craft and architecture than in his students' apparent inability to confront and express their inner feelings, which was precisely what Itten had been trying to achieve in Vienna. Like Gropius, Itten believed that art could not be taught. What could be taught was sensitivity to one's feelings, which—in their view—society (and the traditional art academy) conspired to repress. The path to becoming an artist did not lie in learning rules (the traditional route of the art academy), but in freeing oneself from such constraints and learning to delve fearlessly into one's inner consciousness to release the emotive impulses that lay waiting there. It had been to help the student rid himself of virtually everything he had learned in order to touch his own intuitive sensibility—in a sense, to become a child again—that Itten, at Gropius's urging, had set up his introductory course (*Vorkurs*) in the fall of 1919, based on principles he had applied in his Vienna classes.

Given a totally free hand by Gropius, Itten utilized every device—from breathing and warming-up exercises to the analysis of texts and works of old masters—to push the student to confront his feelings, to imbue in him the "creative automatism" he believed to be a major component of artistic creation. Those who had been exposed to traditional academy training had essentially to unlearn what Itten referred to as "dead convention" in order to "liberate themselves . . . and gain courage to pursue their own work." Although his class met only once a week—on Saturday—it was an intense and grueling experience. For nearly eight hours, as Citroen recalled some years later, Itten "kindled us, shook us up . . . , burst open all the sluices, so to speak, and placed us in a wild whirl of production." *Feeling*, as Weininger later remarked, became the byword of the day. From feeling, the former Bauhaus student declared, came expression. "To be able to work creatively, one had to discover oneself."

Itten utilized rather unorthodox methods to achieve this goal. His class began with relaxation exercises; hands were loosened up, heads massaged.

Large-scale rhythmic drawing followed. After these exercises Itten often proceeded with a formal analysis of a well-known master's work. In May 1921 Oskar Schlemmer (who like Klee would come to the Bauhaus at Itten's suggestion) sat in on one of these analytical classes and described his observations to a friend. Displaying a large photograph of the weeping Mary Magdalene from Matthias Grünewald's Isenheim altarpiece in Colmar, Itten had asked his students to draw what they saw as the essential feature of this monumentally mournful figure. After a few moments, Itten glanced briefly at their work before declaring fiercely, "None of you have any artistic sensitivity at all. You can't draw this," he claimed, pointing toward the figure. "It's undrawable. . . . This is the noblest portrayal of weeping . . . a symbol of the tears of the world. You should sit silently before this and weep yourselves." With that, Itten stormed out of the classroom, slamming the door behind him.

Klee too was fascinated by Itten's gripping pedagogical technique. Sitting in on one of Itten's drawing classes, he described it in a letter to his wife, Lily. "[Itten] walks up to an easel on which there was some paper," he wrote.

> He grasps a piece of charcoal, his body gathers itself, as though he was charged with energy. . . . [He draws] two energetic strokes, upright and parallel to one another . . . the students were instructed to do this as well. The teacher checks their posture. Then he instructs them on the stroke, then he tells them to do the same assignment for homework. It seems to be a kind of bodily massage. . . .
>
> Then he talked a bit about wind, let a few students stand up and describe their impression of wind and storm. After that, he gives the task: the presentation of a storm. [After ten minutes] time . . . [he] checks their results, holding forth in criticism. After this critique they work on them further. One page after the other is ripped up and falls to earth. Some work with such great force that they use several pages of paper at once. After they have all become somewhat tired, he has the beginners take this assignment home with them for further work.

While undeniably effective, Itten's technique—depending on your point of view—was either compelling or brutal. The latter was especially true for those who had already studied at a traditional academy. Weininger recalled how one such student "who thought he knew everything" contended that Itten's assignments were too elementary and beneath his dignity. Itten took care of this, according to Weininger, by "brainwash[ing]" the fellow, working on him so exhaustively that the student eventually came to feel he knew nothing at all. Some students became depressed by Itten's aggressive technique. But all of them emerged changed from the traumatic experience.

In his own way Itten was attempting to carry out Gropius's mandate to create a new type of enlightened individual, in touch with and confident of his feelings, and able to draw on them as a source of artistic creativity. By fair means or foul, every Bauhaus student would be purged of his inhibitions and what Itten considered the rational, materialistic, and technological biases of his Western culture, and brought—or rather, returned—to a childlike state of innocence. "I . . . came to realize," wrote Itten later, "that an inner-directed thinking [meditation] and spiritual energy must counterbalance our outward, technologically oriented point of view." It was this attempt to purify and attain oneness with the self (which Itten, like Gropius, saw as constituting a spiritual or higher state of existence) that had brought him, in 1920, to embrace the teachings of Mazdaznan, an eastern cult based vaguely on Zoroastrianism and other sources.

While Mazdaznan may have simply intensified a process Itten was pursuing at the Bauhaus, its rituals—from a strict vegetarian cuisine to spiritual exercises—threatened "to turn the Bauhaus into a monastery of . . . monks," according to Schlemmer, where "meditation and ritual" mattered more than work. At least they were a colorful lot; every Mazdaznan acolyte had to wear a one-piece work suit of Itten's design.

Left by Gropius to their own devices, Itten and his Bauhaus coterie became more and more immersed in the Mazdaznan nirvana. Described by one of his followers as "[a] saint, a guru," Itten grew increasingly remote and unapproachable and was eventually seen only at his Saturday-morning class and the weekly prayer sessions before disappearing. Two years after the student exhibition of 1919, the Bauhaus was on its way to becoming what Gropius had demanded: an Expressionist mysterium, a "small, secret self-contained . . . conspirac[y] . . .[at whose core was] concealed a mystery, a nucleus of faith."

■

"Ridiculous," the Dutch artist and theorist Theo van Doesburg claimed about Itten and his practices. Invited by Gropius to lecture to the Bauhaus students, van Doesburg arrived in Weimar in January 1921, undoubtedly hoping to receive a Bauhaus teaching appointment. When this did not occur, he surprised everyone by staying anyway and giving public lectures at his studio on Wednesday afternoons.

Despite his heavy Dutch accent, Doesburg was just as charismatic as Itten, and Bauhaus students—who flocked to his lectures—were equally smitten. "[A] fantastic and very interesting speaker . . . incredibly convincing," recalled Weininger, who, despite his Mazdaznan introduction to the Bauhaus, soon found himself leaning toward van Doesburg's rationalistic principles.

Van Doesburg's severe appearance—monocle, homburg, black suit, black shirt, and white tie—contrasted with Itten's flowing monkish robes almost as much as did his artistic theory of order, technology, and the virtues of the square. While Itten preached *feeling*, van Doesburg called for sobriety. Itten wanted the students to let go, van Doesburg urged restraint, objectivity, and the rule of reason, of pure rectilinear forms and primary colors. Itten proclaimed that truth lay within; van Doesburg that it lay without, that it was universal and collaborative. Dynamic and forceful men, they each articulated separate aspects of the Bauhaus's program and attracted worshipful Bauhaus acolytes. "[W]e followed [van Doesburg]," wrote Weininger, "the way the disciples followed Jesus." They preached not simply opposing art but what they saw as opposing truths, and it was a measure of either the extraordinary broad-mindedness or the ambiguity that existed at the Bauhaus in 1921 that they could both exert their influence there simultaneously.

The principles van Doesburg was proselytizing at the Bauhaus were those of De Stijl, a Dutch avant-garde movement that promulgated a geometrically precise, simplified abstract art that had developed out of Cubism in 1917. van Doesburg was the movement's founder, theorist, and leading proponent. His thesis of "lucid tidiness" was worlds apart from the emotive tumult advocated by Itten. Reflecting De Stijl's manifesto of November 1918, van Doesburg claimed that art should reflect technology, which he believed to be the century's dominant trend. The machine, he declared, would replace handicraft.

According to van Doesburg, there was "an old and a new consciousness of the age." The old one, the De Stijl manifesto had declared, was "directed toward the individual. . . . [t]he new one . . . toward the universal." Directly rebutting Itten, van Doesburg asserted that modern artists had to oppose individualism and its arbitrariness. No more craft, no more feelings, no more individualism. "You should work for the world," declared van Doesburg, "not for yourselves. You must ban whatever is individual from your thinking and from your work." Van Doesburg declared that Itten's Bauhaus was living in the past, wallowing in sentimentality and individualism. "With Itten, you are stuck in Romanticism," he said, "and you don't live in the present. I live in the future. De Stijl is a movement that will build for the future."

Gropius had doubtlessly not realized what he was getting into when he invited van Doesburg to lecture at the Bauhaus after meeting him in Berlin in December 1920. Van Doesburg had been on a proselytizing mission through Europe. He had left Holland because the De Stijl group there had essentially disintegrated under his caustic and volatile personality, which antagonized people as much as it charmed them. In 1920 he had been searching for greener pastures to preach his gospel of the square, and the Bauhaus was about as green a pasture as he was likely to find. Shortly after settling in Weimar, van Doesburg had described his plans to his friend the Dutch poet Anthony Kok, his words ringing with characteristically malicious delight.

> At Weimar I have radically overturned everything. . . . I have talked to the pupils . . . [and] have infused the poison of the new spirit everywhere. . . . I have mountains of strength, and I know now that our notions will be victorious over everyone and everything.

Aside from the strength of his convictions and enthralling personality, van Doesburg touched a particularly sensitive chord at the Bauhaus, arriving there just as many students were beginning to question Expressionism, particularly the style's excessive romanticism, its relevancy for a school that promulgated collaboration, and the integration of arts and crafts, its purported link with social change and even its artistic validity. Their doubts reflected a far broader consensus that had already begun in 1920.

The Work Council for Art's (the AfK's) emphasis on Expressionism's tie to socialism in its January 1920 exhibition had led some to question this purported linkage. What precisely *is* the connection between Expressionism and the masses? Their inquiry was particularly pertinent in light of the proletariat's obvious preference for naturalistic genre scenes. Indeed, critics had claimed that Expressionism's exclusivistic and solitary basis ("only I can know my private sufferings") was antithetical to the cooperative, outward-reaching basis of socialism, and that its supporters were not the masses but the "salon Spartacists" of Berlin's fashionable West End.

Such ideological squabbling had not dented the avant-garde's enthusiasm for the style; what finally did was its popularization. What the Expressionists had utilized as symbols of purity, innocence, and the spiritual—jagged, spiky, crystalline forms, as in Gropius's Monument to Those Who Fell in March—now appeared as design elements in advertisements, furniture, even amusement parks. "The Expressionist academy, Expressionist fashion, Expressionist fellow-travelers," one critic lamented, "that catchword *Expressionism* with which the smart art dealers and slick art critics practice their propaganda; would that it was already over!" The Expressionists reacted bitterly to the renovation of the Skala Dance Casino, a Berlin restaurant and nightclub, in a garish pastiche of these forms. Adolf Behne, who denied that the Expressionists had anything in common with such "crooked dance halls," referred to it as a "masquerade."

But postwar Expressionism had been far more than just an artistic style. Its utopian aspirations had formed the ideological bedrock for both the Bauhaus and much of the German artistic avant-garde. These too had collapsed in 1920, when the government—a scant month after the Kapp Putsch—once again turned to their recent adversaries, the Reichswehr and Free Corps, to quell worker unrest. The breakup of the radical German Independent Social Democratic Party (the USPD) at its party conference in Halle in October contributed to the mood of pessimism that helped undermine the Expressionists' utopian dreams. However meager the USPD's political support had been, the avant-garde depended on it.

Having rescued the government during the Kapp Putsch from the excesses of its own rightist allies, the Left—not unreasonably—had expected the Social Democratic government to return to its socialist roots. Counting on such a "leftward drift" and the inevitable resistance of the military, many German workers who had kept their arms continued to battle the Reichswehr and Free Corps into April 1920, most notably in

Saxony and Thuringia. A so-called Red army numbering fifty thousand to eighty thousand strong occupied the Ruhr. Horrified by what looked like another Spartacist insurrection on an even greater scale, the government turned once again to their military cohorts to repress the workers. Their action exposed the government's true colors to the embittered Left, which now abandoned any hope of affiliation.

With inflation and unemployment rising dramatically, disappointment was the least of the burdens German workers had to bear in 1920. In May alone the price of flour rose 100 percent. By July around four hundred thousand were out of work, and unemployment reached 23.5 percent. Kessler and others anticipated a crash and "a new right-wing putsch." The Right's gathering strength had been aided by the Left's inability to reconcile its revolutionary left wing with its more conservative, centrist leadership, which caused it to splinter into irrelevancy in October with the dismantling of the USPD. Most of the Independents moved over to the Communist Party (the KPD), which was itself torn between wanting to follow Moscow (the Comintern) and remaining independent. As slight as the support of the USPD had been, its loss weighed heavily on the avant-garde. After the USPD collapsed, Behne had suggested the AfK be disbanded. Gropius, speaking some months later at the AfK's closing meeting, would specifically cite the loss of its political support as the main reason for the group's demise.

By the end of 1920, just as Itten was deepening and codifying the school's commitment to the style, Expressionism ceased being considered viable as a progressive aesthetic. The Bauhaus—its artistic and ideological premises totally discredited—found itself in danger of becoming outmoded and irrelevant.

If the Bauhaus could no longer claim to be on the cutting edge, or represent a brave new style for a brave new world, what then had it become? "Chaotic," Gropius declared. "A mixed-up mess," Schlemmer echoed. The Bauhaus's essentially inner-directed Expressionistic beliefs remained disconnected from its communal aspirations or its putative emphasis on craft. Barely able to survive its meager funding, the school had been unable to integrate its art classes with its workshops, one of its main goals. Indeed, without money to rebuild the workshops, the Bauhaus could hardly speak of a functioning craft program at all. And without its craft connection, as Schlemmer pointed out, the Bauhaus was just another modern art school. Even Gropius, in 1920, bemoaned the school's lack of achievements.

Given such a state of affairs, the mood at the Bauhaus a scant year after it opened had become glum and sour. Without rules, course requirements, or much work, the student body was uncontrollable. Most of its energies were dissipated in arguments, raucous parties, and pranks, the latter directed with particular glee against the conservative town. The students' nude bathing in the public baths prompted Thuringian authorities to complain about their "endangering public morals"; their splashing paint over one of the old Academy's most venerated statues provoked another uproar.

The Bauhaus's relaxed mores—"to give and take, to live and let live," as the artist Herbert Bayer recalled of his student days—and its emphasis on self-expression had created a community of eccentrics, "some of them strange or just funny." "A fearless band of young people . . . a crazy sampling of modern youth" was how Schlemmer described them. What few rules there were, a former Bauhaus student commented, were usually ignored. "Dogmas were rapidly accepted and even more quickly discarded. Much was begun, but little was completed. . . . There was a lot of amateurish fooling around." Students preferred to meditate rather than work. The Bauhaus, commented Feininger, had become an "unwholesome place."

Its efforts to remove the disgruntled professors and set up a separate art academy for them had added to the Bauhaus's difficulties in 1920. For one thing, many of the faculty opposed the project. Schlemmer, for one, argued that Gropius's analysis of the situation was too "utopian," and that the establishment of a second school would reduce the Bauhaus's already inadequate (and still outstanding) state subsidy.

But the former Academy professors had become as anxious to get out of the Bauhaus as Gropius was to see them leave. Having spent years debating the establishment of a reformed art school and putting themselves on the line with the state authorities in supporting Gropius and his proposed artistic reforms, they felt embarrassed and humiliated by the Bauhaus leader's abandonment of his original proposals, his disparaging comments about their art and teachings, the antagonisms he had aroused within the community, and the controversies the school had become embroiled in.

Depicted as irrelevant and out-of-touch, the professors looked forward to establishing the Old Weimar Painting School to set the record straight. If in the process they could undermine the Bauhaus, so much the better. Goaded on by the rightist press, they missed no opportunity to do so. In an article that had appeared in Bremen's *Weser-Zeitung* on November 5,

1920, the Bauhaus was referred to as a school that "sailed in the most radical channels, both artistically and politically." The differences between its faculty and director, the article declared, had become so serious that the government and state legislature had been forced to intervene.

> The sculpture instructor Professor Engelmann, as well as the painter Klemm . . . have stated publicly that they intend to resign from their posts, since they cannot go along with the aesthetic and political radicalism of the institution, which they consider damaging to its political and artistic standing.
>
> Since, as is well known, the vast majority of Weimar's intellectuals have emphatically spoken out against the Bauhaus's direction, as well as the moral caliber of the students . . . this affair may well hasten the decline and fall of the institution.

Similar articles appeared in newspapers throughout Germany. One periodical referred to the new state art school as "a corrective to the Bauhaus."

Joined by their common desire to part ways, Gropius, the professors, and the rightist parties all worked together with unusual harmony in setting up the new art academy. Gropius had undertaken this venture in the hope of freeing the Bauhaus from local politics. But the adoption of the new school by the Thuringian Right as a central issue in their electoral campaign for the State Assembly in June had accomplished just the opposite. "Bring back the formerly well-known and celebrated Art Academy with its rightful mission," Herfurth's German People's Party (the DVP) urged in an advertisement that appeared on June 6, 1920. "Vote for us," another asserted eight days later, "if you don't want your home[land] to be socialistic! Vote for peace and order."

The Right won on June 20, 1920. Although this victory reflected a marked swing to the Right that had become apparent in the national elections earlier in the month, Thuringia's rightist parties attributed their victory to their anti-Bauhaus campaign. Indeed, the victory initiated a rightist electioneering strategy that would be used again and again until the school's demise in 1933. Armed with their substantial mandate against a fractious and diminished Left, the resurgent Thuringian Right pressed what by now had become its dual ambitions: to reestablish the old Weimar Art Academy, and to get rid of the Bauhaus.

Gropius, either unaware or unconcerned, ebulliently claimed victory when the new art school was established on September 20, 1920. With the departure the following month of Professors Klemm and Engelmann, Gropius, delighted to finally offer the faculty slots to more radical artists, declared the Bauhaus "out of danger." Gropius offered one of these slots to Schlemmer, assuring him that the "reactionaries' stubborn resistance [was] slowly crumbling."

Gropius's optimism, however, proved premature. The Thuringian government's orders for the new school to reoccupy its former quarters currently being used by the Bauhaus, plunged both institutions into a hell of unwelcomed coexistence. Clearly the opposition had not been about to crumble after all. Complaints of inequity—of unequally distributed heat, light, access to the library, canteen, and art materials began at once and would continue for years. Protesting that art could not thrive under such adverse circumstances, Gropius urged a public protest against such "cat and mouse games."

Worse lay in store when the new school opened on April 12, 1921, two years to the day after Gropius's appointment as Bauhaus director had been announced. The new school's name—the State College of Fine Arts—bore a far more substantial title than what Gropius had originally proposed. And thanks to rightist pressure it was specifically set up as a revival of the original Grand Ducal Art Academy, with all the ominous legal implications for the Bauhaus that such a resurrection entailed. Announcements of the new school's opening left no doubt as to its connection with the original Academy. "The State College of Fine Arts in Weimar, founded on October 1, 1860, has reopened," declared a local newspaper. Believing that he had won an uncontested victory, Gropius now realized that he had received a "slap in the face" instead.

The rival school's program also challenged the Bauhaus. Described by Gropius as "a monstrous reactionary creation," the new school declared itself to be a reformed art institution dedicated to the integration of art and craft. In addition to the traditional art academy curriculum, it offered introductory courses in practical crafts such as architecture, decoration, bookmaking, graphics, drafting, photography, illustration, and architectural sculpture, to name only a few—a pointed refutation to those "who maintain that there is nothing left for the graduate of the art academy but to go hungry." In a further dig at the Bauhaus, the program asserted that however one might desire to integrate art and craft (in the form of more advanced craft courses), this remained a goal of the future. "Many have thought about the ideal art school that begins with handicraft training, with the goal of making it into an art. But nowhere has it become a reality." For the time being, the program claimed, one simply had to complete academy training and then go on to craft school, or vice versa.

If Gropius was understandably upset about the new school, the Bauhaus in turn was piqued with him. Not only had he committed an inordinate amount of time to setting up the new school, but his leadership, which alternated between frenetic involvement and inexplicable distance, was provoking increasing complaints. When he arrived at the school, Schlemmer was astonished to discover how unpopular Gropius was among the students. "They claim he is no longer what he was at the beginning, when he lived—and suffered—in true communion with them, a 'Father Gropius.' They say he has changed greatly, that it even shows in his eyes and the expression around his mouth."

These complaints had begun in 1920. Not that Gropius had been doing nothing, but he had been trying to do too much and consequently ignored the school. Gropius had spent most of the year trying to raise desperately needed funds and arouse public support for the Bauhaus. A ceaseless stream of letters to influential individuals, politicians, and critics emanated from his office. He had appeared before the Thuringian State Assembly on July 9, 1920, in another fruitless attempt to settle the issue of the Bauhaus's budget. This had demanded exhaustive preparation, as had his work to set up the new art academy. In addition to this, his architectural practice—one of whose projects had been the fallen workers monument—had picked up and demanded his attention.

Typically, Gropius thrust himself into a whirlwind of activity when he was most depressed. This had been true in 1920, when at various times he described himself as "restless and torn in pieces . . . [and rushing into] a thousand things [in order] to forget." As during the winter of 1918, difficulties with Alma had once again driven him to hyperactivity.

His problems with Alma had to do with his request for a divorce. Although Gropius had initially asked for a divorce in November 1918, when he discovered Alma's liaison with Werfel, the two had been unable to totally break from each other. By 1920 their marriage had settled into a kind of part-time affair. Alma appeared now and then in Weimar to play Bauhaus grand dame and wife to Gropius; her visit during the Kapp Putsch was one such occasion. Then she returned to Werfel in Vienna.

Described by Feininger as "a very lively . . . cosmopolite," Alma had never felt comfortable in Weimar. In 1919 Feininger had referred to her as "visibly bored . . . [and] absolutely unable to become accustomed to life . . . in Weimar." Although Gropius continued to try to obtain a divorce, his efforts had been stymied by Alma's unwillingness to allow him custody of their daughter, Manon ("Mutzi"), which he deeply wanted. Unable to give up Alma or gain custody of his beloved daughter, Gropius felt doubly humiliated, both deprived of his rights as a father and impotent before the "absolute power" she wielded over him, a reversal—he claimed—of "natural law."

Gropius's irresolute attitude toward Alma was apparent in his correspondence with her. His letter of July 1919 asking for a divorce had begun with the word "Beloved." Ambivalent herself, Alma had refused. Gropius oscillated between adulation and despair. By April 1920 he was describing himself as "sitting with a never-ending passion among the ashes." Typically, he viewed his suffering as spiritually productive, declaring that he had "moved up to another stage" after losing Alma's love. Yet her departures after her infrequent visits left him profoundly depressed. "My wife has left me now . . . and I am alone again, deeply depressed and discontented with myself," Gropius wrote in May 1920. "At the moment I am only half a man, but it is not my habit always to complain and therefore I keep silent. . . . I sit deep in the shadows . . . earthquakes shake my soul."

Gropius's dark mood continued into the summer. He described himself as "feeling crippled" and unable to say much good about himself. "Alma tears me to pieces. . . . I lose myself in cynicism. What is holy to me has now turned into a curse and makes me apathetic about life. . . . My child, whom I love, grows and I don't know her. I have an indescribable longing for her." These difficulties, coming as they did during the first tempestuous year of his Bauhaus directorship, no doubt placed great stress on a man inclined, like his father, to depression. The year 1920 had been especially bad. By December he had to admonish himself "to keep a stiff upper lip [so as] not to be defeated." Describing himself as "terribly torn and battered . . . [unable to] find . . . peace," he was at the end of his rope. "[T]he serious conflicts, the unresolvable ones with my wife Alma, and now the continuous blows against the work I have started! I feel as though I'm sitting in an ark."

Although they would eventually divorce, Gropius and Alma would never truly be able to leave each other. His letters to her would always begin with "Liebstes" ("Dearest") and end with "Your Walter." Her signature remained "Alles Liebe Alma" ("All my love"). Their respective spouses, Werfel and Ise (whom Gropius would marry in 1923), would also remain in close touch. In 1926 the young Ise would beg Alma to attend the opening of the new Bauhaus building in Dessau. While it eventually diminished, the bond between Alma and Gropius would never break; nor was he ever able to overcome the double loss of his daughter, first to Alma's custody and subsequently, in 1935, to Manon's premature death.

Gropius's divorce from Alma on October 11, 1920, lifted his gloomy spirits and momentarily inspired an upbeat mood. At a Masters' Council meeting two days later, Gropius vigorously reasserted his directorial voice. He announced that the school had "come to a certain finality," and that it was time to take disciplined action. Gropius presented a veritable cornucopia of proposals. He urged more integration between the workshops and formal art classes; he recommended that examinations be given in the workshop classes and that the initial half-year trial period in Itten's *Vorkurs* be reaffirmed. He complained about the students' glib use of the term *community* (*Gemeinschaft*), their argumentativeness, and their frequent avoidance of classes. "Self-discipline . . . , quietude, and work," Gropius had declared, would mark the Bauhaus.

The uncharacteristic display of directorial drive astonished the student representatives present at the meeting. Nonetheless, they rebelled against Gropius's initiatives, declaring that the situation at the Bauhaus was too "explosive" to push through such aggressive changes. One student leader referred to Gropius's insistence on tightening up the school as "forced labor." Another student, claiming that he found the entire idea of teaching art "preposterous," announced his opposition to the requirement of any course.

By February 1921 what Schlemmer had referred to as "the student chaos" began to alarm Gropius. About twenty Bauhaus students, declaring that "art is a grind" had walked out of the school. The exodus continued in March, which also saw a disheartening drop in new applications. To make matters worse, van Doesburg's criticism of the Bauhaus had grown louder, fiercer, and more indiscriminate. "The Bauhaus," van Doesburg declared, mixes "Expressionist hysteria with a half-baked religious mystique [Mazdaznanism], and elevates it to a dogma." Schlemmer referred to him as one of the Bauhaus's "most vocal opponents." Some Weimar anti-Bauhaus artists, seeing the van Doesburg as a powerful weapon to undermine Gropius and his school, arranged for the Dutch artist to give a series of public lectures at the studio of a Bauhaus student and local Weimar artist, Peter Röhl. The lectures would be widely attended.

By the spring of 1921 the Bauhaus was gravely compromised—artistically, ideologically, morally, and legally. The reestablishment of the old Art Academy had effectively degraded the Bauhaus into little more than a craft school, a *Gewerbeschule* similar to van de Velde's coexistence with the Academy's *Hochschule*. And even here the Bauhaus's craft record was dismal. The mood at the school was more glum than ever. "[T]hings look bad for the Bauhaus!" Schlemmer declared. Itten saw the Bauhaus as "in for a no-holds-barred struggle" with the renewed Academy. Schlemmer, who sensed a "fierce fight" ahead, brooded over the very real possibility of the Bauhaus's "collapse." Student dissatisfaction with Gropius's leadership blossomed into open revolt. "A putsch is brewing at the Bauhaus," Schlemmer commented, admitting that, for the moment, he too had become "a secret putschist." "The best people here," he wrote, "are criticizing Gropius." Drained by the intensifying student attacks, the unrelenting external pressures, the internal quarrels, his own private struggles, and the worsening insomnia that had plagued him since the war, Gropius could no longer lead the battle. That spring Gropius left for a rest cure to Austria's Badgastein in a state of nervous collapse.

Neither Gropius's state of mind nor van Doesburg's attacks had caused all the school's problems. The Bauhaus's difficulties essentially lay in the conflicts inherent in its program, which Itten and van Doesburg's antagonistic theories merely articulated and exposed. Itten's secret brotherhood was irreconcilable with the attempt to unify art and craft under architecture. So too were the school's pursuit of unity with the proletariat, its hoped-for establishment as a prototype art school, not to mention the school's status as a publicly funded institution subject to governmental scrutiny. Van Doesburg's technologically derived notions were incompatible with the school's advocacy of spirit, suffering, mystical fellowship, and nostalgic yearnings for the purported unity of the past (as evidenced in the *Bauhütte*). The Bauhaus of 1921 was the victim of a fundamental predicament symbolized by the coexistence of Itten and van Doesburg and compounded by Gropius's personal problems, along with a radically shifting sociopolitical environment.

And yet Gropius's outlook and temperament played no small role here. Encumbered by his lofty ideals, Gropius seemed unaware of the inherent contradictions between the Bauhaus's ideals and its reality, the divergences between his assertions and acts, between what the school claimed and what was really going on. Having cast his hat in so many rings, Gropius remained notably distant from the school, whether from personal strain or simply from his distaste for being "enslaved to a vision." For whatever reasons, Gropius evinced a near visceral aversion for what he called dogma, consistently preferring anarchy to dictate. "[W]e do not want to promote any dogmas at the Bauhaus," he told van Doesburg. "Each [student] shall develop his own creative individuality." Whether a weakness or a strength, this disposition left a vacuum at the center of the Bauhaus. In calmer times this void could perhaps have tapped a well of creativity; but in 1921 it was filled only with chaos.

9.

From Geist to Gadgets

The Bauhaus Attempts to Change

We step from . . . danger to danger.

—*Lyonel Feininger*

The election in September 1921 of a leftist coalition government in Thuringia radically altered the fortunes of the Bauhaus. Not since the provisional revolutionary government had created the school in 1919 did it enjoy such local sympathy. This shift in the political scene spurred Gropius to undertake aggressive initiatives at the Bauhaus in 1922 that were previously inconceivable. Indeed, the event seems to have colored all his actions that year. But the winds of opportunity that would help create a radically different Bauhaus also bore with them the seeds of disaster.

The new Thuringian government was able to form its scant two-vote majority only with the support of the Communists. The resulting alliance between the moderate and far Left made Thuringia the country's most radical leftist state and created a partnership that many in

Germany, including the national Social Democratic government, most feared. Red Thuringia, as it became known, found itself the object of rabid attention by the nation's conservative press. "A Red majority of two Socialists governs with the consent of the Communists," declared the *Deutsche Allgemeine Zeitung*. In return for this support, the newspaper noted ominously, the Thuringian government promised to pursue "proletarian policies."

Despite the pejorative tone, such an assessment was not entirely unwarranted. Thuringia's government indeed had to placate the Communists, their legislative allies. They did so by appointing Max Greil—a past member of the German Independent Social Democratic Party (the USPD) and an activist educational reformer—as director of the recently created Ministry of Public Education (Volksbildung), the department now responsible for the Bauhaus. Greil, in turn, appointed a Communist adviser.

Greil brought with him a program of radical school reform that was remarkably similar to Gropius's. He wanted to create a unified work school (*Arbeitsschule*) that combined the traditional, university-oriented (and upper-class) *Gymnasium* education with the practical, craft-oriented (and working-class) *Gewerbeschule*. On paper the Thuringian minister's program mirrored that of Ebert's national government. But Greil's will and vigorous leadership—and the votes his government was able to muster—made it likely that he would be able to carry out what the national government merely preached.

Greil presented his radical program to redesign Thuringia's entire school system before the State Assembly in February 1922. Although the Communists' program was even more extreme, they went along with Greil's proposal thanks to the influence of their leader, Dr. Theodor Neubauer, an experienced pedagogue and expert on school issues. Backed by the Communists, the Thuringian State Assembly passed Greil's Comprehensive School Law (Einheitsschulgesetz) on February 24, 1922—the nation's most radical plan for educational reform.

Gropius, who had long hoped to present the Bauhaus as a prototype for a similar reform of the state's art schools with an affiliated leftist government, moved quickly to ally himself with the educational minister. To accomplish this, however, changes would have to be made at the Bauhaus. With this in mind and assuming that Greil's program would be passed by the legislature, Gropius sent a memorandum to the faculty on February 3 announcing a comprehensive reexamination of the Bauhaus. While Greil's plans, along with the school's obvious failings, undoubtedly influenced Gropius's initiative at this time, his personal rivalry with Itten played no small role.

This had not been the first time that Gropius had announced the urgent need to resolve the Bauhaus's mushrooming problems. He had done so many times, but then proceeded to leave matters as they stood. In early March 1921, for example, he had returned to the Bauhaus emotionally fit after his rest cure and again did nothing to improve the situation. Only at the end of the year, in early December—shortly after Thuringia's new government had come to power—did Gropius finally move to bring matters in hand.

Gropius's action was in response to an initiative undertaken by Itten some days before at a Masters' Council meeting, when he had presented his analysis of the Bauhaus's problems. In Itten's view the Bauhaus's difficulties stemmed from two major sources: the incompatibility between its Expressionist and craft aims, and its indecision over whether it was committed to individual creativity or to handicraft. While the creation of the unique, isolated work of art [*Einzelarbeit*] constituted the basis of Itten's own teachings, he recognized that it had little to do with a craft school's need to create prototype models for industrial production. The Bauhaus—despite its manifesto's claims—could not do both, Itten contended. He recognized that the creation of models for industrial production (as embodied in the Werkbund principles of Gropius's original Bauhaus proposal) seemed the best way for the school to earn itself out of its endless financial difficulties.

Itten's blunt assessment at the Masters' Council meeting had surprised no one. His comments at the faculty meetings were consistently succinct and informed. Despite his mystical leanings, Itten possessed a keen analytical mind that perceived issues more objectively than Gropius, who tended to look at matters ideologically and emotionally. Itten was the only professional teacher on the Bauhaus faculty, and he offered the school's only required course.

Burdened as he was with organizational and administrative problems, not to mention his architectural and personal preoccupations, Gropius was only too happy to ignore Itten's increasing absorption with his Mazdaznan rituals and van Doesburg's relentless needling and delegate the running of the school to the commanding and more than competent Itten. But Gropius, like everyone else, also realized Itten would not have minded being the director in name as well as in fact. Schlemmer commented that Itten wanted "[n]othing less than to be at the helm of the Bauhaus."

At a Masters' Council meeting in early December 1921 Gropius told Itten to stick to his teaching, "where he belongs." Gropius's stern reprimand and his sudden move to reassert the leadership he had so willingly relinquished to Itten up to now caught many by surprise. Gropius, Schlemmer declared, was "finally tak[ing] a stand against Itten's monopoly." The options suddenly opened up by a supportive Thuringian government had undoubtedly played a significant role in Gropius's unexpected and uncharacteristic move. So too may he have been influenced by the fact that Wassily Kandinsky, the internationally famous Russian artist, had just arrived in Berlin and had expressed interest in teaching at the Bauhaus. In keeping with Gropius's policy of bringing in artistic "stars" to attract attention to the Bauhaus, Kandinsky's appointment represented a potential plum. As there were a limited number of faculty slots, Kandinsky could come in only if Itten left.

At the close of 1921, then, the embattled Bauhaus had to deal with a fight for power between its two leading figures. "Itten and Gropius are dueling it out," Schlemmer had commented, as he and the rest of the faculty found themselves playing referee. Prone to conceptualize issues within a broad framework, Gropius saw the struggle for the Bauhaus's leadership as a contest between the past (Itten) and the future (himself). Typically, the challenge energized Gropius. "I'm locked in combat with Itten," Gropius declared. "I plan to hold my ground." Such battlefield terminology appeared in the February 3, 1922, memorandum Gropius sent to the Bauhaus faculty. As the leader of the Bauhaus, Gropius declared, he felt obliged to set "the battle's tempo and vigor." Thus charged, Gropius began his reevaluation of the Bauhaus, not with a rigorous and measured analysis of the school's strengths and failings, but with another impassioned "search for unity" that repeated the process that had resulted in the Bauhaus's original program, now disclaimed and wobbly.

The concerns Itten had set forth the previous November were real and urgently needed to be resolved. For many reasons the Bauhaus, as represented in its 1919 manifesto, was not working. Itten recognized that revising the Bauhaus would cost money. While Gropius's highest priority remained establishing the Bauhaus as a prototype for school reform, he seemed to realize that this was a long-term and highly problematic plan.

Government support inevitably brought with it government intervention and control. Ideally, the Bauhaus should be able to support itself (through selling its workshop products to industry) and reduce government subsidy (and control) as much as possible. The goal of Gropius's Bauhaus reexamination was thus twofold. First, to find an artistic direction that would spur the Bauhaus's financial independence; and second, to diminish Itten's influence. Neither of these, however, were mentioned in Gropius's faculty memorandum.

To accomplish these aims Gropius looked to the old Werkbund industrial aesthetic on which he had based his 1916 Bauhaus proposal. He was not alone at this time in harkening back to such an artistic-industrial alliance as the basis of a modern art. So too were van Doesburg and the Russian Constructivists, several of whom were in Berlin at the time. As a matter of fact, Gropius's February memorandum specifically referred to their "parallel efforts," a reference which the school's rightist opponents would never let him forget.

Gropius's typically lofty phrasing—"Today, a creative force is once again winning its way back into an effective dialogue between the artist, industry, and the machine"—transformed the tired industrial aesthetic, the need for money, and the battle for the school's leadership into an exalted-sounding moral and metaphysical enterprise. Where Gropius had earlier sought unity in the creation of utopia, he now sought it—as Schlemmer wryly noted—in the creation of a "[h]eadquarters for superior industrial design." In returning to the industrial basis of the Bauhaus's initial program, the school had not only traveled a long and arduous road for the past three years, but also a circular one.

If the goals of the 1919 Bauhaus had reflected the day's ecstatic revolutionary spirit, the revision that Gropius was proposing in his February memorandum mirrored 1922's more sober mood. The traumas of the war were now receding, and Nietzschean appeals to suffering, the seeking of artistic nurture through confrontations with death, the craving for spiritual unity, and secret conspiracies seemed terribly dated. Expressionism, as a valid artistic style, was essentially finished. Gropius proposed that the school "fit into the rhythm of the competitive world . . . and come to terms with . . . the machine, . . . locomotives, airplanes, factories, American silos and . . . mechanical gadgets for daily use." This was the reality Gropius insisted the Bauhaus had to confront to avoid turning into a "romantic wasteland that has lost contact with the outside world," an echo of van Doesburg's criticism and an unmistakable dig at Itten.

Gropius now condemned what he referred to as "extravagant romanticism" as being "dangerous for our youth."

> Many Bauhaus students worship a Rousseau-esque "return to nature." They want bows and arrows instead of rifles. Why not pick up a stone to throw and go naked? To lead this kind of a life, such a world-denying person should retire to an island.

Despite his references to locomotives and airplanes, Gropius's seemingly new, rationalized approach remained as fervent as had been his earlier allusions to catastrophe, the inner experience, and the transformation of life.

Gropius assigned the specific tactical plan to bring all this about to Otto Dorfner, a "technically extremely competent man" who owned and operated the bookbinding facilities used by the Bauhaus. As both an artist—a book designer—and a successful businessman, Dorfner appeared to Gropius to possess sensitivity to the needs of art and the business sense needed for the school's industrial alliance. By early March Dorfner's proposals were ready. From his suggestions the new Bauhaus would emerge.

Dorfner claimed that the Bauhaus was "too diffuse and unfocused." He proposed that the school concentrate more on its workshops, which he wanted upgraded and made capable of producing prototype models for industry, a so-called Bauhaus collection. To correct the current lack of coordination between the workshops and the art classes, Dorfner insisted that a conscientious workshop program be implemented immediately. He suggested hiring an experienced, first-class business manager as corporation counsel (*Syndikus*) to put the Bauhaus on a proper business footing. Such a business manager would reorganize the workshops into model production centers; act as liaison between the Bauhaus and industry; organize the school as a business and revise the school's bookkeeping practices to clearly separate the school's business and teaching activities; and, in what amounted to a wondrous leap of faith, "make art financially answerable without compromising it."

Given the increased importance of the workshops, Dorfner suggested that the workshop masters be allowed to join the Masters' Council. He argued that the council's current limitation to the artistic faculty, the so-called Form Masters, was a grave mistake. Not only were the workshop heads unable to vote on matters that directly concerned them, but their situation undercut the Bauhaus's basic claim of the equality of art and craft, especially in the eyes of the students.

To help focus the workshops' efforts, Dorfner suggested that the Bauhaus seek a large architectural commission—"such as the construction of a building here in Weimar"—in which all the workshops could participate. Such an enterprise would not only realize the Bauhaus's long-standing claim of organizing the arts through architecture, but also give the public an opportunity to see some tangible results from the school, which up to now had been notably missing.

Gropius, plunging into his full-steam-ahead mode, moved to implement Dorfner's suggestions at once. By the middle of March 1922 Schlemmer wrote of "new waves wash[ing] over the Bauhaus" and of new building plans. A private corporation, Bauhaussiedlung GmbH, was formed to build a Bauhaus housing development. But of all Dorfner's proposals, none was so touchy as the upgrading of the workshops and, specifically, allowing the workshop masters to vote.

The workshop masters heartily agreed with Dorfner. Gropius too recognized the need to raise the status of the Bauhaus workshops. Indeed, he hailed it. "The school is the handmaiden of the workshop, and some day will merge into it," Gropius would declare in 1923. The workshop masters, however, insisted that their voice in running the school equal their heightened status. They demanded membership—with full voting rights—in the Masters' Council. Schlemmer and Itten agreed with them. Itten claimed that denying the craft masters voting privileges would "lead to eventual unrest" and gravely jeopardize the school.

Gropius, however, intractably opposed granting full voting rights to the workshop masters. Referring to the parliamentary system of one person/one vote as a "palpable danger," he refused to budge. The workshop masters' demands, Gropius declared, were simply "unacceptable." But to show his good faith and his desire, as he put it, "to soothe souls," Gropius agreed to allow the workshop masters to sit in on the Masters' Council meetings in an advisory, nonvoting capacity. The workshop masters, however, were as unbending as Gropius on this matter, and they refused to settle for anything less than full voting rights.

The faculty members, always fired up by Gropius's drive, fairly burst with suggestions and advice regarding the school's new direction.

Schlemmer suggested that the Bauhaus's entire program be changed to better reflect the school's new "level-headed and dispassionate" character. His recommendation would culminate in the resounding reformulation of the Bauhaus's program as "Art and Technology: The New Unity."

At the end of March 1922, anxious to begin making contact with industry and also to perhaps raise some scholarship money, Gropius thought of combining the Bauhaus's usual June exhibition with a display of salable objects made by students in the workshops. On second thought, Gropius decided that the students' work was not yet ready for public view, much less sale, and he dropped the idea. But by early May, undoubtedly pushed by financial need, Gropius overcame his hesitations about the quality of the students' works and asked the Ministry of Education for money to expand the June project into a sales exhibit. He gave several reasons for his request. Such an exhibit, he wrote, would let the public see some concrete results of the school's program. It would also establish industrial connections for the school's future orders; arouse interest in the school's products from private sponsors; and benefit Thuringia by "elevat[ing] the entire region's cultural level." While the government granters turned down his request—perhaps because the May appeal came too late for funds to be appropriated for the following month—they were intrigued by the idea of a sales exhibition, with its allure of perhaps lowering their financial contribution. In June they proposed a long-awaited loan to equip the Bauhaus's workshops with the stipulation that the school organize such a sales exhibition the following year. While it would take place on a far more prodigious scale and was now mandated by the government, the goals of what would become the famed 1923 exhibition remained identical to those Gropius had detailed in his initial letter to the ministry.

Apart from the workshop masters, others in the Bauhaus community had reservations about Gropius's proposed changes and his plans for a sales exhibition. Some of the Bauhaus founding principles may have seemed out of touch with the times and excessively romantic, but in general they retained their sway. The Bauhaus community proudly continued to regard itself as a society apart, a spiritually involved group (*seelenhafte Gemeinschaften*) both removed from the rules and traditions of its chaotic capitalistic surroundings and opposed to them. "We had nothing to do with the outside world," one student declared. (While some individuals, such as van Doesburg, viewed this removal from the world as a primitivistic retreat, most at the Bauhaus viewed it positively, if not to the extent of Itten's Mazdaznan group.) However blurred its artistic focus may have become, the heart of Gropius's Bauhaus remained utopian and focused on the future, which many at the school believed the new, essentially pragmatic program rejected. Indeed, Schlemmer referred to the Bauhaus's new program as "turn[ing] its back on utopia."

Many within the Bauhaus community were troubled by Gropius's commercial conversion. The artists were less than thrilled with the idea of being associated with a school whose goal was to make money. Schlemmer thought it "dreadful." Other faculty members were appalled and humiliated. Schlemmer, who expressed the feelings of the artistic faculty, believed that artists should worry about making good art, not about whether or not it would sell. He wondered why artists should try to do something that engineers did better. Bauhaus students claimed that the proposed new program "raped" the inner experience they had been taught to cherish. Feininger felt Gropius was "unquestionably . . . sacrific[ing]" the Bauhaus's development to shortsighted expediency. While he recognized the school's need to show some results to its hard-pressed supporting community and also gain some degree of financial independence, he believed that such a commercial shift was justified only if it averted a total "collapse" of the school.

The artistic implications of the proposed alliance with industry were also worrisome. Schlemmer, for one, wondered what painting had to do with machinery. After Kandinsky became a member of the school's faculty, he too opposed the new course. Having just fled the Soviet Union after the government had adopted a similar program of production art, he admonished the new strategy as "deifying the machine." The artist Gerhard Marcks, another instructor, claimed that human beings were "more important than the successful manufacture of china."

Ideology and aesthetics aside, the proposed shift also prompted practical concerns. How would the Bauhaus, one of whose students had taken a year to complete a metal teapot, deal with issues of profit—industry's primary concern—and with cost effectiveness and competitiveness? How would a business manager, charged with the efficient financial management of the school, respond to such goings-on, and how would Gropius react to the business manager's likely opposition? How could commercial priorities be reconciled to the necessary disinterest of pedagogy? Success in one may, in fact, inhibit success in the other. As an internal Bauhaus report prepared later in the year would argue, a successful business required an obedient and smooth-running organization, all of which sharply differed from the contentious individualism fostered by the Bauhaus, whose whole point was to question everything. And how would local industries react to their taxes supporting a potential competitor, especially during a period of such economic hardship? Despite Gropius's persistent wooing, the Weimar Craft Guild—like most small-industry groups in other areas with arts and crafts schools—had never accepted the Bauhaus. Schlemmer worried that commercial projects would deplete the artists' creative energies. Kandinsky urged caution and suggested that feasibility studies be prepared before anything was negotiated.

Nobody much liked the proposed sales exhibition either. At a meeting held to drum up student support, one student leader referred to it as "totally unrealistic . . . and [revealing] too much wishful thinking about the future." Echoing what Gropius himself had felt some months before, he argued that such commercial expectations demanded too much of the students too soon. Here, too, the faculty agreed. Indeed, Schlemmer, like Gropius, was beginning to feel that the school's fate was riding on the exhibition. "[A] question of survival," he commented in December 1922 about the enterprise planned for the coming year, "of victory or total destruction."

Bolstered by his confidence in the Thuringian government's support and desperate for money, Gropius's plans for the exhibition ballooned, in spite of the pointed questions and reservations. He suggested hiring a special coordinator for the exhibit. Itten, who since June 1922 had been quietly exploring teaching opportunities elsewhere, disagreed, insisting that the hiring of outside experts would negate the point of the exhibit, which was to show what the Bauhaus could do. The Bauhaus, he insisted, should do all the work itself.

Dr. Hans Beyer, the recently hired business manager, agreed with Itten. He also argued that a special coordinator would be too expensive. Beyer, in fact, opposed putting on the exhibition at all, contending that such exercises rarely achieved what they claimed and usually resulted in a large deficit. But the workshop masters remained the most put out. They continued to insist on a voice in the running of the school's affairs equal to their enhanced status.

On the eve of the most monumental change in the Bauhaus's brief history—one that raised all sorts of confounding issues and provoked the nearly unanimous opposition of the school's community, not to mention the preparation of an ambitious, costly, and equally opposed exhibition—the school spent most of 1922 arguing about when and how the workshop masters might participate in a nonvoting capacity in the Masters' Council. The formidable implications of the proposed change were, for the most part, ignored.

Despite the Bauhaus Manifesto's ringing claims about the equality of art and craft, the school's craft masters had long felt like second-rate citizens; that Gropius, in fact, looked down on them. "When Gropius comes into the workshop," one workshop apprentice complained, "you can notice from how he talks that he secretly wants nothing to do with us." But whether they were justified or not, the workshop masters' feelings of inferiority were enhanced by Gropius's adamant refusal to let them vote and his condescending intention to "soothe souls." Insulted, hurt, and angered by what they interpreted as their director's imperious attitude, the workshop masters pushed their demands even harder. Whispered complaints about Gropius's use of publicly subsidized Bauhaus students in his private architectural office began to be heard. Gropius, however, still refused to budge. On July 1, 1922, he sent the finalized new statutes to Greil's Educational Ministry for approval, without the voting rights that the workshop masters were demanding.

When the Bauhaus reopened for its 1922 fall semester, Gropius considered the voting issue closed. At a Masters' Council meeting on October 2 he asked the workshops to immediately prepare "to create prototypes for mass production." He also wanted the students to spend more time in the workshops and less in theory classes, emphasizing once more the school's new craft focus.

The workshop masters were furious that their demands were being ignored and insisted on meeting privately with Gropius on October 4. There Carl Schlemmer, Oskar's brother, who was in charge of the wall-painting workshop, and Josef Zachmann, from the cabinetmaking workshop, leveled serious personal accusations against Gropius and openly questioned the propriety of the state paying the salaries of two of Gropius's private employees (who also had part-time Bauhaus responsibilities), Adolf Meyer and Emil Lange. What they were obviously looking for was a lever by which they could force Gropius to accede to their demands. Gropius instead denounced the accusations as a personal attack and a "conspiracy of unparalleled viciousness."

Having achieved nothing at this private meeting, the workshop masters brought their case before the Masters' Council the following day. There they expanded their charges, accusing Gropius of directorial incompetence and involvement in "intimate and illicit" relationships with female members of the Bauhaus community. To these Dr. Beyer, the newly appointed business manager and corporation lawyer (*Syndikus*) added his own accusations, assailing as "deplorable" the school's administration of its finances.

A Bauhaus committee consisting of two members of the artistic faculty, Kandinsky and Georg Muche, and two workshop masters, Josef Hartwig and Lange, was set up to investigate. On October 13 the committee dismissed the charges (all based on innuendo and hearsay) as blatantly spurious, with the exception of Beyer's and those criticizing Gropius's architectural office. Gropius, who exulted over having made "short work of it . . . and [having] kicked out those violators of the temple," assumed that the matter was settled.

The day after the investigative committee announced its decision, the faculty voted to fire the two workshop master protagonists, Zachmann and Carl Schlemmer, citing their incompatibility with the Bauhaus community. The workshop masters, however, rejected the findings of the committee as biased and incomplete and declared themselves ready to seek other means of redress. On October 16 Schlemmer and Zachmann each addressed formal complaints to Greil's Ministry of Education. Citing persistent doubts, both within the school and without, about Gropius's suitability as director of the Bauhaus, they charged him with incompetence and immoral conduct and requested a formal ministerial inquiry for "possible disciplinary action."

Beyer's accusations, however, were more complex and difficult to evaluate. Unlike those of the workshop masters, his charges were not based on innuendo and gossip but on his own observations. Charges and countercharges were flung back and forth between Gropius and Beyer, who insisted that his criticism of the school's financial management was precisely what he—as the "Bauhaus's corporate head"—was being paid to do. On October 14 both men agreed to allow an audit by an independent, impartial expert. The matter rested there until October 20, when, at a Masters' Council meeting, Beyer expressed his reservations about the value of exhibitions. Gropius's response to Beyer's criticism remains unknown, but it apparently rubbed the business manager the wrong way, for on that date he too filed a formal complaint against Gropius with the

Ministry of Education. Two days later Zachmann, Schlemmer, and Beyer combined their complaints into one, the strength of Beyer's charges bolstering the others' more spurious accusations.

Gropius reacted by firing Beyer, informing the Ministry of Education on October 28 that "because of recent incidents . . . [Beyer] can no longer . . . set foot on the [Bauhaus] premises." Dr. Beyer, whose name had been submitted and appointment approved by the Ministry of Education and who apparently had considerable professional credentials, took grave offense at being dismissed this way. Declaring in a letter to the ministry on October 30 that Gropius's action was "insulting to a person of my position and . . . [thus] invalid," he accused the Bauhaus director, among other charges, of financial incompetence.

Beyer summarized his complaints against Gropius into a list of thirty-eight pointed questions directed at the government. "Is the government aware," he asked, "of the wretched organization of the Bauhaus business office?" He asked if the government knew of and approved Gropius's rejection of enforcing strict attendance in the workshops "despite the repeated pleas by the Craft Masters"; that some artistic faculty members worked part-time for full-time pay; that one of the workshop masters [whom Beyer named] lacked the necessary qualifying examinations; and that two members of Gropius's office received their salaries from the state, despite working "almost exclusively for Gropius's private architectural office."

With the State Assembly scheduled to debate the Bauhaus's budget request for the 1923 exhibition in November, these accusations could not have come at a worse moment. Beyer, Zachmann, and Schlemmer realized this tactical advantage and escalated their attack, deluging various state ministries with incriminating letters. In one letter Beyer accused Gropius of "wast[ing] millions of the State's funds" and noted that he anticipated the loss of millions more due to the workshops' "scandalous" organization. Citing "the grave importance [of this matter] for the entire state budget," Zachmann and Schlemmer a few days later urged the Educational Minister to convene a ministerial-level meeting on the Bauhaus. The magnitude of their accusations swelled with the passage of time.

In December Beyer labeled Gropius's financial bungling "catastrophic" and in need of "rigorous intervention" from the state. He also noted that only seven apprentices from the Bauhaus had been trained over the course of the past three years at a cost to the state of millions of marks. Still without funds or the necessary statutes with which he could approach private industry for support, and with the exhibition scheduled to open in a scant eight months, Gropius spent much of the final months of 1922 frantically rebutting the escalating charges.

The accusations against Gropius attracted allies, both expected and not. Van Doesburg, who continued to fret over not being asked to join the Bauhaus faculty, published a vituperative attack against the Bauhaus in *De Stijl*, in which his colleague, the Dutch painter Vilmos Huszar, accused the school's management of committing nothing less than "a crime against the state and civilization." More probable allies were Dr. Herfurth and his German Nationalist Party (the DNP). Ever watchful of Bauhaus injustices, they took up the complaints after the Thuringian government turned the Bauhaus matter over to the State Assembly.

At a session of the State Assembly on December 16, 1922, Herfurth—speaking on behalf of the DNP—demanded a government investigation of the Bauhaus's financial management to determine if "state funds [were] being handled in the rational manner consistent with state-funded institutions." He based his series of pointed questions on Beyer's queries and demanded a satisfactory answer from the government *before* the State Assembly made any decision about the Bauhaus's financial appropriations, including the funds for the 1923 exhibition.

The government's reply failed to satisfy the nationalists. Herfurth then demanded an interpellation of the Thuringian government "concerning the organization and management of the State Bauhaus" to take place on March 16, 1923. Until then no statutes or funding requests of any sort could be approved for the Bauhaus or its exhibition, scheduled to open four months later. With the accusations now blown up to slanderous proportions, Gropius filed a libel suit against the accusers that began a long legal battle. Embraced with equal fervor by the Right and the nation's press, the lawsuit would titillate the German public for the next five years.

By the end of 1922 the Bauhaus was broke; under legal attack; without its needed statutes; the subject of an embarrassing governmental inquiry; and without any internal consensus. Despite nearly a year of discussion the entire Bauhaus community, students and teachers alike, remained unconvinced about the school's new direction and need for an exhibition.

The collapse of Germany's currency added to the school's woes, mocking any attempt at budgetary planning. In November 1922

Gropius had requested an appropriation from the government of 2.5 million marks to fund the upcoming exhibition. By December he had to quadruple his request to 10 million marks. Schlemmer in December described the Bauhaus's situation as hopeless. "[T]hings look black to me," he confided to his diary. "I [see] the entire Bauhaus teetering along with Gropius."

In 1922, Germany was also teetering. Foreign Minister since January, Walther Rathenau had been murdered by nationalist zealots in June. In October a bloody riot in Berlin between Communists and militant nationalists had left one killed, scores seriously injured, and the nation wondering, as one newspaper commented, if the event was "simply a relapse into revolutionary turmoil or a prelude to new disturbances that . . . would finally drive Germany over the cliff." Gropius, like others, feared civil war.

It was thus at a particularly perilous moment both for the Bauhaus and the country that Gropius, doubtlessly emboldened by the sympathetic Thuringian government, made several highly controversial appointments at the school. He appointed his architectural associate Emil Lange, a politically well-connected member of the German Social Democratic Party (the SPD) to replace the dismissed Beyer as *Syndikus*; and brought in two artists with indisputably Red connections, the world-renowned Kandinsky, fifty-six years old and a recent leader of several important artistic groups in the Soviet Union, and twenty-seven-year-old László Moholy-Nagy, a Hungarian revolutionary and former associate of the Communist leader Béla Kun.

The official announcement of Kandinsky's appointment on July 1, 1922, aroused a predictably outraged response from the Right. "What led to . . . [Kandinsky's] appointment is completely incomprehensible," one of Essen's rightist newspapers commented.

> One asks oneself in vain what Kandinsky, whose orgiastic . . . color mysticism might be at home in the Russian cultural chaos, is doing in an academic appointment in [Weimar], a place ennobled through Germany's classical art. . . . Kandinsky is a Bolshevist, [and] that means an anarchist in both politics and art. Now that the rule of the mob [in the Soviet Union] is slowly causing the leaders to starve, they too are starting to flee. It is understandable that

> Kandinsky has turned his back on . . . Russia, but it is a pitiful
> spectacle [that he has been welcomed] by . . . downtrodden
> Germany.

Gropius, not surprisingly, had expected such a reaction from the Right.
On February 23 he had polled the Bauhaus faculty about Kandinsky's
"Red appearance." Again in June, while awaiting the government's
approval of the new appointment—Kandinsky and the Bauhaus having
already signed a contract—Gropius, worried about "[p]roblems aris[ing]
out of Kandinsky's Russian nationality," had asked the faculty to keep the
matter private.

However bogus the nationalists' Bolshevik accusations may have been,
Kandinsky's Red affiliations were incontrovertible. He had been a particularly prominent leader of several of the Soviet Union's most important
artistic organizations. Although he had been born in Moscow in 1866, he
had lived in Germany for nearly twenty years, having abandoned a law
career at age thirty to study painting in Munich. He had returned to
Russia in 1914 at the beginning of the war when he—like van de Velde—
was declared an "enemy alien."

In January 1918 Kandinsky joined the Fine Arts Division (IZO) of the
People's Commissariat for Enlightenment (known as Narkompros) shortly
after the organization's founding. Some months later Kandinsky was
named director of IZO's theater and film division; he contributed articles
to one of IZO's newspapers. As previously noted, Kandinsky was on the
directing committee of the International Office, the organization set up to
establish contacts with western artists, which had contacted the AfK at the
end of 1918. In February 1919 Kandinsky, along with the artist Alexander
Rodchenko, helped purchase artworks for a new system of museums
organized by IZO. He also helped organize the Fifth State Exhibition of
the New Art's Trade Union of Artist-Painters ("From Impressionism to
Nonobjectivity") held in Moscow.

In May 1920 Kandinsky assumed the directorship of the Institute for
Artistic Culture (Inkhuk) in Moscow and was named honorary professor
at the University of Moscow. The following year he was asked to establish a Russian Academy of the Science of Art (RAKhN), where he headed the physio-psychological division. He became the school's vice president when it opened in October. It goes without saying that none of these
activities necessarily indicates anything about Kandinsky's political con-

victions. But it is understandable how they would be seen in the Red hyperphobic Germany of 1922.

According to his wife, Nina, Kandinsky—like so many other Russian artists in Berlin in December 1921—had come to Germany charged by the Soviet Minister of Culture with gathering and transmitting information about German cultural and artistic events of interest to the Soviet Union. Whether or not he actually did this remains unknown. But, as Nina noted, her husband remained on the payroll of the Soviet government for three months after his arrival in Germany.

Unlike Kandinsky, the far less prominent Moholy-Nagy's Bolshevik sympathies were unequivocal. Fleeing Hungary in the fall of 1919 after the collapse of Kun's Bolshevik revolution, Moholy-Nagy had become the Berlin representative of *Ma* (*Today*), the avant-garde magazine that he and some friends had founded in Hungary. Despite the revolution's failure, Moholy-Nagy's leftist sentiments remained unchanged. "This is our century: technology, the machine, socialism," he had written in *Ma*'s May 1922 issue. "Constructivism is . . . not confined to the picture frame or the pedestal. It expands into industry and architecture. . . . Constructivism is the socialism of vision."

In October, as revolutionary turmoil once again erupted in Berlin, Gropius made another politically controversial appointment, hiring his architectural associate Emil Lange as new *Syndikus*. A year younger than Gropius, the thirty-eight-year-old Lange was bright, energetic, and dependable. As an employee in Gropius's office he would be unlikely to question financial matters as much as his predecessor. He had come to the Bauhaus to head the school's proposed experimental building research center, which never materialized. But Lange's most important strengths— as Gropius stressed at a Masters' Council meeting on October 2—were his socialist party credentials. Lange had been asked by Weimar's workers' groups to represent them in the City Council, a position that Gropius believed would be politically useful for the school, especially with regard to Greil's ministry.

Gropius's confidence in Lange's political connections had not been mistaken. Immediately upon his appointment at the end of October, Lange moved to contact various officials and press organs of the workers' parties. In November he wrote to the chief editor of *Das Volk*, the Social Democratic newspaper printed in the neighboring city of Jena, asking him to help publicize the Bauhaus's forthcoming exhibition in 1923 (*"die entsprechende Propaganda machen zu können"*). As evidence of the Bauhaus's socialistic character, Lange cited the school's "rational organization" and goals as a "national productive institute." A few days later Lange again evoked the school's socialistic spirit in a letter to Social Democratic Party member and Finance Minister Hartmann, asking him to give more support to the Bauhaus, especially with regard to the 1923 exhibition.

Lange introduced Gropius to Theodor Neubauer, the Communist Party's leader and unwavering Bauhaus supporter in the State Assembly. Lange's political efforts would continue in 1923, when he accompanied the Bauhaus leader to a meeting with Neubauer in March to help formulate the party's position on the Bauhaus. Lange also wrote to the leader of the Social Democratic faction in the State Assembly to urge "our party's . . . support of the Bauhaus, as it has done in the past." Considering 1922's turbulent mood, Gropius needed all the political help that Lange could provide.

Gropius also tried to associate the Bauhaus with Greil's school-reform program, even though opposition to it had become apparent shortly after the new government came to power. In November 1921 the German People's Party attacked Greil's proposals to eliminate the compulsory teaching of religion in the schools and some minor religious holidays from the state's calendar as anticlerical. The charge was picked up by rightist newspapers across the nation, who added their voices in condemning "comrades . . . who snubbed the Christian segments of our society." As the birthplace of Luther and the site of Protestantism's triumphant course, Thuringia was especially sensitive to any attempt to remove religion from the schools. One local newspaper referred to the vote as a "rape" of the state's predominantly Protestant population.

Greil's audacious appointment of a Communist adviser to his ministry had also provoked much criticism. Many conservatives viewed the radical Left as little more than Moscow's pawn, and they regarded efforts such as Greil's as the start of the Comintern's expansive ambitions within their country. As one newspaper, shortly after 1921's election, commented, more lay behind "Red Thuringia's mask of democracy and majority decisions."

By the end of 1922 the Right's fears about the ramifications of Thuringia's leftist government seemed justified, at least with regard to Greil's radical school program. As one of "Red Thuringia's" most prominent beneficiaries, the Bauhaus—already suspect in the Right's eyes—

found itself in the midst of a national cultural battle. One Berlin newspaper referred to the Bauhaus as "the most radical art school in the world outside Soviet Russia." The newspaper added that "Weimar's citizens, horrified over what is going on in the van de Velde building, are meeting to swear an oath on Weimar's holy traditions against Gropius's artistic Bolshevism."

Buoyed by the government's support, Gropius and Lange ignored the hyperbole and continued working to secure the Bauhaus's socialist credentials and ties with the Thuringian Left. In an article written for a journal published by Greil's ministry, Gropius specifically cited the similarities of the Bauhaus's practical, hands-on approach and the government's new educational program.

Gropius and Lange, convinced of the "considerable advantages" that such an alliance with the leftist government would bring to the Bauhaus, continued their campaign in 1923, when their efforts began to pay off. In an address before the State Assembly in March of that year, Minister Greil avowed his unequivocal support of the Bauhaus as an example of a "work or production school [*Arbeitsschule*] whose closely connected instruction and productive activity" fell within his own school-reform program. Led by Neubauer, the Communists also strongly supported the Bauhaus at this legislative session, acknowledging the accord of the Bauhaus's goals and status as a production school with those "of the Communist Party." Although his goals for the Bauhaus differed considerably from those of the Communists—Gropius no longer envisioned a radically altered society, nor had he ever advocated any social upheaval to achieve it—the party's public support enhanced the school's linkage with the radical Left in the public's mind.

Greil's ministry supported the Bauhaus with more than words, moving in several areas to integrate the school with the new reforms. Plans were made to utilize the Bauhaus's workshop program as a model for the state, as well as to train Thuringia's crafts teachers. A weeklong vocational school meeting in Weimar in September 1923 was planned to coordinate with the Bauhaus exhibition. Its theme—"The importance of the Bauhaus's training concept for the vocational school"—specifically tied the school to Greil's proposed reforms. Gropius was scheduled to give the meeting's opening address.

By 1923 the Bauhaus was well entrenched within Thuringia's socialist camp. The Right, on the other hand, was garnishing its own support. The powerful local craft union came out in support of Zachmann, Schlemmer, and Beyer and the Right's charges of the school's mismanagement of state funds. These accusations seemed to have their effect, forcing the less committed members of the Left to reconsider their backing of the Bauhaus. Finance Minister Hartmann, the object of one of Lange's petitions, for instance, turned down the school's request for further loans, describing the Bauhaus as "a futile and pointless establishment." Although Herfurth's demand that the Bauhaus be closed was defeated by the majority leftist coalition, his proposal made the Right's ultimate goal unmistakably clear.

The Bauhaus's emphasis on its socialistic character in 1923 reflected less the school's disposition than the realities of Thuringian politics. Indeed, circumstances were pushing the school to affirm socialistic allegiances just when many within the Bauhaus community were accusing Gropius's new program of abandoning such ideals. Despite this discrepancy, Gropius and Lange continued to present the Bauhaus as a socialist institution to Thuringia's leftist legislators and those who influenced their circles. It was with this in mind that Oskar Schlemmer, given the task by Gropius of writing the upcoming exhibition's official program, referred to the Bauhaus as a "cathedral of socialism." "The [State] Bauhaus," Schlemmer wrote,

> founded after the catastrophe of the war, in the chaos of the revolution . . . is becoming the rallying point for all those who, with faith in the future and willingness to storm the heavens, wish to build the cathedral of socialism.

Schlemmer, of course, knew as well as anyone that Gropius was deliberately moving away from this early Bauhaus point of view. The year before, in June 1922, Schlemmer had specifically commented in his diary about the school's new, more utilitarian course: "[I]nstead of cathedrals, the 'Living-machine.'" Since Schlemmer was normally an articulate and precise writer, his rather unconvincing statement, along with his use of the "cathedral of socialism" phrase, may have reflected his unhappiness and lack of conviction over the school's revised program (a Freudian slip, so to speak) as well as the political realities that Gropius and Lange were so openly and aggressively pursuing.

The Right's endless harassment dampened Gropius's quest for government funding. Instead he turned to the public for support, launching a massive publicity campaign for the Bauhaus and its upcoming exhibit. He wrote innumerable articles and delivered lectures all over the country. (It was at one of these lectures, in Hannover on May 28, 1923, that he would spot a beautiful young woman in the audience, Ilse Frank, who would shortly become his wife.) In early March 1923, in the hope of influencing the upcoming budget debate in the Assembly, Gropius sent the Bauhaus's publicity program, along with Schlemmer's statement, to virtually every major newspaper in Germany; every potential political ally in the Thuringian government, including the president of the State Assembly; and all members of the Democratic, Social Democratic, and Communist Parties.

The Left could not have been happier with the Bauhaus's reference to a "cathedral of socialism." Speaking before the State Assembly, Communist Senator Tenner saluted the school for its attempt to create "a socialist cathedral." An unsigned commentator in the *Volksstimme* compared Gropius's emphasis on the spiritually regenerative effect of artistic collaboration to that of Marx.

Predictably, the Right was less enthusiastic. "One reads in the exhibit prospectus," declared a conservative Munich newspaper, "that the state-run Bauhaus in Weimar will be the haven of those forward-looking individuals who wish to build the cathedral of socialism." A Berlin rightist newspaper denounced the school as a center for "heaven-storming socialists, who want to build the cathedral of socialism." For Herfurth and his party colleagues the phrase—coming as it did from the horse's mouth—confirmed what they had been claiming, and Gropius denying, for years.

Gropius, who had apparently not read the pamphlet before it was printed, was surprised and appalled by the Right's reaction. He ordered the remaining copies of the pamphlet destroyed, and he removed the offending reference in the revised version. But too many copies were in the public's hands and the phrase remained attached to the Bauhaus.

10. Victory or Total Destruction

The End of the Weimar Bauhaus

Ah! malheur à celui qui . . . veut boire l'idéal dans la réalité!

[Ah! How unhappy are those who . . . want to drink the ideal
in reality!]

—Alfred de Musset

In early January 1923 Gropius sent yet another urgent petition to Minister Redslob. With the opening of the Bauhaus exhibition only six months away and the Thuringian government unable to provide any funds until the various claims against the school were settled, Gropius had turned to a private bank consortium to loan him the needed ten million marks. Before committing themselves, however, the banks insisted on a letter of support from the National Cultural Minister; and it was this that Gropius now begged from Redslob. "Would you please be so kind to help me out again by sending such a reference as soon as possible?" he pleaded. Redslob agreed, and Gropius received his loan.

It was with Gropius's next request that the Minister drew the line. In a letter on January 8 a euphoric Gropius, having received the banks' financial commitment, asked Redslob to invite no less a personage than President Ebert to become the patron of the exhibition and help fund it as well. The request not only astonished Redslob—"I would never do this," he replied—but moved him to declare the inappropriateness of asking the president of the Reich to chair a local exhibition. "You ask him yourself," Redslob brusquely replied.

Perhaps in his more subdued moments Gropius might have agreed. But the challenge of developing the Bauhaus's new direction and exhibition had charged him up. The more impediments and difficulties that fell across his path, the more driven he became and the more his plans grew. In 1923 the Bauhaus's difficulties ballooned. The ongoing governmental investigation was the least of the problems the Bauhaus faced. The faculty and most of its students still opposed the school's new business-oriented course and its readiness for a major exhibit. But far and away the most formidable problem confronting the Bauhaus was Germany's economic collapse.

This situation had come about due to the country's snowballing indebtedness and its resultant dangerously weakened currency. Faced with a citizenry that could still barely accept their nation's defeat, the government was reluctant to impose the stringent measures that might have controlled the financial free fall. The situation was compounded by the refusal of various German constituencies, such as labor or the industrialists, to carry their share of the financial burden to help ameliorate the situation, insisting that others do it instead. The industrialists, who feared heavier taxes as much as the government's sequestering of their assets, wanted labor to give up its gains of 1918, such as unemployment benefits, the right to collective bargaining, and the eight-hour workday, which labor—of course—refused to do. The Right was equally unrealistic. Some urged defiance of the Allies' claims; others demanded that the reparation payments be reduced or eliminated. Some even wanted to renew the war.

The financial crisis—which had been brewing since 1914, when Germany removed its currency from the gold standard in order to borrow funds for the war—had escalated dangerously in 1922. As the Allies saw it, Germany was deliberately debasing its currency to sabotage its reparation payments. Anxious to hold on to the value of their compensation, they tightened their demands. Raymond Poincaré of France threatened to seize the Ruhr, Germany's industrial heartland, unless the country brought its currency under control. Germany's printing presses worked feverishly to turn out increasingly devalued bills; meanwhile workers, facing growing unemployment and breadlines, took to the streets to protest their hardships and anger toward a government that appeared to be catering to the industrialists' interests. On December 26, 1922, a destitute Germany was declared in default of its reparation payments.

By January 3, 1923, $1 (U.S.) equaled 7,525 marks. On January 11, as expected, French and Belgian troops moved into the Ruhr, and President Ebert convened a series of emergency cabinet meetings to try to come up with a response. Toward the end of the month, in the midst of these urgent meetings, Ebert received an invitation from Gropius—who had obviously ignored Redslob's advice—to become a patron of the Bauhaus exhibition in Weimar. Understandably, the beleaguered Ebert turned it down.

Gropius's invitation to Ebert was only one instance of his attempt to defy the day's harsh realities. Between early January and the beginning of February 1923, as the mark collapsed by more than 400 percent, Gropius relentlessly pursued funding and prestigious sponsorship for the Bauhaus exhibition. Right up until the opening of the exhibition, Gropius sent out hundreds of fund-raising letters to every industrialist, banker, art collector, and culturally involved person that he knew, and many that he did not know, both in Germany and abroad. Letters were sent to former patrons, such as Carl Benscheidt, for whom he had built the Fagus Shoe Last Factory. Americans, such as Gropius's friend Herman Sachs, head of the Dayton (Ohio) Museum of Art, and Katherine Dreier, whose Société Anonyme was giving Kandinsky his first one-man show in America in March 1923, received letters too. So did so-called dollar kings John Rockefeller, Henry Ford, "Willy" Hearst, and Paul Warburg. Except for those sent to people he knew personally, such as Benscheidt, most of Gropius's requests were ignored or, as with Ford and Warburg, politely turned down. His appeal to the avant-garde philanthropists in other German cities proved equally fruitless. "Stuttgartners are not interested in contributing to Weimar enterprises," one Stuttgart businessman starchily replied.

The nearly insurmountable problems the Bauhaus faced in 1923, not to mention its own internal dissension, drove Gropius to distraction. To shore up the school's leftist political support in the state legislature to try to win some funds, he emphasized the Bauhaus's socialistic instincts. This, in turn, decreased its appeal to the capitalists from whom he was also seeking funds. Forced by the vagaries of public finance and politics to find financial support wherever he could, he resolved this dilemma by empha-sizing the varying (and often conflicting) aspects of the Bauhaus's pro-gram—old, as well as new—to different groups. At varying times and to varying observers, Gropius would present the Bauhaus as a trade school dedicated to increasing profitability; an experimental internationalist community of artists dedicated to bringing about a world without borders; a nationalistic enterprise that would advance Germany's economic inter-ests; a craft school for artists; an art school for "enlightened" craftsmen; and a publicly funded institution responsive to the needs of its supporting community. This, of course, was in addition to his earlier depictions of the Bauhaus as a secret sect attempting to transform a materialistic and profit-oriented society; a community of artists who willingly and joyfully subsumed their artistic autonomy before a "conductor" architect; an egal-itarian artistic community where all the arts were equal; a response to the artists' desire for relevance and integration into society, and to the new call for radical social upheaval; and a conspiratorial mysterium disdainful of a supporting public that the school viewed as philistine and bourgeois. If Gropius's strategy made little sense, it measured the hour's despera-tion—and worked.

Meanwhile, Zachmann, Carl Schlemmer, and Beyer were pursuing their charges with equal relentlessness. While even the most zealous Bauhaus opponents recognized the spuriousness of Zachmann and Schlemmer's accusations, Beyer's charges were a different matter. The Right had always used the state's funding powers to stymie the Bauhaus. Herfurth's accusa-tion, then, at the formal interpellation in the State Assembly on March 16, 1923, that the Bauhaus had mishandled public funds and was persistently indifferent to the state's limited financial resources—was simply a Beyer-enhanced version of the Right's long complaints.

Here—as Gropius and Lange, the school's new business manager, both recognized—the Bauhaus was indeed vulnerable. Beyer's abrupt departure had left the Bauhaus's financial records in shambles. Current accounts were neither correct nor up-to-date, and the vouchers needed to set up a new accounting system were at the government's revenue office and unavailable. Desperate to move forward, Gropius responded by continu-ing—indeed, expanding—his plans, which overburdened the school's already disorganized accounting system. The Bauhaus's inadequate and overworked administrative staff was equally stretched. In addition to preparing detailed responses to the government's investigation, they now had to deal with the building of a private home for the upcoming exhibition, the so-called Haus am Horn, as well as set up a new production department and establish a private corporation to develop standardized housing.

Gropius, deeply involved with the Bauhaus's overall plans and thinking that Lange was looking after financial matters, did not pay much attention to the school's account books. But even under normal circumstances Gropius preferred to involve himself more "in the ideal aspects of things" than in the nitty-gritty of finances. Beyer would not be the only one to speak of Gropius's financial indifference. Wilhelm Necker, who came to the Bauhaus as *Syndikus* in June 1924 from the Thuringian State Bank, also described attempts to discuss financial matters with Gropius as "tricky business."

Given Gropius's harried schedule and apparent disinterest in reconciling either the school's ambitions or the scope of its planned exhibition with economic realities, Lange soon abandoned as hopeless any effort to get the Bauhaus's bookkeeping under control. By July 1923 the school's financial record-keeping would crumble under the strains of inflation, directorial indifference, and the imminent opening of the exhibition. Lange would be content to merely jot down financial transactions on loose sheets of paper. And even the most orderly bookkeeping could not have coped with what was happening in Germany.

By early April it was obvious that Germany was facing financial catastrophe. "What is to happen," lamented a financial expert to Harry Kessler, "if in a few weeks the dollar rate of exchange races up to a hundred thousand marks . . . ?" By July the rate exceeded 350,000 marks. At the end of the month $1 bought 6,400,000 marks. Schlemmer received an advance of 2.5 million marks in a packet of bills as thick as two fists, and brooded over whether to buy a tie with the money or a book, which now cost 6 to 8 million marks. In October $1 would be worth more than 25 *billion* marks. Banks would run out of money, and Schlemmer, who considered himself lucky to be able to collect his advance of 500 million marks, would dye old gloves rather than spend the 250 million marks to buy a new pair. A cup of coffee cost 17 million marks.

A mark cost more to print than it was worth. Workers were paid twice a day. Given half an hour off, they would run out and try to barter the funds before the value diminished. People carried their money to banks in huge wicker laundry baskets. Lifetime savings were cashed in for a loaf of bread. Some did not even have money for this. Berlin was jammed with starving people. Breadlines grew longer; malnourished and sickly children grew weak, and their growth slowed. Moholy-Nagy, who had arrived at the Bauhaus in April 1923, made collages out of the worthless bills.

But not everyone suffered. Many people, in fact, made millions. Those who had tangible assets could secure loans and pay them back with increasingly worthless funds. Unaffected as well by the inflation were those who had access to foreign funds. The Russian artist El Lissitzky, who was visiting Germany at the time, described how a Count Kielmansegg exchanged twenty-five dollars for more than twenty-five million German marks. In fact, most German industrialists were doing better than ever, expanding their businesses on cheap loans and paying their workers—and their lenders—with increasingly worthless money. They sold their goods abroad cheaply and received payment in hard currency. These were the individuals to whom an increasingly agitated Gropius turned for private contributions. Carl Benscheidt contributed five hundred thousand marks between January and March, and an additional one million in April. A twenty-dollar contribution in July from the industrialist Hermann Lange—a notable art collector and important patron of the architect Mies van der Rohe—was converted into more than three million marks.

Understandably, with the economy collapsing, not all promised funds came through. And much of the money that did come in—such as the ten-million-mark advance that Gropius secured from the Thuringian government at the end of May—was worth so little that it hardly alleviated any financial pressure. By June Gropius was referring to the exhibition's state as "disastrous."

Gropius's appeals became increasingly frantic, as he literally had to beg people for money. By mid-July he had to raise thirty million marks within fourteen days simply to carry out what had already been started. Lack of money, however, was not Gropius's only worry. Rainy weather was hindering the drying of the Haus am Horn that the Bauhaus had built, and the exhibition opening had to be pushed back to August 15, one month later than planned.

Despite Gropius's frenetic publicity efforts, he could hardly arouse much interest in the Bauhaus exhibition. Germany was in a glum and distracted mood. The presence of foreign troops on their soil depressed and humiliated people. The revolting inequity between those who were starving and those who were making millions did nothing to lift their disposition. Pensioners and workers of all parties and social classes—blue- and white-collar alike—angrily watched years of hard work and frugal savings being wiped out overnight. From Right to Left, people felt betrayed and abandoned by the government, the traditional centrist parties, and, most ominous, by democracy itself. The militant Right—where the name of Adolf Hitler was attracting increasing attention—was growing rapidly. In early April 1923 it was believed to number about 110,000 men, including much of the Reichswehr. Anger exploded into the streets. Provoked by an ever more fanatical and well-armed Right, workers demanded access to arms to defend themselves.

From the East, Moscow watched all this with covetous eyes. Hoping to attract disaffected German nationalists to its fold, the Soviets declared a new policy of "national Bolshevism" and sent in Communist agitators to rile up the disgruntled citizens even more.

By July 1923 one hundred thousand German workers were out of work and riots broke out around the hungry and desperate country. Feininger described the dark cloud that hung over Germany as "awful." In Bavaria, proliferating nationalistic groups formed a *Kampfbund* (fighting group) with Hitler's National Socialist Party; in neighboring leftist Thuringia, workers again demanded to be armed. The national government, worried about an imminent return to the revolutionary situation of 1918, responded by banning demonstrations by both Right and Left, a prohibition that was routinely ignored. On July 23 a leftist demonstration in Frankfurt am Main led to an especially savage political murder. On July 27 the Communists flouted police bans and organized rallies in Potsdam, Hamburg, Bremen, Cologne, and Munich, which ended up in bloody rioting.

On August 11, as strikes continued to spread across the country, Chancellor Wilhelm Cuno's government fell and Gustav Stresemann, a former monarchist turned republican, was named Chancellor. Alarmed conservatives demanded the establishment of military rule. Worried this might happen, and seeing an opportunity in the deteriorating social conditions to spark a general revolt, the Communists launched strikes the following day throughout "Red Thuringia" (and neighboring Saxony), where they enjoyed the most official support.

The strikes hit Weimar particularly hard. Hungry people were stealing shoes from outside hotel doors and stripping roofs of their lead, letters of their stamps, and doors of their handles in an attempt to get their hands on anything that could be bartered for food. Butter and poultry were no longer available at any price. At the Bauhaus striking workers threatened to halt the exhibition's last-minute preparations. Only the intervention of Neubauer—after a desperate plea from Gropius—allowed the work to go on. With no trains running, people had difficulty getting to the exhibition. But at one o'clock on Wednesday afternoon, August 15, 1923—as Communist-led riots surged throughout Germany and the new Chancellor struggled to save the country's constitutional government—Gropius opened the Bauhaus's exhibition before a diminished but nonetheless glittering audience of local and international notables. There in the school's vestibule, a formal, pin-striped-attired Gropius proclaimed a new artistic unity.

Considering the circumstances it was astonishing that anyone was there at all. But from all over Europe they had come: composers Igor Stravinsky and Paul Hindemith; and J. J. P. Oud, the famed Dutch architect. From Berlin came Reichs Minister of Art Redslob; industrial leaders; and some of the city's most important architects: Peter Behrens, the brothers Bruno and Max Taut, and Ludwig Mies van der Rohe. Also Thuringia's Secretary of State; Max Greil, the Minister of Education; and senators from the State Assembly. Ordinary people came too. Fifteen thousand people in all would visit Weimar between August 15 and September 30, 1923, to see the Bauhaus exhibition, whose theme was "Art and Technology: The New Unity."

This exhibit would become one of the most famous events in the annals of twentieth-century art. Here on display were the Bauhaus's attempts to create a new and truly modern art by uniting the meaningfulness of art with the efficiency of the machine. Not even the casual visitor could overlook the exhibit's theme, for it was displayed in brilliantly designed posters everywhere—from Weimar's railway station to flags that decorated the school's exterior. Inside the Bauhaus school building, designed some ten years earlier by van de Velde, various walls were decorated with vivid red-and-black posters and abstract reliefs by artist and faculty member Joost Schmidt. Down the stairwell, in niches, and along hallways danced Oskar Schlemmer's giant marionettelike figures in delicately colored murals and sculptural reliefs.

An exhibit of Bauhaus faculty art appeared in one of Weimar's local museums. Since the faculty now included—in addition to the previously mentioned Schlemmer and Schmidt—Kandinsky, Klee, Feininger, Moholy-Nagy, Georg Muche, and Lothar Schreyer, this in itself constituted a major artistic event. But, as might be imagined from the artists involved, the unity heralded by the event's slogan was nowhere apparent. In fact, the show was marked more by an extraordinary diversity than by any outstanding stylistic similarity. Nor, with the exception of Moholy-Nagy's art, was the influence of technology discernible.

The exhibit's purported theme was also hardly evident in its main section, the student-designed Bauhaus products, such as kitchenware, textiles, cupboards, lighting fixtures, chairs, tables, radiators, rugs, coffeepots, and teapots. These were the designs Gropius hoped to sell as prototypes for mass production and also show off the school's accomplishments. Most of the objects were bulbously curved and harshly angled, more revealing of Expressionistic angst than the stark, geometric simplicities of machine technology. For every stripped-down, machine-planed product displayed, there were twice as many terra-cotta pots—perhaps even more—whose tormented forms made them ill-suited for mechanical reproduction.

This discrepancy between the exhibition's stirring slogan and what was on display did not escape the critics' attention. "Misleading" was how one critic characterized the slogan. The quality of the students' work was also faulted as "crude and not well thought-through," an appraisal which even Gropius had to admit was correct.

The only evidence of stylistic unity and industrial influence existed within the exhibition's two architectural sections: the simple, white-walled, flat-roofed building known as the Haus am Horn (designed by Muche and built near the school), in which many of the student objects were displayed; and an international architecture show that formed part of the main exhibition itself. Surprising inclusions in a school that had no architecture department, both the house and the architecture show reflected Gropius's particular interest more than the Bauhaus's accomplishments. Displayed in this architectural show-within-a-show were projects by Frank Lloyd Wright, Le Corbusier, the Dutch J. J. P. Oud, and G. T. Rietveld, along with works by such prominent German architects as Mies van der Rohe, Eric Mendelsohn, Hans Poelzig, Bruno and Max Taut, and Gropius himself. In Muche's Haus am Horn industrial influence and the overall aesthetic unity of what was clearly a new building style was evident in the simplified, clean-cut, sharp-edged planes. While the architecture (outside of Muche's house) had virtually nothing to do with the Bauhaus or with the exhibition's two main goals of making money from sales of student products and showing the school's accomplishments to Weimar's doubting taxpayers, it did create the impression that the Bauhaus was participating in a broad new cutting-edge international artistic style, an association the school would always retain.

For the most part, then, whatever stylistic unity and technological influence was revealed by the Bauhaus exhibit derived less from what the school was producing than from a building by one of its faculty members (Muche) and the designs of architects, none of whom—with the exception of Gropius—had anything at all to do with the Bauhaus. As critic Walter Passarge observed, in terms of its declared theme, the exhibition's (and the Bauhaus's) "real heart" lay in architecture, a subject that was not even officially taught at the school.

If anything, the exhibition demonstrated a schism at the heart of the Bauhaus, between its preaching of artistic unity and its practiced diversity. Indeed, Gropius prided himself on the artistic variety the Bauhaus harbored, of which its disparate artistic personalities—Itten, Moholy-Nagy, Kandinsky, Klee—spoke eloquently.

The exhibition could be no more than what the Bauhaus itself was in 1923. Neither will nor energy could overcome the confusion; the lack of money, consensus, and coordination between theory and practice; and the incessant political interference. Nor could Gropius's will and drive overcome the country's dire state. With press attention diverted by the national crisis, the exhibition received hardly any coverage. Particularly disappointing to the Bauhaus was industry's lack of interest, which was due in part to the continuing economic collapse, as well as the school's indifference to the bottom line. Although Gropius, despite intensifying faculty disapproval, continued to pursue commercial support after the exhibition, the anticipated orders never materialized to any great extent. "Sale of Bauhaus goods . . . slight," Gropius's new wife, Ise, would comment after her husband's return from the Leipzig fair.

Not surprisingly, the exhibition ended up being a financial catastrophe. An astonishing number of people had attended, but the strikes and the ballooning price of tickets and train fare kept many others away, some of whom demanded refunds. The giving away of 124 free tickets to members of the Thuringian ministries and legislature—the most important arbiters of the Bauhaus's fate—wiped out any slender hope of making money. There was not even enough left to dismantle the architectural exhibits, whose models needed to be crated, shipped, and properly insured. Gropius had to ask the Thuringian government to cover the remaining expenses of "approximately" seven billion marks, which Beyer lost no time in reminding the authorities that he had predicted the year before.

Thuringia's leftist coalition government was having its own problems. The economic collapse and accompanying wave of social unrest had pressed them and their neighboring socialist government of Saxony to try to broaden their constituency by seeking support from the increasingly discontented bourgeoisie, those stable, thrifty, middle-class Germans now impoverished and made hungry by the horrific inflation. This attempt to reach out to the bourgeoisie repelled the Communist members of their coalition, who in the beginning of September 1923 withdrew their support, thus depriving both the Saxon and Thuringian governments of their majorities. Forced to accede to the Communist demands, both governments formed new, more radical leftist governments. On September 11 a new Thuringian State Assembly was formed, with the Communist Party and Social Democratic workers holding the majority.

To Moscow this was a not-to-be-missed opportunity. With the dollar buying 142 million marks on October 1, 1923, and Germany edging toward economic disintegration, Moscow instructed the country's Communist leadership to launch a German revolution from Saxony and Thuringia, whose new Communist coalition governments offered the most hospitable setting for the Red agitators. Since they were trying to gain support from the now rioting workers, the Communists made no secret of their plans. On October 8 a Communist Party member of the Reichstag warned the national legislators of the coming revolution, and *Die Rote Fahne*, the Communist newspaper, printed appeals to the starving and angry workers. Two days later the newspaper published a letter to the editor declaring that "[t]he approaching revolution in Germany is the most important world event of our time." It was signed by Joseph Stalin.

On October 16 the Communist Party entered the Thuringian government with three ministerial appointments. Albin Tenner, the Communist representative who had delivered the party's statement supporting the Bauhaus in the State Assembly on March 16, became Minister of Economics. Neubauer was appointed Privy Councillor (*Staatsrat*). With Greil continuing as Education Minister, the Bauhaus now enjoyed a receptive Thuringian government, although Gropius, who married the twenty-six-year-old Ilse (whose name he later changed to Ise) Frank that day, was probably not too concerned at the moment about such matters. In November, with inflation at its height—more than 130 *billion* marks were needed to buy $1—the Thuringian government, nervously glancing at neighboring and increasingly rightist Bavaria, acceded to workers' demands to form armed "defensive" units.

Not all German Communists, however, were happy with the Comintern's intervention. Many of them refused to subordinate their nation's interests to Moscow's dictates and spent nearly as much time battling their line-toeing comrades as they did in attending to their agitational tasks. The united, Comintern-led Communist conspiracy that figured so prominently in the radical Right's propaganda was more an attempt to exploit people's fears than a true mirror of the situation. The German Communists were, in fact, bitterly divided and fragmented. Not all of those who formed part of the Thuringian government, agitated among the workers, or armed themselves, did so at Moscow's behest.

The rightists were similarly fragmented. Not all of them—the Bauhaus opponents, for instance—were fascists, protofascists, or racist fanatics. Many individuals, especially those who opposed Greil's school reforms, were simply afraid of any more changes in their already drastically altered lives. They opposed only certain aspects of the radical leftist government's programs. A strong rightist victory in July's election for the Parent's Council in the Thuringian city of Altenburg, for example, was due less to nationalistic sentiments than genuinely deep resentment against Greil's policies. The more fanatical rightist groups flourished in Bavaria, and it was they who began to eye the arming of leftist workers in neighboring Thuringia with increasing hostility.

On November 2, 1923, Stresemann and Ebert—anxious to preempt a rightist Bavarian strike—ordered the Reichswehr to occupy Saxony and Thuringia, an act entirely in keeping with the national Social Democratic government's antileftist sentiments. The Reichswehr, whose sympathies lay openly—especially in Bavaria—with the Right, banned the Communist Party, along with the armed workers' groups, and arrested forty workers in Weimar. On November 8, Hitler and his National Socialist Party's Beer Hall Putsch in Munich tried and failed to overthrow the Bavarian government. That same day the Reichswehr—whose presence in Weimar, the state's capital, remained especially heavy—imposed martial law in Thuringia and pressured the newly formed leftist state government to distance itself from the Communist members of its coalition. Four days later the Communists retaliated by canceling their affiliation with the Social Democrats.

Unimpeded by legal restraints, the army moved relentlessly and brutally against the Communists and those suspected of Communist activity, treating both agitators and former Communist members of the government alike. Neubauer (who would later be murdered by the Nazis) and others were arrested and criminal proceedings instituted against them. Others fled the state. One of those marked by the Reichswehr for suspected Communist activity was Gropius.

Gropius had been informed of the impending action against him. On the evening of November 22, 1923, he appeared on Feininger's doorstep to ask his friend to hold on to two small twenty-two caliber guns that he normally kept at home. At ten-thirty the following morning, six soldiers accompanied by a Reichswehr officer appeared with a search warrant at Gropius's home. The soldiers' gruff attitude, the "dramatic manner" in which they carried out their search for incriminating material—indeed, the act itself—outraged the former officer. Complaining that the search had been initiated by "unverified, malicious and irresponsible" denunciations, Gropius immediately protested to General Hasse, the military commandant of Thuringia, and General von Seeckt, the Reichswehr commanding officer in charge of the campaign. Von Seeckt was not only unmoved, but offended by what he claimed were Gropius's insults to himself personally and to the army. He replied with a libel suit against Gropius, contending that he had witnesses' testimony to prove that he and other members of the Bauhaus "were close to the Communist Party."

The false and flagrantly malicious charges outraged Gropius, who initially wanted to fight them. Second thoughts prevailed, however, after he consulted some Social Democratic Party (SPD) notables. Not only would it be futile, they argued, for him to plead his case before the rightist-biased Thuringian judicial system (now firmly controlled by the Reichswehr), but the fact remained that as inaccurate as the charges may have been, the Bauhaus would have trouble disproving them. Putting aside the revolutionary circumstances of the Bauhaus's birth and the political innuendoes of its original manifesto (especially the version published in the *Vorwärts*), they cited Gropius's and Lange's recent and highly touted overtures to the Left; their close association with Neubauer and the Communists; the party's long-standing support; the Bauhaus's strong identification with Greil's radical and controversial education-reform programs; and its well-publicized depiction of itself as "a cathedral of socialism." Compounding the difficulties of any such defense were the presence on the faculty of the Russian Kandinsky—whose high profile in the Bolshevik government would impede his efforts, as late as 1927, to gain German citizenship—and the Hungarian Moholy-Nagy, whose Communist sympathies were well known within the Bauhaus community. Gropius realized how untenable his situation had become. He apologized to von Seeckt, who accepted the Bauhaus director's assertion that he had intended no offense, and the matter was dropped.

On November 24 the new Thuringian government replaced its Communist ministers at the Reichswehr's "request." Deprived of its coalition partner and ruling majority, the Thuringian government was unable to gain acceptance of its ministry lists, a deadlock—along with the Reichswehr's campaign—that strengthened the rightist parties. The following week the rightist parties moved a vote of no confidence against the government, forcing the Social Democratic Thuringian government to resign and the State Assembly to be dissolved. The Communists, now pushed underground by the Reichswehr ban, increased their provocations in Thuringia and throughout Germany. A prominent Thuringian businessman was attacked in his home. In Berlin, Communist-led demonstrations had to be dispersed by armed force.

Responding to this growing civil disorder, the Thuringian Right—the Democratic (DDP), Nationalist (DNP), and People's (DVP) Parties—formed a Law and Order Alliance (Ordnungsbund). They campaigned on a vigorously anti-Communist theme, in which—as usual—the Bauhaus played a prominent role. "Craftsmen, businessmen, members of the retail trade!" declared an election appeal. "The goal of the socialist-communist government is to clobber us [*Niederknüppeln*]. [Their programs] deliberately attempt to destroy the hard-working middle class. . . . Think of the Bauhaus." Their campaign succeeded. In the elections of February 1924 the rightist alliance won a legislative majority and became Thuringia's new Law and Order regime (Ordnungsregierung). Like Minister Greil, who on February 24 was dismissed from office, the Bauhaus's days in Weimar were numbered.

Gropius, along with everyone at the Bauhaus, realized this. But however much he recognized the futility of the battle—he had earlier compared it to pushing against "a wall of mud"—and despite faculty opposition, Gropius continued to seek private industrial support for the Bauhaus's workshops, in the hope of keeping them out of the government's control. Morale at the school, normally poor, sank even lower. Feininger told Gropius that he wanted to leave, a decision he later reconsidered. Schlemmer, describing himself as exhausted and depressed, claimed that he no longer cared what happened to the Bauhaus.

Thanks to Beyer's accusations, the government had asked the highly regarded Treasury to scrutinize the Thunringian State Bauhaus's accounting practices. Its review appeared in August 1924. The Treasury's scathing denunciation of the Bauhaus's financial practices offered the hostile regime the legal weapon it had long been seeking. The report sealed both Gropius's attempt to gain private funding and the school's fate.

On September 18, 1924, the Thuringian Ministry of Education informed the Bauhaus that faculty contracts would not be renewed after they terminated on March 31, 1925. Unable to raise the private funds that would guarantee faculty salaries and the school's continued existence, Gropius in December 1924 announced the dissolution of the Weimar Bauhaus as of the end of March 1925.

Divided, contentious, and battered by a storm of controversy, the Bauhaus would leave Weimar as it had lived there.

11.

"Those Happier Shores"
Young Americans Meet Europe

Never, if you can help it, miss seeing the sunset and the dawn.
And never, if you can help it, see anything but dreams
between them.

—*John Ruskin*

Dollarlande," as America was called, even among wealthy Berliners, was exactly what the Berlin art dealer J. B. Neumann had been looking for in 1923. There Neumann hoped to find "a pot of gold" for the artists he represented, such as Paul Klee, Edvard Munch, and his favorite, Max Beckmann. Like many Europeans, Neumann entertained some exaggerated ideas about America, "all frontier, raw and wild," he would later recall. The mentioning of his German galleries in a 1921 report of Katherine Dreier's Société Anonyme had led Neumann to believe that his name was well known among the "people who counted in New York." But, arriving there, he learned that no one knew either him or his artists. "[Max] Beckmann was a 'nobody' and I was less," he later commented. America was not ready for the mostly Expressionistic German art that he exhibited in 1924 in his gallery, the New Art Circle Gallery on New York's 57th Street. For the most part, he found, art collectors preferred Rembrandt to Schmidt-Rottluff. By 1926 Neumann was both disappointed and financially strained.

Georg Muche, the German artist and Bauhaus faculty member, visited the United States in 1924 and also noticed a gap between American and European culture. "Forget Europe if you want to stay in America," he wrote to Gropius.

> America does not need European art and European artists. . . . For better or worse, one has to surrender to America. . . . Either become an American in America or remain a European in Europe. It is not possible to please America as a European.

But Muche, who was in America for only a few weeks, would return to Europe, not unthankfully one imagines from his comments. Neumann, anxious to escape marital problems in Germany and find his pot of gold, chose to stay. His enterprise would ultimately be rescued by Alfred H. Barr Jr., who—gangly and emaciated-looking at the age of twenty-four—hardly looked like anyone's savior. In July 1926, about to teach a college course on a modern art he had barely seen, the young Barr needed help; and no one at this time in America was better placed to introduce the young enthusiast to modern German art than Neumann, who knew virtually everyone of any cultural note in Germany. In 1927 his letters of introduction would open doors throughout Germany for the young art historian. In a sense the two men would save each other. Neumann, elated to meet an American enthusiast, gave Barr his first real acquaintance with someone who had participated in the German modern art wars; while Barr—three years later, as director of the Museum of Modern Art and a devoted purchaser—would help to rescue Neumann's financially floundering gallery. Barr was able to get German books on contemporary art that he needed for his course and from Neumann learn about Gropius and the Bauhaus.

While America had not suffered Germany's angry modernist struggles or its accompanying social and political upheavals, its own encounter with modern art—replete with words such as *subversive* and *crazy*—remained only slightly less heated. This cranky dialogue had begun in February 1913, with the opening of a contemporary-art exhibition in

New York's Armory, and continued as the show subsequently traveled to Chicago and Boston. One critic had referred to the Cubist-Futurist art on display as "unwholesome [and an art] of morbid hallucination or sterile experimentation" that denied society's values—indeed, those "of life itself"—in the name of individualism. The writer of this critique was Princeton's Professor Frank Jewett Mather, the school's "expert" on modern art and a later teacher of Alfred Barr.

Although exhibitions would gradually familiarize Americans with European modern art, the outraged, sarcastic tone that marked Mather's comments remained. In 1926 the art critic of the *Boston Herald* would describe van Gogh as "a crazy galoot . . . [whose paintings] resemble the crude, elemental 'expressions' which nit-wits affix to sidewalks, fences . . . and elsewhere—especially elsewhere." While such diatribes often provoked those few Americans who collected modern art to equally surly rebuttals, they would imbue in Barr's modernist pursuits a messianic zeal not unlike that of Gropius.

Those few Americans who dared to collect such art were exposed to similar slurs. Alfred Barnes was so offended by his fellow Philadelphians' derision of his collection of modern art when it was exhibited there in 1923 that he set up his collection in quarters that he had purchased the year before in the Philadelphia suburb of Merion, locked the door, and virtually threw away the key, making it almost impossible for anyone to go look at the art. Claribel Cone, who with her sister Etta had accumulated a major collection of modern art, was so disgusted by her native Baltimore's lack of appreciation for her art that when she died, in 1929, she instructed her sister to look elsewhere to leave the collection if the city's attitude did not improve.

The Bolshevik revolution in 1917 added a new dimension to the antimodernist tirades. What had earlier been seen as perverse, outrageous, and threatening to society was now transformed into Communist subversion perpetrated by a group of dangerous Reds. An anonymously written brochure had accused an exhibition of Impressionist and Post-Impressionist art put on by the Metropolitan Museum of Art in 1921 of being part of a worldwide conspiracy to break down "all law and order and the revolutionary destruction of our entire social system"; code words, of course, for left-wing art. "[D]egenerates . . . [making] ku klux criticism," had been New York lawyer and modern art collector John Quinn's equally outraged reply.

If modern art was ever to be accepted in America, it had to be removed from the implications of social or political reform that had played so determining a role in its development in Germany. This J. B. Neumann—"the art dealer of the revolution"—quickly learned. And except for occasional slipups, as when he would describe modern German artists in 1931 as "left-wing painters," so too did Alfred Barr.

Born on January 28, 1902, in Detroit, Michigan, to Alfred H. Barr Sr., a Presbyterian minister with strong missionary interests, and Annie Elizabeth Wilson Barr, Alfred Jr.—like Gropius—was the eldest of the family's two sons. In 1911 the family moved to Baltimore, where Dr. Barr was appointed minister of the city's First Presbyterian Church. Similar, as well, to Gropius in Berlin, Barr grew up in the establishment circles of the day, where money mattered less than breeding, bloodlines—there was a Castle Barr near Prestwick, Scotland—and certainly in Barr's case, brilliance. A tight and cozy little world where only certain clubs, professions, religions, and schools would do, Barr's society was as prescribed in its own way as Gropius's. Both men assumed the privileges of their class as they sought to break down its prejudices.

Just as Gropius was expected to perform his military service with an elite unit, so too was Barr expected to join the ministry or make his name in law, banking, or academia after completing his education at Harvard, Princeton, or Yale. Barr's was a coddled and secure world of teas and long, lazy luncheon parties; debutante balls; country summers; and lush university campuses whose ivied gardens—in Barr's case, Princeton's—were imported from Europe, which still served, as it had traditionally done in America, as a distant but powerful fount of culture. Barr's social milieu was as close to an aristocracy as America would ever produce, and like most aristocracies it detested threats to the status quo.

While this close-knit, almost incestuous world more often than not led to dilettantism, supercilious smugness, and a boozy brain, it also—as Sir Isaiah Berlin has noted—produced Edith Wharton, F. Scott Fitzgerald, and Franklin Roosevelt; gave to America—in Princeton's Allen Marquand and Paul J. Sachs of Harvard—some of its most influential scholars; and granted to talented men like Barr and his friends Henry-Russell Hitchcock and Philip Johnson the freedom and grace to pursue the new, the radical, and the untried. But unlike Gropius's Germany, Barr's world had remained relatively intact, without the violent rupture that the

Bauhaus leader's generation had suffered in 1914, with all its profound emotional, social, political, and artistic ramifications.

In addition to their social backgrounds, Gropius and Barr shared a similar assumption that an underlying unity lay behind reality's dizzying diversity. While Gropius's belief stemmed from the German idealistic tradition, Barr's originated less from this—although it was certainly reflected in his Ivy League education—than from a compulsion to categorize and find connections between things that would later culminate in his rigorous mapping of modernism, in which the Bauhaus would form an integral part. This categorizing trait revealed itself early in Barr's childhood, when he collected stamps, botanical specimens, and—as his high school paper noted—"many other oddities"; sighted birds, keeping track of the dates and locations; classified butterflies and prehistoric animals; and learned the names of all the kings and queens of England along with their major achievements. Few things escaped Barr's intellectualizing and charting bent. Each Saturday at the age of ten, Barr would write a poem of precisely "five verses [and] four lines." War, too, fell under his rationalizing instincts. He remained fascinated throughout his life by military history, war's intellectualized distillation. At Princeton he planned to major in paleontology, a scientific discipline based on categorization.

Barr's intellectualizing bent was balanced by his aesthetic sensitivity; he almost painfully "felt" art. "How can you be pessimistic if you open the shutter of your soul to beauty," the twenty-year-old Barr asked a friend, asserting that such a notion was "not theory or preaching . . . [but] pragmatic—a form of religion." In 1926 Barr would describe his reaction to a Corot painting as "hurt[ing] . . . [making] my throat feel queer and my eyes smart." Yet as deeply felt as it was, the aesthetic experience never entirely satisfied Barr, who exhibited a visceral need to explain.

Graduated at sixteen as class valedictorian from Boy's Latin School, Baltimore's most prestigious private school, Barr went off to Princeton in September 1918 with his childhood friend Edward King. There he encountered the classical education of the elite American Ivy League schools, a deracinated, "timeless and placeless" scholarly world that recognized no native culture, no social or political roots, nor conveyed any sense that a culture grew out of some sort of situational context. It was from such a purely intellectualized perspective—devoid of social and political considerations—that Barr would come to perceive European modernism and, within it, the Bauhaus.

Serene and isolated in suburban New Jersey, Princeton's idyllic campus exemplified this rarefied aestheticism. Its buildings—a historically dizzying pastiche of Tudor England, Renaissance Tuscany, Fontainebleau, Venice, and High Gothic England—reflected little about its local community. Known as Collegiate Gothic, the High English Gothic style was especially popular at the Ivy League schools for its reminiscence of England's Oxford and Cambridge. At Princeton actual building fragments from those hallowed institutions were embedded within some of its building's walls. Pretentious and picturesque, Princeton went to often ludicrous extremes to maintain its image. Barr later commented about how "one carefully cracked pane" in each casement window of his imitative Gothic dormitory was supposed to suggest antiquity.

Like the Collegiate Gothic campus, what students studied—in Barr's case, ancient and medieval art, Italian painting, Shakespeare, Greek, Latin, and philosophy among other subjects—similarly ignored local context. Barr's colleague and later collaborator Henry-Russell Hitchcock, who received a similar education at Harvard, subsequently complained how little, if anything, "many Americans of that . . . period [including himself] . . . knew of the American cultural achievements of the nineteenth century." Since many of their professors—especially in the Ivy League's art history departments—often came from privileged backgrounds, the system perpetuated itself. The founder and head for forty years of Princeton's art history department was Allan Marquand, the son of a wealthy New York banker, who had been one of the founders of New York's Metropolitan Museum of Art. Marquand's family had endowed his chair at Princeton, and Marquand himself funded much of the department's expenses out of his own pocket. Although he retired as head in 1920, during Barr's sophomore year, Marquand continued his affiliation with the department. Barr took several courses with him and wrote various papers under his supervision, including his master's thesis. When he returned to Princeton as a teaching assistant in 1925, Barr again worked with Marquand.

A similar situation existed at Harvard, where Barr pursued his graduate studies. Harvard's counterpart of Marquand was Paul J. Sachs, the son of Samuel and Louisa Goldman Sachs of Goldman, Sachs Company, the New York banking house. After graduating from Harvard in 1900, Sachs became a partner in the family bank and worked there until 1916, when he accepted a position as lecturer in art at Wellesley College. In 1923 he joined the Harvard faculty, becoming associate director of Harvard's Fogg Museum, whose collection—like Marquand at Princeton—he personally enriched. In 1924 Barr took two of Sachs's old master drawing courses, and during the fall semester of 1926–27 he sporadically attended Sachs's famed museum course. If the tenets of Gropius's Bauhaus emerged out of the trenches of war, Barr's interpretation of them developed within a milieu of elegant lunches at Sachs's home in Cambridge, one of the city's eighteenth-century showplaces, where, as a classmate of Barr's recalled, discussions would be held *after* lunch, "in the best Harvard tradition."

While not every member of Princeton and Harvard's art history departments was a financial scion, their world—like that of the students they taught—was small, tight, and rarefied. When Barr was unable to obtain a grant to study contemporary art abroad in 1927, Sachs personally arranged for funds to be made available to him. Two years later, as one of the Museum of Modern Art's founding board members, Sachs would offer twenty-seven-year-old Barr as a candidate for the museum's directorship.

Thus, similar to Gropius's classical education (against which he and his Bauhaus sought to rebel), Barr's intellect formed far from the harsh realities of the street. Custom and his relatively limited social milieu rendered him essentially disinterested in the social context out of which Europe's much-admired cultural achievements emerged. Unlike Barr, Gropius—in line with the long-standing concerns of the European avant-garde—had early discerned this to be a deficiency; his awareness of the gulf that existed between art and everyday reality had been amplified by his experiences with war and revolution. While Gropius and his peers viewed art as an instrument of social change, Barr and his American colleagues saw it much as a panorama of aesthetically pure, socially irrelevant jigsaw parts, of which only a key was needed to fit them together into what was assumed to be an entirely comprehensible entity. For Barr this key was provided in his junior year at Princeton by Professor Charles Rufus Morey, Marquand Professor of Art and Archaeology and a specialist in medieval art.

Morey, whose books on the subject remain seminal works to this day, did not teach medieval art in the traditional American way of focusing on the most important works of a particular style or period. Morey saw *all* manifestations of medieval art—from the tiniest ivory to the most monumental church—as reflecting a singular civilization that was defined by the Christian faith. It was an all-embracing approach both in terms of what it examined—popular folk art as well as traditional masterworks—and where it looked, beyond traditional Europe to the entire Mediterranean area and Asia. Morey saw medieval art much as a transparent, spiritual vessel, something to be looked *through* in order to see the important truth that lay behind it, from which its significance derived. This truth, for medieval art, was its Christian spirit, whose "communion with the infinite . . . the initial and essential content of medieval art," as Morey wrote, "the modern soul still seeks to recover."

"Communion with the infinite" was the Barr family's trade. Not only was his father a Presbyterian minister, so were both his grandfathers and his mother's brother; and it could not have been easy for the young prodigy to have turned away from this family tradition. While paleontology had initially satisfied his categorizing urges, Morey's interpretation of art as "a form of religion," as Barr commented, fulfilled his sense of beauty and the "great beyond." Morey's comprehensive view provided him with a way to reconcile his aesthetic, sanctimonious and categorizing instincts, and toward the end of the spring semester of 1920—while taking Morey's course—Barr changed his major from paleontology to art history.

Like Gropius, Barr would become an impassioned proselytizer of modernism. But Barr's messianism would not stem from any desire to change the world—like Gropius's—but from his desire to enlighten his fellow art historians and subsequently the American public, a view essentially aesthetic at heart. Aside from Morey's course, Barr was sharply critical of the way Princeton's art history department depicted art as a series of more or less stylistically connected—but otherwise isolated—aesthetic objects, an approach the school shared with American colleges of its day. The art history department's neglect—indeed, its scorn—of contemporary art, which Princeton again shared with its fellow American institutions, also bothered Barr. Mather, for example, who taught Princeton's course on modern painting, made no effort to hide his disparaging views. According to Barr, who took the course in 1921, Mather began his survey as far back as he could—with the seventeenth-century art of Rubens—and ended it peremptorily in 1900 "with a few superficial and often hostile remarks about van Gogh and Matisse." At Vassar College, where he taught the history of art from 1923 to 1924, Barr encountered a similar attitude.

It had been his professors' unabashed "ignorance . . . [and] contempt" for modern art that initially piqued Barr's interest in the subject. "Old gray beard laughed," commented Barr about Morey's reaction to a talk that the young art historian had given on modern art. Curious to find out more about this much-scoffed-at art, Barr turned to articles that appeared in such contemporary journals as *The Dial* and *Vanity Fair* with their fuzzy black-and-white photographs. Except for a visit that he made with Mather to the Metropolitan Museum exhibition of Impressionist and Post-Impressionist art in 1921, Barr did not see much original modern art and had little opportunity to compare what he read with what he saw. But this hardly seemed to matter to this blazingly intelligent and confident young man, who once described Isadora Duncan as "America's greatest living artist," without—as he freely admitted—ever having seen her dance. Barr's experience of modern art for most of the early 1920s would be similar, his opinions derived from contemporary avant-garde publications. Understandably, such views would often be considerably off the mark. From German avant-garde journals, for example, he learned "something of the culture of the Weimar Republic . . . and their hospitality toward modern art," a comment about which one can only surmise Gropius's reaction.

Toward the end of his senior year at Princeton Barr decided to specialize in contemporary art and, similar to what Morey had done with medieval art, attempt to unify its diverse manifestations by discovering its singular spirit. That he had not yet seen much of the vast panorama of contemporary art that he was going to "de-code" did not dissuade him. Modern art, he decided, was essentially monovalent, its singular spirit—as with Morey's medieval art—expressing itself in every artifact of modern civilization, from its masterworks to its comic strips. National and stylistic differences would be explained as local variants of this singular spirit, and the art in which this generic, transcendental idea could not be detected or comfortably fit would be ignored.

Given the situation of the day, Barr's art education necessarily assumed a dual course: academic studies oriented almost wholly toward traditional art history, and modern art pursued on his own. By the spring of 1922—the year he graduated Princeton and began graduate studies there—he was familiar with a variety of avant-garde art magazines. Between 1923 and 1924, when he taught art history at Vassar College, Barr's acquaintance with actual modern art broadened. Katherine Dreier's Société Anonyme presented an exhibition of Kandinsky paintings at Vassar in November 1923. In April the following year Barr himself mounted an exhibition there of sixty-one works of modern European art. The exhibit brought him in touch with several New York galleries from which he borrowed art, including J. B. Neumann's newly opened New Art Circle.

In the summer of 1924, having saved much of his Vassar earnings, Barr set off for his first trip to Europe with his boyhood friend Edward King. Despite his deepening commitment to modern art, he did not travel to any of its centers, such as Holland, Berlin, or Weimar, or to the France of Picasso and Le Corbusier, of whose epochal book on modern architecture, *Vers une architecture*, published in 1923, he as yet knew nothing. Nor does his correspondence suggest any particular search for the European avant-garde. Instead, guided by Professor Mather's suggestions and a twenty-one-year-old Baedeker guidebook, Barr and King embarked on a traditional grand tour, traveling from Paestum to Pompeii and up the Italian peninsula to Paris and Chartres. What Barr experienced was not the contemporary Europe of Matisse and Mussolini but the aestheticized world of Morey and Mather, the visual equivalent of those culturally displaced old world fragments that Princeton had so reverentially embedded in its ivied walls.

Barr returned to Harvard to continue his graduate education, but, lacking money, he could stay there only one year. In the fall of 1925 Barr returned to teach at Princeton, where in early 1926 he received an appointment to teach art history (including a course on modern art) later that year at Wellesley College. While his exposure to contemporary art had broadened considerably by now—he had become acquainted with Corbusier's writings and visited the Barnes Foundation and various New York art galleries—Barr still remained essentially unacquainted with the continent's spirit, whose artistic outline he was now formulating. This, however, did not seem to constrain him in planning the scope of his course, which he described as "contemporary painting in relation to the past, to other arts, to aesthetic theory, and to modern civilization." Barely four years after he had begun, and without direct experience of its European centers or participants, Barr had essentially completed his mapping out of twentieth-century art.

What seemed to disturb Barr more than his lack of firsthand visual experience with the art he was about to teach was his lack of slides and good color reproductions. The only reproductions he had were the blurred journal photographs; it was in the hope of securing slides and color photographs, as well as some German art books for his students to read, that he contacted Neumann in July. Although he would prove himself to be an indispensable fount of information about German modernism for the young American art historian, Neumann in the final analysis only filled in the colors of a European modernism whose outline Barr had already drawn.

Although Barr's monumental schema of modern art would not appear until some years later, he had already formulated his basic concept of European modernism as a thrust toward the abstract. In an astonishing diagram that would appear in conjunction with the Museum of Modern Art's Cubist art exhibition in 1936, the vast range of European modernism would be depicted as a maze of arrows and boxes connecting various *isms*, in which the Bauhaus (located on the diagram's lower right side) would be shown as an offshoot of Constructivism, Suprematism, and the Machine Aesthetic, not unlike a chemical chart's depiction of how water is formed out of hydrogen and oxygen. From the Bauhaus a segmented arrow leads to Modern Architecture.

Barr's Wellesley course was based on these reductivist principles. In line with Morey's perception of an aesthetic laser beam that illuminated all currents of medieval civilization, Barr's course encompassed not only the masterworks traditionally included in such courses—the forerunners of modern art, such as Cézanne, Seurat, van Gogh, and Gauguin, and the style's contemporary manifestations, such as Cubism and Futurism—but also architecture, theater, modern music, and common everyday objects, such as cereal bowls, refrigerators, filing cabinets, cartoons, advertising, movies, and comics. Visits to the five-and-dime stores to find well-designed objects were as important as trips to museums.

It was in this sweeping aesthetic context that the Bauhaus first appeared in Barr's writings. In order to find out what his entering students knew about modern art, Barr in the fall of 1926 devised an entrance examination, one of whose questions asked, "What Is the Bauhaus?" The answer, in the later published version of the questionnaire, declared the Bauhaus to be a "publicly supported institution for the study and creation of modern architecture, painting, ballet, cinema, decoration and industrial arts." According to Barr, the Bauhaus was an institution dedicated to exploring what he had defined as modernism's two main abstract strands: the machine-inspired geometrical (exemplified by Moholy-Nagy) and the nongeometrical, personified by Kandinsky. This view—which made the Bauhaus the apotheosis of Barr's aestheticized perception of modernism—reflected Gropius's highly publicized claims of artistic unity, which in fact bore little resemblance to the real institution.

Believing that modern architecture similarly partook in this singular reductivist spirit, Barr asked his friend Henry-Russell Hitchcock, a young Harvard graduate student in architectural history whom he had met in Sachs's museum course, to lecture his students on the subject. As Neumann had done in art, Hitchcock filled in the considerable gaps that existed in Barr's knowledge of contemporary European architecture and influenced his views of Gropius and the Bauhaus.

A year younger than Barr, Hitchcock had entered Harvard College planning to study architecture. Circumstances, however, tripped him up, and his architectural ambitions went the way of Barr's pursuit of paleontology. He became instead an architectural historian. Like Barr, he was influenced by one of America's greatest medieval scholars, Professor Kingsley Porter, who—like Princeton's Morey—imparted a breathtaking immediacy to medieval culture. That contrasted strikingly with the grim and irrelevant architectural studies that Hitchcock took during his senior year between 1923 and 1924 at the Harvard School of Architecture. Like Gropius, Hitchcock believed that he had learned nothing useful at architecture school, including nothing about modern architecture.

Whatever interest he may have had at this time in modern architecture remained secondary to his main studies. Although he visited Europe twice in the early twenties—a biking tour in 1922 and a year abroad on a fellowship between 1924 and 1925—Hitchcock paid little attention to modern architecture; he did not see Le Corbusier's L'Esprit Nouveau pavilion at the International Exhibition of Decorative Arts in Paris in 1925.

In need of funds when he returned to Cambridge that fall, Hitchcock left the Architecture School and turned instead to studying architectural history with Kingsley Porter at the Graduate School, where he was able to earn some money as a part-time tutor in the fine arts department. Only around late 1926, when he read Le Corbusier's *Vers une architecture*, did Hitchcock begin to turn his attention "almost exclusively" to modern European architecture. It was thus with only a few month's serious immersion in the subject that Hitchcock lectured Barr's Wellesley students on modern architecture at the end of the spring term of 1927.

Like Barr and Gropius, Hitchcock also viewed modernism in salvationist terms. While Gropius wished to save society and Barr modern art, Hitchcock wanted to save American architecture from its propensity to cloak its modern buildings in historical styles, as in New York's Woolworth Building and Ritz Tower. In an article that appeared in

September 1927, titled "The Decline of Architecture," Hitchcock suggested that a building's design should reflect its practical demands. Rather than quoting misleading historical references, he espoused a reductive, structuralistic view that elevated the simple factory above the ornamented church—similar to Gropius—"and the average bathroom . . . [above] its accompanying boudoir." Hitchcock, however, like Gropius, recognized the limitations of a purely engineering solution; the simple factory shed was not enough. "We must accept all of technics," he wrote, "but we need not accept that technics are all."

By 1928 Hitchcock moderated his insistence on pure function to include the essentially rationalistic and French architectural qualities of order, proportion, and massing associated with the École des Beaux Arts in Paris, on which most of the local European architectural academies had based themselves. In this, Hitchcock reflected the influence of Le Corbusier, whom he also emphasized in his lecture to Barr's Wellesley class.

In *Vers une architecture* Corbusier declared that the century's greatest architectural triumphs were not its architecture but its engineering products, such as the factory, the American silo, the automobile, and the airplane. A house, wrote Corbusier in a much-quoted axiom, "is a machine for living in." Reflecting the French tradition, Corbusier also acknowledged the importance of formal harmonies, writing that "[a]rchitecture [is] the masterly, correct and magnificent play of masses brought together in light." Hitchcock, heeding Corbusier's advice to listen to American engineers rather than American architects, took Barr's Wellesley students on field trips to several of Boston's railroad stations and factories. By 1927, thanks in great part to the influence of Hitchcock/Corbusier, Barr—whose first article on architecture now appeared—was, as he put it, "beginning to learn something about recent architecture." It was through such Corbusian "eyes" and theory that he would come to interpret and criticize the entire range of modern architecture, of which Gropius's Bauhaus would be a major exemplar.

But there was another side to Corbusier's architectural theories—the social context—that both Hitchcock and Barr, and subsequently most American architects, ignored. Referring in his book to society's being "profoundly *out of gear*," Corbusier laid the blame for the day's "unrest" on architecture, "specifically its insensitivity to people's needs." "Architecture or Revolution," the European Corbusier had written.

Primed by their culture and education toward a socially disembodied aesthetic view, Hitchcock and Barr ignored Corbusier's reference to revolution, out of whose admiration or fear so much of Europe's modern artistic spirit—including the Bauhaus—had largely developed. For Barr and Hitchcock, art and culture were respites from the noise of distant, dirty, and often violent streets, not their reflection. While both Barr and Hitchcock would modify their view of modernism many times over, it would never lose its aesthetic focus and power—as Kingsley Porter had written of the Gothic cathedral:

> to lift the mind entirely from the cares and thoughts of the world, *de materialibus ad immaterialia transferendo* . . . to call forth within the soul a more than mortal joy, until for the moment the material world is forgotten, and the mind is carried captive to that strange shore of the universe which is more of the mould of Heaven than of Earth.

Within a startlingly short time after being introduced to modernism, Hitchcock and Barr believed they had identified the style's aesthetic core. Based on unerring eyes and a command of language that was as bold as it was meticulous, their assertions appeared startlingly obvious and convincing to Americans who remained essentially ignorant of contemporary European culture. At the center of this aesthetically reductivist style—where, according to Barr, "the various abstract currents alive in Germany after the War, together with influences from Holland and Russia, were united"—was the Bauhaus.

In 1927, thanks to the largess of Paul Sachs, who arranged a stipend for a year of travel and study, Barr was able to make his second trip to Europe. Joined by his Harvard roommate Jere Abbott, the two young men set off to explore what their friend Hitchcock referred to as "those happier shores" of the European avant-garde, carrying letters of introduction from Sachs, Dreier, and Neumann. On December 4, nearly a year and a half after Barr had formulated his views about the Bauhaus, he and Abbott arrived for their first visit to the school. However, it was not to Weimar that they went, but to the town of Dessau, the new home of the Bauhaus, where one year earlier—to the day—the school had triumphantly opened the doors of its new glass building to world acclaim. But now, once more the focus of a bitter election, the Bauhaus was again breaking down.

Bauhaus students playing soccer; Bauhaus building, Dessau, in background (Photo T. Lux Feininger. Courtesy Harvard University Art Museums.)

Walter Gropius as a
cadet in the Fifteenth
Hussar Regiment,
Wandsbeck, 1904.

Poster by Max Pechstein, 1918. The legend reads "The National Assembly; cornerstone of the German Socialist Republic," the latter being the official designation for the Weimar Republic (Courtesy Archiv für Kunst und Geschichte, Berlins.)

**Soldiers on the ruins
of the Palace, Berlin,
December 24, 1918
(Courtesy Bundesarchiv).**

**People standing on the ruins
of their home destroyed in street
fighting, Berlin, March 1919
(Courtesy Bundesarchiv).**

Johannes Itten, 1921 (Courtesy
Bauhaus-Archiv, Berlin).

**Walter Gropius, Director of
the Bauhaus, 1920 (© Foto
Atelier Louis Held, Inhaber
Eberhard Renno, Weimar).**

Theo van Doesburg, Weimar, 1922 (Courtesy Stedelijk Van Abbemuseum, Eindhoven, The Netherlands).

Oskar Schlemmer, 1925 (Courtesy Photo Archiv C. Raman Schlemmer, Oggebbio, Italy).

The dedication of Walter Gropius's Monument to Those Who Fell in March, Weimar, May 1, 1922 (Courtesy Stadtarchiv Weimar).

Student-designed pottery for Sale, Bauhaus exhibition, Weimar, 1923 (Courtesy Hochschule für Architektur und Bauwesen Weimar).

The Reichswehr occupying Weimar, November 1923 (© Foto Atelier Louis Held, Inhaber Eberhard Renno, Weimar).

Fritz Hesse, mayor of
Dessau, 1925 (Courtesy
Stadtarchiv Dessau).

The opening of the Bauhaus,
Dessau, December 1926
(Courtesy Harvard
University Art Museums.)

Hannes Meyer, during the 1920s (Courtesy Bauhaus-Archiv, Berlin).

Members of the Bauhaus at a party in Georg and El Muche's home, Dessau, July 2, 1927 (Courtesy Bauhaus-Archiv, Berlin).

Ludwig Mies van der Rohe (Courtesy Bauhaus-Archiv, Berlin).

Birthday party for Walter
Gropius in the Bauhaus canteen,
1924 (Courtesy Hochschule für
Architektur und Bauwesen Weimar).

Bauhaus students urging Dessau's workers to attend the KPD election rally on August 10, 1930 (Courtesy Hochschule für Architektur und Bauwesen Weimar).

Bauhaus students participating in KPD demonstration, Dessau, 1930 (Courtesy Hochschule für Architektur und Bauwesen Weimar).

The Bauhaus school building taken over by the Nazis, Dessau, circa 1936 (Courtesy Stadtarchiv Dessau).

12. | "Dessau Impossible"

Oh, Weimar! Sweet nest, with what have they exchanged you?

—Oskar Schlemmer

Dessau was not the type of city one would naturally associate with the Bauhaus. Until the school arrived there in 1925, most Dessauers had never heard of it. An industrial city of approximately fifty thousand inhabitants lying between Magdeburg and Leipzig about one hundred miles southwest of Berlin, the town's main appeal lay in its bucolic setting between the Muldau and Elbe Rivers and its two-hour proximity by train to Berlin. Apart from its highly regarded musical and theatrical traditions, Dessau was considered one of Germany's less important cities. Kandinsky's first impression of the city was "not so hot," an opinion that almost everyone else at the Bauhaus would come to share. Klee never got used to living there. Feininger thought that even Weimar looked good by comparison. Anticipating affil-iation with a larger, more sophisticated metropolis, such as Frankfurt or

Munich, Gropius—away from Weimar when he learned of the city's offer—cabled "Dessau impossible."

Like Weimar, Dessau had once been a princely seat, the capital of Anhalt, Germany's smallest state. The city's decline had begun in the beginning of the nineteenth century; by mid-century it was marked by ruined houses and streets. While Dessau had never enjoyed the weight of Weimar's Goethean past, it did have a notable liberal tradition, of which its citizens remained proud and which continued under Mayor Fritz Hesse's leadership. Until recently this legacy was symbolized by two buildings, the enormous brick Ducal Palace and the Friedrich Theater, which it directly faced across Kavalierstrasse, the city's main street. The theater embodied an especially vital heritage. Its acclaimed performances made Dessau a nationally recognized musical and theatrical center, in spite of its decline. The city's musical director, Franz von Hoesslin—who had come to Dessau in 1923, following the departure of the renowned Hans Knappertsbusch—had introduced the music of Hindemith, Bartók, Schoenberg, and Kurt Weill, its native-born son of a local cantor, to the Dessau community.

On January 25, 1922, a flash fire reduced the theater and the city's pride to a heap of smoldering ashes. In an article that appeared in a local newspaper the next day, Mayor Hesse expressed the city's grief. "Our pride and joy . . . now lies in ruins," he wrote. Declaring that Dessau without its theater was unimaginable, Hesse vowed to quickly remedy the situation. For a variety of reasons, however—mostly a lack of money—the theater was not rebuilt. Dessau's depressing confrontation with its past was aggravated by the palace across the street. The city's largest building, it had stood unused and empty since the forced resignation in November 1918 of Prince Aribert, its last ducal occupant. Argument over what to do with the abandoned hulk—too big and too costly to be turned into a museum—divided the town. In 1925, when Mayor Hesse invited the Bauhaus to come to Dessau, the city's theater remained a ruin and the Ducal Palace had only recently been torn down to create a city park. It was in an effort to restore Dessau's lost cultural sheen that Hesse had courted the Bauhaus. Most of the city's inhabitants, however, saw it as an attempt to replace their treasured past.

The idea of bringing the Bauhaus to Dessau had first come to Hesse in late December 1924, when he read in a Berlin newspaper about the school's leaving Weimar. Not only did the school's much-publicized advocacy of an alliance between art and commerce seem to particularly suit Dessau's growing industries, but Hesse thought the school might attract similar artistic enterprises to Dessau and transform the city into a world-class cultural center. These were fleeting thoughts, however, and Hesse at first did nothing. Only after Fritz von Hoesslin, who had read the same article, called him the next day to suggest what Hesse himself had thought did the mayor move.

The morning after Hoesslin's call, Hesse telephoned Ludwig Grote, Dessau's thirty-two-year-old Art Curator, to ask his opinion. Grote, who was responsible for the town's artistic matters, was intrigued by the prospect of boosting the town's artistic reputation and hopefully its art collection, as well as getting to know some of the famed Bauhaus artists. The young curator jumped at the idea, volunteering to go to Weimar to look things over and explore the school's feelings about coming to Dessau. His visit to Weimar in early February 1925 strengthened his opinion of the Bauhaus's cultural significance, a view he conveyed to Hesse. "The Bauhaus's importance to Dessau can hardly be estimated," he enthused. With his convictions confirmed by Grote's observations, Hesse—taking the art historian with him—now visited Weimar himself.

Forty-four-year-old Dessau-born Fritz Hesse was one of the most successful politicians in the city's history, as politically as he was culturally astute. In 1908 Hesse had been one of the founders of the short-lived Democratic Coalition (Demokratischen Vereinigung) in Berlin, and subsequently in Dessau. A leader of Dessau's liberal German Democratic Party (the DDP) since its founding in December 1918, he had been elected the city's mayor for a twelve-year term in February of that year. His formation of a successful coalition government with the German Social Democratic Party (the SPD) and single representative of the German Communist Party (the KPD) had given Dessau a liberal, socialistic reputation throughout the country.

As successful as he was, Hesse had many political enemies, including the powerful rightist opposition—a coalition of the German People's Party (the DVP), the German National People's Party (the DNVP), and the House and Property Owners Association. He knew what hard calculations and maneuvering lay ahead if he were to realize the costly dream of bringing the Bauhaus to Dessau. Until he could assure himself of enough votes to contain the opposition's inevitable objections, he could not commit himself further to the Bauhaus. Only when Dessau's two building administrators approved his plan did he feel confident enough to make an offer.

And a generous offer it was: an annual budget of one hundred thousand marks (thanks to rigid economic controls, Germany's inflation had ended by 1924 and its currency had stabilized); abundant workshop space; assurances of a prominent Bauhaus voice in the city's cultural affairs; and housing (including their own studios) built for the masters according to their own plans. Most important, the school would be taken over by the city of Dessau and administered by its City Council (rather than by the state, as in Weimar), whose sympathetic support Hesse's majority coalition assured. To the Bauhaus faculty—dazzled simply by the prospect of being able to work in peace—Hesse's offer seemed almost too good to be true.

Committed now to bringing the Bauhaus to Dessau and confident of his ability to control the City Council, Hesse agreed to every request the faculty made. Feininger, who disliked teaching and preferred to act as a mentor to his devoted group of students, was particularly touched by the mayor's willingness to support him in this role; Thuringia had never accepted the idea of nonteaching faculty at a publicly supported school. The lure of being able to freely pursue their art; Hesse's enthusiasm; and the city's proximity to Berlin convinced the faculty that Dessau was more suitable than other, more cosmopolitan cities the Bauhaus had been considering. "They want us and need us," exulted Feininger, his feelings shared by most of the Bauhaus faculty. "[T]hey plead with us. . . . We have an open checkbook there [*ein voller Kredit dort*] and [none of Weimar's] . . . musty tradition."

Pressured by the termination of the Bauhaus's contract with Thuringia on March 31 and the need to have a new contract begin on April 1 if the faculty and subsidized students were not to scatter to the winds, the negotiations with Hesse moved at a frantic pace. Some Bauhäuslers had already made other arrangements. Most of the workshop faculty had chosen to remain in Weimar at the Bauhaus's replacement academy—renamed the State College for Crafts and Architecture—which was to reopen in the Bauhaus's vacated quarters under the leadership of the architect and former Work Council for Art (AfK) member Otto Bartning. Some of the long-disgruntled faculty had used the school's closing in Weimar as an opportunity to leave the Bauhaus. Gerhard Marcks, who had never masked his opposition to the school's new industrial orientation, was going to Halle, and not too unhappily it appeared. "Thank God, [the Bauhaus is] behind me," he declared to Feininger. Klee, Schlemmer,

Kandinsky, and Feininger were all thinking of doing the same. Feininger was being wooed by Weimar's College of Fine Arts; Schlemmer by Bartning's school; and Klee was negotiating with Frankfurt. But Hesse's offer put those who had not committed themselves into a euphoric mood and made the others reconsider. Moholy-Nagy was so excited that he wanted to accept the offer right away.

If Hesse was looking for culture and the artists for peace, what Gropius wanted no one knew. On February 2, 1925, the Bauhaus leader left for a month's vacation. He was not there when Grote visited or later when Hesse came. Nor was he around during most of the negotiations, which were handled on the faculty's behalf by Kandinsky and Muche. Only when the negotiations were effectively completed, at the end of February, did Gropius return to Weimar. His frantic (and futile) struggles to save the Bauhaus by partially privatizing the workshops had exhausted him, and urged by the faculty, he had taken a month's rest. Although telegrams kept him informed of the goings-on, Gropius had occasionally been inaccessible. "[G]ood Gropi isn't here, and is nowhere to be reached!" wrote Feininger on February 18, as the faculty found itself having to decide about Dessau on its own. On February 19 Kandinsky and Muche went to Dessau to look over the situation there. The following day, unable to get in touch with Gropius, the faculty, ecstatic over Dessau's offer, wired *their* acceptance of the proposal and prepared to move, with or without their leader.

That they would even consider this revealed how disenchanted with Gropius's leadership they had become by 1925. Many, including Schlemmer and Feininger, blamed Gropius to a large extent for the Bauhaus's embattled state in Weimar. Gropius's single-minded pursuit of a machine-based art (not to mention his pursuit of industrial contracts) over the faculty's strenuous objections continued to polarize the school and intensify the artists' disgruntlement, a situation that no one expected the move to Dessau to change. If anything, Schlemmer expected the school's new direction to become more pronounced there. This general disillusionment with Gropius's leadership was not just an issue of artistic differences. Any art school worth its salt has that. It was due rather to his undisguised advocacy of one line (the industrial/technological) over any other, and his indifference to the threat that this approach represented to the artist members of the faculty. "[W]hy bedeck this mechanization with the name of art, as the all-powerful brand of art of our times and even more of the future," lamented Feininger to his wife. "Is that the atmosphere in which painters like Klee and a few of us can flourish? Klee was entirely depressed yesterday."

Yet, in spite of their exasperation with Gropius, most of the artists stayed at the Bauhaus, a tribute to both their strong communal spirit and personal devotion to him. For despite their complaints, they respected Gropius's idealism, enthusiasm, and tenacity and, like so many others, felt drawn to his warm, magnetic personality.

Given the artists' and Gropius's divergent points of views, their objectives for the school understandably differed. When Gropius returned at the end of February, he added new issues to those that the artists had already resolved during the nearly concluded negotiations. Gropius remained as deeply committed to the Bauhaus's attempt to meld industrial principles to those of art as he had earlier been to its Expressionistic phase, and his experience with Weimar had left him determined to avoid being totally dependent on the public purse. He thus insisted that a part of the school be allowed to operate as a profit-making enterprise and have access to local industries. Even though Hesse agreed to these demands, Gropius still could not bring himself to accept Dessau's offer. His reluctance and the mayor's by now total commitment to bringing the Bauhaus to Dessau at nearly any cost—"They seriously want to have us immediately," Feininger commented—gave the Bauhaus a decided tactical advantage, for Hesse wanted the school more than Gropius wanted him.

What finally pushed Gropius to accept Dessau's offer was Hesse's promise of architectural commissions, something that had played no role in Hesse's original interest in the school, or in his initial offer, made before he had even met the architect. Neither had it been relevant for the faculty with whom the city had negotiated. For Gropius, who had originally wanted but never received this guarantee from Thuringia, having the opportunity to build remained as fundamental as the need for the school to earn money. His wife, Ise, whose diaries faithfully mirrored Gropius's views, referred to Dessau's building promises as the city's "main attraction," a point she reemphasized in a subsequent letter to Gropius's mother. "[T]he Bauhaus will build itself," she wrote. "That of course has a certain appeal and reconciles us somewhat to its being a small city. Overall, the industry there is very potent . . . and a lot will be built in the future, so we will get quite a lot to do."

Not only did Hesse promise Gropius that he would be allowed to build the new masters' quarters, but—after determining the inadequacy of the current available space to house the proposed merger of the Bauhaus with Dessau's Vocational School—an entirely new school building as well. He also guaranteed Gropius an inside track on future city building projects, of which workers' housing comprised one of the city's and Gropius's priorities.

Despite the criticism that his intermingling of his private architectural practice with the publicly subsidized school had provoked in Weimar, Gropius, to the faculty's astonishment, moved to repeat this in Dessau. "Where will the Bauhaus architecture school be? Again only a private office," commented Schlemmer. But Dessau, perennially plagued like most German cities by a shortage of low-cost housing, thought the use of Gropius's architectural office was fine, especially given his well-known interest in mass production (known as rational or serial building) as a way of lowering construction costs. The city, in fact, underscored this point. "In Gropius, a leading architect of industrialized building techniques, is coming to Dessau," hailed Grote in an article that appeared in a local newspaper on March 10, noting that "workers' housing and factories will be able to be built with this type of low-cost . . . building." But while the city father's admired Gropius's well-known advocacy of industrialized building methods, Dessau's local building trades—like their counterparts elsewhere—felt threatened by the application of industrial techniques to their basically handicraft industry. Nonetheless, his enthusiasm for serial building did bring him the support of one of Dessau's and its state of Anhalt's most powerful political figures, Heinrich Peus, the so-called grand old man of Anhalt socialism.

At sixty-three, Peus—the state leader of the Social Democratic Party and publisher of the party's local newspaper, *Das Volksblatt*—was Hesse's most important ally on the City Council. A longtime socialist—he had been a member of the prewar Reichstag—Peus was deeply committed to workers' housing. It was known as his "pet idea." While Hesse saw the Bauhaus's move to Dessau as sparking the city's cultural rebirth, Peus viewed it as giving new impetus to the creation of low-cost housing, an idea which alone pushed the feisty political veteran to support the school. "If you don't bring them to Dessau, then we [the SPD] will!" Peus bellowed at Hesse and his fellow DDP members of the City Council after speaking with Gropius during a visit to the Weimar Bauhaus by Dessau's legislators in early March. After this visit Peus became one of the most vigorous advocates of the Bauhaus's move, although his reasons for supporting the school figured little in the mayor's invitation and not at all to the school's faculty. Sensitive to Peus's importance, Gropius courted him assiduously.

Despite Hesse's promises and the rosy scenario he presented, the Bauhäuslers—their school still split over its industrializing and profit-making direction—anticipated little from their new home, aside from perhaps more peace. In February 1925 Feininger referred to the prospective move as the "second edition of the Bauhaus struggle . . . that none of us [will] begin . . . with entirely light hearts." His apprehensions grew as the move loomed closer. By March Feininger almost feared the move to Dessau. Of all the participants only Hesse (who knew nothing about the school's internal divisions) remained confident about the move, certain that he could keep the Dessau Bauhaus from becoming "a pawn of political infighting, as it had been in Weimar."

In all likelihood Hesse was also unaware of how opposed Dessau's craft unions were to industrializing their trade, which since 1923 had been how Bauhaus described its workshop program. Their opposition, however, became evident on Wednesday, March 11, 1925—one day after notice of the Bauhaus's prospective move had appeared in the local newspapers— when Dessau's craft unions distributed hostile brochures that had been sent by their counterparts in Weimar. Why, asked their pamphlet, does Dessau need another arts and crafts school when it already has a proven and successful institution? And who, they asked, is going to pay for this? Taxes will surely have to be raised, the pamphlet asserted. By March 16, as Hesse worked to line up his majority support for the City Council's vote on March 19, the school's projected move—known as the "Battle Around the Bauhaus"—had become the subject of heated full-page debate in Dessau's newspapers.

Could Dessau afford the approximately 100,000 marks per year to support this school? asked one local newspaper. Its readers were well aware that lack of money had lost them their palace and was preventing the reconstruction of their theater. The newspapers also called attention to the Bauhaus's embarrassingly small number of students, only 82 in September 1924, down from its initial enrollment of 150 in 1919. Noting that only 7 of these students came from Thuringia, the source of the Bauhaus's financial support, a "concerned" engineer whose letter appeared in a local newspaper questioned the school's claim of significant local industrial backing. One can only conclude, he commented, that the six-year-old school was not providing its graduates with training that its locally supporting industries found useful. If this was so, he then asked how a subsidy of 100,000 marks could be justified for so problematic a school. Dessau's local arts and crafts school, he noted, enrolled 900 students, whose subsidy of 150,000 marks came out to 167 marks per student. The Bauhaus, on the other hand, would cost 1,000 marks per student, even generously assuming that the school could attract 100 students.

A German National Party (DNP) representative on Dessau's City Council raised another sensitive issue, asking why the city was looking for new—and costly—cultural endeavors when it neglected what it had, most notably its famed theater. "So what if the Bauhaus puts Dessau at the very pinnacle of artistic developments in Germany," he argued. The theater was where the city had demonstrated its leadership for a hundred years. "Rather first class in one area," he commented, "than mediocre in many!"

Shocked by this surge of criticism, Hesse's coalition partners began to waiver in their support. Hoping to reignite enthusiasm, Hesse asked Gropius to give a lecture on Saturday, March 14—a few days prior to the scheduled City Council vote—before an invited audience of about one thousand of Dessau's most important citizens. Once again the opposing Dessau trade union was ready. Standing in the doorway of the auditorium, its members gave out fliers titled "The Bauhaus Hoopla" ("*Der Bauhaus-Spuk*"), another rehash of Weimar's complaints. Weimar's entry into the Dessau scene jolted and depressed Gropius, who blamed factions from that city for firing up the growing community outcry. Believing then that the issues being raised in Dessau's local press were spurious, Gropius, in his address, ignored them. His speech received generally favorable reviews. But Gropius's refusal to deal with these concerns failed to placate the faltering City Councilors, and Hesse found himself as uncertain of his coalition partner's vote after the speech as before.

Hesse was pushing so hard for the Bauhaus and was so totally identified with its cause—the school would soon be known as "Hesse's baby"—that the mayor now found his own political standing as much at stake as the school's move. Uncertain about being able to muster his majority, Hesse rescheduled the vote from the March 19 to March 23. A telegram of support from the Berlin Architects' Association signed by several well-known personalities, including Peter Behrens, Ludwig Mies van der Rohe, and Otto Bartning (Gropius's successor in Weimar) helped boost the councilmen's spirits. Though Hesse remained unsure of his coalition partners' inclinations, he could not ask for another postponement. The first had already demonstrated his inability to control his coalition. A second request would destroy him as well as the Bauhaus. When he entered City Hall that morning, Hesse still had no idea what he was going to do. Only one week remained before the Bauhaus had to leave Thuringia. By the time he reached the meeting chambers he reluctantly decided that an adjournment was "the only way out."

Waiting for him at the entrance of the meeting hall was the leader of the SPD faction, Herr Sinsel. "Mr. Mayor," he called out, "we have agreed to the takeover of the Bauhaus." A lecture to the doubting coalition by a Dessau art historian and SPD member, Dr. van Kempen, had convinced the members of the school's merits. Sinsel announced that they were ready to vote unanimously to adopt the proposal. With the Bauhaus validated and his own political standing safe, the mayor pressed forward with the vote. The proposition was simple and straightforward. The Weimar Bauhaus would fuse with the city's vocational school; Gropius would be appointed director of the joined institutions; the current director of the vocational school would be put on pension (to which he willingly agreed); contracts for the director and faculty would be limited to five years and the budget would not exceed one hundred thousand marks per year.

Hesse realized, however, that construction of a new school and the appropriation of its funding could jeopardize the whole proposition. A master parliamentarian, he decided to shove aside these "unresolved remaining details" and delegate their resolution to the Finance Committee, a nine-man group (including himself) that he could more easily control than the entire Council. Four and a half hours after it convened, the Council voted: twenty-six in favor and fifteen (the entire rightist coalition, as in Thuringia) opposed. Precipitously and with what some would later claim to be parliamentary sleight of hand, the Bauhaus was coming to Dessau.

The school arrived there in its usual tumultuous and "boiling" state, according to Feininger and Ise. Apart from the faculty's ongoing doubts about joining art and industry, the contentious issue at the moment was the new direction of the workshop's educational program. Should the workshops be primarily directed toward teaching basic artistic principles? Or should they focus on commercial considerations, such as the designing of salable products for the marketplace; identifying, testing, and establishing standards or prototypes for industrialized production; and the basics of assembly-line techniques, cost reduction, and marketing principles? For someone like Kandinsky, who was form master for the wall-painting workshop, financial and practical considerations of producing models suitable for commercial production *had* to be secondary to the teaching of artistic principles he believed were applicable to all the workshops.

Principles aside, there were practical difficulties as well. What should be done with those workshops, such as stained glass, that were unsuited for large-scale commercial development? Students in the stone-sculpture workshop produced gravestones, a product hardly suitable for industrial production. On the other hand, toys made in the wood-carving workshop proved highly successful. So too did lamps, ashtrays, and teapots, among other items, produced by the metalworking class.

Some of the faculty, such as Schlemmer, griped that they were depleting their creative energy in trying to come up with salable models. "Everywhere the same complaint," Ise bemoaned. "[T]oo much time spent on the commercial aspects and too little time for private work." And it wasn't just the painters. Marcel Breuer, now a young master, complained to Gropius that the school's commercial pursuits were impeding its artistic inventiveness, experimentation, and much vaunted quest for "the totally new idea," an inherent conflict he doubted the Bauhaus would ever be able to overcome. Gropius, as usual, denied this.

As if these issues of art versus commerce—the heart of the new Bauhaus—were not sufficiently formidable in themselves, Gropius's attention to them was distracted by his architectural projects, most notably the masters' villas and school building and the chaotic state in which his architectural office arrived in Dessau. His longtime associate Adolf Meyer had left with the closing of Gropius's Weimar office. Just before the move, so too had Carl Fieger, another experienced member of his atelier. Given Gropius's drafting deficiencies, not to mention all his other activities—lecturing, running the school, and writing numerous articles—he was, perhaps more than most practicing architects, very dependent on experienced help. Ernst Neufert, described by Ise as "an excellent worker," took over Meyer's position as head of the office and was placed in charge of the new Dessau buildings. He would last only a year. On April 1, 1926—four months before the completion of the masters' villas and eight before the inauguration of the school building—he too left Gropius's office, surprisingly enough, to join Bartning at the Bauhaus's replacement school in Weimar.

This absence of a full and experienced staff in Gropius's office could not have come at a worse moment. In addition to the Bauhaus buildings, Gropius's atelier was busier than ever. Ise described it as a volcano out of which "project after project is thrown up." The strain on Gropius was obvious and a source of constant worry for Ise. "[T]here is so much to do right now and he can't do it all with new people. . . . [He] is losing a lot of weight," she confided to her mother-in-law. To her diary Ise despaired even more. "G. has to do all the work himself," she wrote, "and is very worn out." By the fall she would describe Gropius as working himself to death.

Absorbed by these architectural tasks in addition to his other activities, Gropius loosened even more his normally forbearing style of leadership. After all the frenetic maneuvering to install the Bauhaus in its new home by April 1, Klee and Kandinsky did not show up in Dessau until mid-June, appearing at the school only after the younger masters staged "a palace revolt." When they did arrive, their request to teach only two times every other week further ruffled the feathers of Dessau's officials. Adding to Gropius's burdens and distracting him even more from his administrative duties was the fact that the Bauhaus had neither an accountant nor a business manager when it arrived in Dessau, and he had to assume these jobs himself.

Thus to the Bauhaus's already frayed and contentious state, along with Gropius's usual indifference to the artists' concerns and inclination to ride above controversy, was now added directorial neglect. Alarmed over the deteriorating situation and perhaps feeling a certain sense of responsibility for the Bauhaus's decision to come to Dessau, Kandinsky began to lobby among the students and other faculty members for the school to return to artistic rather than commercial priorities.

Kandinsky, an imposing and professorial man, was not someone with whom one trifled. In fact he was Gropius's right-hand man, the school's de facto director just as Itten had been. Kandinsky had never hesitated to express his opinions to Gropius, who was thus well aware of the Russian artist's views favoring art over commercial considerations. Gropius also knew that Kandinsky had taken to propagating his opposing views within the school. Soon, whenever student complaints began to surface, Gropius blamed Kandinsky. Indeed, Kandinsky had the solid support of all the painters on the faculty; Klee, in fact, was working actively with him. "Apparently there is a quiet understanding between Moholy and

Muche to put the workshop work into the background [and] to take up positions like Klee and Kandinsky," wrote Ise.

The situation outside the Bauhaus was similarly troubled. The Right was outraged when it learned that the Finance Committee had authorized the city to build the Bauhaus school at a cost of 680,000 marks. Claiming that only the full City Council had the right to vote such an expenditure, they disputed it forcefully at a City Council meeting on June 22, 1925. The Finance Committee responded by noting that the City Council had authorized their action at its March 23 meeting. But the rightist coalition insisted that they had authorized only the subcommittee to decide whether or not such a building *should* be constructed. Supported by his sturdy SPD (and single Communist) majority, Hesse overrode their objections. But the Right, who was beginning to see this issue as a useful propaganda tool against both Hesse and the Bauhaus, had made its point. Thanks to their incessant harping on what was basically an issue of parliamentary procedure, many Dessauers would come to see the Bauhaus not only as a costly thorn, but possibly an illegal one as well.

Trouble was also brewing with the construction of the masters' villas, begun before the school building and the contested appropriation. The contractors charged that Gropius's specifications for the houses had been inaccurate and they had to hike their construction costs to protect themselves. They threatened to air their complaints before the public, an action which Hesse—in enough trouble with the Right—wanted to avoid at any cost. The construction workers added their voices to the fray. Like their colleagues in Weimar, handicraft trade unions for the most part never supported the Bauhaus. From the start they were among the school's most vigorous opponents. The building trades remained essentially a handicraft industry, and like their colleagues in other cities they worried that Gropius's well-known advocacy of mass-production techniques for building construction would reduce the need for union labor. Anxious to discredit both Gropius and his revolutionary building theories, the construction trade workers went on strike over the summer in sympathetic protest with the contractors.

Undoubtedly provoking their wrath was the villas' enormous size, doubly irritating at a time when Dessau was suffering a severe housing shortage. Even Gropius himself seemed startled by the "disproportionately large" villas. Schlemmer, visiting the just-completed houses in early

October, was also "shocked" by their size. He described the "whole thing [as] incredible," and worried about what would happen after Dessau's homeless poor came to stare at "the Lord Artists sun[ning] . . . themselves on the flat roofs of their villas." After moving into one of these houses, Kandinsky whitewashed the glass-walled stairwell, not just to protect his privacy but also to avoid being stoned—or worse—by Dessau's angry workers, who had apparently begun resorting to sabotage. The window-panes in Gropius's house were repeatedly smashed. T. Lux Feininger, Lyonel's son, was nearly electrocuted by improperly installed wiring when he stepped out of the bath in his new house.

Dessau's local architects, upset over having been excluded from the profitable and noncompetitive building commission of the masters' villas, were also grumbling. After all, they argued, it was their tax money that was going to pay the outsider Gropius's fees. The Bauhaus school building was the last straw. When its construction began on September 28, 1925, they went to the public with their complaints. Seeing the widening controversy as a way to enlarge its readership, a local rightist newspaper, the *Anhalter Woche*, took up the architects' cause. Where was the City Council? asked the newspaper. "How did we get these buildings and who gave the city administration the right to use the city's resources to build them? The building should be stopped at once!"

The harshness of the criticism took Gropius aback, and his reaction, as usual, was echoed by Ise. "[I]ncredible agitation against the Bauhaus in the city," she commented. Even Hesse, in spite of his careful planning, was surprised. No one was quite certain how to contain the controversy. Some city officials wanted the Bauhaus to placate the townsfolk through lectures or an exhibition. Hesse counseled the opposite. "Just keep quiet," he said, "the best course is to remain invisible!" Calls to impeach the mayor and send "the whole Bauhaus packing" now began to be heard. With Dessau becoming more and more reminiscent of Weimar, Gropius fell into a gloomy state, his depression deepening with the formation of an anti-Bauhaus Citizens' Alliance (Bürgerverein).

Ise dismissed the growing controversy as a "storm in a teapot." But Hesse, who saw the booming readership of the now vehemently anti-Bauhaus *Anhalter Woche* as a barometer of the town's growing hostility, was becoming troubled. So too was Gropius, who once again watched his Bauhaus become a political football for the opposing parties. The German National People's Party (the DNVP) recognized this as well. Seeing the swelling opposition as a convenient anti-Hesse tool, the party went on record as opposing the Bauhaus at a well-attended meeting on October 22, 1925. To issues such as the so-called illegality of the Finance Committee's actions, the controversy surrounding the masters' villas, and the enterprise's "exorbitant" costs they now added Gropius's "high fees" and the question of whether or not a new school was even needed. "Before the Bauhaus came here," declared a speaker at the meeting, "no one spoke of needing a new school." In light of the townspeople's increasing concern, a party representative suggested that the Bauhaus issue be quickly cleared up "by means of a nonpolitical assembly." He urged the audience to attend the upcoming meeting of the Citizens' Alliance.

Sponsored as it was by the House and Property Owners Association— part of Dessau's rightist coalition—the Citizens' Alliance hardly qualified as a nonpolitical organization. At its first meeting on October 30, 1925, the Alliance brought up another popular irritant, the supposed financial burden that the Bauhaus was imposing on Dessau. Citing the doubling of taxes since 1913 and the inability of local businesses and individuals to obtain loans from cash-drained banks, the group blamed the expensive Bauhaus for "ruining" Dessau's economy. "The city should make sure that its citizens can earn a living," declared one of the speakers, "before taking on additional obligations." Another speaker labeled the Bauhaus "the final straw breaking Dessau's cup of discontent."

These highly publicized complaints were directed toward influencing a City Council meeting of November 5, 1925, where the Right, reacting to the purportedly illegal action of the Finance Committee, submitted a motion demanding the immediate cessation of all Bauhaus construction. Hesse's coalition was able to defeat the motion. But seven months after the school's arrival the Bauhaus issue was now, as a local newspaper observed, "out of control"; and Dessau's animosity to the school surged in vitriolic counterpoint to their economy's miserable state.

Two years after recovering from devastating inflation, Germany was now suffering another economic blow. This time a depression was once again putting people out of work. If economic conditions had been better, Dessauers might not have cared about the Bauhaus. But given the nearly intolerable situation that existed in 1925, they cared too much. The sudden death on February 28, 1925, of fifty-four-year-old Friedrich Ebert— shortly after Grote's initial visit to the Weimar Bauhaus—removed from the public scene whatever pallid remnants remained of the country's revolutionary hopes. Likewise, the election of seventy-eight-year-old Field Marshal Paul von Hindenburg on April 27—just as the Bauhaus was settling into its new home—revealed the country's increasingly conservative turn. "All the philistines are delighted about Hindenburg," Kessler observed in May after the new president's swearing-in. Most German liberals felt the same. Ise wrote, "Farewell progress, farewell vision of a new world . . . Hindenburg, alas!"

The exalted moral enterprise on which a war-torn generation had staked its hopes and established a republic—and Gropius a Bauhaus—was now being dismantled. As Germany's economy once again failed, so too did the country's sputtering experiment with parliamentary government. Between December 1923 and the end of June 1928, six cabinets would govern the country.

Describing the country's state of affairs as "catastrophic" in November 1925, Schlemmer was awed by Dessau's willingness to accept a project like the Bauhaus "in times like these." Forced to watch every penny, Gropius at the end of the month asked the Bauhaus faculty to waive 10 percent of their salaries—he imposed the same on himself—to help support the school's workshops, which still could not find sufficient industrial support. By December, few individuals remained untouched by hardship.

The situation worsened in 1926, just as the Bauhaus's buildings were going up. On January 1 Dessau's businessmen described themselves as "terrified" by what awaited them in the coming year. Unemployment benefits ran out for many Dessau workers, and the financially strained city began to distribute bread and milk. Ise could no longer pay the family's bills. In February she lamented their "[g]reat financial worries." Dessau's permanent postwar army of 4–6 percent unemployed surged ominously. By May 1 the economic crisis forced Junkers Aircraft Company, one of the city's main employers, to lay off 25 percent of their workers, an especially severe blow to the local economy that one newspaper described as "dangerous." Desperate for revenue and unable to demand higher taxes from politically powerful industry, the city government raised individuals' taxes again, forcing many people to borrow against their increasingly mortgaged property from the cash-depleted banks and inspiring more invective against the Bauhaus from Dessau's House and Property Owners Association. As the city's funds shrank to precipitously low levels and its construction of new subsidized housing fell to a postwar low, the Bauhaus's monumental constructions rose from Dessau's dusty and increasingly impoverished plains.

As usual, the economic strains nurtured the growth of political extremism. In Dessau, as throughout Germany, meeting halls and streets again reverberated to the sounds of serious, bloody clashes. On June 9, 1926, Communists disrupted a speech being given by NSDAP Reichstag member Gregor Strasser in Dessau and attacked the audience with beer glasses and broken chairs. On June 19 thirty people were injured, five or six seriously, when members of two violent extremist veterans groups, the Red Front Line Soldiers' Union (Rotfrontkämpferbund) and the Steel Helmets (Stahlhelm) confronted each other in a Dessau suburb with bricks, wooden boards spiked with protruding nails, and kitchen knives. Despite Gropius's strict prohibition, the intensifying economic crisis was arousing the students' political sympathies. As Dessau's unemployment rate soared above 10 percent, some of the students and younger masters no longer attempted to hide their deepening Bolshevik convictions, which, to Gropius's distress, Kandinsky some months later would report to the mayor.

Toward the end of June the disgruntled building contractors union— again protesting the excessive construction costs of the Bauhaus masters' villas—published their complaints in all of Dessau's newspapers. Although no figures were published to either prove or (on the Bauhaus's behalf) dispute the accusations, the public's speculation was aroused. The contractors once again threatened to stop construction. In July Schlemmer declared the anti-Bauhaus attacks worse than anything the school had experienced in Weimar.

Having worried and struggled over the Bauhaus for more than a year now, Hesse was exhausted. Ise described him as "wan and tired." Gropius too was depressed, weary, and feeling put upon. "G. is worn out," Ise commented. "The whole thing is getting too much for him." The only group that seemed to be thriving in Dessau was the Right. Looking toward the November 1927 elections for city council, the Right saw the growing Bauhaus controversy as an anti-Hesse bounty that they intended to use to their advantage.

The horse on which they would try to ride to victory would be the Törten housing project. This commission for the construction of sixty homes for a workers' housing development, to be built in the Dessau suburb of Törten, had been given to Gropius in April 1926 as part of the building package that Hesse used to lure him to Dessau. While the Bauhaus, in fact, would have very little to do with either this project or the other buildings going up in Dessau, the Right's relentless references inevitably linked them with the school.

By the time the Törten plans came up for approval before the City Council on June 25, 1926, the Right, picking up the contractors' complaints, severely questioned Hesse's giving so large a commission to Gropius. The day before this meeting, an article written by Dessau city architect Kurt Elster and appearing in a local newspaper had defended (and thereby enhanced) the contractors' complaints. "How can the city justify giving a new commission to an architect whose current constructions are so controversial?" Elster had asked. If the city insists on "giving Gropius a monopoly on its constructions," Elster continued, "then the city is morally obligated to its tax-paying citizens to do so only after an investigation of his current, problematical constructions reveals that the complaints are baseless."

At the July 25 meeting the rightist councilmen continued the challenge. "What has Gropius achieved so far to be given such a commission?" asked one city councilman, who, to the Right's undisguised glee, was none other than Heinrich Peus. Gropius and the Bauhaus's most vocal supporter a scant year earlier, Peus was now obviously having second thoughts. A long-standing advocate of workers' housing, Peus may have been upset that Gropius had not consulted him on the project. Peus was particularly bothered by Gropius's design of sixty identical houses, which he claimed did not reflect people's differing needs. He accused the mayor of being "too fixated on Gropius." Referring to another Elster objection, Peus asked why this commission had been awarded without competition. If the city wants to support its own, he argued, it should give Gropius the chance to prove himself with twenty houses, not all sixty. Peus had other, even more substantive complaints. Gropius had submitted no cost analysis nor any practical information, such as the materials with which the homes were going to be built. "Are the houses going to be built from steel or concrete slabs?" Peus asked. "There's nothing here," he disgustedly declared about the unaccountably thin proposal.

The members of the rightist coalition could hardly contain themselves. "Ach, Peus, you helped bring the Bauhaus here. . . . Victory for the Right!"

chided a DNP member. "Now that the Bauhaus is here with their bag of tricks (*Bauhausrummel*), Peus is losing his courage," admonished another.

Claiming that "Bauhaus theory and Bauhaus practice are far apart" and that such an ill-conceived proposal would result in defective buildings and cost the city more money, DNP representative Seiss suggested the Bauhaus prove itself without city subsidy. Hesse made no attempt to counter these arguments, claiming instead that the city's need for quickly built, inexpensive houses overrode such undeniably persuasive objections. Having recorded their complaints and not wishing to damage their coalition, Peus and his Social Democrats ultimately voted to approve Gropius's building of the Törten project.

For Dessau as well as Gropius, Törten embodied long-held but somewhat divergent ambitions. While both were committed to urgently needed low-cost housing, the project represented a particular opportunity for Gropius to demonstrate his as yet unproved theories about erecting cheap housing based on principles of mass production—in essence, the architectural summation of his Bauhaus vision. Gropius's proposal, however, bore profound implications, not only for construction workers but for the construction process itself.

The adaptation of traditional building techniques to those of mass production was a formidably complex issue involving the rethinking, developing, and testing of every aspect of housing construction, from technique to materials. Despite considerable attention to this issue in the professional journals, no one really knew if industrialized techniques would work on building sites or exactly how much they would reduce costs, if, indeed, at all. For all Gropius's writings and efforts by others in the field—such as Martin Wagner, Ernst May, and Bruno Taut—serial building, as this type of construction was known, remained a highly theoretical undertaking. While various housing projects had experimented with one technique or another, none had successfully applied factory principles to all aspects of construction, from start to finish. The vigorous national opposition by the construction workers' unions made local governments hesitate to grant the large sums of money needed for such experimentation. The industrialized techniques that Gropius planned to utilize at Törten remained for the most part untried.

By 1926 the application of technology to building mass housing had become Gropius's main architectural preoccupation. Despite the uncertainties, he was anxious to display the results of his much-vaunted theories in time for the December opening of the Bauhaus school building. Begun in mid-September, several of the homes would be ready for the Bauhaus's inauguration at the end of the year.

Hesse had given the Törten commission to Gropius to fulfill one of his promises to the architect. But the mayor—worried by the school's growing controversiality and seeing the commission as a good opportunity for the Bauhaus to mend its diminishing goodwill within the community— wanted the students to participate in the design too. Surprisingly, considering his lifelong advocacy of collaboration, Gropius vetoed this notion, arguing that such a project demanded a single architectural vision; that the students had no practical experience in such matters; and that without its own architectural department, the school had no legal basis on which to undertake such a collaboration. The year before, Gropius had similarly denied Muche and Breuer's request to collaborate on the designs of the villas and school building, justifying his decision then with the need for speed and precision, which, he declared—pre-empted "experiment[ation]." Although Hesse and most everyone else in the community considered Törten a Bauhaus project, the school would be involved in the design of only a few interior furnishings.

Within the Bauhaus, students griped that Gropius's architectural preoccupations were distracting him to an unacceptable degree, and they began to drop out of the school at an alarming rate. Anxious to put these complaints to rest, Gropius responded by inviting two students over to his house for lunch twice a week, an exercise that did nothing to resolve the real issue. Indeed, in what Ise described as "a very productive period," Gropius continued to work "incessantly" on his plans for mass-produced housing.

The Bauhaus, however, needed its director's undivided attention more than ever. The school was now divided into two distinct camps: those mostly younger masters, such as Moholy and Breuer, who pursued the creation of model household objects suitable for industrial production; and the mostly older painters, such as Feininger, Klee, Muche, and Kandinsky, who opposed such commercially mediated creating. Much like a chess game, the loss of even one member within each camp was severely contested. Kandinsky, for instance, worried about losing his ally in the aesthetic war, Muche, and accused Gropius of not working hard enough to try to keep Muche at the Bauhaus. Kandinsky's assessment proved correct. For on November 2, Muche declared that his basic artistic ideas no longer coincided with those of Gropius and announced his departure.

Believing that the Bauhaus's problems were soaring out of control, Kandinsky—who brooked no nonsense normally—moved to save the school. He continued to express his concerns to Gropius, but he also met with the mayor from time to time, of which Gropius was aware. Kandinsky may have doubted the mayor's appreciation of the artistic issues dividing the school, and he spoke mostly to Hesse about Bolshevism's inroads within the school, his firsthand experiences in the Soviet Union making him all too aware of the difference between Bolshevism's lofty promises and its harsh reality. Since their initial meetings, Kandinsky and Hesse had grown quite close. Both lawyers, they found in each other a thoughtful, sober, and trusted confidant in whom they could share their growing misgivings about Gropius and his Bauhaus. It would be to Kandinsky that Hesse would turn in the critical period that lay ahead.

But at the dedication of the new Bauhaus building on December 4, 1925, not a trace of the school's tremulous state was visible to the fifteen hundred guests who gathered in Dessau that day. It was not apparent in its lofty publicity rhetoric; the sprawling glass-walled Bauhaus building that glittered in the pale wintry sun; or in Gropius's welcoming address, delivered before a sea of well-known personalities from the worlds of art, academia, and politics who came from all over Europe to pay homage to a man and an enterprise about which many had dreamed but few had dared to realize. From Paris, Amsterdam, Russia, Switzerland, and Berlin they came, jamming themselves into the auditorium, across the stage, and in side rooms, the entryway, and the stairwell. Representatives of the Anhalt government were there; so too were members of the Prussian Art Administration and, as always, Art Minister Redslob. For Gropius—so moved that he could barely speak—it was a moment of undeniable triumph.

Seven and a half years ago, he declared in his opening address, the Bauhaus had begun its search for the singular, universal, and collectively achieved spatial unity (*Raumgestaltung*) that underlay all contemporary creativity. Directed toward improving society, the task, Gropius declared, had been pursued by the Bauhaus with persistence and "unwavering determination." While few could quarrel with such stirring ambitions, those among the crowd who knew the Bauhaus best understood the gap that existed between these aspirations and the reality of the school's situation. Like ripples emanating from a stone dropped into water, which expand the farther they get from their source, so too did admiration for the Bauhaus increase the more distant its source was from the school. From faraway America would come the Bauhaus's greatest praise. The most dubious remained those within Dessau, Weimar, and the Bauhaus's own walls.

13. | Dessau 1927

A Critical Election

Dieu est mort! le ciel est vide—
Pleurez! enfants, vous n'avez plus de père.

[God is dead! Heaven is empty—
Weep, children, you no longer have a father.]

—Gérard de Nerval

He had been through "hell's doors [and] survived," Gropius said of himself shortly after the dedication, his comments as appropriate to the extensive celebrations as to the year's travails. But what greeted him in January 1927 was not a victor's triumph but the school's near collapse; and Gropius plunged into a dark depression. "[T]ired . . . run down . . . depressed and listless" was how Ise described him in January and February. Kandinsky was opposing his choice of Hannes Meyer, a Swiss architect, to head the school's new architecture department, and Hesse—also "at the end of his rope"—was unaccountably grumpy toward him. One month after the school's dedication the Bauhaus's honeymoon in Dessau was decidedly over.

Hesse's sullen mood was provoked by a report he had received in the beginning of January 1927. He realized that the Bauhaus would be a pivotal issue in the coming November election. Anxious to avoid the official inquiry his opponents were sure to demand about the supposed cost overruns for building the masters' villas and the school, Hesse had ordered the city's accounting office to prepare an objective and thorough review. What the accountants uncovered neither exonerated Gropius nor gave Hesse and his Democratic coalition what they were looking for, most notably the opportunity to expose their opponents' spurious accusations and collect much needed political capital. Instead they discovered an astonishing overrun of one hundred thousand marks on the buildings, just as the opposition was claiming!

Everyone recognized that the November elections were critical. They would determine not only party control of Dessau's City Council, but also Hesse's political fate, and with it that of the Bauhaus. The mayor, unable to understand how such an oversight could have happened, was as baffled as he was furious. Like everyone else in Dessau, Gropius was well aware of these charges. Hardly a day had passed since construction began that the local newspapers had not aired complaints. Picked up by the rightist coalition parties, protests against Gropius and the Bauhaus had become Dessau's fastest growing industry, spawning the stunning growth of the Citizens' Association and two local newspapers, the *Anhalter Woche* and the *Central-Anzeiger*. Thanks in part to the public's rising hostility to the school, the coffers of the various right-wing parties were overflowing. Even strangers to Dessau, such as the American journalist Dorothy Thompson, who visited the Bauhaus in the spring of 1926, noticed the townspeople's opposition to the school. The city and the Bauhaus had impressed her, and she praised them as prototypes of "the new Germany." But she also noted the impression of many Dessauers that the Bauhaus people were "completely crazy" and their mayor "irresponsible and wasteful" for bringing the school there.

Gropius knew all this. According to Ise, he was simply "beside himself" over the accounting office's report. He worried that it would damage his relations with the mayor. Gropius blamed the errors on oversights and ledger mistakes by his architectural office manager, Ernst Neufert. Ise, perhaps more realistically, attributed them to overwork. But whatever their cause, Gropius's assessment of their repercussions was right on target: such "miscalculations," he realized, were sure to undermine the mayor's trust in him and "complicate" an already difficult electoral battle. They did far more than that. Hurt and resentful, the mayor could not forgive Gropius's blithe disregard for the fact that he and the Bauhaus were partners of sorts; if it failed, Hesse—who had risked so much on the school's behalf—went down too.

Gropius's dismissive attitude toward what he considered lesser matters was nothing new. After all, Nietzsche had praised the strong, not the careful; and from Gropius's miscalculations in Behrens's office to his lackadaisical control over the Bauhaus's finances in Weimar, inattentiveness to detail had stalked his career. He had never been able to reconcile his Bauhaus ambitions with the financial constraints of the day. This was apparent in Weimar, as he relentlessly pursued the 1923 exhibition in the face of economic catastrophe. In Dessau he could not keep the school's construction expenses under control or the Bauhaus workshop costs anywhere near their earnings.

The Bauhaus workshops—the critical core of a school that sought to bind practical craft training with artistic theory in the hope of realizing a new creative unity—had always been a problem both pedagogically and financially. These pedagogical difficulties increased in 1923, when the workshops had to teach students how to make not only artistic objects but also salable ones. In his proposal of March 1922 Otto Dorfner, who had originally developed the program to turn the school into a profit-making enterprise, had warned of the problems the workshops faced in trying to combine aesthetic training with successful business practices. After all, a well-designed artistic object is not intrinsically more salable if it is too expensive, or ill-suited for assembly-line production, or does not particularly suit some well-defined need. To avoid this, Dorfner had urged that the workshops' commercial aspects be clearly separated from teaching activities, and that the workshops be organized as proper businesses. None of these recommendations had been heeded. Since the workshops' birth as semicommercial enterprises in 1923, no week seems to have passed without someone—Breuer, Muche, Klee, or Kandinsky—complaining to Gropius about the difficulties of trying to simultaneously search for basic artistic principles and making salable, machine-reproducible objects.

The workshops had also been a serious and constant drain on the Bauhaus's finances. In December 1922 Emil Lange, whom Gropius had appointed as the school's *Syndikus* after Beyer's departure, had urged the school to reconcile its "unrealistic expectations" with economic realities. This too had never been done. By 1927 the situation had become critical.

"There is just not enough money to cover all ends!" lamented Ise in early January 1927. "The situation is very precarious." Despite the breast-beating and Gropius's frequent meetings with the mayor, the situation remained unresolved and soon became desperate. Citing the school's seriously compromised financial situation, Dessau's advisors, including the mayor, urged that one or more of the workshops be temporarily eliminated.

Gropius was reluctant to do this. Neither was he able to significantly cut workshop costs. He preferred instead to look for other ways to reduce expenses, such as asking the faculty, himself included, to accept "voluntary" pay cuts. But these were difficult times, and what Gropius asked the faculty members to do would have involved considerable sacrifice. The resistance with which Kandinsky and others greeted Gropius's proposal did little to improve the school's sour mood or the workshops' financial state. Gropius's constant demand for money, along with his unwillingness or inability to manage it, became an increasing irritant to the put-upon faculty and Hesse. To the mayor's chagrin, it also became a bounty for the school's—and Hesse's—opponents.

The political ramifications of the Bauhaus opposition had already become painfully obvious in November 1926—one month before the dedication of the Bauhaus school building—when the Citizens' Association was able to attract an audience of one thousand to its meeting. There, Georg Büchlein, a local businessman and founder of the group, had read excerpts from a vicious anti-Bauhaus brochure (known as the "Yellow Brochure" for the color of paper on which it was printed) that initially appeared in Weimar in 1924, like much of such scurrilous material. Büchlein neglected to mention that Gropius had filed a still-pending libel suit against the brochure's publisher; instead he presented as fact its descriptions of Gropius as "dishonest" and an artistic failure whose every wrinkle on his "sly, furtive face revealed that he was a thief, an intriguer, and a coward."

Compounding the deception, the *Anhalter Woche* and the *Central-Anzeiger*—competing against each other in anti-Bauhaus invective—published these accusations again as fact. Torn between ignoring the slander or giving it wider notice by responding, Gropius, along with Dessau's City Administration (led by Hesse) and a similarly libeled member of the City Council, DNP Representative Theiss, brought criminal charges of "provocative defamation" against Büchlein and the two newspapers. Although the highly publicized case would be resolved in Gropius's and

Theiss's favor at the end of June 1927, it provided Dessau with seven months of titillating speculation and heightened the mayor's apprehensions.

Aiding Büchlein's cause was his association with Konrad Nonn, an engineer and member of the Prussian Building Administration; editor of the Prussian Finance Ministry's prestigious architectural journal, the *Zentralblatt der Bauverwaltung*; and longtime Bauhaus opponent. Nonn was resolutely opposed to Gropius and his school, and he used his prestigious position and professional stature to add weight to his often bogus accusations.

Büchlein's and Nonn's hatred of Gropius and the Bauhaus prompted a natural alliance. Büchlein's open wallet funded reprints of Nonn's sordid articles throughout the country, while the affiliation with Prussian Ministerial Councilor Dr. Engineer Nonn gave a certain stature to Büchlein's loudmouthed but otherwise forgettable Citizens' Association. Backed by Büchlein's funds, Nonn became the spokesman for many of the groups that opposed the Bauhaus: the politically powerful building-trades unions, who felt threatened by modernism's advocacy of mechanized building technology; the political parties who sought to gain support from the resentments of these increasingly vocal groups; and the rapidly growing numbers of individuals for whom any attempt to modify the status quo was seen as subversive.

Like the brochure that Büchlein quoted at the November 1926 meeting of the Citizens' Association, Nonn's charges against Gropius and the Bauhaus had also originated in 1924. But again like the pamphlet, they had found little resonance outside of the school's local Weimar opposition. To those inclined to read his articles, Nonn's technique was as deceptive as it was compelling. Proceeding from what appeared to be objective and technical criticism—of building techniques or what he perceived as design flaws, as well as the Bauhaus's pedagogical irresolution—Nonn, in increasingly mocking and pejorative tones, deduced evidence of insanity and cultural destructiveness. The Bauhaus's "lamentable results," he wrote in a 1924 article, made "a laughingstock of all that is German." The appearance of his articles in respected professional journals gave spurious credibility to his purportedly objective criticism, despite his use of such obviously unprofessional terms as "oddities," "crass negation . . . of reason," "lamentable," and "scandalous."

In an article titled "Update on the Bauhaus," which appeared in the *Zentralblatt der Bauverwaltung* on March 9, 1927, Nonn turned his

attention to the new Bauhaus school building and what he termed
"Gropius's basic errors." He began in typically sober fashion by criticizing purely technical details, such as the "improper" installation of the
building's flat roof and the attachment of the heating system to a glass
wall, which he predicted would require ten times more fuel to heat in the
winter. An orgiastic condemnation followed. Referring to this type of
architecture as "misguided," Nonn denounced the Bauhaus's entire arts
program as "nonsensical" and based on producing hypnotically induced
trance states on the hapless students, for whom, he claimed, "medical
help" often had to be sought. Büchlein, who was running for Dessau's
City Council, was delighted. He paid for reprints of the article to be distributed throughout Dessau.

Adding to Hesse's concerns was his city's—indeed, the entire country's—shift toward the right, a reactionary turn that would be highlighted
by a visit of President von Hindenburg to Dessau in June 1927. While
every Dessauer would agree it was a day to remember, exactly why would
be far more divided. For some, Hindenburg was nothing more than an
apolitical, aged hero, even a source of embarrassment. Others, as the
Anhalter Anzeiger declared, saw him as representing a victory for
"German interests . . . [that would certainly] exert its influence on . . .
local politics." Indeed it would. A few days after the president's visit, a
local right-wing militia group known as the Stahlhelm (Steel Helmets),
condemned as "lies" Germany's responsibility for the war and asked
Anhalt's rightist parties to draft legislation ordering the compulsory
arrest, imprisonment, and withdrawal of civil rights "for life" of anyone
who asserted this.

This nationalistic temper was not limited to Dessau, the state of Anhalt,
or even politics. Visible already with Hindenburg's election in 1925,
Germany's reactionary turn was also reflected in its increasing hostility
toward the avant-garde. "Times are bad for modernism," Schlemmer
wrote that year to the German painter Willi Baumeister, a concern he reit-
erated three days later when he referred to the "momentous . . . rejection
of . . . abstraction in art." Thanks in large part to Gropius's publicizing
efforts and the country's awareness of the controversies that plagued the
school, Germany's attitude toward modernism inevitably reflected on the
Bauhaus. By 1926 most of increasingly conservative Germany had come
to share Weimar and Dessau's animosity toward the school. "Every
German seems to despise the good things that are happening in Dessau,"

Feininger lamented in August of that year.

Gropius, however, had expended ceaseless energy in trying to link the Bauhaus with a broad progressive international spirit. He reasserted this at the Bauhaus's dedication ceremonies in December 1926, when he spoke of the school preparing its students for the "new world" and "modern life." While Gropius's efforts to link the school with a universal modernist spirit undoubtedly enhanced the Bauhaus's international stature, it also put the school at considerable risk in its own country when many of his compatriots began to question and reject such values. As Germany became increasingly self-absorbed and preoccupied with "German interests," the Bauhaus found itself regarded as a cantankerous symbol of current discontent, markedly out of step with Germany's sullen, escapist, and accusatory mood.

Hesse could not do much about the country's disposition, but his government's ability to build low-cost housing offered him a powerful election-year weapon; and it was in the Törten housing project that he sought election help. The spring of 1927 had seen Törten's first residents move in. There were varying complaints: built-in cupboards whose proportions made little allowance for their bulky furniture; a nearly five-foot-high windowsill on the upper floor that kept most people from being able to look outside; an improperly functioning heating system; a bathtub that stood in the middle of the kitchen; and, in place of a bathroom, an outhouse in the garden. Yet, the low price, which even ordinary workers could afford—a full 10 percent to 15 percent lower than similar housing—compensated for such inconveniences.

Hoping to gain much needed political capital, Hesse wanted to commission the project's second phase of 156 homes as quickly as possible. But because of Gropius's alienation of Peus, the mayor found himself in a quandary. To award the commission to Gropius would undoubtedly affront Peus, who remained adamantly opposed to the Bauhaus director's participation. Yet to placate the SPD leader by giving it to another architect would be to admit that commissioning Gropius for the initial project had been a mistake and jeopardize not only himself and his coalition government but also Gropius and perhaps the entire school, with whom the housing development had become inextricably—if incorrectly—entwined.

What swayed Hesse to remain with Gropius was the architect's prominence within the National Commission for Standardization, popularly known as the RfG, a national governmental agency responsible for awarding large federal subsidies to experimental mass housing projects. Gropius's ability to claim grants for the second project, as he had done for the earlier one, drove Hesse to risk Peus's wrath and give the commission for Törten II to the Bauhaus leader.

Unfortunately, Büchlein and Nonn also saw Törten as a ticket to victory. Similarly realizing that it was Gropius's influence within the RfG that gave him an inside edge on the commission, they—like Hesse and Gropius—vigorously lobbied their supporters within the national government. A committee from the RfG had come to Dessau in early February 1927 to inspect the nearly completed houses of Törten's first phase to help them decide whether or not to subsidize the project's next stage. Toward the end of March Büchlein sent reprints of Nonn's "Update" article to every member of the Reichstag, which funded the RfG, and the Minister of Labor, under whose wing the RfG operated.

Gropius and Hesse, realizing the grave threat Nonn posed, tried to have him removed from his prestigious platform. On March 15, 1927, Gropius received "very promising, if not absolutely certain" assurances that Nonn was on his way out of the Prussian Ministry of Finance because of his attack on the Bauhaus. Nonn's demotion has "already been signed by the minister," Gropius was advised on March 28. Hesse too was leaving no stone unturned. On March 28 he wrote to a minister (unnamed by Ise, who wrote of the episode) "asking him to have the attacks on the Bauhaus stopped." On April 2 the mayor visited the Minister of Finance in Berlin, who also assured him of Nonn's imminent demotion. Based on this assurance, Hesse that same day gave Gropius the go-ahead to build the second phase of Törten.

Dessau could not afford to build these houses without the federal subsidy; and until the RfG specifically committed funds for the project, Hesse could not publicly announce its start. Without this boost, as Hesse was more and more coming to realize, the election would probably be lost. But Hesse and Gropius's presumption of RfG support was premature. Thanks to Büchlein's and Nonn's successful lobbying, nearly three months elapsed after the RfG visit to Dessau in February before Gropius, on May 24, received verbal assurance of the commission's commitment for a 350,000 mark subsidy. "The effect here in Dessau," commented Ise, "will be very favorable." Again, the joy proved hasty. It was not until mid-July that Gropius received this commitment in writing, again provoking sighs of relief within the Bauhaus and Ise's rejoicing over her husband's successful "coup." But once again the elation was short-lived. Toward the end of August several rightist parties, joined by Nonn and some members of the Citizens' Association, petitioned the RfG, the Reichs Ministry of Labor, and the Reichstag to revoke the promised funds at once.

With Hesse and Gropius again reassured by their allies within the federal government of Nonn's imminent departure, Ise remained staunchly optimistic. "The payment of the 350,000 marks is only a question of time now," she confided to her diary on August 26, dismissing Nonn and Büchlein's efforts to torpedo the RfG's subsidy. But a report in a local newspaper on September 1, 1927—its source cited as someone within the Labor Ministry—noted that the RfG merely made its recommendations to the Labor Minister, who subsequently accepted or rejected them. Despite the signed approval that Gropius had received in July, the article declared that the RfG had not "definitively committed funds to any construction project," nor had the minister approved any such allocation. Reports to the contrary, declared the newspaper, were simply mistaken.

In the Bauhaus itself the situation was no less grim. Gropius and the artist faculty remained at loggerheads over the school's commercial direction. Gropius, however, burdened by his growing difficulties with Hesse, could no longer tolerate the artists' perpetual complaints. In his view the artists' purely aesthetic interests made them totally unsympathetic to his utilitarian priorities. The artists, Gropius believed, simply had no idea of what he was trying to accomplish at the Bauhaus and were thus totally alienated from the school's central purpose. Referring to the Bauhaus as "confused" and unable to settle into "the core of [its] real work," Gropius blamed the artists. "G. plans to tell the masters that he will have to resign if he continues to get so little collaboration," Ise commented. "Klee and Kandinsky are totally uninformed about the critical situation; they read no papers and bury themselves in their studios. It seems that the time of the painters at the Bauhaus is going to end." Ultimately, however, Gropius could not bring himself to remove them. He decided instead to reduce their influence by bringing in another faculty member who shared his own commitment to the utilitarian principles of the Bauhaus's "real work."

An important change that had taken place at the Bauhaus had given Gropius the tool with which he could accomplish this. In October 1926, seven years after founding the Bauhaus, Gropius was finally able to address a major absence in the school's structure. Embarrassing for an institution bearing the name Bauhaus (*Bau*, to build; *Haus*, house), there had never been a school of architecture to teach students how to build houses or, for that matter, any other kind of building. Now at last a fortuitous turn of events allowed Gropius to set up such a department in the school.

In the spring of 1926 Dessau's Building Trades School, which shared the Bauhaus's premises, had an enrollment of only seventeen students. Knowing that Hesse was keen to have the Bauhaus students take part in the Törten project, Gropius used this argument to try to persuade Hesse that it would make sense to close down the Building Trades School and start an architecture department at the Bauhaus incorporating the Building Trades School students. This graduate-level, studio-type program could take on its own commissions without having to depend on Gropius's private office. That way the Bauhaus architecture class could participate in the city's building projects and develop various types of models for industry and craft. The possibility of allowing the students to participate in municipal commissions convinced Hesse. In October 1926 the new department was established and the Bauhaus was reorganized as a College for the Visual Arts (Hochschule für Gestaltung).

To head the department and to be the additional faculty member who would bolster the utilitarian principles of the Bauhaus's "real work," Gropius had wanted to appoint the young Dutch Marxist architect Mart Stam. Twenty-seven-year-old Stam was not only the youngest architect chosen by Mies van der Rohe to participate in Weissenhofsiedlungen, the prestigious architectural exhibition that would open outside of Stuttgart in the summer of 1927, but also "the most radical, politically as well as architecturally." Stam's leftist politics were less apparent from what he said or wrote than from what he did and with whom he was involved. Stam was closely associated with El Lissitzky, the Russian Constructivist and dedicated Communist. Known as "Lissitzky's Dutch disciple," Stam—like his Russian mentor—was committed to the principle of collectivity. Stam also worked closely with the Swiss Marxist architect Hans Schmidt. In 1930 the two would join a team of architects and engineers— led by Ernst May, the leftist architect from Frankfurt am Main—to travel to the Soviet Union, where they would work for several years as advisers in domestic architecture and city planning.

In 1924, influenced by El Lissitzky, Stam, and Schmidt, along with several members of the Swiss Werkbund Collective, established a Swiss

Constructivist group known as ABC. The group also published a journal, titled *ABC—Contributions to Architecture* (*ABC—Beiträge zum Bauen*), which promulgated the group's hard-line doctrine of Marxist antiaesthetic functionalism (usefulness mattered more than beauty in art) that sought to replace "the handcrafted by the mechanical; the capricious [and] individual by the collective and standardized, [and] the . . . fortuitous by the precise."

Stam, however, who claimed he was not interested in teaching, turned down Gropius's persistent requests to join the Bauhaus. In Dessau for several days in December 1926 during the Bauhaus's celebrations with two of his fellow ABC members in tow—the Swiss architect Hans Wittwer and his partner, Hannes Meyer—Stam once again turned down Gropius's offer. Subsequently Gropius, who had never before met Meyer, shifted his focus to Stam's thirty-seven-year-old friend. So compelling was the ABC connection that Gropius, writing to Meyer some days later, did not ask the personable Swiss architect if he was interested in such a position but offered it to him outright. "After having met you here," Gropius wrote, "I immediately wanted to ask you to take over this project, should you have the desire and tendency for it. . . . At any rate, I must initiate this architectural community as soon as possible and would be very happy if you would say yes." It had clearly been Stam's ABC association that interested Gropius, for in the same letter he offered the position to Hans Wittwer should Meyer decline.

Meyer had left no doubt about his unabashed adherence to ABC principles. In his letter to Gropius of mid February 1927, in which he accepted the position, he wrote, "The basic tendency of my teaching will absolutely be functionalist, collectivist, and Constructivist in the sense of ABC and 'The New World.'" The latter was an article he had written in 1926 that made clear how closely he identified his views with those of ABC. In this article Meyer, like ABC, advocated strict utility, collectivity, uncompromising rationality, and social conscience. Collectively achieved and collectively directed, art and architecture were to be used to organize and transform society. "The work of art . . . as 'l'art pour l'art' is dead," Meyer asserted. Art, he declared, is "a technical process, not an aesthetic [one]. . . . Function times economy . . . use plus cost." Meyer, who considered himself a philosophical—rather than a political—Marxist, viewed art primarily within its social function. He saw society as an organic continuum, all of whose parts—economic, social, political, and artistic—interconnect.

Since Gropius was ostensibly bringing in Meyer to restore the Bauhaus's "real work," one might reasonably assume that he believed this to be represented by Meyer's (and Stam's) collectivist, utilitarian, and socially directed point of view. But since 1919 the school had not articulated such an unabashedly socialistic program. Even then its declaration had been more rhetorical than overt. The hasty and embarrassed removal in 1923 of Schlemmer's "cathedral of socialism" phrase had ended any further socialistic reference in either Gropius's or the Bauhaus's numerous publications. Had Gropius abandoned the school's original socialistic goals? Or was he simply displaying judicious restraint—a tactical retreat, so to speak—in the face of the country's conservative turn and the school's need to find corporate support? Peter Hahn, the director of the Bauhaus Archive in Berlin, has suggested that Gropius's socialistic goals never disappeared; they simply moved underground, a furtive response to changed circumstances. He claims that Gropius shifted the program to "Art and Technology" in 1923, in part to rid the school of its overemphasis on romanticism, as well as to better implement these social ideals.

In contrast to the disinterest that Gropius often displayed with regard to finances and building specifications, he exhibited undeviating tenacity in his social quest. He referred to this as "the longer breadth," and prided himself on his patience in this regard. Ise specifically commented about Gropius's unusual ability to "watch and wait." Although it may seem as though Gropius has abandoned his plans, she wrote, "he [suddenly] pulls the stubborn mule out of the stable." Gropius's vigorous pursuit of Stam and Meyer and his desire to return the school to "its real work" suggest that social usefulness and purpose remained a basic if publicly unacknowledged underpinning of his Bauhaus, a quality the faculty artists, by virtue of their aesthetic orientation, neither realized nor understood.

But this is not to suggest that Gropius was *only* interested in utility. His Bauhaus straddled both usefulness and beauty, however conflicting these ideals may have been. (Beautiful art is not necessarily useful, nor useful art beautiful. In his creation of a work of art an artist—or architect—usually has one or the other criterion in mind.) Gropius always seemed reluctant to come down totally on one side or the other. As late as 1927, for example, one of the Bauhaus's English-language publicity brochures would assert that objects had to serve their purpose well, be "cheap," and also be "beautiful."

Meyer, far more polemical and unswervingly utilitarian than Gropius, did not feel this way at all. He did not even try to mask his contempt for the Bauhaus's sullying of its utilitarian objectives with what he called the school's "aestheticism." In a letter to Gropius in early January 1927, Meyer had criticized the school's "aesthetic bias" as "mere superficialities," citing as an example "the very basic principles" of Breuer's work. In fact Meyer had been disturbed by far more than the absence of strictly utilitarian criteria at the Bauhaus. He had deplored, as well, the school's lack of an undeviating social conscience and the precision, order, and organization demanded by ABC. Aside from its "collectivistic" community and a few elements he called "ripe for development"—such as a steel house built by Muche in 1926 with Richard Paulick, "parts" of Schlemmer's stage works; Kandinsky's and Gropius's basic theories— Meyer had found nothing he particularly liked at the Bauhaus.

Despite his own ambivalence about the virtues of beauty versus usefulness in art, Gropius was anxious to diminish the Bauhaus's aesthetic emphasis about which Meyer complained. He moved quickly to secure the Swiss architect's appointment, informing the faculty of his interest in hiring Meyer at a Masters' Council meeting on January 14, 1927. No one objected, except Kandinsky, whose experience with Bolshevism had sharpened his instincts in such matters. "Too theoretical," Kandinsky had declared about Meyer, pointing also to what he called his "outspoken communistic tendencies." Insisting that Meyer's beliefs were "quite unpolitical," Gropius had dismissed Kandinsky's concerns. Soon Moholy-Nagy—up to now the Bauhaus's preeminent Constructivist and cringing under Meyer's accusation of "romanticism"—had added his opposition to Kandinsky's. But these objections were also brushed aside. After another visit to the school, when he met with members of the faculty, students, and Mayor Hesse, Meyer advised Gropius of his decision to come to the Bauhaus. Ise, desperate to relieve her exhausted and overburdened husband, had commented: "Thank God!"

In mid-February 1927 Gropius asked Hesse to approve the new Bauhaus appointment, enclosing with his letter a curriculum vitae he had asked Meyer to prepare. It was a detailed document that emphasized, among other things, Meyer's broad educational background—studies in various German cities, Belgium, and England—and his interest and experience in communal housing projects in Switzerland and Germany. It noted he had no political affiliation and explained his architectural orientation as collectivist and utilitarian. Although he had emphasized it in the letter to Gropius that had accompanied his curriculum vitae, Meyer made no mention of his ABC affiliation.

Also unmentioned to either Hesse or Gropius, was Meyer's increasingly political turn, which he confided in a letter to the painter Willi Baumeister. He had reached "a turning point" in his life, Meyer had commented, and found himself drifting more and more to the left. Ignorant of this, as well as the Swiss architect's pronouncedly Marxist bent, Hesse approved Meyer's appointment. Meyer also commented to Baumeister that he now believed his "New World" article to be "too mild." Nevertheless, he included a copy of it to the mayor in early March. On April 1, 1927—the day before Hesse commissioned Gropius for Törten II—Meyer arrived in Dessau.

By September 1927 the Törten commission was turning into a debacle. The Labor Minister finally approved the RfG's subsidy for Törten that month, but he did it in a way that rendered it useless. Whether he was influenced by Nonn's articles or by the growing political clout of the building trade unions, the Minister set so high a rate of interest on the grant that the city could not accept it (to do so would have made such housing too expensive for workers). This turn of events shocked and humiliated Gropius, an RfG founding member. With no new work coming into his architectural office, he had also been counting on the Törten commission financially. Politically disarmed two months before the election, Hesse was furious; and despite Hesse and Gropius's continuing appeals, Nonn could neither be removed from his influential position nor silenced. He was free, as Ise commented several days before the Dessau election, to continue to dump his "buckets of dirt on the Bauhaus."

Hesse's opposition, however, no longer needed Nonn's scurrilous support; for Dessau, like the rest of Germany, was once again facing economic crisis. At the City Council meeting on November 4, 1927—the last before the elections—Hesse was forced to acknowledge that the city had no money to rebuild their theater "in the foreseeable future." Within two months fifty thousand workers would be on strike in Anhalt and Saxony, six thousand in Dessau alone, not a few sympathetic Bauhaus students demonstrating with them. Given so catastrophic a situation on the eve of the election, the Bauhaus's costs to the city loomed larger than ever. To deflate this volatile issue Hesse, responding to an anticipated petition by the Property Owners' Party for an accounting of the Bauhaus's construction costs—finally released the figures. He had been able to reduce them to an overrun of 5 percent for the Bauhaus school building and 3 percent for the masters' houses, extra costs he described as "normal."

But given the day's depressed economic state, any overcost was grist for accusations of financial irresponsibility. Opposition to the city's continued support of the supposedly profligate Bauhaus became the focus of the Right's campaign. "Exactly how much does the Bauhaus cost the city?" asked a longtime German People's Party opponent of the Bauhaus, who also wanted to know if these costs included Gropius's architectural fees. As a municipal employee, he argued, Gropius should never have charged the city for his services in the first place. If these buildings—which by now included Törten—had been designed by municipal architects there would have been no fees, he contended. Despite the lack of any objective evidence to prove such a contention, the impression now arose in Dessau that Gropius had become rich on the city's buildings, especially through his earnings from Törten. Ise bitterly attributed the accusation to Peus.

As the election neared, the piercing and often embarrassing questions mounted. What exactly has the Bauhaus achieved? asked several members of the rightist coalition at the City Council meeting on November 4, 1927. Where are their workshops' contracts? How many have they signed and with what industries? How come the city's subsidies have not diminished as the Bauhaus had promised? Why are Bauhaus-designed products better than others and what industries have acknowledged this? Are their products any cheaper than those produced by traditional methods of manufacture? Did the mayor know of the financial accusations that Thuringia had made against the Bauhaus? If he had, why were they ignored? If he had not known about them, why not?

The impact of these ceaseless accusations on the public was as obvious to the Bauhaus as to the mayor himself. "[T]hings are going to be hot for [the mayor]," wrote Schlemmer just before the election. Like everyone else, he foresaw "a swing to the right and bad times for the Bauhaus." So defensive was Hesse about these accusations that he could bring himself to respond to them only a scant thirteen days before the election, doing so not at a public forum but before a friendly meeting of his own German Democratic Party. But Hesse, like his coalition partners, had already conceded the election's loss. What no one anticipated was by how much. The results were devastating. Hesse's DDP lost half its seats on the City Council, falling from four to two. The various coalition parties on the Right gained two seats, going from fifteen up to seventeen; and the Left coalition of the SPD and Communists was reduced from twenty-one to nineteen. As the *Anhalter Anzeiger* triumphed, it was unquestionably "a bourgeois result."

Bitter and blaming the Bauhaus for his party's defeat, Hesse by December 1927 could no longer contain his anger toward Gropius. Ise described Hesse's behavior as "hardly bearable." She wrote, "[Hesse's] relations with the Bauhaus are now very negative. . . . He is taking on an almost impersonal, cold attitude that makes it almost impossible for G. to go on working with him." Gropius realized that Hesse had lost faith in him and would be happy to see him go. This, plus his inability to silence Nonn or move the RfG or the Labor Ministry to release the funds for Törten at a reasonable rate, put Gropius in a grim mood. "[T]hings can't go on this way," he confessed to Schlemmer.

The two young American visitors who arrived on December 4 for a visit, however, noticed none of this. Writing to J. B. Neumann eight days later about the Bauhaus's cordiality, Alfred Barr enthused about the "wonderful time" he had there. Barr and his friend Jere Abbott were long gone from Dessau by January 18, 1928, when the newly rightist-leaning City Council turned its attention once more to Törten. Soon to be known as Dessau's *Schmerzenskinder* (children of misery), Törten had experienced an unanticipated rise in costs. This, plus the appearance of certain difficulties that were coming to light at the housing development—such as frozen pipes due to the defective heating system—led its members to accuse Gropius of "irresponsibility [and professional] failure." They demanded to know who would pay for repairs. Although the Bauhaus had had little to do with Törten, the Right seized the opportunity to censure the school. "The Bauhaus," claimed Deputy Seiss, "has disappointed all expectations and must be acknowledged as a complete flop. I believe that now is the moment to dissolve the institution."

Five days earlier, unknown to the city councilmen, Gropius had privately informed Hesse of his intention to leave the Bauhaus. The hint of legal action, along with Hesse's antagonism, had become too much when added to the years of stress to which he had been subjected. He knew that he could not possibly remain any longer. Only after the RfG and Labor Ministry finally approved Törten's subsidy at more reasonable rates did Gropius, on February 3, 1928, announce his decision to the school. A public announcement was made on February 6, along with the naming of Hannes Meyer as the school's new director.

The Gropius era of the Bauhaus was over. While the school's subsequent directors would all leave their marks on the Bauhaus—refining, extending, or altering Gropius's program—the school would never lose its founder's visionary imprint or the inherent contradictions that similarly marked the man. While the conflicts at the core of the Bauhaus have long been recognized and rightly attributed to many of its time's political, social, and artistic circumstances, the degree to which they mirrored its creator's own internal state has been less acknowledged. Whether or not Gropius was aware of these bipolar forces that characterized his personality (and subsequently the school) is unknown. But he did recognize— indeed, cherish—his ability "to leave everything in suspension, in flux."

This quality could be seen, as could so many of his personal characteristics, both positively and negatively. For one, it produced a vacuum at the Bauhaus's center that some interpreted as a void, an absence that was filled by a group of outstanding artists. Others, such as the artist Josef Albers, saw it as a "serenity" that permitted such diverse artists as Kandinsky and Klee to pursue their own ways without paying attention to what anyone else was doing. The weaver Anni Albers, Josef's wife and a former Bauhaus student herself, was even more emphatic. Referring to it as a "creative vacuum," she considered it to be Gropius's greatest contribution, responsible for the "richness of invention" that came out of the Bauhaus. Other contradictory aspects of Gropius's personality were similarly reflected at the Bauhaus and produced as many admirers as detractors.

He was both an autocrat (as shown by his intransigence with regard to the craft masters' voting rights) and a tolerant democrat who hesitated to impose his views on others. He could be maddeningly passive when vigorous action was demanded, and near manically combative when cool-headedness would have been preferred. He professed himself a rationalist, and indeed his Bauhaus has been remembered as the apotheosis of modernism's purported rationality. But in practice Gropius seemed to have had little faith in reason, ascribing his moments of success to his iron "will power," rather than to sound and superior argument. He also rarely acknowledged rationality in the views of those with whom he disagreed. It is difficult to discover anyone who opposed Gropius's ideas whose arguments he recognized.

In fact the quality that probably marked him more than any other was his verve. Gropius, who once described himself as "a shooting star," was a truly driven man. He perpetually oscillated between passion and lucidity, tumult and order, verbosity and conciseness. Happiest when he was "weaving together a thousand threads," Gropius could hardly stay quiet for a second. When he did slow down he often fell into dark despair.

Never once over the course of his nine-year directorship of the Bauhaus did Gropius doubt his cause's worth. He saw himself, as he once put it, "standing on the front line fighting for truth." This conviction imbued in him an imperturbable sense of righteousness and near-messianic fervor. It turned those who opposed him into false idols whose arguments he could simply dismiss. It also allowed him the mesmerizing assurance to "stand above" careful analysis, professional rigor, the school's perpetually disorganized state, and reality's constraints to keep the Bauhaus going in the midst of often unimaginably adverse circumstances. These dual and contradictory aspects of Gropius's personality resulted in a complex and turbulent Bauhaus. While Gropius's passionate commitment undoubtedly fueled much of the Bauhaus's achievements, his need for confrontation and for proving himself by surmounting obstacles burdened it as well.

Part of Gropius's ambivalence stemmed from political and social circumstances. He was undoubtedly a rebel, but he was also a Wilhelminian. He had spent the first thirty-five years of his life under the reign of Kaiser Wilhelm II. Gropius was already thirty-one years old in 1914 when he went off to serve in the First World War, an experience that would push him, like so many of his contemporaries, to severely rebel against the mores of his youth. Out of this questioning he had founded the Bauhaus. But Gropius could never entirely shed the past's values and points of view (such as the quest for unity, or the certainty of a singular "Truth"), and although he unequivocally looked ahead and sought to defy the authoritarian mindset, he did so through the idealistic and moralistic lens of his Wilhelminian past.

Gropius's uncanny ability to simultaneously straddle these two worlds with equal conviction led one family member to speak of his "peculiar [ability] to walk along the edge between the past and the future." He was truly, as the architectural historian Julius Posener once remarked, a "man in the middle," with one foot forward and the other facing backward. The quandary posed by trying to challenge the past while continuing its principles and prejudices would haunt Gropius and the Bauhaus, as it would their times.

Yet however conflicting and problematical Gropius's sense of social purpose and yearning for wholeness may have been, or however much his personal propensities may have caused the school to occasionally over-reach and expose itself to all sorts of charges, he ignited the Bauhaus with a questing spirit that would remain the school's ultimate legacy and assure it a unique place in the history of its time.

Subsequently, under Meyer the Bauhaus would seriously try to mend the breach between its head and its heart, between its longing for spiritual unity and its need to eat. Meyer would align the school's curriculum with its aims and produce models for industry. For the first time in its history the Bauhaus would even make some money. Meyer would get both Mart Stam and Hans Wittwer to teach at the Bauhaus one week each month. He even managed to keep its name out of the newspapers, a not inconsiderable achievement given the school's history. But it would be too little too late. For by the time Meyer got the Bauhaus in order, the Depression had begun and he, like Germany, was searching for more radical solutions.

14. | **Triumph of the Right**

All dangerous precedents originate in good causes.

—*Julius Caesar, according to Sallust*

In early 1929, unemployment in Dessau soared and the city's workers, intensifying their massive strikes and demonstrations of the year before, took to the streets in protest. Similar actions were taking place throughout the country. The government, once again seeing these activities as an omen of revolutionary mayhem, applied increasingly repressive measures against the mounting insurrection. They banned Communist organizations, such as the newspaper *Die Rote Fahne* and the Red Front Line Soldiers' Union, and jailed many left-wing journalists. Workers, outraged by the government's antilabor bias and deteriorating economic conditions, confronted the police with mounting violence. On May 1 a particularly brutal confrontation in Berlin between the police and demonstrating workers left more than forty people dead. At a rally held five days later in front of

Dessau's City Hall, State Assemblyman Paul Kmiec—a Communist Party representative and committed supporter of the Bauhaus in Dessau's City Council—accused the Social Democratic government of "murdering" workers. By July the number of jobless workers in Dessau had soared ominously and so too did street demonstrations, in scenes that were repeated around the country. Such was Germany *before* October 28, 1929, when the New York stock market crashed and the Depression officially began.

The government's ban succeeded in preventing public gatherings of the more militant leftist groups, but it could not suppress all demonstrations. Toward the end of 1929 Dessau's workers and Communists would again march through the town, carrying huge red signs that declared "Down with fascism!" and "Only civil war can defeat imperialism." Joining the singing and holding banners, as they had done in workers' demonstrations the year before, would be Bauhaus students—up to 60 percent of the student population, it has been estimated—of which not a few were members of the school's Communist cell.

The Bauhaus's first Communist cell had been set up in the summer of 1927. However, the school had long harbored radical leftist students. Indeed, their sentiments had predominated the Weimar Bauhaus. A portrait of Lenin hanging on the wall is clearly visible in a photograph taken of a student celebration of Gropius's birthday in 1924. But active political participation seems to have been disorganized and negligible. Only nine students (out of a total enrollment in Weimar of six hundred) appear to have belonged to the local Communist Party. The move to Dessau in 1925 disrupted whatever political activity had existed within the Bauhaus. But once settled into their new home, the students' political sentiments were riled up by the growing distress of Dessau's unemployed, and by 1926 radical leftist leanings reemerged in force. This, plus the contacts made with local workers' organizations and the German Communist Party (the KPD), had moved Kandinsky to complain to Mayor Hesse in November of that year about Bolshevism infiltrating the school.

The Bauhaus's first KPD cell—soon to be known as kostufra (*kommunistische Studentenfraktion*)—was organized in July 1927 by the student Bela Scheffler, with the help of Dessau's Communist Party. The group's initial activities—collecting signatures to protest the conviction of Sacco and Vanzetti in the United States, seeking donations of clothes and money for striking coal workers, and enrolling members in workers' assistance organizations—had been innocuous enough. But aided by the skilled support of the local Communist organization, the Bauhaus cell soon emerged into a highly organized and efficient unit whose open, aggressive, and uninhibited proselytizing among the students gave it a profile and influence that far exceeded its numbers. So emboldened had the group become by January 1928 that its student representatives felt free to demand the establishment of an acknowledged cell within the school, which was refused.

In 1928, under the leadership of Albert Burke, the Bauhaus Communist cell had fifteen members, approximately 10 percent of the student body. About a quarter of the students did not belong but supported the cell's activities. Instructed and sustained by the local KPD organization, the Bauhaus students' group—now the strongest and best organized in the school—had the full status of an operating Communist cell.

A series of interviews published in a 1928 edition of *Bauhaus*, a school journal that Meyer used to "propagandize" the school's aims, reveal the students' increasing politicization. The radical leftist sentiments, however, of the journal's editor Ernst Kállai should be kept in mind in interpreting interviews that he himself conducted, edited, and published. In one of these interviews student Max Bill, for example, praised technology for its liberating potential but condemned its use by capitalism to subjugate people. In response to the question of why she had chosen to study at the Bauhaus, Lotte Burckhardt replied that it was the school's interest in "the lack of public housing and social conditions on the whole" that had drawn her there. While she asserted that no one came to the Bauhaus for political reasons, she did insist that concern about housing and social conditions necessarily involved politics. "We cannot build houses based on conditions that do not exist. But proper social conditions do not just happen on their own. Work and quality of life must go hand in hand."

The Bauhaus Communists and their sympathizers did not confine their activities to the school. They participated in all the workers' actions in Dessau, including the May 1, 1929, celebrations there; some were even present at the deadly battle that took place that day in Berlin. Along with most of the student body the Bauhaus Communists commemorated the anniversaries of the October and November revolutions in the Soviet Union and Germany, respectively; the Knapp Putsch; the Fallen Workers of March; and the deaths of Liebknecht and Luxemburg. Since the students' political instruction could not take place "officially" within the Bauhaus, kostufra operated covertly. Meetings and guest lectures by such visiting Marxist scholars as Herrmann Duncker usually took place outside the school's premises. An architectural teacher from the Soviet Union, Professor Ludwig, spoke at Hannes Meyer's home. Announcements of these lectures did not appear in the school's journal *Bauhaus*, the normal vehicle for such events.

The students' radical political sentiments often infiltrated their work. This too was surreptitious and executed outside the school. Two Communist students, Philipp Tolziner and Tibor Weiner, for example, intrigued by how people would live in a socialist society, worked on an experimental project in 1929, titled "Living in Socialism," in Tolziner's apartment. Ludwig Hilberseimer, whom Meyer had brought to the Bauhaus in the spring of 1929 to teach architecture, admired their project and suggested having it published in an architectural journal, but only if all references to socialism were eliminated. The two young radicals, as Tolziner later wrote, "of course" refused.

While Gropius had insisted that no political activity take place within the Bauhaus, he had remained as laissez-faire about what students did off-campus as he had been about their class attendance and course requirements. He personally never endorsed the harsh precepts of Bolshevism. But in this, as in so many other areas, he was a "man in the middle." Bolshevism's general condemnation of capitalism's injustices, its advocacy of collectivity, utility, and the need for social change had struck a sympathetic chord in Gropius. Gropius's "Red" sympathies—expressed most overtly in the version of the Bauhaus Manifesto that had appeared in the socialist press, in his participation in the AfK and in his attempt to bring in such Marxist-oriented architects as Stam and Meyer—never entirely disappeared, however much circumstances may have inhibited their expression.

In 1921 Gropius had invited the painter Heinrich Vogeler, a fellow AfK participant and an early member of the Communist Party, to lecture at the Bauhaus. Concern, however, about community reaction had made him subsequently rescind the invitation. Five years later Gropius's surprisingly meek response to Kandinsky's complaints about Bolshevik activity within the Bauhaus also suggested a certain ambivalence. Meeting with a student representative of kostufra in response to Kandinsky's charge, Gropius did not insist that the group stop its activities, as one normally might have expected. Instead he merely asked its members not to take "advantage of his own obliging attitude." But what Gropius had tolerated, Meyer encouraged; and it was the new director's well-recognized support, along with the developing economic crisis, that helped sway many Bauhaus students to embrace Bolshevism's aims. For them, kostufra did not so much mark a change in the Bauhaus's longtime social commitment as its fulfillment.

Gropius's social compassion had been tempered by his equal commitment to the search for an underlying aesthetic unity. A Bauhaus product, under Gropius, had to be beautiful and "typical," as well as useful. Meyer, however, harbored no such dualism. In this of course Meyer was deluding himself. The Bauhaus products under his directorship were as beautiful as they were useful. Meyer simply refused to acknowledge that aesthetic considerations impinged on his utilitarian canon; he sternly insisted that art should only concern itself with society's organization and needs. As Meyer put it, "[e]very [artistic] creation must acknowledge life." As an art school then, the Bauhaus in his eyes was essentially a social enterprise whose goal was to create "a harmonious form of society." Above all Meyer insisted that the artist had to serve the people. "We strive," he wrote in 1929, "to consider people's lives as much as possible,"

> to gain the greatest possible insight into people's souls,
> the greatest possible understanding of people's organization.
> as creators
> we must serve this people's organization.

With this view in mind Meyer, in January 1928—while Gropius was still there and with his approval—had begun to refocus the Bauhaus's artistic training toward the study of man's needs, how they were expressed and how society should accommodate them in order to be able to artistically respond to them. Thus to the study of design principles Meyer added sociology, psychology, and economics. Thanks to his rigorous analysis the Bauhaus curriculum began to assume a coherence and consistency it had never known before. Under his leadership the Bauhaus changed essentially into a school of architecture—that most practical of arts—and industrial design, where its repute would ultimately remain. In addition to the changed courses, the artistic faculty was required to teach regularly and more frequently.

Meyer's changes were most evident in the reorganized workshops. Here Gropius's search for an object's singular "valid" nature was put aside; students now learned how to cut product costs and develop models that suited industrial production as well as meet "the needs of the . . . proletariat." "Popular necessities before elitist luxuries" became the workshop motto. In 1928, with the workshops geared to such pragmatic concerns as cost analysis and adaptation to mechanical processes, industry started to take notice of their products and work with them to develop their special interests. This, of course, was what Gropius had always wanted. But Gropius had straddled the fence between aesthetics and practicality, constrained as much by his own inclinations as by those of the artist members of the faculty. The workshops under his directorship had never been able to devote themselves entirely to industry's purely practical interests. Meyer's workshops realized what Gropius had always intended. Among other commissions, lucrative contracts were negotiated for inexpensive plywood and laminated wood furniture, standardized lamps, wallpapers, carpets, exhibition designs, and advertising. Even Dessau's newly rightist City Council, as hostile as ever toward the school, could find little to complain about. To Hesse's relief, Meyer, who had arrived at the Bauhaus "as good as unknown" to members of the City Council, remained that way, and for the first time in its turbulent history the school's opponents were quiet.

But Meyer's tighter focus on practicalities and his fixation on utility and social purpose—which he referred to as "productive pedagogy"—exposed one of the Bauhaus's long-standing fault lines, most notably the painters' irrelevance to industrial production, which they had felt since the 1923 adoption of the new technological line. Even Gropius had recognized this when he considered purging them from the school in 1927. But Meyer, more extreme in his ideology than Gropius and also more unbending in his implementation of it, did not hesitate to openly question the artistic faculty's relevance to his program. After all, what had Klee, Kandinsky, Feininger, and Schlemmer to do with easing workers' lives or designing cheap lamps? Indeed, what did any studio art or easel painting have to do with this? Under Gropius this dilemma had provoked endless bickering, pedagogical incoherence, and artistic disgruntlement. Under Meyer it turned into open warfare.

The boundless and genuine sensitivity that Meyer displayed throughout his life for the socially deprived—indeed for mankind *in general*—was nowhere evident in his relations with individuals. On a personal level he displayed the delicacy of a hammer, behaving often thoughtlessly and with cruel indifference. He was, as Konrad Püschel (a Bauhaus student and Meyer enthusiast) described him, "a personality of extremes." Meyer thought nothing about ridiculing those with whom he disagreed. His relentless derision of the artists began with his first visit to the school in December 1926 and never stopped. Shortly after arriving at the Bauhaus Meyer had referred to Klee as being "in a perpetual trance." Kandinsky soon joined his pantheon of ridicule, bringing Ise to characterize Meyer's attitude toward these two artists as "astonishing." Meyer could not understand what they were doing at the school and bluntly said so. But his most brutal comments had been reserved for Gropius, whose artistically biased Bauhaus Meyer had lambasted in 1928 for being "trapped in formalism." A bitterly mocking poem appeared in 1929.

> *We search for*
> *no bauhaus style and no bauhaus fashion*
> *no stylish simplicity or superficial ornament*
> *plays of horizontal or vertical and neoplastic pap.*
> *we search for*
> *no geometric or stereometric forms,*
> *distant from life and devoid of function.*
> *we are not in timbuktu:*
> *ritual and hierarchy*
> *do not dictate our creation.*
>
> *We despise every form*
> *which prostitutes itself in becoming formula.*
> *. . . The new [Bauhaus]*
> *. . . is not concerned with talented elite.*
> *It despises ape-like spiritual agility as talent,*
> *. . . the danger of the sect:*
> *inbreeding, egocentrism, unworldliness [and]*
> *ignorance of life.*

Rigid, tactless, and unrestrained, Meyer had not been the artists' choice to succeed Gropius as the Bauhaus's director. Klee and the painter Hinnerk Scheper, both of whom objected to Meyer's dogmatic and inflexible manner, had opposed him. So had the artist Joost Schmidt. Moholy-Nagy, no longer able to stand being under the same roof as Meyer, resigned from the Bauhaus when Gropius did. Albers thought Meyer was belligerent and inflexible, while one of the Bauhaus students characterized

Meyer's appointment as catastrophic and worried that it would precipitate the school's downfall.

So obviously unwanted by their new director, the artists almost longed for the good old days of Gropius's "honest indifference" toward them. "The painters are merely tolerated as a necessary evil now," Schlemmer wrote. Meyer's hostility toward abstract art (because workers could not understand it) further antagonized the artists. The battle between Meyer and the artists emerged into the open in 1929, when Ernst Kállai attacked the artistic *Vorkurs* taught by Klee, Albers, and Kandinsky as useless and mere compensation for their artistic neuroses.

Meyer's increasing politicization, which he also made no effort to conceal, further aggravated the artists. Kandinsky had recognized Meyer's political leaning early on, but others came to see it as well. In November 1927 Breuer, complaining to Gropius about Meyer's taste for political polemic within the Bauhaus's courses, questioned its appropriateness in a school that was not "planning to establish a new world order."

Other faculty members also felt Meyer's political sting. When his theatrical productions were condemned as "irrelevant, formalistic, [and] too personal," Schlemmer, in charge of the Bauhaus Theater, replied that political productions belonged in Russia and refused to politicize the school's theater. "Don't ask me to draw like George Grosz or do [theater] like Piscator," he said, referring to two well-known leftist cultural figures. Unable to budge Schlemmer, the students—with Meyer's support—had set up a second Bauhaus theatrical group in 1928 to put on Soviet-inspired "collective" productions, one of which Schlemmer described the following year. The subject of the student production, Schlemmer wrote, was "a soviet republic of the Bauhaus," whose masters, known as "capitalistic kings . . . [are] deposed and stripped of their privileges." Apart from annoying the faculty, Meyer's ideological priorities increasingly permeated the Bauhaus curriculum. In his 1929 diatribe against the *Vorkurs* Kállai suggested that "serious" students should instead study "historical theories on a materialistic social basis."

Finding their situation intolerable, the artists began to leave in earnest in 1928. After Moholy-Nagy, Breuer and the graphic artist Herbert Bayer also left that year. Schlemmer departed in October 1929. In early 1930 so would Feininger and Klee. Of the Bauhaus's artistic faculty only Kandinsky and the painter and young master Josef Albers remained. With Kállai's indictment ringing in their ears, they too realized that their days were numbered. But what could they do about it? Burdened as he was with Dessau's crushing social problems, Mayor Hesse could hardly be expected to sympathize with their complaints. After the harrowing financial turmoil of the Gropius years, Hesse was pleased with the financial stability that Meyer had brought to the school, which—for the moment— had managed to quiet the Right's complaints. After all, Meyer was the Bauhaus's director, and he would surely not tolerate political interference with what were clearly his rightful prerogatives. Albers and Kandinsky realized it was not they who had to be eliminated from the Bauhaus, but Meyer himself.

The growth of political extremism at the Bauhaus between 1929 and 1930 reflected more than Meyer's intensifying political convictions. It mirrored the country's disenchanted mood that was bloating the membership rolls of extremist parties, Right and Left. For nearly ten years, since the founding of the Republic, Germany had lurched—almost absurdly—from socialist republic one day to industrial and military autocracy the next. An increasing number of Germans, believing that republican democracy had been foisted on them unwillingly by a victorious and much despised Entente, were coming to reject representative government. Compromise was neither recognized nor respected; and without compromise, democracy's unaccustomed and frequently resented machinery could not work properly. The Republic, its economic capabilities burdened by the harsh reparation payments, functioned perpetually on failure's edge. To people's fear that the whole system did not work—loudly nurtured by the Communists and Nazis alike—was now added economic collapse. Only in utopian schemes like those of Gropius and Meyer—and Hitler—could Germans imagine a functioning, much less optimistic, future.

Driven by economic misfortune, Germany's shift toward radicalism gathered speed in 1929, the intensifying economic hardships heightening the extremists' appeal. They fared poorly in the early part of the year; by year's end, however, and into early 1930 they achieved impressive gains. At a gathering in Dessau in March 1929 a Nazi speaker mercilessly condemned Germany's political system and announced the imminent arrival of a "savior" who would bring back civic order and eradicate unemployment in Germany, as Mussolini had done in Italy. By the end of his speech the hall was empty and a planned discussion had to be canceled. Six months later, however, the same message brought the Nazis 11.3 percent of Thuringia's vote for the State Assembly. The result not only gained the NSDAP the opportunity to be represented in a state government for the first time in Germany, but granted unheard-of legitimacy and notice to a party that till then had been considered maverick.

The KPD experienced a similar surge. It too found scant public support for its calls for mass demonstrations in 1929. An action planned for August 1 produced embarrassingly poor turnouts; a subsequent one in Dessau on August 4 had to be canceled. Yet by March 1930, with nearly three million unemployed—almost five hundred thousand in Berlin alone—the KPD began to attract an increasingly large audience.

Vitalized by the country's social unrest in early 1930, the radical Right and Left pursued their activities with renewed assertiveness. As one Bauhaus student put it, "[T]he moment had come to move beyond intellectual dalliance or mere sympathy. It was time to act." His words had a particular urgency considering that Thuringia, Anhalt's neighbor and the Bauhaus's initial site, had just installed the nation's first Nazi government. On January 23, 1930, with the NSDAP's proportion of the vote entitling it to two ministries within Thuringia's new government, Wilhelm Frick, the party's local head, took both appointments for himself, the Ministries of the Interior, which controlled the state police, and Education. Frick announced that he intended to show the nation what the Nazis meant by moral and spiritual renewal.

This radicalist surge was reflected in the Bauhaus, where the school's Communists began to openly assert themselves. Meetings that had earlier taken place surreptitiously outside the school now gathered within. While not every Bauhaus student belonged to the thirty-six-member KPD cell, the majority of students endorsed Meyer's increasingly radicalized aims. Still supported by Dessau's local Communist Party, the Bauhaus's Communist cell (kostufra) emerged solidly as the school's most decisive and intellectually dominant internal group. Despite its relatively small membership, kostufra organized the students' political education; controlled the management of the student canteen; supported candidates' applications, especially those from working-class families; collected funds to help support them; canvassed all new students for party membership; and helped to further radicalize most of the Bauhaus's student body as well as its director, Meyer. Some kostufra members participated in the Dessau KPD's militant activities, including those of the banned Red Front Line Soldiers' Union.

Few Bauhaus students could remain aloof from politics. They felt isolated from the majority who followed kostufra's lead, and as a result often found it easier and more socially acceptable to simply follow the Marxist line. Reflecting the country's newly urgent mood, Meyer in early January 1930 moved to aggressively reformulate the curriculum for the coming winter term. One of his planned revisions, as Kállai had suggested some months before, was to eliminate the painters.

On March 1, 1930, at the Bauhaus's Carnival Party, Kandinsky and Albers found the opportunity to do something about their increasingly tenuous situation. Of all the school's activities, the Bauhaus's famed parties had achieved unanimous and nearly legendary acclaim. For a few exuberant hours the Bauhäusler forgot their usual bickering; their uninhibited antics, imaginative decor, and costumes enchanted guests both of Right and Left. The March affair was no exception. Three bands played, including the Bauhaus's own; fabulous costumes and drinks abounded, and students entertained by dancing, singing, and every now and then acrobatically flipping about the room. A carousel set up on the stage of the lecture hall was much in demand. By eight o'clock the school's beautifully decorated rooms were filled. Guests included Anhalt's President Deist and other members of the state and local governments, as well as Mayor Hesse. Normally surly in its coverage of Bauhaus activities, even the *Anhalter Anzeiger* commented about the evening's convivial spirit.

The student canteen downstairs—transformed for the evening into a beer cellar—was kostufra's domain. There spirits were even higher, and festivities continued until the early hours of the morning. Around midnight a group of boozy students gathered around the bar to sing, Polish lullabies first, then "The Internationale." Emotions soon got carried away. Raising their beer steins, the students cheered the Soviet Union and "our German comrades!" Guests watched in dismay. Not only did the incident sour an otherwise splendid evening, but it provided the local newspapers with eye-catching headlines. "Soviet Hammer-and-Sickle over Dessau," blared the *Anhalter Anzeiger*.

Kandinsky, who had continued to express his concern to Hesse and Grote about the school's increasingly "Red" tone, was aware of their fears of a Bolshevist Bauhaus. This Carnival incident—blown up for all it was worth by Dessau's anti-Bauhaus newspapers—confirmed his allegations. Supported by Albers, Kandinsky complained to Grote that Meyer was doing nothing to stop these radically leftist students from propagandizing within the school. Grote, alarmed by Kandinsky's charge and the press coverage, conveyed the accusations to Hesse.

Hesse was surprised. His feelings toward Meyer were essentially positive. He was grateful to Meyer for his quiet stewardship and successful financial management of the school, which allowed him to attend to Dessau's pressing social and economic problems. Convinced that Meyer was "in no way politically engaged," Hesse disagreed with Grote's and the faculty's misgivings. But his colleague's disclosure did make him recall Meyer's having recently asked him if Communists would be allowed to study at the Bauhaus. At the time, Hesse had attributed the question to the Swiss architect's unfamiliarity with German politics. Hesse, expressing the Bauhaus's and Dessau's long-standing liberal traditions, had replied that the students' political opinions were their own private concern, as long as they refrained from political activity at school. But aside from this, Hesse had no reason to quarrel with the Bauhaus director. The mayor was in no mood to ruffle the Right's relative quiescence, and he doubted neither Meyer's loyalty nor his ability to maintain control of the school.

Nonetheless, Hesse did meet with Meyer to convey his associate's complaints. Meyer admitted that what Grote had said was "in some measure, true." But he claimed he was as anxious as anyone to avoid the dangers of politicization, which he agreed would disturb the Bauhaus's work. The two men decided to post an announcement to Bauhaus students warning them that political activity within the school was forbidden. Meyer's banning of the Bauhaus's Communist cell and expulsion of several of its leaders reaffirmed Hesse's confidence in him and throttled Kandinsky's and Albers's plans.

Meyer's relationship with the Bauhaus had never been marked by candor, however. Neither Gropius nor Meyer had been completely forthright in their disclosures to the city administration, nor had Meyer told the Bauhaus director about his increasing politicization. This pattern of deception continued. Dessau's officials knew nothing of Kandinsky's and Albers's real reasons for trying to get rid of Meyer, who himself was acting furtively. Contrary to what Hesse believed, Meyer did not ban the Communist cell. He informed kostufra's leaders of the mayor's demands, and *they* decided to dismantle the group. They replaced it with various Marxist "working teams," which the director allowed. The expelled Bauhaus students remained in Dessau and continued their activities at the Bauhaus through the local KPD.

The temptation to act surreptitiously, to disguise and try to save one's own interests even if they ran counter to those of the majority, permeated the Bauhaus as it did the politics of the Weimar Republic at this time. Eleven years after their founding, both the Weimar Republic and the Bauhaus lacked any firm sense of communality. They remained disgruntled conglomerations of antagonistic interests: labor against industry; the military (along with the president) against the republicans; the architects (Gropius and even more so Meyer) against the artists. Dissatisfied, suspicious, and resentful of others' aims, none were willing to compromise or sublimate their own claims to a greater good. Just as Kandinsky and Albers sought to save the Bauhaus for their interests, so too were Hindenburg, the Communists, and the Nazis—their objectives couched in mutually contradictory guises of salvation—working to *save* Germany for theirs.

On April 1, 1930, the Thuringian State Assembly passed Frick's Ordinance Against Negro Culture and Germany learned what the Nazis meant by cultural salvation. Modern art and architecture was defined as "Negro culture," a racist program that Frick backed with several appointments. Hans F. K. Günther, the author of a 1926 book, *Race and Style*, that racially linked architecture and style, was appointed to a professorship at Jena over the objections of university officials. To head the Bauhaus's successor arts institution in Weimar (from which Otto Bartning was ousted), Frick appointed Paul Schultze-Naumburg, a native Weimar architect and the author of various racist architectural tracts. For the first time Thuringia and Germany realized that for the Nazis—as a building trade journal put it—flat roofs equaled flat heads.

One month later, on May 1, 1930, the Bauhaus Communists unveiled their program in a newsletter titled *Simple and Joyful*, published by the school's banned Communist students and printed in the offices of Dessau's KPD. Addressed to the students, the pamphlet declared "open warfare" on those who sought to "apply the beautiful pure Bolshevist Bauhaus idea to the . . . rotten bourgeoisie." In a notably belligerent tone, it asserted that the aestheticism advocated by the artistic masters (i.e., Kandinsky and Albers) was "training [the students] not to serve human progress, but to be bourgeois" and was turning the Bauhaus into

a barracks in which the bourgeoisie drills its cadres to suppress the masses, prepare for new wars, ideologically defend its exploitative [policies], and [in general] dress up its parasitic existence . . . in order to make "creative individuals" . . . who will serve the bourgeoisie and provide them with . . . clever, piquant [and] refined . . . Bauhaus originalities . . . in the cultivation of a reactionary Bauhaus spirit.

"Comrades!" the pamphlet continued, "there is no common Bauhaus idea linking you and the Masters' Council."

We take from the Bauhaus what is useful for our lives and our struggle, and we conduct a ferocious battle . . . side by side with the revolutionary proletariat. On which side of the barricades do you stand?

The Right's reaction to the publication was swift. Writing in a local newspaper, one outraged Dessau citizen referred to the Bauhaus as "Bolshevikia," whose warnings from Weimar the city had ignored. "It is Herr Hesse," the writer declared, "who is really responsible for Dessau's takeover of the Bauhaus, and it is he who will have to bear its political repercussions." The Bauhaus Communist cell, he went on, not only obviously continued to exist despite the ban, but it was pursuing the Bolshevik cause "more energetically than ever. . . . In view of the fact that the Bauhaus costs the city of Dessau hundreds of thousands [of marks] . . . are we not justified in asking how the mayor, the school's director, and the Masters' Council intend to end this situation?"

Anhalt's Educational Minister, Professor Blum—one of the school's initial enthusiasts and main supporters—now added his concern about the Communist activity within the Bauhaus to that of Kandinsky, Albers, and Grote. Gropius was following these troubling events from Berlin. On May 5, 1930, Hesse again met with Meyer, this time in the presence of Grote and Anhalt Minister Blum. In response to their questions, Meyer admitted his commitment to "philosophical Marxism." He acknowledged its unavoidable influence on his leadership of the Bauhaus but again asserted his appreciation of the need to keep politics out of the Bauhaus. Nobody, he declared, could stop him from teaching "a Marxist theory of design." Dr. Blum accepted this. Grote did not. Accusing Meyer of being a Communist, he told the Bauhaus leader that he was compromising them all.

Hesse felt terribly let down by Meyer's admission. No longer caring about the difference between *Kultur* and *Partei* politics, between a Bolshevist and a philosophical Marxist, Hesse explained to Meyer that the SPD—the school's core support—would "never tolerate a Communist-led Bauhaus." Hesse still believed that Meyer occupied a "certain high moral ground," and he hoped that the Bauhaus director—like Gropius—would recognize the impossibility of his position and resign. Meyer, however, refused, a decision that put Hesse in a real bind. According to the terms of Meyer's agreement with Dessau, his contract was automatically renewed after April 1, 1930, unless the city notified him to the contrary by October 1, 1929, "at the latest." To terminate his contract after April 1 required six months' notice. Gropius, however, was urging them not to dismiss Meyer until a replacement could be found. Hesse had no recourse but to ignore the terms of the contract and wait. Once again, the saving of the Bauhaus was postponed. But events taking place in Berlin would force Hesse's hand.

There President Hindenburg was working to correct what he similarly considered to be an untenable situation, namely the inability of the SPD-dominated Reichstag to come to terms with the rightist parties on a variety of issues, from the control of soaring unemployment to a painfully renegotiated reparations agreement known as the Young Plan that would remove foreign troops from the Rhineland. Thwarted by what he saw as an obstructionist Reichstag, President Hindenburg had initiated a covert and complex scheme to override it. He had long been doing this through emergency decrees. But such a strategy was risky in that it could be overruled by a majority vote of the Reichstag. Unwilling to compromise with the SPD, and disregarding the principles of proportional party representation within the cabinet that was the backbone of parliamentary democracy, Hindenburg and the group of mostly military men around him worked out a plan in 1929 to set up a presidentially appointed governmental cabinet of rightist inclination (without including the majority SPD), known as the Presidential Cabinet.

When on March 12, 1930, the Reichstag ratified the Young Plan, which the President and the Right had adamantly opposed, Hindenburg moved to put his scheme into effect. He forced the resignation of Chancellor Müller's government, and over the objections of the majority SPD then called upon the Center Party's Heinrich Brüning, who had previously agreed to Hindenburg's antidemocratic plan, to form a new government.

With this clandestine plan in mind, Chancellor Brüning on April 1 warned the Reichstag that he would dissolve the legislature and demand new elections if it did not pass his program for fiscal reform as submitted, without modifications or amendments. The Reichstag members, who received his program's initial installments in June, ignored his threat.

The higher taxes and lowered benefits proposed by Brüning's program agitated the middle class and the workers alike, and as unemployment soared, so too did civil unrest. On Sunday, June 15, 1930, seven days before local Saxon elections, Nazi and Communist election rallies in the town of Eythra, near Leipzig, ended up in a brawl that left three dead and many injured. Similar clashes took place in Berlin, Cologne, Mannheim, Magdeburg, and in the Mansfeld region, where coal workers were waging a desperate strike. "Fratricidal War" headlined one newspaper, its words reflecting the country's growing apprehension over the prospect of Germans once again firing at their fellow countrymen. In the Saxon elections for State Assembly on June 22, 1930, the Nazis repeated their Thuringian electoral victory. Benefiting from the country's increasing fears of chaos and opposition to the Young Plan, they gained an astonishing 14.4 percent of the vote and were now Saxony's strongest party after the SPD.

The Nazis' gathering strength hardened the resolve of the Communists, who were themselves—to a lesser degree—benefiting from the increasing social unrest. Claiming they had to defend themselves against intensifying Nazi attacks, the Berlin KPD called on all workers—employed or jobless, regardless of party affiliation—to create Red factory defense forces. The Right interpreted this as little more than a subterfuge to re-create the banned and fearsome Red Front Line Soldiers' Union.

The intensification of the Communists' actions were reflected within the Bauhaus. Despite the ban on political activities, students participated in various strikes—of coal miners in Mansfeld and Rheinland-Westphalia, and of metal workers in Berlin. They also solicited donations for the International Workers' Aid Society (Internationale Arbeiterhilfe, the IAH), a fund established to aid the distressed families of striking workers. A student delegation traveled to Waldenburg in Silesia, where they handed over the school's collection of money and clothes to the hard-pressed strikers. Albers, who was still trying to mount a case against Meyer, kept tabs on these activities and conveyed his findings to Grote. "[Fritz] Kuhr is the leader of a Marxist work team, of which we already have three," he wrote on June 20, 1930. "The second is led by [Natan] Borowski."

On July 5 the leftist *Magdeburger Tribüne* reported that Bauhaus students had contributed funds to striking coal miners, and its account was picked up by the *Anhalter Anzeiger* three days later. On July 14 the latter newspaper subsequently reported an additional Bauhaus contribution of 155 marks, of which Meyer was purported to have contributed 50 marks. Despite the report's buttressing of the case that the city was trying to make against Meyer's politicization of the school, the effort to dismiss him was stymied by an inability to find a successor. In Berlin Gropius was conducting an urgent search.

Considering Meyer's reference to the former director's Bauhaus as "egocentric, inbred, and elitist" the year before, Gropius could not have found this task to be particularly onerous. His initial choice to head the school, whom he had suggested in May—Otto Haesler, an architect from Celle—had turned down Grote's offer. In early July Grote had suggested that Gropius come back. But Gropius was not interested in returning to the helm. As the search went on, events in Berlin imposed a new urgency on the Bauhaus situation.

On July 16, 1930, the Reichstag ignored Brüning's threats and turned down his program for fiscal reform. The government responded by decreeing the rejected proposal into law. At the SPD's insistence the Reichstag subsequently voted to nullify the law in a majority vote that astonishingly brought together the Social Democrats, Communists, most of the German National People's Party, and the Nazis. Brüning, who had planned his unconstitutional action all along, now dissolved the Reichstag. He reissued the invalidated decree in a more drastic form, and in the face of mounting social strife—unemployment was soaring toward three million—and indisputable evidence of increasing Nazi electoral appeal, he ordered a new Reichstag election for September 14, 1930.

Blamed by Right and Left extremists alike for the country's wretched state of affairs, the SPD could not have faced a national election at a more vulnerable moment. The recent electoral gains of the Nazis and Communists had come out of their increasingly disgruntled and diminishing constituency. To the Nazis—and to an increasing number of Germans in general—the SPD represented little more than the KPD's "pale Red brother." As usual, what they feared most of all was the formation of a united revolutionary front between the SPD and the Communists.

An SPD conference held in Württemberg revealed their concern to be real. To more effectively combat the fascist surge, the SPD urged its worker supporters to "[r]each out fraternally to Communist workers" and create a united front. The sudden calling in mid-July 1930 for elections within two months heightened these fears of a unified Left. In Dessau these fears focused on the Bauhaus and its much publicized Communist activities. What boded even worse for Hesse and the school's SPD supporters was the Social Democrats' apparent toleration of them.

"It seems strange," wrote Wilhelm Karius, a rightist member of Dessau's City Council, "that the mayor has only just now noticed the Bauhaus's director's Marxist stance and the . . . fact that the [school] is run on purely Communist-Marxist lines." Given the new situation, Hesse and the SPD's apparently lax behavior with regard to the supposed Bolshevik threat that had hung over Dessau since at least the beginning of March, if not earlier, made them very vulnerable with regard to the Bauhaus. Just as circumstances had five years earlier pressed the mayor to bring the Bauhaus to Dessau, perhaps in haste they now pushed him to act in a way he might never have done had he been less compelled.

The time had passed for genteel exploratory letters such as Grote had earlier sent Haesler. Only desperation could have moved Gropius toward the end of July 1930 to appear in the office of Ludwig Mies van der Rohe to literally beg the forty-four-year-old Berlin architect to take over the Bauhaus's leadership. "Unless you take it over, it will collapse," urged Gropius.

Both temperamentally and philosophically, Mies (as he was generally known) was not the most obvious choice. Essentially a solitary and contemplative architect whose handful of elegant, reductivist designs would set the standard for the century's architectural preoccupations, he was little concerned with collaboration, social usefulness, collegiality, or democratic consensus, the bedrocks upon which the Bauhaus stood. His architecture, including his rare workers' housing, such as the housing development on Berlin's Afrikanischestrasse of 1926/1927, dealt with aesthetic, not social, issues. In response to complaints that his buildings were too costly for workers, Mies replied, "Pay them more money!" If Meyer represented the utilitarian and socially grounded branch of Gropius's philosophy, Mies just as unswervingly and dogmatically represented its other side, the quest for a single underlying aesthetic.

Meyer was certainly not a collegial individual. But his radical moves, such as eliminating the painters' course, were backed by the majority of students. Mies would not even seek the students' consensus. A man of few words, he preferred to envelop himself in a cocoon of green Havana cigar smoke and vinous—preferably Rhine wine—ponderation, in the often pained recollection of his students. It was difficult to imagine him traveling around the country publicizing the Bauhaus, wooing politicians and important supporters, or seeking business for the school's teapots. Mies expressed himself through his charcoal crayon and piercing architectural conceptualizations. While this may have been a blessing for an architect, it was hardly pertinent for the head of a controversial pedagogical institution, who had to spend most of his time oozing bonhomie and mediating incessant feuds.

Aside from belonging to the Friends of the Bauhaus—a group of well-known individuals whose names Gropius periodically drew upon to support the school—and participating in the architectural portion of the 1923 exhibition, Mies had never had much to do with the Bauhaus. But if Gropius and the Dessau authorities were looking for someone to convincingly depoliticize the Bauhaus, someone whose artistic integrity and disinterest in politics were acknowledged by Right and Left alike, they could not have chosen a better-suited German architect.

Gropius and Mies had been rivals for nearly twenty-two years, since 1908 when Mies had chafed under the supervision of the three-years-older Gropius in the office of Peter Behrens. They would remain rivals until their deaths in 1969. As with so many such relationships, they were in many ways mirror images of each other. Gropius had been born into privilege and prosperity and bore a name long honored in German architecture. Mies had come from a humble background. He learned his trade not as Gropius had done, during bored passage through eminent *Hochschulen* with paid draftsmen in tow, but through calloused hands-on apprenticeship, first by working at the side of his stonemason father in Aachen, then at craft schools, and finally in Behrens's office. Gropius had the haute bourgeois bearing that Mies craved. The Dutch *van der* that he added to his mother's name *Rohe* bore a faint though unmistakable flavor of the German aristocratic *von*. But Mies had the drawing talent—indeed the architectural genius—that Gropius so painfully knew he lacked. While more diplomatic than Hannes Meyer, Mies was no particular admirer of Gropius's architectural talents. Mies thought Gropius's Dessau school building was "pretentious." He did, however, admire Gropius's invention of the name "Bauhaus."

Gropius's coming to Mies and the latter's acceptance must have involved a considerable swallowing of pride for both men: Gropius to acknowledge that he needed Mies, and Mies to take up the reins of what even he admitted was his rival's greatest accomplishment. But with the Depression having dried up many of Mies's commissions, the pay offered in Dessau proved a potent antidote to his bruised ego. This, plus the agreement to let him keep his private architectural practice in Berlin and appear at the school only two or three days a week, moved him to accept. A preliminary contract was signed. With Mies now set, Hesse could move against Meyer.

Hesse's action would become one of the most challenged and contentious episodes in Bauhaus history. Hesse, Meyer, Gropius, and Grote would publish accounts of it periodically throughout their lives, offering conflicting explanations, justifications, and refutations of what purportedly transpired. Hesse, for example, claimed he was accompanied by Grote when he arrived at Meyer's office on the afternoon of July 29, 1930, to demand his resignation. Meyer claimed the mayor came alone. Such conflicting accounts marked Meyer's entire association with the Bauhaus, and it is in an effort to avoid the embellishments and justifications of hindsight that discussion of this event has been confined to contemporary accounts wherever possible.

Hesse, who appeared in Meyer's office unannounced, moved right to the point. He declared that contributions to the International Workers' Aid Society constituted a banned political activity within the school and demanded Meyer's immediate resignation. The Bauhaus director was shocked, unable to grasp how so innocuous an act—in fact a venerable Bauhaus tradition—represented a "political" activity and the basis for his resignation. Hesse, who had assumed that Meyer would realize the hopelessness of his situation, had not even considered the possibility that Meyer might refuse to resign. "Our common interest in the Bauhaus *demands* your unconditional resignation," declared Hesse to a stupefied Meyer.

Still unable to comprehend what was going on, Meyer asked for some time to think. A second meeting was set up for July 31, two days hence.

Confronted by Meyer's unanticipated obstreperousness, the mayor now faced the discomforting fact that what he was attempting to do—not unlike Brüning's and Hindenburg's maneuvers—was legally questionable. The October deadline to notify Meyer that his contract would not be renewed had long since passed. With elections coming up in September,

Hesse had to get Meyer out of the Bauhaus as quickly as possible. The mayor could not afford to wait the required six months. Anxious to bolster his tenuous case, Hesse sought faculty support during the two-day interim. But this proved difficult, as most everyone was away on summer vacation and had to be reached by mail. Meyer, in the meantime, used the two-day period to garner kostufra's support among the students who had remained at the school over the summer.

The more Meyer thought about what was going on, the more incensed he became. Convinced he was being treated unjustly, he canceled the meeting scheduled for July 31. Hesse replied by announcing Meyer's resignation that same day and the appointment of Mies as his successor. The following day Meyer announced his *refusal* to resign and requested an immediate inquiry by Blum's state Ministry of Education. As his student supporters mobilized for a student strike at the beginning of the fall semester, Meyer initiated a massive, international campaign to arouse support.

"I just want to tell you briefly that they decided to 'let me go' today," wrote Meyer to Karel Teige, editor of the Czech newspaper *Red*. "They are using the [summer] holidays to eliminate me." Response to Meyer's charges was immediate. "Grotesque . . . and a sign of our tumultuous time," declared the critic Josef Gantner. "Unbelievable . . . a mark of Germany's entire political structure," commented the director of Zurich's Craft School and Museum. By August 6 Meyer was referring to his dismissal as demonstrating "Dessau's culturally reactionary lust for murder." By the end of the month it had become a "stab in the back"; and by October, an example of "the [Bauhaus's] fascistization."

Meyer's fellow architects, such as J. J. P. Oud and Hermann Finsterlin, quickly offered their support. Referring to Meyer's Bauhaus as "a healthy, idealistic, and humanitarian creation within . . . a warehouse of relics," Finsterlin claimed he was not surprised by the news.

For Dessau, the Bauhaus was a curiosity, an amusement. As long as it was harmless, it was regarded as a mere freak show. If it had been allowed to unleash itself as an aggressive, independent organism, it would have been dangerous. Anything radical or extreme is inadmissible. . . .

You, Hannes Meyer, could have regenerated the Bauhaus and made it powerful. We are terribly saddened to survive you after this destruction.

Critics, too, added their support, publicly condemning the manner in which Meyer was dismissed. In an article prepared for the *Neue Zürcher Zeitung*, Gantner described Meyer's attempts to reorganize the Bauhaus as a "very logical expansion of Gropius's ideas on increasingly serious social problems." He questioned whether any school could attempt to deal with such issues in a capitalistic society. Gantner went on to declare the manner of Meyer's ouster as "no less backward . . . and anticultural than the measures taken by the reactionary government of Thuringia against the Weimar Bauhaus."

Understandably, it was mostly the Left who defended Meyer, especially Communist organizations in Germany and the Soviet Union. *Die Rote Fahne* lumped Meyer's dismissal with the increasing censorship; banning of revolutionary books, brochures, films, and theatrical plays; and the imprisoning of fifty-three Communist editors, contending they all constituted part of "Germany's increasing cultural reactionism."

The issue of Meyer's dismissal was mushrooming into a political cause célèbre. Unhappy about exposing it to the cauldron of Anhalt politics in a state inquiry at such a politically sensitive moment, as Meyer had requested, Hesse convinced Meyer to settle their dispute by arbitration, a route that would allow him to "resign" rather than undergo a more humiliating dismissal. An arbitration panel, chaired by Minister Redslob, was set up in early August 1930. At the hearing Hesse shifted his stance to one that was more legally defensible. He now claimed that Meyer's Marxist philosophy had precluded him from controlling the Bauhaus's increasing politicization. This, claimed Hesse, had not only interfered with the school's work, but also damaged the reputations of the institution and the city. Hesse asserted that he had therefore acted on behalf of the school's and the city's best interests.

The issue would be resolved in early November 1930, when the panel found neither Meyer nor Hesse at fault. Meyer would be affirmed as a cultural and not a political Marxist, and Hesse's action, while overly hasty, would be declared to have been done with good reason. Not to have done so, the panel argued, "would have jeopardized the further existence of the Bauhaus." Although the mayor's action was considered "justifiable," Dessau would be ordered to pay Meyer compensation of four thousand marks, and the matter remained out of the courts.

Until this resolution, however, Meyer was out of both money and a job. Perhaps inspired by an upcoming trip planned by Stam and a group of leftist German architects and engineers, Meyer—declaring himself "happy to have escaped the half-heartedness of my life [in Dessau]"—decided to go to the Soviet Union. He would leave in early October, accompanied by ten to twenty of his Bauhaus student supporters, whom he described as "the best of the `Marxist' Bauhaus." The rest of his student supporters—the overwhelming majority of the Bauhaus's students—returned to Dessau in early September to rile up their fellow students and confront Mies.

They were met sympathetically by most of the Bauhaus students, who were outraged over the circumstances of Meyer's dismissal and the fact that they had neither been consulted in this nor in the hiring of his successor. If unloved by most of the faculty, Meyer had been enormously popular among the students. They admired his social compassion, his insistence that art had to be based on social concerns—particularly meaningful during such difficult times—his keen pursuit of collectivity in an otherwise hierarchical academic world, and his encouragement of their participation in all aspects of the school's affairs, the latter as cherished by the students as it had been abused by kostufra. Student representatives had always participated in the general meetings of the Masters' Council, but only under Meyer had the Student Council's voice truly equaled that of the faculty and in some instances exceeded it, to the faculty's dismay. Accustomed to this role, the students were devastated at having been ignored with regard to such critical decisions.

Ostensibly replaced by the so-called Marxist working teams, kostufra remained the dominating presence at the Bauhaus. Camouflaged and surreptitious, it operated essentially as before the ban. Its members continued to lead the Student Council, and it was they who were planning the student strike. Instead of openly within the school, they met now in student apartments. Their journal *Simple and Joyful* still tried to churn up student wrath. "[H]err kandinsky," declared an article in issue number 3,

> is it true that you or your wife . . . spread the news about hannes meyer's contribution to the "red relief" to the proper quarters, so that it could appear in the newspapers?
>
> herr kandinsky, is it further true that you already knew about the things that were going to happen here before you left for your summer vacation?

Kostufra's members, trained by the local KPD, were virtually professional agitators. Feeding upon the students' genuine misgivings, they organized a student strike to begin on September 3, 1930, the opening of the fall semester. But like Hesse, the SPD, and the Right, their eyes were focused as much on the upcoming critical Reichstag election as on the Bauhaus.

The leftist press hailed the continuing but no longer secret Communist presence in the Bauhaus. "Forces are at work within the Bauhaus that are stronger than any director of the moment," declared the *Magdeburger Tribüne*. The newspaper noted that the change of director "by no means" meant the end for the Communists there. "Hannes Meyer," the *Die Rote Fahne* asserted, "should be honored that the revolutionaries among the Bauhaus's students are on his side." The participation of Bauhaus students in a large Communist election rally held in Dessau in August was prominently covered by the local newspapers, along with their banner that declared, "Down with cultural reaction at the Dessau Bauhaus."

The Communists' continuing prominence within the Bauhaus enraged the Right. Commenting that the change of directors had altered nothing, Karius declared that Meyer's dismissal had been little more than a subterfuge, a "scapegoat for the Bauhaus's scandalous state of affairs" through which the mayor was trying to appease the anxious population. The Bauhaus situation, he asserted, remained essentially unchanged. It is up to the mayor, Karius warned, to make sure that the book on the school's radicalization was not simply closed for the time being, but for good. Playing on people's fears of a united revolutionary front, Karius accused Hesse of being more or less captive to the Communists. "The Bauhaus . . . is indissolubly linked to Bolshevism," he continued,

> for which it is consciously paving the way by destroying our national culture. . . . The Bauhaus's Communist cell, which even the SPD acknowledges cannot be eradicated, is instead proliferating and increasingly taking possession of the student body. . . .
>
> Mr. Mayor, . . . take the decisive step before it is too late, and let the Communist Bauhaus go.

Pressed by the upcoming election, both Right and Left moved to stamp their competing claims on the increasingly unsettled community. A lecture given by Meyer in mid-August at the Association of Revolutionary Artists (ARBKD) offered the *Anhalter Anzeiger* the opportunity to accuse Meyer of being "a Communist, who actively turned the Bauhaus into a purely Communist institution." Again asserting that Meyer's sacking had done nothing to diminish the school's Communists, the newspaper charged that the Dessau Bauhaus remained a Communist cell.

On September 3, 1930, as Dessau anxiously watched Nazis and Communists electioneer in the streets with knives, broken chairs, and heavy chains, the Marxist leaders of the Bauhaus's striking students, holed up in the student canteen, greeted the new director, Mies van der Rohe, and the Masters' Council with their demands. In keeping with the Bauhaus's tradition of student self-rule, they insisted that Mies meet with them to discuss the Bauhaus's future and show them his work so they could judge his "suitability." After the students rejected the masters' request for the names of those who had written about Kandinsky and had harshly criticized Meyer's dismissal in *Simple and Joyful*, Mies, backed by the mayor and the studentless Masters' Council, refused to have anything more to do with them and broke off all discussion.

On September 8, six days before the election and with the students still on strike in the canteen, the Masters' Council, chaired by Mies—and with Mayor Hesse present, but still without any representatives from the Student Council—ordered the immediate closing of the Bauhaus. The old statutes were declared null and void and new statutes instituted. The entire student body of 170 was dismissed. Each student was told to reapply and submit to a personal interview with Mies when the new term began on October 21. Those who chose to reregister would have to sign a regulation swearing, as Püschel put it, "to keep their mouths shut" and their opinions to themselves. Politics "of any kind" was prohibited. Kandinsky and Albers's *Vorkurs* was restored and Meyer's planned replacement course eliminated. All residents of the student studios were ordered to immediately vacate their premises. A police deportation order was issued for five foreign students. Given twenty-four hours to leave Dessau, they were told "never to return."

Mies's actions enraged the Left. The Communist *Die Rote Fahne* claimed them to be nothing less than an attempt "to wipe Meyer's spirit and all traces of his work off the face of the earth." Gone from the Bauhaus and observing the goings-on from Breslau, Schlemmer saw them indicating the school's shift from Left to Right. For the embittered students, they marked the end of "the Bauhaus's saddest chapter."

On September 14, with more than three million unemployed, the largest turnout of voters since 1918 delivered an astonishing electoral success to the Nazis. As Gordon Craig has noted, Brüning's hopes to establish a strong moderate Right never materialized. While he and the Hindenburg group had anticipated a repudiation of the SPD-dominated Reichstag, they had hardly expected an increase from 12 to 107 in the number of seats held by the Nazis. A gain unprecedented in German parliamentary history, it made the Nazis the legislature's second-largest party after the SPD. The KPD also benefited from the social crisis, increasing their seats to 77. Although its 143 seats kept the SPD the Reichstag's strongest party, its loss of ten seats signaled a terminal decline.

In October both the Bauhaus and its homeland set out in new directions. In Weimar the Thuringian government obliterated the frescoes that Schlemmer had painted in the Bauhaus's vestibule for the 1923 exhibition; it also removed seventy modernist paintings by Barlach, Dix, Feininger, Klee, Kandinsky, and Schlemmer, among others, from the city's museum collection. On Monday, October 13, the new Reichstag opened to the sound of shattering glass. Jewish-owned department store windows were smashed by Nazi thugs who rampaged through the heart of Berlin shouting "Germany awake!" and "Death to the Jews!" Two days later the Dessau police moved to deport other foreign students who continued to engage in agitational activities in the Bauhaus.

On October 21, 1930, the Bauhaus's new semester opened with each student having vowed personally to Mies to forego political activity. Declared now an institution dedicated to the "handicraft, technical, and artistic training of students," the Bauhaus, like the Weimar Republic, turned its back on one failed and disreputed utopia to pursue another. Schlemmer, as usual, recognized this. "Our beloved Bauhaus," he declared, "seems to . . . be headed for new shores."

15. | Death and Transfiguration

> We observed [a] very *soignée* lady [at the Museum of Modern Art confronting] a huge and rather grim-looking porcelain insulator—the kind they use for attaching high-tension cables to the poles. She stared at it for some time, digesting its meaning, then turned with a sort of rapt look and said "Superb!"
>
> —*Review of "Machine Art" show at the Museum of Modern Art,* The New Yorker, March 17, 1934

The economic crisis that appeared to be leading Germany to revolution—or as Schlemmer worried, to war—was in America creating an unaccustomed mood of doubt and depression. Americans may have been singing "Time On My Hands," one of the year's most popular songs, but as breadlines spread throughout cities across the country, they were learning that jobless inactivity did not lead to love (as the song's lyrics implied), but to hunger, anxiety, and disgrace. On both sides of the ocean, 1930 was a year of breakdowns: of nerves in America, of society in Germany.

The gleaming new Cord convertible that glided toward the docks on New York's West Side in early June did not seem part of this depressed and broken world. One of the best-designed and most costly cars, it bespoke a world of wealth and privilege little touched by the day's harsh realities. Stowed in the ship's hold that would bear it and its owner—twenty-four-year-old Philip Johnson—across the Atlantic, the car would elegantly transport him and his guest, twenty-seven-year-old Henry-Russell Hitchcock, whom he was meeting in Paris, across a Europe heaving on the edge of catastrophe. Newspapers told them about this world. But thanks in part to their Harvard idealism, which tended to isolate European culture from its social and political context, they paid no particular heed to the warning signs. "'Political' didn't mean anything to me," Johnson later remarked. They would make a notable-looking team, the red-bearded, scholarly, and rather somber Hitchcock—now an assistant professor of art history at Wesleyan College—and the blond, handsome, and high-spirited Johnson, newly graduated cum laude from Harvard.

Unlike his mentors Barr and Hitchcock, Johnson had spent much of his youth in Europe and was as much at home there as in his hometown of Cleveland. His father, a lawyer named Homer Johnson, had been a member of the Wilson administration, and young Philip—fluent in French and German—had lived in Paris briefly and gone to school in Switzerland. Although Johnson had seen most of Europe's architectural monuments, he had never formally studied art history. It was not until he met Barr at his sister Theodate's graduation from Wellesley College in 1929 that he began to pursue the subject on his own. Told by Johnson of his interest in modern architecture and his visit to Weissenhoffsiedlung two years before, Barr suggested that he look into Hitchcock's writings. Inspired by Barr's enthusiasm and authoritative knowledge, Johnson read Hitchcock's works, most notably his 1928 article on J. J. P. Oud, and experienced what he called a "Saul-Paul" conversion that offered a focus for his keen mind and irrepressible energy. It changed his life.

Ten years earlier Gropius had experienced a similar conversion that had launched his career and, finally, the Bauhaus itself. Barr's aesthetic course was similarly set after he too experienced what his close friend and classmate Edward King characterized as a "vision." Thus, Gropius, Johnson, and Barr had all grounded their involvement in an artistic style that would come to be defined by its rationalistic traits after experiencing innervating, empowering, and distinctly nonrational transfigurations that imbued in them all never before experienced strength and convictions. But, while Gropius's conversion had come from the terrors of his wartime experiences, Johnson's and Barr's had come from neither life nor art but from art's cerebral cousin, the intellectual constructions of art history, an essential difference that highlighted the basic breach that existed between the Bauhaus (as well as much of modern European architecture) and the formalistic focus of its messianic American interpreters.

In his review of Hitchcock's book *Modern Architecture: Romanticism and Reintegration*, published in 1929, Barr suggested that the author himself could have used such an inspirational spark. The review appeared in the spring of 1930, just before Johnson and Hitchcock's European trip, and while Hitchcock was pleased by Barr's overall praise, he was deeply dejected by his mentor's trenchant complaints. Barr, since July 1929 the director of the newly established Museum of Modern Art in New York, was basically interested in *converting* people to his new religion of modernism. Hitchcock, ever the scholar, was more interested in *explaining* it, and it was precisely his sober, objective tone to which Barr objected. "Too erudite for the ordinary reader," Barr complained, declaring himself surprised and "a little disappoint[ed]" by Hitchcock's restrained and "discriminating mildness." Barr also criticized Hitchcock's "rather conscious Spenglerian melancholy," the meager number of illustrations, and the lack of analytical attention paid to Gropius's Bauhaus building in Dessau, cited by Barr as modernism's "most imposing single achievement." Barr claimed the book would be more appreciated in Europe than in the United States.

By nature introspective and pessimistic, Hitchcock took Barr's comments to heart. He and Johnson spent much of their time in Paris in June debating what to do. They decided to work together to correct the book in line with Barr's criticism. They would rewrite it in a more popular tone and add more illustrations. Heeding Barr's suggestion regarding its aptness for Europe, Johnson would translate it into German and seek a German publisher. The two men decided to spend the next three months traveling through Europe searching for buildings to include in the book. Subsequently Johnson would go by himself to Czechoslovakia and Austria, and Hitchcock would scout out England.

On July 7, 1930, Hitchcock and Johnson met Barr in Hamburg and excitedly informed him of their plans. Barr was enthusiastic. He was traveling with J. B. Neumann to help select works of art to be shown at the museum's planned exhibition of German painting and sculpture the following year, and with Cary Ross, a poet and member of the Museum of Modern Art circle. Meanwhile, Johnson's participation was noticeably altering the project. His ebullient nature was lightening the text's previously somber tone, and topics closer to his heart—such as construction, new materials, and functionalism—were being added. The focus, as well, was being directed more toward "the fundamental aesthetic, especially the style," as Johnson described it.

German publishers, however, did not share Johnson's enthusiasm and turned down their proposal. One might reasonably presume that Germany, as one of the cradles of modern European architecture, would understand its own architecture better than some youthful foreigners. But neither Hitchcock nor Johnson saw it that way. Indeed, they felt just the opposite. In their view Americans' artistic opinions were free of national bias and were thus more valid than those of the German publishers. Their rejection, then, neither altered their views nor diminished their confidence in their self-proclaimed propagandizing mission. Instead they decided to explain modern architecture not to the unappreciative and subjective Europeans, but to their own fellow countrymen, whom as Hitchcock had written in 1929 possessed a "purer" aesthetic conscience than the Europeans. "[T]o the great disappointment of our German . . . friends, who think of nothing but sociology," Johnson wrote to J. J. P. Oud, he and Hitchcock would continue their stylistic approach and "make propaganda" for modern architecture in America.

Johnson was struggling to develop his own ideas apart from those of Hitchcock and Barr. The aesthetic partiality that he expressed in his letter to Oud, however, reflects a view shared by his two mentors. Hitchcock thought modern European architecture was obsessed with sociology, a subject he considered more appropriate for "battle cries and . . . manifestos" than for building. America, Hitchcock claimed, did not have this bias and was thus more open to architecture as art. Hitchcock also believed that Europe overemphasized technology and utility. Barr emphasized style and what he referred to as modernism's essential aesthetic unity in the series of lectures on modern art and architecture that he gave in the spring of 1929 at Wellesley College. In May, Barr devoted an entire lecture to the Bauhaus. In this talk, titled "The Bauhaus at Dessau: An Academic Experiment in Constructivism and Expressionism," Barr identified the Bauhaus as modernism's paradigm.

Barr's proselytizing instincts and his desire to gain converts sometimes got in the way of scholarly objectivity. Having depicted the Bauhaus as the epitome of an aesthetically oriented modernism, Barr seemed reluctant to acknowledge the antistylistic shift the school had taken under Meyer.

Thanks to his correspondence with Feininger, Barr kept informed as to what was going on at the Bauhaus. He was well aware that Meyer had been the school's director for more than a year and that Gropius was no longer around. Yet in his Bauhaus lecture Barr described Gropius as the school's "guiding genius and one of [its] chief executives." He vigorously criticized Meyer's utilitarianism for its disinterest in "formal beauty," and he identified the Swiss architect only as a member of the school's architectural faculty. Such a misleading emphasis might have been meaningless had Barr not been appointed that July to head New York's new Museum of Modern Art, a position that imbued on his convictions the cachet and authority that America accorded the museum's Rockefeller founders. In turn, Barr would base the museum's organization and philosophy on his perception of the Bauhaus.

While Barr (and with him Hitchcock and Johnson) considered their aesthetic perception of modernism to be "purer" and thus superior to that of Europe, it was, as far as the Bauhaus was concerned, only the Werkbund half of Gropius's original conception they were considering, the other being the search for utopia. In fact the school had never achieved the aesthetic unity Gropius so endlessly proclaimed in Bauhaus publicity material and Barr appropriated. In 1929 Barr's aesthetic view bore practically no resemblance to Meyer's resolutely unformalistic school. The current director's view of the school was not simply different from Barr's, but indeed contradicted it. In May 1929 Barr described the Bauhaus as an attempt to reveal a new form of art. In Dessau the following month, a lecturer invited by Meyer praised the school for trying to seek "a new form of life."

This divergence hardly concerned Johnson, who on August 5, 1930— accompanied by Jan Ruhtenberg, one of Mies's associates—drove down from Berlin to visit the Bauhaus for the day and await the school's new director, Mies. It was Johnson's second visit to the school, and it would be as fleeting as his first had been the previous October, when he had gone at Barr's suggestion. Then, reflecting his mentor's high opinion of the building, Johnson had looked only at the Bauhaus architecture. Writing to Barr from Dessau, Johnson described himself as "thrilled" to see the building, which he declared to be "magnificent . . . [and] the most beautiful . . . [I] have ever seen." What the Bauhaus as a school was doing did not interest him. He did not visit the workshops or meet Director Meyer. Johnson had similarly ignored the day's ferocious political clashes. A remarkably fast learner, Johnson, who had met Barr only a few months before, had become a converted member of the tribe by October 1929.

Now, one year later, Johnson remained as disinterested in the striking workers and extremist partisans who were battling in Germany's streets as in the Bauhaus student leaders who, closeted within the school's canteen, were planning their revolt against the new director. In turn, the Bauhaus hardly noticed him. The periodic visits by these ardent, charming, and very different American youngsters became almost routine.

Barely older than the Bauhaus students, these Americans were different indeed. Mies's closing of the school in September moved student Konrad Püschel to barely constrained fury. "Sometimes I'm so angry I could break . . . windows," he wrote on September 17, 1930. But the same event aroused Johnson's enthusiasm. "[Mies] has closed the Bauhaus for a month," Johnson wrote to Oud on the same day,

> because the students were so politically minded after the regime of Hannes Meyer that they thought they would continue to run the school along their programmatic lines. Mies says he has no interest whatsoever in politics or programs but only in beautiful buildings, so he has closed the school. I have great hopes for the Bauhaus if Mies can once [sic] get his start there.

What Johnson did not know was that Oud seemed to have agreed with Püschel. One month earlier the Dutch architect had conveyed his sentiments to the ousted Bauhaus director, writing "all the best, dear Hannes Meyer, and a warm handshake."

Unlike his predecessor Meyer, who had arrived at the Bauhaus virtually unknown, Mies by 1930 was one of Germany's best known modernist architects. His luxurious German Pavilion, built for the Barcelona Fair in 1929—with its dazzling onyx and marble walls and chromium-plated columns—was one of the first buildings to reveal the new architectural style's suitability for something other than cheap, usually poorly constructed workers' housing. His ideological leanings, however, were less well known, aside from a nonpolitical reputation that allowed him to accept commissions (and criticism) from Left and Right. Mies's Liebknecht-Luxemburg memorial of 1926 had been acclaimed by the Left and denounced by the Right. It would become one of the first monuments the Nazis demolished after they came to power. On the other hand, the Left interpreted Mies's participation in the 1930 competition for Berlin's Memorial for the War Dead as indicating his reactionary leanings. Even the Communist newspaper *Die Rote Fahne*, normally unequivocal in its opinions, could not make up its mind about Mies.

So pervasive was the German association of modern architecture with the Left that in 1930 the newspaper linked Mies with Gropius as belonging to those "progressive" architects who did not mind denying their own radical principles when they worked for the German bourgeoisie. Yet in an earlier article titled "Cultural Reactionism and Architecture" *Die Rote Fahne* referred to Mies's replacement of Meyer as reflecting the same rightist cultural tendencies as Frick's replacement in Weimar of the "progressive" Otto Bartning with the "pure-blooded" Schultze-Naumburg. In fact, the newspaper speculated that Mies might turn out to be nothing more than a "'modernized' Schultze-Naumburg," an opinion shared by the Bauhaus Communists and many students. Schlemmer, too, had seen Mies's appointment as indicating the school's rightward turn.

Granting a certain hyperbole in the day's use of such terms as *Right* and *Left*, Mies's personification of the singular artistic genius—what Meyer and the Left condemned as subjective and individualistic—and his lack of appreciation of, indeed his opposition to, the notion of collectivity and egalitarianism did implicitly contradict two of socialism's basic tenets. This impression was strengthened by his vigorous refutation of social priorities in architecture. Mies, nearly alone among his peers, refused to cloak architecture in the ideological mantle of "sociology" that Hitchcock berated. Mies believed that architecture had only one purpose—to spatially express the spirit of the times—and "nothing else." His uncompromising pursuit of the aesthetic ideal—often at the expense of utility, as well as the client's comfort, desires, and pocketbook—was notorious. "Anything less than perfection is unacceptable," he would later declare.

Mies particularly emphasized this point in a speech before the German Werkbund in Vienna on August 1, 1930, the day Meyer's resignation and his appointment were announced. "The new age is a fact," he declared. "It exists entirely independently of whether we say yes or no to it." Events, he claimed, took their inevitable and value-free course, and he urged acceptance of the day's social and economic conditions.

Such neutrality infuriated the Communists, who saw society as a fight to the death between the abusers and the abused, the haves and the have-

nots. The Bauhaus students, themselves committed to changing these conditions, were outraged. Who but a "self-centered person who has lost all
contact with the rest of the world . . . [is] able to view the world in this
way," the Communist student journal *Bauhaus* had commented about
Mies's speech. And to whom, they had asked, did his "we" refer? If Mies
meant the "alienated artists," then he was correct. But if he was referring
to the capitalists or the proletariat, the age indeed mattered. It was not the
metaphysical "nonsense" contained in such a statement that had most disturbed the article's writer, but the fact that it had been made by the
Bauhaus director. "The statement becomes a program, and we have to
take a stand on it," the article declared. To the students' angry defiance
over what had happened to Meyer they now added their hostility to what
their new director represented.

For Johnson, on the other hand, Mies confirmed his aesthetic creed of
"the whole style and nothing but the style." Johnson's appreciation of
Mies had intensified after he saw Mies's just-completed Tugendhat House
in Brno, just over the Czech border, where he had driven after leaving the
Bauhaus. The Tugendhat House, an example of the luxurious, no-
expense-spared construction at which Mies excelled, proved a revelation
to Johnson, whose attraction to architecture, especially after meeting
Mies, became nearly rapturous. Intellectually challenging, elegant, yet
austere, the Tugendhat House was architecture worthy of an aesthete's
dreams. In his September 17 letter to Oud, Johnson extolled the building's
grandeur, luxe, and finish. "It has cost so far nearly a million marks, so it
ought to be good," Johnson remarked, citing the baronial dimensions of
the nearly ninety-foot-long main room, the chrome-clad steel posts, the
nearly thirty-three-foot-long glass wall, and a curved wall of rare wood.
Mies's building was to the cracked walls, skimpy rooms, and six-foot-high
ceilings of workers' housing as Johnson's Cord convertible was to a
Model T Ford. "Cheap, cheap, cheap," was Johnson's dismissal of mini-
mal housing, which not only comprised the overwhelming majority of
German modern architecture (that he and Hitchcock were preparing to
"sell" to America) but provided its raison d'être for so many of its prac-
titioners, including Gropius and Meyer. For Johnson cheap workers'
housing simply represented the first step in a stylistic development that
culminated in Mies. Or as Johnson would assert the following year, Mies
was "far past the stage in which the architect sees the house as the cheap-
est and best-planned expression of the needs of its inhabitants." Cheap

housing that reflected its inhabitant's needs, Johnson declared, was something Communists most appreciated. His implication was clear. Communists might design workers' housing, but artists—like Mies—designed architecture.

Johnson returned home at the end of August 1930 "a violent Mies man," as he put it. He commissioned Mies to design his New York apartment and subsequently sought commissions for him from the Rockefellers, as well as from the Aluminum Corporation of America, in which his family held substantial shares. Although Hitchcock, in his *Modern Architecture,* had referred to Mies's "extraordinary imaginative power," he had accorded him far less note than Gropius. This book would go through many transformations before it finally appeared as *The International Style.* But none would matter more than the emergence of Mies as the quintessence of architectural modernism, a momentous change that was specifically Johnson's contribution. This perception of Mies appeared to confirm the Americans' aesthetic interpretation of modernism and ignore the slight they had received from German publishers.

Barr had thought about putting on an architecture exhibition ever since he became the Museum of Modern Art director the year before, and by the fall of 1930 Hitchcock and Johnson's book project expanded to include this goal. In December 1930, some months before the revised book's first draft was completed, Johnson submitted his initial proposal for the exhibition to the museum's trustees. The proposal would go through several versions and resubmissions, but certain elements remained intact. Modern architecture would be presented as a worldwide, essentially aesthetic phenomenon, whose range—as Johnson noted in his proposal—encompassed the construction of cheap houses in Frankfurt and mansions in Paris. Little attention would be paid to the social and political context out of which this architecture had emerged.

In Germany, however, where another million people were unemployed by the end of 1930, social context was difficult to ignore. Impoverished and frustrated by the government's inability to stop the precipitous economic decline, people were more and more taking matters into their own hands. Gunfire, robberies, industrial unrest, political terrorism, and bloody street fighting between the Nazis' storm troopers and the Communists had become daily occurrences. By 1931 moderation was vanishing in Germany, and with it support for the political center that Hesse's German

Democratic Party (the DDP) represented. It was with grave misgivings that Dessau's mayor anticipated the City Council election in October 1931. His liberal coalition had dominated Dessau politics for thirteen years. Now, four years after the last election, Hesse worried that he would not even be able to hold on to his party's already diminished status.

To no one's surprise, the election triggered the usual Nazi assault on the Bauhaus. With Dessau's budget deficit running over two million marks— the Bauhaus's subsidies this year fell below the 1929 level—and nearly twelve thousand of its citizens out of work, the Nazis found even larger and more sympathetic audiences than usual for their accusations of the immorality of allowing German comrades to go hungry "while foreigners are handsomely paid with the taxes of a starving nation." They urged the immediate cessation of all Bauhaus funding and the dismissal "without notice" of all foreign teachers. To this usual litany of the Right's demands they added their own distinctive twist by insisting the Bauhaus building be demolished.

The Nazis' efforts were unintentionally aided by Mies's inability to sup press the Communists in the school. Mies's failure did not come from want of trying. He did not hesitate to impose iron-fisted measures. Believing that the subject of one student's painting (abortion, then illegal in Germany) was too controversial for Dessau's edgy citizens, Mies ordered it removed from a school exhibition. He also refused to grant travel permits to students who wanted to hear a lecture given by Hannes Meyer in Leipzig, the Swiss architect having returned briefly to Germany for a speaking tour. Only conservative speakers were invited to address the Bauhaus. The subject of one of these, given by the sociologist and philosopher Hans Freyer, was "Revolution from the Right." Bauhaus brochures now stressed the school's teaching of apolitical design.

While he pushed the school's Communists further underground, Mies failed to brake their activities. With nearly one in ten Germans out of work by the end of the year, and fascism on a seemingly inexorable rise, the students found it repugnant, if not intolerable, to be told to park their political passions outside the classroom. Mies's efforts to neutralize the Bauhaus remained futile against the weight of the school's tradition, reputation, and the day's feverish political mood. His actions assuaged neither the students—the overwhelming number of whom remained sympathetic to the Communists—the Nazis, nor the community, as the results of Dessau's October 25, 1931, election soon revealed.

The election confirmed Hesse's worst fears. The Right emerged with a majority of nineteen, of which fifteen belonged to the Nazis. The Left was reduced to seventeen representatives—thirteen from the Social Democratic Party (the SPD) and four from the Communist Party (the KPD). Like most of the country's other centrist bourgeois parties, Hesse's DDP lost both its seats. The liberal coalition between the Social Democrats and the DDP that Hesse had established in Dessau in 1918— which had brought in and supported the Bauhaus—was finished. Mies's ability to move against the school's Communists was also severely hampered. For without the Social Democrats, the Bauhaus was more dependent than ever on the City Council's four Communist votes. Given this state of affairs, the Bauhaus at the end of 1931 found the Nazis controlling its destiny and the Communists (with their four critical votes) its purse strings and most of its students' hearts.

Most Bauhäuslers had not taken the Nazis' anti-Bauhaus threats too seriously, believing them to be so much campaign jargon. They were thus surprised when the Nazis moved on the school at a City Council meeting on January 21, 1932. After electing a Nazi Gauleiter by the name of P. Hofmann, a committed opponent of the "Bolshevist Bauhaus," to head the Council, the Nazis demanded the Bauhaus be closed on April 1; all foreign teachers be immediately dismissed; funds previously earmarked for the school be transferred to the Welfare Office for relief of the unemployed; and its school building be demolished. The entire fifteen-member Nazi block voted for the proposal. But the SPD representatives, the Communists, and the four so-called Magistrate members put together a majority of twenty-five and the proposal was defeated.

The Bauhaus's electoral difficulties, however, were far from over. Elections for president and State Assemblies loomed in the spring of 1932. Hindenburg, again running for the presidency, was opposed by three candidates, the Communist Ernst Thälmann; the nationalist candidate— Theodor Düsterberg—whose party, the German Nationalists (the DNP), had previously supported Hindenburg; and the still relatively unknown Adolf Hitler. Given the country's dire straits and the Nazis' proven ability to capitalize on them, many citizens were terrified. "Who knows what political developments the spring will bring?" wrote Schlemmer in early February. If the Nazis came to power it would mean the end of "Eastern Bolshevist Jewish Marxist art," he predicted, mocking the party's lingo for modern art, which the Bauhaus had come to epitomize. It was perhaps this as much as the narrow victory by the school's supporters in the recent City Council session that led Schlemmer to describe the Bauhaus as "permanently endangered."

The Bauhaus's Communists and their supporters, however, were concerned less with the school's fate or its reputation than the possibility of a fascist triumph. They defied Mies's ban on political activity and engaged in a spirited if subversive electioneering campaign, mostly producing posters and pamphlets. On the night before the elections the lighted windows in the school's atelier displayed the number 4, which everyone who passed by knew referred to the KPD's Line 4 on the ballot.

None of the presidential candidates gained a clear majority in the March 13 elections. Hindenburg received only 49.6 percent of the vote, Hitler slightly over 30 percent, and the Communist Thälmann 13.2 percent. Although Hindenburg would easily win an absolute majority of 53 percent in the runoff vote on April 11, he felt insulted by having to submit to a second round of votes. Harboring a deep resentment against Hitler, Hindenburg allowed himself at year's end to fall prey to a foolish scheme by one of his associates, Franz von Papen. Contrived to hem Hitler into a coalition cabinet, von Papen's plan backfired and instead— as Gordon Craig has noted—allowed the former lance corporal to ascend to the Chancellorship on January 30, 1933. Of more immediate concern to the Bauhaus, however, were the signs of how far Right Dessau had swung since the school arrived there in 1925. While the city virtually matched the national proportion of votes cast for Hindenburg (49.6 percent for the nation, as opposed to Dessau's 49.51 percent), their 40 percent support of Hitler was 10 percent higher than the nation's.

This shift boded ill for the SPD and thereby the Bauhaus in the April 1932 election for the Anhalt State Assembly. Although the Bauhaus was funded by the city, the state's SPD majority had always extended what Hesse termed a "protective hand" over the school, and the mayor frequently turned to them to help bolster the school's often wavering SPD supporters on the City Council. But now the party, believing its longtime support of the Bauhaus had contributed to the party's defeat in the City Council elections of the year before and was thus harming its interests, tried to distance itself as much as possible from the school. The Nazis, however, also realized this. As the SPD watched in impotent horror, the Nazis once again focused their electoral assaults on the "Bolshevik" Bauhaus and its SPD "friends." Still "violently politicized" and on the verge of losing its SPD support, the Bauhaus could no longer tolerate Communist activity, no matter how surreptitious. Whatever the ramifications with the City Council's Communist members might be, Mies had to move against the Bauhaus's Communist cell.

The opportunity presented itself over the question of how to distribute the income that the school received from licensing its products. This income, thanks to the city's severe reduction of its subsidy, had become the Bauhaus's major source of financing. It was also, however, the source of a long-standing dispute between the faculty and the students, the former wanting more of the income to go toward their salaries, the latter urging more of the funds for student-assistance programs. On March 18, 1932, student leaders called for a meeting in the school's canteen—their traditional turf—to discuss their demands, a gathering which Mies banned and the students defied. Mies ordered the students to leave the canteen. Again they refused. In response, Mies turned to the Dessau police, who in the early morning of March 19 forcibly removed the students. Fifteen students were expelled from the school. When one of them—Isaak Budkow—reappeared, Mies called in the police again, and he was jailed for four weeks.

Mies's actions threw a pall over the school that never disappeared from its participants' memories. For behind the Bauhaus's incessant squabbling lay the school's long-cherished image of itself as a utopian bulwark against a crass and uncaring society. This image—the impetus that had kept the school going in the face of endless opposition—was, for many Bauhäuslers, decimated by Mies's act. In their eyes little separated Mies's use of police force against his own students from the black shadow of fascism that was descending over the country. For most Bauhäuslers, as for twenty-two-year-old T. Lux Feininger, who had spent most of his life at the school, Mies's deed spelled the Bauhaus's "absolute end."

As the Bauhaus withered in Germany, its effigy rose in New York, an important centerpiece of the Museum of Modern Art's "Modern Architecture—International Exhibition," which opened on February 9, 1932, and closed on March 23, four days after the police raid in Dessau. A model of the Bauhaus—and photographs of various other buildings by Gropius in Dessau—dominated the exhibition's first large hall. The main gallery, however, was devoted to models of impressively luxurious single-family homes: Mies's Tugendhat House; Le Corbusier's Villa Savoie; the

House on Mesa by Frank Lloyd Wright; and Oud's project for the Johnson family, which was displayed as the House at Pinehurst. Abounding in servant and guest quarters, none could even remotely be considered an average family's home. Wright's house, which featured a three-car garage, billiard room, several maids' rooms, and an artificial lake-type pool, was estimated to cost nearly twenty times that of the average home in 1931. The implication of the exhibition's layout was clear. The aesthetic principles displayed in the Bauhaus building culminated in these costly villas, an ironical commentary considering Gropius's castigation some years earlier of the "adoration of power and material things."

The display of mass housing was relegated to a secondary area, without any acknowledgment that the desire to provide adequate low-cost housing had been the original impetus for the elegant and costly homes exhibited out front. The exhibition's list of patrons—a dazzling array of dukes, princes, viscounts, and baronesses—further severed the style from its original desire to overthrow the status quo and contributed to what would become the American association of architectural modernism with prestige and "class." Whatever sociological and political principles the style may have originally embodied were not simply imperceptible but alien to the refined aesthetic principles espoused by the exhibition and Hitchcock and Johnson's book. The exhibition, as was noted, made modern architecture "safe for millionaires." It was a lesson America's corporate captains would soon absorb.

Opening as it did in the Depression's darkest days, the exhibition of beautiful buildings that few could afford proved less than compelling to most Americans. Only 33,000 people attended the exhibit over its six-week duration. In 1929, by comparison, the Metropolitan Museum's exhibition "Architecture and the Industrial Arts" received 186,000 visitors. Johnson, who had worked unpaid for a year and a half on its preparation, was crushed by the public's tepid response. Perfunctory newspaper attention added to his disappointment. One critic referred to "Miss van der Rohe, famous German draftsman."

The exhibition's aesthetic viewpoint would be reinforced by several of the museum's later shows, most notably the Cubist and Abstract Art exhibition of 1936 and the Bauhaus exhibition of 1938, which would securely anchor the school within Barr's overall artistic constellation. Thanks mostly to Johnson, Mies replaced Gropius as the quintessence of the new architectural style; and from the 1932 exhibit on, Gropius would be essentially presented by the museum in terms of his architectural and aesthetic contributions to the Bauhaus.

The museum's view—which differed so radically from the beginnings of European architectural modernism—contrasted no less emphatically with the circumstances that were leading to modernism's end there. By mid-1932 Germany was plunging ever deeper into an economic morass. In Dessau alone the unemployment rate approached 33 percent; and the Nazis continued to reap the rewards of people's long-standing resentments, frustrations, and need to lay blame.

Mies's severe measures against the students on March 19 did nothing to reassure the apprehensive Dessau community or Anhalt's beleaguered SPD campaigning for the State Assembly. The Nazis were now soothing people's nerves. On April 23 the nationalist parties won a tremendous victory in the state. With twenty seats—to the Left's sixteen—the nationalists emerged as the legislature's majority. The Nazis, winning fifteen of the Right's twenty seats, were now the Assembly's largest single party. The SPD-DDP coalition that had long ruled Anhalt was replaced by a fascist-nationalist coalition, and a Dr. Freyberg, a former lawyer from Quedlinburg and an NSDAP member, replaced Bauhaus supporter Deist as the state's chief executive. Despite the duplication of this nationalist victory throughout the nation—the Nazis won majorities in all state assemblies except Bavaria—Anhalt's embittered Social Democrats, having already suffered the loss of their majority on Dessau's City Council, blamed their defeat on their longtime support of the controversial and now prodigiously unpopular Bauhaus.

With the Nazis in control of both the Dessau City Council and Anhalt's State Assembly, it became obvious that the Bauhaus's days in Dessau were numbered. Despite this, Hesse and Grote worked desperately to stave off what they knew would be the Nazis' certain attempts to close the school. Letters were sent to "enlighten" the Nazis about Mies and the new Bauhaus. Hesse met with Anhalt's Minister President Freyberg and proposed that he visit the Bauhaus to see for himself what the school was doing. The school, Hesse suggested, would mount an exhibit specifically for this purpose. Freyberg agreed to the idea but insisted on bringing an art expert with him. His choice—none other than Paul Schultze-Naumburg, the Weimar architect who had ordered the destruction of Schlemmer's fresco and the removal of modernist works of art from

Weimar's local museum—sickened Hesse and everyone at the Bauhaus.

The Bauhaus now began the charade that marked its final sputtering days in its homeland. Only Mies, virtually alone among the Bauhäuslers, took the exhibition seriously. Confident that he could convince the Nazis that the Bauhaus was politically innocuous, he earnestly set about organizing the exhibition, planned for early July 1932. Most everyone else, however, saw it as a farce and—to Mies's annoyance—resisted his careful preparations. Kandinsky deliberately included some old geometric abstract paintings that he knew would antagonize Schultze-Naumburg. The Communist students complained that the exhibit was a pointless sham and threatened to boycott it. One student caught up by the protest inserted a thick slice of ham under glass at the last minute. Mies expelled both student and ham. On July 8, their decision already made, Freyberg and Schultze-Naumburg peremptorily walked through the exhibit.

Despite this setback, efforts to save the school continued. Grote tried to go over Freyberg's head by appealing to the party's upper echelon. In a series of letters that he wrote to several of the Nazis' main supporters, he described Mies as "a fascist" and "German architect" whose building stressed "the spiritual values which Moscow's Marxism condemned." Suggestions of keeping the Bauhaus going under a different name were purportedly derided by the Nazi's chief cultural spokesman, Alfred Rosenberg, who claimed that the school could not escape its "ominous associations."

On August 22, with the entire SPD block abstaining, the Dessau City Council voted to terminate support of the Bauhaus as of October 1. Only Hesse and the four Communist members of the Council voted against the Nazi proposal.

To everyone's surprise Mies fought tenaciously to keep the Bauhaus open, driven perhaps as much by his sense of justice as by his insistence on convincing the Nazis that modernism (at least his apolitical version) represented no threat. In October he tried to remove the Bauhaus from political interference by reopening the school in Berlin as a private institution, dipping heavily into his own personal funds to do so. Mies continued to expel obstreperous students and applied all kinds of strong-arm attempts to maintain control. Understandably, his efforts aroused considerable student opposition, especially among the more leftist. In November one student, Gerd Balzer, complaining about Mies's "absolute dictatorship," declared that the term *freedom* no longer applied to the Bauhaus.

Another student, Hubert Hoffmann, griped that "[s]omething is rotten in the Bauhaus." But as controversial as Mies's efforts were, in the end they accomplished nothing. On April 11, 1933, three months after Hitler became Chancellor, the Gestapo raided and sealed the Bauhaus's new Berlin premises.

Mies still refused to concede the school's closing. He made heroic and personally dangerous appeals to Alfred Rosenberg and the head of Berlin's Gestapo. But none of this could temper the Bauhaus's fate. It was clear from what Rosenberg had said about the futility of changing the school's name that the Bauhaus, as Schlemmer commented, was paying for its "past sins," for its audacity in having dared to propose itself as a vehicle for its country's spiritual transformation, a role which the Nazis were now assuming. Fourteen years before, Gropius had stormed into Weimar in the hope of creating his purifying and exclusionistic vision of a better society; in 1933 the Nazis sought theirs. With political power now in their hands, the Bauhaus—in July of that year—closed its doors.

Epilogue: The Bauhaus in America

We live in a time of flux. . . . There are . . . no new religions, no new puritanism, no new Marxism, no new socially conscious morality that can give discipline, direction, or force to an architectural pattern. Today we know too much too quickly. It takes moral and emotional blinders to make a style. One must be convinced one is right. Who today can stand up and say: "I am right!" Who, indeed, would want to?

—*Philip Johnson*

The convulsive forces that expelled the Bauhaus from Weimar, Dessau, and finally Berlin ultimately also expelled the Republic, Gropius, Mies, and such faculty as Kandinsky, Feininger, Klee, Breuer, Albers, and Moholy-Nagy, to name only a few. Not everyone, however, fled. Schlemmer for one could never bring himself to leave Germany. He earned a precarious living under the Nazis, initially as a housepainter and subsequently working in the color laboratory of a lacquer factory that a German industrialist had set up to help support some of the country's persecuted artists. Exhausted and depressed, Schlemmer died in 1943 at the age of fifty-five. Kandinsky sought refuge in Paris, and Klee returned to his native Switzerland. But most of the others, including Gropius, Mies, Feininger, Breuer, Albers (and his wife, the weaver Anni Albers), Moholy-Nagy, Walter Peterhans (brought in by Hannes Meyer to teach photography), Ludwig Hilber-seimer, and the graphic artist Herbert Bayer, along with a considerable number of Bauhaus students, all went to the United States. Aided by their prodigious talent, the Museum of Modern Art's enthusiastic and presti-gious patronage, and the cultural and economic dominance that America assumed in the postwar world, the Bauhaus would leave its most enduring mark in America.

Unlike the story of what happened during the fourteen years of the Bauhaus's existence in Germany, which has never before been completely revealed, what followed after the school closed its doors and began its tri-umphant course elsewhere in the world has been fairly well documented. Nevertheless, the Bauhaus story is not complete without a brief look at the great success that the school had in America and what happened to the story's main characters there after the school closed down in Berlin.

The America in which the Bauhaus flourished was very different from the Europe in which it was founded. Beginning with the end of World War I, when the Bauhaus began, Europe entered into an era of competing ideologies. These opposing *isms* of the period—fascism on one side and socialism and communism on the other—not only determined how peo-ple understood the world, but confronted each other with the fervor of religious warfare.

To a large extent the United States escaped this ideological battlefield (with the exception, perhaps, of certain intellectual circles in New York, like the *Partisan Review* crowds who were still mentally tethered to Europe). Pluralistic, practical-minded, and individualistically inclined, America regarded ideologies suspiciously. The Bauhaus, of course, was a product of ideology, and when it came to America—where the design and building of houses and objects are not politically charged issues—it had to be stripped of its ideological guise to be understood.

Curiously, what had seemed to be its core in Europe turned out to be irrelevant in the far more pragmatic atmosphere of America. The Bauhaus that Gropius created was hardly what America subsequently imagined it to be, except perhaps in its last few years under Mies. Indeed, one might argue that the European Bauhaus as a definable and consistent enterprise never existed, with the exceptions of a brief year or two under Meyer and subsequently Mies; although the idea of a single modernist architectural movement certainly did exist. But Gropius's Bauhaus, along with much of European modern architecture, meant something far more than the stark and simple technological style that America imagined. It meant to change the world through how it looked and lived. Thanks to America's misinterpretation, the Bauhaus achieved this. Ironically, America's stripped-down version of the Bauhaus—the one devoid of ideology—turned out to be much more powerful than what the school really had been.

What exactly happened in the transfer to the New World may be seen in some statements made by Moholy-Nagy—one of the German Bauhaus's most ideological members—before and after his immigration to America. In 1922 (the year that Gropius first met him), Moholy-Nagy unabashedly described himself as "fighting for the realization of a communist way of life." Two years later, as a controversial member of the Bauhaus faculty, he continued to speak this way, expressing his pleasure in having been "given the privilege . . . to translate revolution into material reality." Such references disappeared, however, in 1937, when Moholy-Nagy emigrated to Chicago to establish what he called the New Bauhaus. As its name suggested, this new school specifically modeled itself after the Bauhaus, particularly its Dessau version. Among other courses, it offered workshop training in photography, industrial and stage design, architecture, and town planning. No program that Gropius would set up at Harvard, Albers at Black Mountain College in North Carolina, or Mies at Chicago's Armour Institute would so conspicuously attempt to emulate the Bauhaus curriculum to the extent of Moholy-Nagy's school. In 1938, one year after his emigration to America, Moholy-Nagy explained the basis of the New Bauhaus education as emanating from the "need [for] new men with new mentality." What specific mentality he was referring to, however, remained undefined. No mention of Left or Right; and certainly no talk of revolution. In such a similarly innocuous way, the chameleonlike Bauhaus—having already shed its various skins in Weimar, Dessau, and Berlin—wondrously adapted to its changed American circumstances.

In this, as might be expected, Gropius played a major role. After leaving Germany in 1934 he settled first in England and then—in 1937—went to Harvard to head the architecture department of its Graduate School of Design. He held this position until 1952. At Harvard Gropius trained many of America's best-known architects, among them I. M. Pei, Paul Rudolph, Edward L. Barnes, and—surprisingly, in light of his declared allegiance to Mies—Philip Johnson. (Asserting that he had no taste for the rigors of Mies's pedagogical style, Johnson insists that he did not go to study with Gropius. He returned to *Harvard*.) Gropius, who was forty-nine when he arrived in America, made no attempt to reestablish a Bauhaus in the New World. For one thing, Harvard was a far cry from Weimar Germany; so too were its relatively affluent graduate students from the Bauhaus's motley crew of revolutionaries. Unlike their European predecessors, American architectural students were more interested in acquiring a profession than in overturning society.

In one area, however, Harvard resembled Europe, and that was in how it taught architecture. Like other American schools, Harvard's traditional architectural program emphasized the logic and proportions of classical building systems that characterized the French École des Beaux-Arts. Little more than a decade before Gropius arrived, Harvard's program had driven a bored Hitchcock to pursue architectural history instead. In Europe a decade before that, Gropius had suffered through his own ennui. It had been partly to counter such an obsolete architectural teaching program and provide students with more hands-on building experience that Gropius had encouraged the Bauhaus's architectural students to work in his atelier.

Gropius gradually changed Harvard's traditional design program, reorienting it away from the conventional formal concerns of the Beaux-Arts toward an emphasis on practical building solutions that utilized industrial technologies. In Chicago, where Mies headed Armour Institute's School of Architecture (later known as Illinois Institute of Technology), he did much the same. It was in this radical shift in architectural training that the Bauhaus would leave its most durable imprint in American architectural education. Eventually every architectural school in the United States would adopt a similar program.

The Bauhaus would also emerge in America as a potent force in the teaching of design, particularly in the adaptation of form, material, and structure of household objects to industrial processes. This reorientation of how design was taught ultimately resulted in simplified, standardized, and cheaper goods, a result that Gropius had originally envisioned but had been unable to achieve in Germany.

Soon after Gropius arrived he helped bring over Breuer and Herbert Bayer, both of whom went on to long and productive American careers; Breuer as a teacher and architect, and Bayer as design consultant and art director of J. Walter Thompson advertising agency and several important corporations. As always, Gropius's heart remained in the practice of architecture, and in 1938 he set up an architectural partnership with Breuer (who also had a teaching appointment at Harvard) that lasted until 1941. The combining of a private practice with Gropius's teaching responsibilities raised as many eyebrows at Harvard as it had done earlier in Weimar and Dessau; which the former Bauhaus director—as he had done before—ignored. In 1946 Gropius established the Architects Collaborative.

Architecturally, Gropius never reached the heights in America that he had achieved in Germany with his Faguswerke and the Bauhaus building. Apart from his home in Lincoln, Massachusetts (designed in collaboration with Breuer), Gropius enjoyed numerous commissions both in the United States and abroad. Among his best-known buildings are the Harvard Graduate Center in Cambridge, Massachusetts; the U.S. Embassy in Athens; and the Pan American Airways Building in New York City, none of which could be considered outstanding. Indeed, the oversized Pan Am building (built between 1958 and 1963) not only damaged Gropius's architectural reputation but also exposed some of the limitations of the so-called Bauhaus style, such as its difficulties in dealing with monumental scale and its tendency to ignore architectural context.

Gropius continued to pursue many of his interests in America, particularly that of prefabrication. Although nothing much came of this during his lifetime in the United States—he was initially constrained, like everyone else, by wartime restrictions of material and money, and afterward by difficulties of production and finance—his numerous writings on this did help to spur subsequent development. Today nearly one in three new single-family homes in America are factory-built and more than 7 percent of the population live in them. As Gropius predicted (but at the time was unable to prove), these homes cost roughly about half as much as traditional homes. Several American cities are now studying the feasibility of using such factory-produced housing for the poor. One journal recently referred to factory-built housing as fast "becoming part of the American experience."

Having lived in Nazi Germany for one and a half years before he fled, Gropius had well learned the need to erase both the Bauhaus's (and his own) "Reddish" stain. This effort too continued in the United States, which harbored its own fears of Bolshevism. If not life-threatening as in the Third Reich, a Red association of any hue in America was no asset to anyone, especially a newly arrived immigrant.

The Museum of Modern Art's ideologically "pure," aesthetically sanitized, Miesian perception of the Bauhaus, however distorted it may have been, fit in perfectly with this historical whitewash. In 1938 the museum staged a Bauhaus show organized by Gropius, his wife, and Herbert Bayer, now new and grateful U.S. residents. This exhibition further ratified the view of a sanitized Bauhaus. Hannes Meyer's name would virtually disappear in America, his contribution to the Bauhaus barely acknowledged by the exhibition or its accompanying book, whose time span was arbitrarily restricted to the Gropius years.

The Nazi persecution of the Bauhaus—and modernism—mobilized still more American sympathy for both. "New York Holds Exhibit of Art Barred by Nazis," declared one American newspaper. No one seemed to ask what specifically about modernism it was that the Nazis so opposed. It was assumed the Nazis' attitude was simply part and parcel of their general cultural boorishness.

Gropius was particularly fortunate in finding so compatible a champion as Barr. Despite the nearly twenty-year disparity in their ages—Gropius was born in 1883, Barr in 1902—the two men had much in common. Both elder sons of privileged and conservative families, they were messianic proselytizers of radical change. They understood each other. They saw themselves and their creations in essentially salvationist terms: Barr wanted to save art and Gropius to save society. For both, art possessed the qualities that religion had lost; it was both redemptive and morally improving. Unfortunately, as the twentieth century's grim history reveals, such salvationist urges were not confined to these two titanic creators of our modern vision. There was another, less benign aspect to the belief that a singular way existed, that certain endowed individuals were capable of understanding it and had the right to impose it on others.

Gropius died at the age of eighty-three on July 6, 1969, an American citizen for twenty-five years and a revered and world-honored figure. England and America had bestowed on him their nations' highest architectural awards. So too, in 1958, did his native Germany.

Although Gropius complained about the stylistic overemphasis of the "International Style," he never precisely delineated the Bauhaus's social ideology that this phrase overlooked. After Gropius died, his wife, Ise, picked up the Bauhaus torch. Until her death in 1983 she would perpetuate the school's myth in America with even greater single-mindedness than her husband, her opinions bolstered by the Museum of Modern Art.

Having come to the Bauhaus in 1923 as a naive twenty-six-year-old, Ise had never known the circumstances of the school's impassioned origins nor as her diaries indicate did she reveal any particular insights or opinions apart from those of her husband. In spite of these shortcomings, Ise established herself as the inescapable sentry through which all Bauhaus inquiry had to pass, quickly and often testily contradicting any intimation that the Bauhaus might have been something other than an artistic Parnassus or her husband less than omniscient. Few articles or books on the Bauhaus could appear without invoking her commentary and, usually, her wrath. She refuted the architectural historian Reyner Banham's contention that architectural courses had only been introduced by Meyer. What Banham meant, of course, was that such classes were only *formally* introduced under Meyer. Ise labeled Sybil Moholy-Nagy's assertion that Gropius had been pressured out of the Bauhaus as "totally false," claiming instead that his departure had come "as a complete surprise" to Mayor Hesse.

Mies, who continued to try to sell modernism (and himself) to the Nazis, did not leave Germany until 1937, when he went to direct Armour Institute's School of Architecture. (He too had been considered by Harvard to head its architecture department but he lost out to the more personable and better-known Gropius.) While Mies would vehemently (and rightly) deny any Bauhaus influence on his style, by bringing along with him two former Bauhaus faculty members, Ludwig Hilberseimer and Walter Peterhans, he ensured a prominent Bauhaus presence at his school. This was reinforced by four young Americans who had (briefly) studied with Mies at the Bauhaus in Germany—Bertram Goldberg, Howard Dearstyne, John B. Rodgers, and William Priestley—all of whom continued off and on to work with him in the United States.

Unlike Gropius, who left his major architectural achievements behind him in Germany, Mies achieved new heights of architectural creativity in America, most notably with his Seagram Building in New York City and his Farnsworth House in Plano, Illinois, to name but two of his many buildings. He participated in various postwar German projects, such as the National Gallery in Berlin. While Gropius became known in America mostly for his Bauhaus contribution, Mies was revered for his subtle, rigorous, and exquisitely refined architecture. When Mies died on August 19, 1969, just more than a month after Gropius, he too had become an icon in his time, the recipient of Gold Medals and the American Medal of

Freedom. Conditioned by the Museum of Modern Art's view, the American public came to look at Mies's architecture as the apotheosis of what is popularly known as the Bauhaus style.

Gropius really started this identification of the Bauhaus with international modernism in 1923, when he included the architecture show in the school's general exhibit of that year. But while it participated in the movement, the Bauhaus certainly did not invent modernism. Indeed, architecture was only one of several important European developments in which the German Bauhaus partook. Among others were the development of prefabricated housing, the attempt to integrate hands-on craft training with artistic theory, and the design of household goods with machine technology. Here too the Bauhaus was more part of these developments than their originator. Despite this, Gropius's linkage of the Bauhaus with the broad European international modernist movement succeeded in America beyond his imaginable dreams.

Stripped of its ideological base—"a new architecture for a new age"—this less-is-more so-called Bauhaus building style thrived in America for very pragmatic reasons. It was relatively cheap, easy to build, and—important to real estate developers—easy to copy. Adding to its appeal, the style bore a bona fide pedigree from the Museum of Modern Art, the country's most prestigious arbiter of the avant-garde. In the 1960s a booming postwar America adopted this stripped-down, no-nonsense modern style for housing developments and colossal glass-walled skyscrapers that sprouted across the country. Thanks to new technology these modern skyscrapers assumed a gargantuan scale that was hardly imaginable to its European creators during the twenties. Highly visible symbols of American prosperity and power, these skyscrapers were adopted around the world, from Bombay to Buenos Aires.

But modernism's simplicity and apparent ease of reproduction was deceiving. For deprived of its generating ideology, the reductivist, almost formulaic Bauhaus style was uncommonly dependent on the sheer talent of its designers. With the deaths of Mies van der Rohe and Gropius in the late sixties the Bauhaus lost both its major designing genius (Mies) and most committed proselytizer (Gropius). Stripped of both a sustaining ideology and prodigious talent, the American version of the reductivist modernist style appeared simplistic and prissily puritanical—if not downright boring. Toward the end of the sixties, even the architectural critic Ada Louise Huxtable, one of the foremost and articulate admirers of international modernism, admitted that she too was becoming bored by "Bauhaus blue."

Surprisingly enough, one of the first to recognize this was none other than Philip Johnson, who had done so much to create and propagate the style. A restless and inexhaustible personality and an unparalleled presence on the American architectural scene, Johnson had spent much of the century helping the country discover the new and the naughty. Sometimes he went overboard. In 1934, for example, Johnson, then director of the Museum of Modern Art's architectural department, discovered politics with the same zeal that he had embraced a so-called de-politicized Bauhaus and international modernism a scant five years earlier. Johnson and a museum colleague, Alan Blackburn, resigned from the museum to found their own neo-Nazi political party, which they called the National Party. Johnson's political reveries eventually faded, and in 1943, having received his architectural degree from Harvard, he returned to "pure" art. But around 1960 Johnson experienced a similar about-face with regard to modernism. With characteristic cheekiness he began to refer to his earlier aesthetic modernist enthusiasms as "those dear, dead days." In 1984 Johnson's Chippendale-roofed AT&T Building in New York sounded the death knell to America's fifty-year flirtation with the so-called Bauhaus style.

Created to herald the worthy life, modernism's pristine canon had little truck with life's muddy footprints or misplaced socks. Without its supporting ideology, the Bauhaus style in America lacked substance, becoming little more than a throwaway, Kleenex style, rejectable when the next and equally transient architectural trend came along. Tired of Barcelona chairs, glass walls, and all-white rooms? the *New York Times* recently asked. "Get yourself a dog," the newspaper urged, advising those in the "know" to envelope their rooms in "velvet darkness" and let their shedding dog's fur assert "nature's messy vitality."

Today in America, reminiscences of the past—Doric columns, bay windows, and Greek temple fronts—are all the rage. "Retro" has become the "visionary," and the so-called classicists who build in this bizarrely backward style are hailed as the true radicals of their time. The Walt Disney Corporation, no longer satisfied with creating fantasy parks, is now building a "fantasy" community for twenty thousand residents near Orlando, Florida. Named "Celebration," this re-creation of an imaginary America in "the good old days," complete with front porches and clean streets, is selling out as fast as Disney can build it. American architectural students are flocking to Europe to soak up the Old World's curlicues, towers, and turrets that their forebears rejected and are demanding traditional classical training in their architecture schools, which hasten to add them to their programs.

Despite what these events seem to suggest, along with the very public wranglings that fill the pages of the daily press and professional journals alike, America's adoption of the Bauhaus style has not come to an end. America's most thoughtful and talented architects, such as Frank Gehry and Richard Meier, as well as many notable colleagues abroad, such as the English Norman Foster, the Japanese Arata Isozaki, the Swiss Mario Botta, and the French Christian Portzamparc and Jean Nouvel to name but a few, are all continuing to refine, reexamine, and reinterpret the modernism the Bauhaus came to exemplify; all are producing diverse, dynamic, and responsive modernist buildings.

Perhaps what America may be turning away from is its own particularly limited and biased view of a modernism stripped of its generating forces. Barr thought Europe exaggerated politics; perhaps one might argue just the opposite, that America inflates the artistic, the style without its substance. What has become clear is that America has interpreted European modernism and the Bauhaus to suit itself. It has seen only half its face. What Barr praised in the Bauhaus and modernism and America appropriated—the engineer's aesthetic, its reductivist concerns, and lack of historical resonance—are precisely those qualities that are now being criticized. Perhaps modernism's purported failure in America may really be a failure of comprehension, a mistaken or rather a too narrowly interpreted and aestheticized view.

On the other hand, if European modernism seems to have fallen victim to America's impatience with ideology, this in itself is not necessarily bad. The vigorous artistic debate, for example, that is going on in America at the century's end—between those who look backward over their shoulders toward a nostalgic past and those who confidently face ahead—bears an uncommon resemblance to what went on in Wilhelminian Germany as well as the Weimar Republic. But on closer view it is not the same. For however heated the arguments may be today, no one is suggesting that one position or another is more virtuous, more Left, or—heaven help us— more American. This too is part of the Bauhaus story. And considering what went on in Europe at the Bauhaus and elsewhere in the first half of the twentieth century, this might even be considered progress.

Appendix: Abbreviations in Notes

AA	*Anhalter Anzeiger*
AAA	Archives of American Art/Smithsonian Institution–
AHB	Alfred H. Barr Jr., papers, microfilm
JBN	J. B. Neumann, papers, microfilm
RI	Reginald Isaacs, papers
W&IG	Walter and Ise Gropius, papers (microfilm, unless otherwise noted)
IG/d	Ise Gropius diary, English translation, 1924–1929 (microfilm, 2393)
AfK	Working Council for Art
AHB	Alfred H. Barr Jr.
AM	Alma Mahler
AM/g	Alma Mahler Gropius
ARD	*Anhaltische Rundschau*, Dessau
AZC	*Allgemeine Zeitung*, Chemnitz
BAA	*Berliner Abend-Ausgabe*
BA/B	Bauhaus-Archiv, Berlin
F/1	File Bauhaus Weimar, Bauhaus-Presse 1919–1924
F/2	File Bauhaus Weimar, Bauhaus-Presse 1923, Bauhaus-Austellung
F/3	File Bauhaus Weimar, Bauhaus-Presse 1924

F/4	File Bauhaus Dessau, Bauhaus-Presse
F/5	File Bauhaus Dessau, Presse Vorträge, Walter Gropius
F/6	File Bauhaus Dessau, Presse, 1927
F/7	File Bauhaus Weimar, Bauhaus-Presse, July 1922–May 1924
F/8	File Presse 1923, Bauhaus-Austellung I
BA/D	Bauhaus-Archiv, Dessau
BAUW	*Bauwelt*
BBC	*Berliner Börsen-Courier*
BLA	*Berliner Lokal-Anzeiger*
BLZ	*Braunschweigische Landeszeitung*
BMP	*Berliner Morgenpost*
BT	Bruno Taut
BTB	*Berliner Tageblatt*
BZM	*Berliner Zeitung am Mittag*
CA	*Central Anzeiger*, Dessau
DAM/HM	Deutsches Architekturmuseum, Nachlass Hannes Meyer (Frankfurt am Main)
DAZ	*Deutsche Allgemeine Zeitung*
DDP	Deutsche Demokratische Partei
DESAN	*Dessauer Anzeiger*
DESZEIT	*Dessauer Zeitung*
DK	*Das Kunstblatt*
DLND	*Deutschland*, full name *Allgemeine Thüringische Landeszeitung Deutschland*
DN	*Dresdner Nachrichten*
DNP	Deutschnationale Partei
DNVP	Deutschnationale Volkspartei
DRF	*Die Rote Fahne*, Berlin
DS	*Der Sturm*
DTZ	*Deutsche Tageszeitung*, Berlin
DV	*Das Volk*
DVP	Deutsche Volkspartei
DWB	*Die Weltbühne*, Berlin-Charlottenberg
DZ	*Deutsche Zeitung*, Berlin
FH	Fritz Hesse
FJ	*Freie Jugend*

FM	Fritz Mackensen
FREI	*Die Freiheit*
FZ	*Frankfurter Zeitung*
GB	*Germania, Berlin*
GC/HM	Getty Collection, Hannes Meyer Collection
GSS	Grossherzogl. Saechs. Staatsministerium, Abteilung des Innern und Äussern
HA	*Hamburger Abendblatt*
HM	Hannes Meyer
HRH	Henry-Russell Hitchcock
IG	Ise Gropius
JBN	J. B. Neumann
JF	Julia Feininger
KEO	Karl-Ernst-Osthaus-Archiv, Hagen
KMW	Kultusministeriums, Weimar (See also THAW)
LAB	Landesarchiv Berlin
LF	Lyonel Feininger
LFHU	Houghton Library, Harvard University, Cambridge, Lyonel Feininger Collection, Feininger Correspondence 1883– , Vol. II.
LH	Lily Hildebrandt
LNN	*Leipziger Neuste Nachrichten*
MC	Minutes of Masters' Council meeting, Bauhaus
Mies	Ludwig Mies van der Rohe
MNN	*Münchner Neuste Nachrichten*
MOMA	The Museum of Modern Art, New York
JBN	Special Collections, J. B. Neumann Collection
MSG	Manon Scharnweber Gropius, mother of Walter Gropius
MW	Walter Müller-Wulckow
MZ	*Magdeburger Zeitung*
NB12	*Neue Berliner 12-Uhr Zeitung*
OM	Otto Meyer-Amden, friend of Oskar Schlemmer
OS	Oskar Schlemmer
PJ	Philip Johnson
Rfg	Reichsforschungsgesellschaft für Wirtschaftlichkeit im Bau- und Wohnungswesen
RI	Reginald Isaacs

RUND	*Rundschau*
RWZE	*Rheinisch.-Westfael. Zeitung, Essen*
SA	Société Anonyme
SAW	Stadtarchiv Weimar
SDA	Stadt Dessau Stadtarchiv
Ber	"Berichte über die Verwaltung und den Stand der Gemeindeangelegenheiten," 1913 bis 1933
Gemein	"Gemeinderatsprotokolle, Dessau 1923–1925," [minutes of the meetings of the Dessau City Council]
vol. 51/Gemein I	"Gemeinderatsprotokolle, Dessau 1928"
vol. 51/Gemein II	"Gemeinderatsprotokolle, Dessau 1929 bis 1933"
vol. 53/Fin 1	Dessau, "Sitzung des Finanzausschusses 1925–1929"
vol. 53/Fin 2	Dessau, "Sitzung des Finanzausschusses 1931–1932" (errata—includes meetings 1925/1926)
SMB/ZA	Staatliche Museen zu Berlin/Zentralarchiv
SOZMON	*Sozialistische Monatshefte*
SPD	Sozialdemokratische Partei Deutschlands
SSR	*Sächsische Rundschau*
THAW	Thüringisches Hauptstadtarchiv Weimar (Landeshauptarchiv)
+RS	Document includes reverse side
B	Bauhaus Abteilung
GKA	Gebietsregierung, Kultusabteilung
GSS	Grossherzogliches Saechs. Staatsministerium, Innern und Äussernabteilung
HFBKW	Staatliche Hochschule für bildende Kunst, Weimar
KGBSW	Kunstgewerbeschule, Weimar
KMW	Kultusministerium, Weimar
TFM	Finanzministerium
TVB	Volksbildungsministerium C; Abteilung Wissenschaft und Kunst
TLZ	*Thüringerische Landeszeitung*
TS	Tut Schlemmer
TT	*Thüringerische Tageszeitung*
TVB	Volksbildungsministerium, Weimar

USPD	German Independent Socialist Party
VB	*Volksblatt*
VdV	Henry van de Velde
VPAM	Alma Mahler letters, Special Collections, University of Pennsylvania, Van Pelt Library
VRTS	*Vorwärts*, Berlin
VSTM	*Volksstimme*
VZ	*Vossische Zeitung*, Berlin
VZB	*Volkszeitung*, Berlin
WG	Walter Gropius
WGHU	Walter Gropius Papers, Arbeitsrat für Kunst file, Houghton Library, Harvard University
WHAB	Hochschule für Architektur und Bauwesen, Weimar
WLTB	*Die Weltbühne*
WZ	*Weimarische Zeitung*
WZB	*Weser-Zeitung, Bremen*
WZHAB	*Wissenschaftliche Zeitschrift der Hochschule für Architektur und Bauwesen, Weimar*
ZBW	*Zentralblatt der Bauverwaltung*

Notes

3   *"the fragmentation of the German people"*   OS, diary, June 1923,
     Oskar Schlemmer, *The Letters and Diaries of Oskar Schlemmer,*
     ed. Tut Schlemmer, trans. Krishna Winston (Evanston, Ill.:
     Northwestern University Press, [1972] 1990), p. 139.
    "[a] true child of the German Republic"   Hannes Meyer,
     Edificación, 1940, DAM/HM.
    a "microcosm" of what was happening in the Reich   AA,
     7 May 1930.
    "the circumstances and means of our time"   Walter Gropius,
     "Das Manifest der neuen Architektur," in *Stein Holz Eisen* 40,
     no. 109 (5 August 1926): 198, AAA, W&IG, 2275.
    broad cultural scene   IG to Marcel Franciscono (Urbana, Ill.),
     15 January 1972, AAA, W&IG, 2271.
4   *"the continuous and tense" interaction*   Peter Gay, *Weimar
     Culture: The Outsider as Insider* (New York: Harper & Row,
     1968), p. 119.
    "curious and persistent" parallels   "Bauhaus Conflicts Seen
     Now," microfilm of typed manuscript of broadcast transcript of
     BBC, Third Programme, prerecorded London: 16 October

1968; transmission: 25 October 1968; George Baird, compiler and narrator, AAA, W&IG, 2281.

4   *very pressures*   Frank Whitford, *Bauhaus* (London: Thames and Hudson, 1984), p. 9.

1. YOUTH, WAR, AND REVOLUTION

5   *a much-treasured record book*   Reginald Isaacs, *Gropius: An Illustrated Biography of the Creator of the Bauhaus* (Boston, Toronto, London: Little, Brown, and Company, [1983] 1990), p. 1.

6   *Schinkel's career*   Unable to support himself in the early years of his architectural practice, Schinkel often supplemented his meager income by painting and designing. It was in this capacity that he became involved with the Gropius family, designing curtains and a proscenium for the Gropius dioramic theater owned by Wilhelm Ernst, which achieved the effect of three-dimensionality through changing lights and moving sculptural figures accompanied by music and words. The family commissioned Schinkel to create a proscenium for the theater and he subsequently provided sketches for the diorama itself. In addition, the family provided exhibition space for his paintings at their annual Christmas exhibitions from 1807 to 1815. The popularity of the Gropius diorama and Schinkel's well-known participation in it helped bring his name to the public and launch his career. For more detailed information, see Isaacs, *An Illustrated Biography*, p. 2.

a timid and depressed man   WG to Klaus Karbe, 5 May 1967, AAA, RI.

a civil servant in the Prussian State Building Department   Klaus Karbe (Berlin) to RI, 29 June 1965, AAA, RI.

7   *"merely adequate"*   IG/d, 11 April 1926, AAA, W&IG.

"iron willpower"   Ibid., 20 May 1925, AAA, W&IG.

tolerant   WG to Manon Gropius Burchard, 16 February 1963, AAA, RI.

frank, and liberal   Klaus Karbe (Berlin) to RI (Berlin), 29 June 1965. English translated typescript, AAA, RI.

indestructibly kind   WG to Manon Gropius Burchard, 16

February 1963, AAA, RI.

7 *"his loved ones' pride and joy"* Luise Hönig Gropius (Berlin) to WG, 12 May 1905, AAA, 2270.

"battered by a cruel life" MSG (Berlin) to WG, 24 May 1915, AAA, RI.

Frank Lloyd Wright's work . . . and she accompanied him AAA, RI, Notes.

8 *a bridge across the Rhine* AAA, RI; see Julius Caesar, *The Conquest of Gaul*, trans. S. A. Handford with revs. Jane Gardner (London: Penguin Books, [1951] 1982), pp. 95–96.

commanding officers' praise WG (Wandsbeck) to MSG, 9 September 1904, AAA, RI.

"shamefully insulted" WG (Berlin) to MSG, 29 August 1907, AAA, RI.

"[a] strong, straight-ahead character" Werner Hebebrand, interview with Reginald Isaacs, Hamburg, undated, AAA, RI.

9 *"the simplest thing . . . could be so bad"* WG (Medina del Campo) to MSG, 21 October 1907, AAA, RI.

rarely lifted a pencil . . . Architects' Collaborative Winfried Nerdinger, *Walter Gropius* (Berlin: Gebr. Mann Verlag, 1985), pp. 29–31.

10 *a "support activity"* Ibid., p. 29.

"the lifelong air of a missionary" Ibid.

challenge to stay dynamic WG to "Ekart" (Behne), 16 September 1919, THAW/B, 6/13.

preparing "for battle" . . . strength of the opposition WG to Redslob, 13 January 1920, THAW/B, 6/205–206.

"measur[ed] up to this struggle" WG (Weimar) to AM/g, 12 July 1919, AAA, RI.

danger LF to JF, August 1924, LFHU, 24/29.

split personality Nikolaus Pevsner, "Any Old Bauhaus?" *The Listener* (24 January 1963): 160.

"great inner agitation" Fritz Hesse, *Von der Residenz zur Bauhausstadt* (Bad Pyrmont: privately printed, 1963), p. 200.

"carried us all away" George Adams, "Memories of a Bauhaus Student," *Architectural Review* 144, no. 859 (September 1968): 192.

"a true, upright man" LF to JF, May 1919, LFHU, 19/16.

11　*hired draftsman in tow*　Nerdinger, *Gropius*, p. 29.
　　"work with my draftsman"　WG to MSG, 16 June 1906, in ibid.
　　latest European and American publications . . . interesting lectures
　　　　AAA, RI.
　　Gropius's fault　Nerdinger, *Gropius*, p. 29.
　　"forgo any further collaboration"　WG to Osthaus, 5 March
　　　　1910, ibid.
　　"burning sense of social responsibility"　Pevsner, "Any Old
　　　　Bauhaus?" p. 160.

12　*come to recuperate*　Karen Monson, *Alma Mahler: Muse to
　　　　Genius* (Boston: Houghton Mifflin Company, 1983), p. 104.

14　*"hammering heart"*　WG (Le Quieux) to MSG, 26 September
　　　　1914, AAA, RI.
　　"a lousy, dirty field soldier"　Ibid., 7 October 1914, AAA, RI.
　　"before everything [fell] apart"　Monson, *Alma Mahler*, p. 164.
　　"The shock was terrible"　WG (Laître) to MSG, early January
　　　　1915, AAA, RI.

15　*"A hellish dance began"*　Ibid.
　　"The best are dead"　WG (Laître) to MSG, undated (believed to
　　　　be 5 or 6 January 1915), AAA, RI.
　　"completely unlearned [how] to sleep"　WG (Wisch) to MSG, 16
　　　　January 1915, AAA, RI.

16　*"rouses people"*　WG (Vosges) to MSG, December 1915, AAA, RI.
　　just the wife of a junior military officer　AM/g (Vienna) to WG,
　　　　undated (believed to be late September 1915), AAA, RI, quoted
　　　　in Reginald R. Isaacs, *Walter Gropius: Der Mensch und sein
　　　　Werk*, vol. 1 (Berlin: Gebr. Mann Verlag, 1983), p. 156.
　　"totally . . . unwritten page"　Ibid.
　　sexually repressed maestro　"In a most interesting foray into his
　　　　life, we have analyzed his condition, especially his Maria
　　　　Complex [*Mutterbindung*, or Oedipus Complex]" (Sigmund
　　　　Freud to Theodor Reik, in Françoise Giroud, *Alma Mahler;
　　　　oder Die Kunst, Geliebt zu Werden* [Vienna: Paul Zsolnay
　　　　Verlag Gesellschaft GmbH, 1989], p. 117).

17　*Gropius walked away*　In Isaacs, *An Illustrated Biography*, p. 49.
　　slowly falling apart　WG (Vienna) to Karl Ernst Osthaus, 19
　　　　December 1917, in Isaacs, *An Illustrated Biography*, p. 54.
　　"thundering hunger"　In Seth Taylor, *Left-Wing Nietzscheans:*

The Politics of German Expressionism, 1910–1920, vol. 22 of
Die Nietzsche-Forschung (Berlin: Walter de Gruyter & Co.,
1990), p. 187.

17 growing desperate   Ernst Toller, I Was a German: The Political
Turmoil in Germany During and After World War I; The
Autobiography of a Revolutionary, trans. Edward Crankshaw
(New York: Paragon House, [1933] 1991), pp. 130–31.

existing Bismarckian order   Gordon A. Craig, Germany,
1866–1945 (New York: Oxford University Press Inc.,
1978), p. 363.

"monarchical-conservative elements in Europe" . . . inciting
revolution   Ibid., p. 103.

"deluge of patriotic abuse" . . . even persecution   Ibid., p. 94.

"the red menace"   Bismarck, ibid., p. 93.

"an un-German madness" . . . equal of bestiality   Heinrich von
Treitschke, ibid., pp. 95, 145.

18 "must be destroyed"   Ibid., p. 264.

threatened to refuse responsibility   Ibid., p. 379.

conquest, annexation, and defense   Ibid., p. 358.

19 compared war to Christmas   In Craig, Germany, p. 339.

Thomas Mann "joyfully" anticipated   Thomas Mann, Briefe,
1889–1936 (Frankfurt am Main: S. Fischer Verlag GmbH,
1961), p. 115.

indispensable reading   According to Joachim Burchard (nephew of
Walter Gropius in Hannover) and his mother, Mrs. Manon
Burchard, Gropius's sister; undated, AAA, RI.

"resurrections"   Friedrich Wilhelm Nietzsche, "Thus Spoke
Zarathustra: Second Part" in The Portable Nietzsche, ed. and
trans. Walter Kaufmann (1954; reprint, New York: Viking
Penguin Inc., 1982), p. 224.

"mute"   in Toller, I Was a German, p. 93.

"livid with rage"   WG (the Vosges, field headquarters) to MSG,
17 August 1916, AAA, RI.

20 unable to paint   Schmidt-Rottluff to LF, 27 August 1920,
LFHU, 20/15.

vowed revenge   Adolf Hitler, Mein Kampf, trans. Ralph
Mannheim (Boston: Sentry, Edition, Houghton Mifflin, [1925]
1943), pp. 204–206.

20 *mood of the troops* WG (the Vosges, field headquarters) to MSG,
17 August 1916, AAA, RI.

"I defend no ideals . . . disgust and contempt for people" George
Grosz, *An Autobiography*, trans. Nora Hodges (1946; reprint,
New York: An Imago Imprint, 1983), p. 98.

German "Kultur" In Taylor, *Left-Wing*, p. 190.

healthy enough Carl Zuckmayer, *A Part of Myself* (London:
Secker & Warburg, 1970), pp. 177–78.

"hare who roars like a lion" Harry Graf Kessler, *Tagebucher:
1918–1937* (Frankfurt am Main: Insel Verlag, 1961), p. 92.

21 *"dancing star"* Nietzsche, "Human, All-Too Human," *The
Portable Nietzsche*, p. 129.

intellectual change In Magdalena Droste, *Bauhaus: 1919–1933*,
trans. Karen Williams (Berlin: Bauhaus-Archiv Museum für
Gestaltung, Berlin, Benedikt Taschen Verlag GmbH & Co. KG,
1990), p. 16.

"a whole new world" Toller, *I Was a German*, p. 99.

"ruined as an artist" WG (Vienna) to Karl Ernst Osthaus, 19
December 1917, in Isaacs, *An Illustrated Biography*, p. 54.

"tough peacetime battles" WG (between Soisson and Reims) to
MSG, 7 January 1918, AAA, RI.

22 *"weaklings and pigs"* WG to MSG, undated (believed to be
January 1 or 2 February 1918) AAA, RI.

"stink of money" Richard Fischer, "Field of Honor," *Menschen*
1, no. 3 (15 March 1918): 1.

in this offensive Craig, *Germany*, p. 394.

"lost, lost, lost" WG (Breitenstein) to MSG, 11 June 1918,
AAA, RI.

23 *between life and death . . . weak calls* AAAs RI; see also Isaacs,
An Illustrated Biography, p. 1.

"the latest wave of voices" WG (Wallergasse) to AM/g, 23 July
1918, VPAM.

take stock of his life AAA, RI.

Nietzsche's claim "[T]hat the creator may be, . . . suffering
is needed and much change. Indeed, there must be much
bitter dying in your life, you creators." Nietzsche, "Thus
Spake Zarathustra: Second Part," *The Portable
Nietzsche*, p. 199.

23 *"I have found a way"* WG (Wallergasse) to AM/g, 23 July 1918, VPAM.

24 *source of all higher thought* Oswald Spengler, *The Decline of the West*, ed. Helmut Werner, English abrev. ed. Arthur Helps, trans. Charles Francis Atkinson, 2 vols. (New York, New York and Oxford, England: Oxford University Press, 1918 and 1922, one-vol. ed. 1991), pp. 89–90.

"all for nothing" Toller, *I Was a German*, p. 137.

"we are going under, friends" In Craig, *Germany*, p. 482.

"Pan-German-militaristic-conservative combine" Ibid., p. 395.

25 *"The Red flag is over Berlin!"* VRTS, 9 November 1918.

"Red-ness of the time" . . . *"Socialismus asiaticus"* Ibid., 5 and 6 November 1918.

26 *nervous German government* Ibid., 9 November 1918.

infuriated Ebert Gay, *Weimar Culture*, p. 11; see also Craig, *Germany*, 401–402.

comical circumstances Gay, *Weimar Culture*, p. 11.

government of the people VRTS, 10 November 1918.

27 *taut faces* Count Harry Kessler, *The Diaries of a Cosmopolitan: 1918–1937*, ed. and trans. Charles Kessler (London: Weidenfeld and Nicolson, [1961] 1971), 11 December 1918 (Berlin), p. 39.

"to participate in the revolution" WG (Berlin) to Karl Ernst Osthaus, 23 December 1918, in Herta Hesse-Frielinghaus, ed., *Karl Ernst Osthaus, Leben und Werk* (Recklinghausen: Bongers, 1971), pp. 470–72; also in Isaacs, *An Illustrated Biography*, p. 63.

"strike while the iron is hot" Ibid.

"secret wing beats" Nietzsche, "Thus Spake Zarathustra: Third Part," *The Portable Nietzsche*, pp. 269–70.

2. THE BEAUTY OF EFFICIENT FORM: TYRANNY, TREASON, OR SALVATION? BACKGROUND TO THE BAUHAUS

28 *taking over his position* Henry van de Velde, *Geschichte meines Lebens* (Munich: R. Piper GmbH & Co., KG, [1959] 1986), p. 501.

dropped out Obrist's negotiations did not get very far, while

Endell remained in the running until the beginning of January
1916, when negotiations with him were broken off. GSS, 14
January 1916, THAW/HFBKW, 100/1.

28 *resign his directorship* GSS to FM, 24 September 1914,
THAW/HFBKW, 168/9.

29 *handling the actual hiring* FM to GSS, 22 December 1914,
THAW/HFBKW, 168/14–17.

closure of van de Velde's school VdV to WG, 8 July 1915, in
Hans M. Wingler, *The Bauhaus: Weimar, Dessau, Berlin,
Chicago*, ed. Joseph Stein, trans. Wolfgang Jabs and Gilbert
Basil (Cambridge, Mass.: The MIT Press, 1969), p. 21.

expanded to include architecture FM to WG (on Western front),
22 November 1915, THAW/HFBKW, 179/7.

at least double VdV to WG, 8 July 1915, in Wingler, *The
Bauhaus*, p. 21.

30 *expanding the seminars into a school* Ibid.

he had begun negotiations FM to WG, 14 October 1915,
ibid., p. 22.

31 *Such an arrangement* FM to GSS, 22 December 1914,
THAW/HFBKW, 168/14–17.

Now the idea was FM to WG, 22 November 1915,
THAW/HFBKW, 179/7.

remain relevant See Theophile Thoré (W. Bürger, pseudonym),
"Nouvelles tendences de l'art" (1857), p. ix.

Manet complained In Otto Friedrich, *Olympia: Paris in the Age
of Manet* (New York: Harper Collins, 1992), p. 7.

32 *functional priorities* John Ruskin, *The Art Criticism of John
Ruskin*, ed. and intro. Robert L. Herbert (Garden City, N.Y.:
Anchor Books, Doubleday & Company Inc., 1964), p. 3.

a remarkable prophecy Oscar Wilde, *Impressions of America*,
ed. and intro. Stuart Mason (Sunderland: Keystone Press,
1906), p. 24.

"turned to iron" Friedrich Naumann, "Was ist eine Maschine,"
cited in *Naumann Buch* (Göttingen: Vandenhoeck und
Ruprecht, 1903), p. 84.

the Kaiser's personal request Eckart Muthesius, "Muthesius,"
Muthesius in England, p. 6, catalogue published by the
Architectural Association, *Hermann Muthesius, 1861–1927*.

See also Joan Campbell, *The German Werkbund: The Politics of Reform in the Applied Arts* (Princeton: Princeton University Press, 1978), p. 12; and Introduction by Stanford Anderson, "Style-Architecture and Building Art: Transformations of Architecture in the Nineteenth Century and Its Present Condition" by Hermann Muthesius, Texts and Documents, The Getty Center Publication Programs, The Getty Center for the History of Art and the Humanities, p. 2.

32   *his real job*   This was Henry-Russell Hitchcock's view; Posener disagrees (Julius Posener, "Muthesius in England," catalogue published by the Architectural Association, *Hermann Muthesius, 1861–1927*, p.6).

33   *dreaded socialism*   Julius Posener, *Anfänge des Funktionalismus.; Von Arts und Crafts zum Deutschen Werkbund* (Frankfurt am Main: Ullstein, 1964), p. 224.

"economic power"   Ibid.

integral to Germany's . . . economic policy   Ibid., p. 76.

35   *"Let's go!"*   Filippo Tommaso Marinetti, "The Founding and Manifesto of Futurism" (1909), in *Futurism and Futurisms* (New York: Abbeville Press, [1909] 1986), p. 514.

Boccioni . . . and Ezra Pound's   Marjorie Perloff, *The Futurist Moment: Avant-Garde, Avant Guerre, and the Language of Rupture* (Chicago: The University of Chicago Press, 1986), p. xix.

36   *radically altered priorities*   Hermann Muthesius, *Stilarchitektur und Baukunst: Wandlungen der Architektur im XIX. Jahrhundert und ihr heutiger Standpunkt* (Mülheim an der Ruhr: K. Schimmelpfeng, 1902), p. 94.

a "mighty tree"   Spengler, *Decline*, pp. 411–13.

"real physical pain"   Ruskin, "The Cestus of Aglaia," *The Art Criticism*, pp. 145–46.

a world engulfed   Ruskin, "The Eagle's Nest," ibid., pp. 148–49.

"gloomy beacon"   Charles Baudelaire, "Exposition universelle, 1855," *The Painter of Modern Life and Other Essays*, ed. and trans. Jonathan Mayne (New York: Da Capo Press, [1863] 1964), pp. 125–27.

"the great disease"   in Anne Coffin Hanson, *Manet and the Modern Tradition* (New Haven: Yale University Press, [1977] 1979), p. 15.

37 *"exactly alike"* Ibid., pp. 10–12.

"Beware of the modern" Ibid., p. 4.

more on the fine than the practical arts The artistic issues
involved in the machine aesthetic remained mostly confined to
the Werkbund.

"foreign ones forced on us" quoted in James Joll, "Revolt in
Munich!" *The New York Review of Books* 38, no. 7 (11 April
1991): 23.

"ridiculous fad" In Peter Paret, *The Berlin Secession: Modernism
and Its Enemies in Imperial Germany* (Cambridge, Mass.:
Harvard University Press, 1980), p. 65.

envy belied their complaints Ibid., p. 186.

38 *slander and treason* Max Liebermann, *Die Phantasie in der
Malerei* (Frankfurt am Main, 1978), p. 49.

German moral and patriotic ideals Henry Thode, *Schauen und
Glauben* (Heidelberg, 1903), in Paret, *The Berlin Secession*, p.
111.

the nationalistic spirit of German art Karl Storck, "Deutsche
Kunst," *Deutsche Welt* 8, no. 2 (1905), in Paret, *The Berlin
Secession*, p. 177.

"dangerous dilettante" In Paret, *The Berlin Secession*, p. 209.

"a sin against the German people" Joan Weinstein, *The End of
Expressionism: Art and the November Revolution in Germany,
1918–19* (Chicago: University of Chicago Press, 1990), pp. 1–2.

39 *a racist dimension* In Paret, *The Berlin Secession*, p. 68.

"I don't want to say Jews" Ibid., p. 110.

40 *arouse the masses* In Taylor, *Left-Wing*, p. 36.

equivalent revolutionary acts Erich Mühsam, *Revolution* 1,
no. 1 (15 October 1913): 2, in Weinstein, *The End of
Expressionism*, p. 15.

"You mongrels" Johannes Becher, "Song of Freedom,"
Revolution 1, no. 1 (15 October 1913): 2, ibid.

"artfully demolish their comfort" In Taylor, *Left-Wing*, p. 44.

41 *"Secessionist junk"* In Paret, *The Berlin Secession*, p. 106.

Kollwitz, denied the award Ibid., p. 112.

ruining . . . German draftsmanship Ibid., p. 158.

to public attention WG, "Monumentale Kunst und Industrie,"
address delivered at Hagen, 29 January 1911, in Helmut Weber,

Walter Gropius und das Faguswerk (Baumeister–Bücher, 3: Munich, 1961), p. 27, BA/B.

42 *He would not "compromise"* WG (in Field) to FM, 17 December 1915, THAW/HFBKW, 179/11–12.

"[M]ake demands" AM/g to WG, undated (believed to be late fall 1915, as Mackensen had written in mid-September), VPAM, quoted in Isaacs, *Walter Gropius: Der Mensch*, p. 151.

depressed and . . . "desperate" WG to Karl Ernst Osthaus, 23 December 1918, in Hesse-Frielinghaus, *Osthaus*, pp. 470–72.

"apathy in the streets" Hjalmar Schacht, *My First Seventy-Six Years* (London: Wingate, 1959), p. 149.

43 *few could figure out what was going on* OS to OM, mid-December 1918, Schlemmer, *Letters and Diaries*, p. 63.

some absurd crime film Kessler, *Diaries*, 12 November 1918 (Berlin), p. 11.

his rebelliousness had become pronounced See Gropius's reference to saving himself for the coming peacetime battles (WG [between Soisson and Reims] to MSG, 7 January 1918, AAA, RI).

a speech he gave at the Leipzig Trade Fair WG, "Die Überwindung des europäischen Krämertums: Voraussetzung für eine Kultur," address, Leipzig Trade Fair, winter 1918, AAA, W&IG, 2275.

anguished over being forgotten WG (Berlin) to Karl Ernst Osthaus, 23 December 1918, in Hesse-Frielinghaus, *Osthaus*, pp. 470–72.

only hope was Weimar WG (Berlin) to MSG, undated (believed to be early December 1918), in Isaacs, *Walter Gropius: Der Mensch*, p. 189.

the city's Craft Guild had rejected R. Alander (Member, Board of Craft Guild for Grossh. Sachsen Handwerkskammer) to GSS, 15 March 1916, memorandum, THAW/B, 3/14–15.

"my many efforts . . . have unfortunately failed" FM to GSS, 24 March 1917, THAW/HFBKW, A100/21.

44 *The Academy . . . could not make up its mind* GSS [sig. Rothe?] to Direktion der Grossherz. HfbK (FM), 10 October 1917, THAW/HFBKW, 184–186/498.

"I would prefer it" WG (Berlin) to MSG, undated (believed to be early December 1918), in Isaacs, *Walter Gropius: Der Mensch*, p. 189.

44 *a preliminary agreement* WG (Berlin) to Herr Kaemmer, 31
   March 1919, THAW/B, H75/11. Gropius referred to his earlier
   agreement in this letter.
   "beyond imagining" WG to MSG, undated (believed to be early
   December 1918), in Isaacs, *Walter Gropius: Der Mensch*, p. 189.

3. A FRAGILE MOMENT: WEIMAR, GROPIUS, AND THE AVANT-GARDE

46 *trailblazing hub* VdV, *Meines Lebens*, p. 209.
   a grandiose plan Ibid., pp. 222–23.
   Count Harry Kessler Ibid. Kessler was commonly believed to be
   the son of Kaiser Wilhelm I, begotten by the seventy-year-old
   monarch during a visit to the Paris Exposition in 1867. Kessler
   was born the following year in Paris.
   "struggles, intrigues, and dangers" VdV, *Meines Lebens*, p. 224.
47 *"[T]heir . . . opposition . . . cannot harm us"* Ibid.
   Kessler plunged into his task Ibid., p. 226.
   undisguised hostility Ibid.
   Prominently seated . . . raised van de Velde's hopes Ibid., p. 215.
48 *look for his successor* Ibid., p. 373.
   "follow the German spirit" FM to GSS, 26 July 1916, memorandum, THAW/HFBKW, 100/18–19.
   expanding the handicraft department GSS (sig. Rothe?) to
   Direktion der Grossherz. HfbK (FM), 10 October 1917,
   THAW/HFBKW, 184–186/498.
   greater emphasis on practical crafts training FM to GSS, 17
   October 1917, THAW/HFBKW, 184–86/515–24.
49 *"guide the spirituality"* Ibid.
   unwavering monarchists Gitta Günther and Lothar Wallraf, eds.,
   Geschichte der Stadt Weimar (Weimar: Hermann Böhlaus
   Nachfolger, 1975), p. 516.
   The Kaiser abdicated Ibid., p. 520.
   so quietly Ibid., p. 521.
   unswerving loyalty Ibid., p. 522.
50 *how alienated he had become* WG (Berlin) to MSG, 17 March
   1919, AAA, RI.
   "only what is coming down" WG to MSG (Berlin), late January

1919, in Isaacs, *An Illustrated Biography*, p. 63.

50   *"overthrow [the] old . . . conceit"*   Nietzsche, "Thus Spake
Zarathustra: Third Part," *The Portable Nietzsche*, p. 308.

51   *a messianic community . . . to create an ethical world*   Iain Boyd
Whyte, *Bruno Taut and the Architecture of Activism*
(Cambridge, England: Cambridge Urban & Architectural
Studies, Cambridge University Press, 1982), p. 90.
"neither the mentality of [the] trade union"   Kurt Hiller,
"Ortsbestimmung des Aktivismus," *Die Erhebung* 1 (1919):
363, in Whyte, *Taut*, p. 100.

52   *"the foundations of an enlightened society"*   WG to Ernst Hardt
(Weimar), 14 April 1919, AAA, RI (Grundstein einer Republik
der Geister), in Isaacs, *Walter Gropius: Der Mensch*, p. 208.
the new political situation   In Whyte, *Taut*, p. 95.
political aims   Ibid.
moved to strengthen the group's solidarity   Ibid.
"a dirty word"   OS to OM, 22 November 1918, *Oskar
Schlemmer: Tagebuch, 1907–1918, 1919–1923, 1924–1927*,
unabridged diaries, typed manuscript, BA/B.

53   *Gropius apparently joined*   The precise date of Gropius's involvement with the AfK remains unclear. He was long believed to
have founded the group. But correspondence and the absence
of his name among the list of founding members on the publication of the AfK's program in early December seem to indicate
that Gropius came to the group shortly after its founding. A letter to Gropius's mother mentioning his interest in the AfK is
undated but—according to Isaacs—is believed to date from
December 1918. "I have come to orient myself and to take part
in the new artists' organizations," wrote Gropius. "I shall have
a meeting with Heinrich Tessenow and Bruno Taut concerning
the Arbeitsrat für Kunst right now" (WG [Berlin] to MSG,
undated [believed to be December 1918], in Isaacs, *An
Illustrated Biography*, p. 64). In his letter of December 23 to
Osthaus, Gropius mentions having joined the AfK (Hesse-
Frielinghaus, *Osthaus*, pp. 470–72).
it now appears to have been founded by . . . Bruno Taut   Gropius
and Adolf Behne have been variously considered to have initiated
the group. Marcel Franciscono, *Walter Gropius and the*

Creation of the Bauhaus in Weimar: The Ideals and Artistic Theories of Its Founding Years (Chicago: University of Chicago Press, 1971), p. 128, cites Lothar Lang as claiming that Behne actually conceived the AfK. But neither Behne's nor Gropius's names were on the lists of members published, along with its program, in *VRTS* and *FREI* on 11–12 December 1918, respectively. Whyte (*Taut*, pp. 96–97) asserts that it was in fact Taut who founded the AfK.

53   *to transform society*   BT, "An die sozialistische Regierung," *SOZMON* 24, no. 15 (26 November 1918): 1050, microfilm.

Taut's ideology . . . more developed   See Whyte, *Taut*, pp. 11–12.

what the revolution brought to architecture   Taut, "What Does the Revolution Bring to Architecture?" *VRTS*, 18 November 1918.

A convinced Nietzschean   In a letter of 8 June 1904 to his brother Max, Taut wrote "I've read Nietzsche's *Zarathustra* over the last 3 months—a book of enormous and serious vitality. I've learnt a lot from it" (in Whyte, *Taut*, p. 85). Citing the German philosopher as his authority, Taut also quoted Nietzsche's "Schopenhauer als Erzieher" in *Die Stadtkrone* (Jena: E. Diederichs, 1919), p. 57; see also Whyte, p. 48.

"sad, lonely artist"   Taut, "What Does the Revolution Bring to Architecture?"

"great cultural construction"   Taut, "An die sozialistische Regierung," p. 1051.

54   *"priest who serves God"*   Taut, "What Does the Revolution Bring to Architecture?"

neither culture nor art   Taut, *Die Stadtkrone*, p. 59, in Whyte, *Taut*, p. 52.

"what religion once meant"   John Schikowski, "Revolution and Art," *VRTS*, 14 November 1918.

"the kingdom of heaven"   Heinrich Tessenow, *Handwerk und Kleinstadt* (Berlin, 1919 [written in 1918]), p. 4, in Whyte, *Taut*, p. 106.

"We roam in chaos"   WG, "Die Überwindung."

"a fantastic construction"   Taut, "What Does the Revolution Bring to Architecture?"

a physical and *moral enterprise*   Taut, "An die sozialistische Regierung," p. 1050.

54   *"builders of a new culture"*   Ibid., p. 1051.
     "great spiritual idea"   WG, "Die Überwindung."
55   *"crystal symbol of a new faith"*   In Wingler, *The Bauhaus*, p. 31.
     "luxury for the rich"   Taut, "What Does the Revolution Bring to
     Architecture?"
     unified mankind   Taut, "An die sozialistische Regierung," p. 1050.
     "without . . . presumptuous class distinctions"   In Wingler, *The
     Bauhaus*, p. 31.
     "teaching, religion, and art"   Taut, "An die sozialistische
     Regierung," p. 1050.
     "That's what we are fighting for"   WG, "Die Überwindung."
56   *Taut's AfK agenda*   BT, "A Programme for Architecture," in
     Ulrich Conrads, ed., *Programs and Manifestoes on 20th-
     Century Architecture*, trans. Michael Bullock (Cambridge,
     Mass.: The MIT Press, 1970), p. 41.
     "influence the government"   BT address, "Protokoll der
     Vorstandssitzung des Werkbundes von 30 Juli, 1919," in Hesse-
     Frielinghaus, *Osthaus*, p. 476; also in Whyte, *Taut*, p.99.
     "The revolutionary gentlemen"   Hermann Schmitz, *Revolution
     der Gesinnung!: Preussische Kulturpolitik und
     Volksgemeinschaft seit dem 9. November 1918* (Neubabelsberg:
     privately printed, 1931), pp. 50–51.
     "a purely fortuitous accident"   VRTS, 14 November 1918.
57   *a future socialist society*   Wilhelm Hausenstein, *Der nackte Mensch
     in der Kunst aller Zeiten und Völker* (Munich: R. Piper & Co.,
     1913), p. 192; in Weinstein, *The End of Expressionism*, p. 12.
     some sort of danger   BTB, 11 November 1918.
     dated and obsolete   For more information, see Whyte, *Taut*, p. 108.
     "I regard the Werkbund as dead"   WG (Berlin) to Osthaus,
     23 December 1918, in Hesse-Frielinghaus, *Osthaus*,
     pp. 470–72.

4. STORMING INTO WEIMAR: THE CITY AS RELIC OR HARBINGER

58   *relatively conservative*   Karl-Heinz Hüter, *Das Bauhaus in Weimar*
     (Berlin: Akademie-Verlag, 1976), pp. 13–14.
     nor had they belonged   Günther, *Geschichte*, p. 516.

59 *stopped its presses*   Ibid., p. 517.

petitioned the state authorities   They also suggested that the
Assembly be located in Weimar, citing the city's importance to
German culture. Faculty of HFBKW to Baudert (Weimar), 30
November 1918, memorandum, THAW/HFBKW, 184–86/632.

"dangerous fire"   Günther, *Geschichte*, p. 517.

Weimar chosen . . . as the site   Under normal circumstances the
National Assembly would have met in the Reichstag building in
Berlin. But the building had been heavily damaged during the
November revolution, and the ongoing civil unrest had made it
impossible to secure it properly for the gathering of the contro-
versial national legislative body.

60 *simply to a buy railroad ticket*   WG (Berlin) to Herr Kaemmer, 31
March 1919, THAW/B, 75/11.

61 *"total change" . . . "radical transformation"*   WG,
"Die Überwindung."

courtiers administering revolutionary governments   Decree. Die
provisorische republikanische Landesregierung [sig. Baudert] to
Staatsministerium, Finanzen/Direktion HFBKW, 10 December
1918, THAW/HFBKW, 184–86/26.

the "Weimar Bauhaus"   See A. Behne (AfK stationery) to WG
(Staatl. Bauhaus-Weimar), 8 January 1919, THAW/B, 6/06;
and A. Behne to WG (Staatl. Bauhaus-Weimar), 13 January
1919, THAW/B, 6/08. See also a letter to the AfK membership
on 13 January 1919 that refers to the "Weimar Bauhaus"
(THAW/B, 6/09).

asking for his advice   WG to Ernst Hardt, 16 January 1919,
AAA, RI.

"Your Excellency"   WG (Berlin) to Baron von Fritsch,
31 January 1919, THAW, Hofmarschallamt 3707, LVII,
No. 1; 1917–1919, 125.

62 *a return to power*   Franz Pfemfert, "Nationalversammlung ist
Konterrevolution!" *Die Aktion* 8, no. 49/50 (30 November
1918): 611–12, in John H. Zammito, *The Great Debate:
"Bolshevism" and the Literary Left in Germany, 1917–1930*
(New York: American University Studies, 1984), p. 25.

63 *"I don't want politics"*   Thomas Mann, *Betrachtungen eines
Unpolitischen* ([1918] 1956), p. 253; also quoted in Craig,

Germany, p. 415.

63 *having accomplished nothing* Adolf Behne, "Unsere Moralische
Krisis," *SOZMON* 25, no. 52 (20 January 1919): 34, microfilm.

a private, separate world WG to Osthaus, 2 February 1919, in
Whyte, *Taut*, p. 115.

"Let them rule" BT, "Der Sozialismus des Künstlers," *SOZMON*
25, no. 52 (24 March 1919): 259–62.

the Hohenzollerns *VRTS*, 16 December 1918.

64 *the "preservation of our German-ness"* *DAZ*, 13 January 1919.

"Save our country" Ibid., 14 January 1919.

"Whoever follows Liebknecht" Ibid., 15 January 1919.

Gropius took over WG to Dr. Valentiner, 18 February 1919,
BA/B, in Whyte, *Taut*, p. 116; see also WG (Berlin) to
Kommerzienrat Arnhold, 23 February 1919, BA/B, in which
Gropius refers to himself as the AfK's director.

"The AfK gives me real joy" WG (Berlin) to MSG, 17 March
1919, AAA, RI.

65 *"the beginning of the end"* WG, address delivered before a meeting of the AfK, Berlin, 22 March 1919, in *Arbeitsrat für Kunst,
1918–1921* (Berlin, 1980), p. 106.

"a new spirituality" WG, "Baukunst im freien Volksstaat." The
typescript of a substantially similar version of this article, titled
"Der freie Volksstaat und die Kunst" (BA/B, GN 2/3), was written in March 1919.

the government could no longer be counted on Ibid.

second revolution to which Gropius . . . alluded WG to Ludwig
Meidner, 26 February 1919, BA/B.

"not that of the Cossacks" Walther Rathenau, in Hermann
Schmitz, *Revolution*, p. 11. Rathenau, son of Emil Rathenau,
the founder of the huge AEG corporation (Allgemeine
Elektricitäts-Gesellschaft), was a founding member of the
Democratic Party (DDP) and briefly Foreign Minister until his
assassination in 1922.

"fanciful" WG to Professor Weiss, 9 April 1919, BA/B.

or guild WG (Berlin) to Adolf Behne, 6 March 1919, BA/B.

"sweep[ing] aside the divisions" WG, AfK address, 22 March 1919.

"private, separate world" WG to Osthaus, 2 February 1919, in
Whyte, *Taut*, p. 115.

65 *"a conspiracy"*   WG, AfK address, 22 March 1919.

66 *"supported by all the people"*   WG, "Baukunst im freien
    Volksstaat."

   Gropius explained this idea   WG, "Was ist Baukunst?" *Weimarer
    Blätter* 1, no. 9 (1 May 1919): 220, AAA, W&IG, 2275.

   reappear virtually unchanged   The Bauhaus Manifesto declared:
    "Architects, sculptors, painters . . . [t]ogether let us desire, con-
    ceive, and create the new structure of the future, which will
    embrace architecture and sculpture and painting in one unity"
    (in Ulrich Conrads, ed., *Programs and Manifestoes on 20th-
    Century Architecture*, Michael Bullock, trans. [Cambridge,
    Mass.: The MIT Press, 1970], p. 49, and Wingler, *The
    Bauhaus*, p. 31).

   the Bauhaus emerged   Early that month, preoccupied with setting
    up the Bauhaus, Gropius had asked Adolf Behne to take over
    the day-to-day management of the AfK (WG [Berlin] to Adolf
    Behne, 6 March 1919, BA/B). Although Gropius remained
    nominally the AfK's leader, the organization was in fact run by
    both men, and Behne's input was significant for both the AfK
    and the Bauhaus. How the public came to perceive the AfK—
    which would bear heavily on their view of the Bauhaus—was
    as much the result of Behne's efforts as of Gropius's.

   natural leader   WG, "Baukunst im freien Volksstaat."

   essentially Nietzschean perspective   See Nietzsche, "Wir
    Künstler," in *Die fröhliche Wissenschaft*, vol. 4, Werke [Leipzig,
    1906], p. 59.

67 *"Artists are brothers"*   Adolf Behne, "Vorschlag einer
    Brüderlichen Zusammenkunft der Künstler aller Länder," *SOZ-
    MON* 25, no. 52 (19 March 1919): 156.

   fellow artists in Russia   Report ("Sehr geehrter Herr") to mem-
    bers of the AfK, sig. A. Behne, 17 June 1919, copy received
    by WG, BA/B.

   "things got started"   Behne, "Vorschlag," p. 157.

   Bähr   Christian Schädlich, letter to author, 7 October 1992.

   to maintain contacts   Christina Lodder, *Russian Constructivism*
    (New Haven and London: Yale University Press, 1983), p. 234.

   "progressive fighters of the new art"   Ibid.

   "News from Russia"   OS to OM, 25 January 1919, Schlemmer,

Letters and Diaries, p. 65.

68 *a wire to Moscow* AfK (Berlin), "In der Anlage zwei
Programme," Telegramm nach Moskau, 26 January 1919,
BA/B, typescript.

Lack of a translator WG to Ludwig Bähr, 4 February 1919; also
Ludwig Bähr (Dresden) to WG, 9 February 1919, BA/B.

an AfK response AfK, "Aufruf an die revolutionären Künstler
Russlands," 25 March 1919, *Arbeitsrat für Kunst, 1918–1921*,
p. 112.

according to Harry Kessler "In the afternoon, at the Kaiserhof, I
was introduced to Markovski, the Soviet government representative, who had remained here in secret. Gropius was there
too" (Kessler, *Diaries*, 24 March 1919 [Berlin], p. 91.)

"Comrades, this, our handshake" AfK, "Aufruf," p. 112.

69 *"choking the life out of art"* WG, "Baukunst im freien
Volksstaat."

"revolutionary proletariat" BT, "Idealisten," review of the
Exhibition of Unknown Architects, *FREI*, 28 March 1919.

70 *no less confrontational* WG, "Was ist Baukunst?"

"subversive of all existing values" Walter Riezler, "Revolution
und Baukunst," *Mitteilungen des Deutschen Werkbundes*, no.
1, 1919, p. 20.

Kessler, for example Kessler, *Diaries*, 9 February 1919 (Berlin), p.
66, and 20 February 1919 (Berlin), p. 70.

"faith in [Russia]" OS to OM, 12 April 1919. Schlemmer,
Tagebuch.

71 *"I am convinced that Bolshevism"* Heinrich von Gleichen, *Der
Bolshewismus und die deutschen Intellektuellen*, (Leipzig,
1920), p. 50, cited in Anneliese Schmidt, *Der Bolschewismus
und die deutschen Intellektuellen, Äusserungen auf eine
Umfrage des Bundes deutscher Gelehrter und Künstler* (Leipzig,
1922), p. 5.

"deluxe editions" Protocol of meeting of Business Committee of
the Artistic Work Community of the AfK, Berlin, 18 November
1919, p. 108, BA/B.

proletariat representatives WG to Meidner, 26 February 1919,
BA/B; see also Protocol of meeting of business committee of the
Artistic Work Community of the AfK, 18 November 1919.

71 *Meidner*   Ludwig Meidner, "An Alle Künstler, Dichter, Musiker,"
    An alle Künstler!, pp. 7–8, in Weinstein, *The End of
    Expressionism*, p. 56. Meidner's article also appeared in the 5
    February 1919 issue of the USPD's *FREI*.

72 *"go to the devil"*   WG (Berlin) to Ewald Dülberg (Oberhambach),
    3 April 1919, BA/B.

    His Weimar idea . . . was "not a minor one"   WG (Berlin?) to
    Ernst Hardt, 14 April 1919, AAA, RI.

    the resulting institution   "Proposed Budget for the Art Academy
    and the School of Arts and Crafts in Weimar, 1919–1920," WG
    budget estimate submitted to HFBKW, THAW, unregistered
    documents, budget estimates October 1913–May 1922; highly
    edited version in Wingler, *The Bauhaus*, p. 26.

    the combined schools   Some months later Gropius would try
    without success to bring the Weimar School of Architecture
    and Civil Engineering as well as the former Grand Ducal
    Drawing Academy under Bauhaus influence. WG to
    Hofmarschallamt (Weimar), 2 May 1919, memorandum,
    THAW/B, 20/01.

    his expansive plans   WG (Weimar) to MSG, undated (believed to
    be the last week in May 1919), AAA, RI.

    the beginning of civil war   Kessler, *Diaries*, 6 March 1919
    (Berlin), pp. 81–82.

73–74 *J. B. Neumann . . . similarly hailed*   AAA, JBN, N69–96, p. 4.

74 *"further radicalize" the AfK*   WG (Berlin) to Adolf Behne, 6
    March 1919, BA/B.

    Bolshevism had come to Germany   Kessler, *Diaries*, 8 March
    1919 (Berlin), p. 82.

    66 percent of their votes   Günther, *Geschichte*, p. 532.

75 *Landauer . . . had particularly influenced Taut*   For more informa-
    tion on Landauer's influence on BT, see Taylor, *Left-Wing*, p. 47.

    Taut and . . . Tessenow   Whyte, *Taut*, p. 118.

    "new era of human history"   Gustav Landauer, "Entwurf zu
    einem Kulturprogramm" (April 1919), in Whyte, *Taut*, p. 118.

    Berlin looked like a battlefield   Kessler, *Diaries*, 8 April 1919
    (Berlin), p. 93.

76 *viewed them with hope*   OS to OM, 6 May 1919. Schlemmer,
    Tagebuch.

76　*a euphoric Kessler*　Kessler, *Diaries*, 12 April 1919 (Berlin), pp. 94–95.

　　"no final peace can be made"　DLND, 12 April 1919.

5. A HORNET'S NEST: TRADITION MEETS THE NEW, CHANGED WORLD

77　*"Miserable, disastrous"*　Leonhard Schrickel, *DLND*, 14 December 1919, BA/B, F/1.

　　"enormous bitterness"　LF to JF, May 1919, LFHU, 19/10.

78　*"the Weimar Academy . . . stood in sharp contrast"*　In Wingler, *The Bauhaus*, p. 25.

　　von Bode's approval　Ibid., p. 33.

79　*"its Expressionist 'genius'"*　LF to JF, 21 May 1919, LFHU, 19/4.

　　"old, reactionary fumblers" . . . "wallpaper designs"　Ibid.

　　"renewed and strengthened"　Ibid., May 1919, LFHU, 19/10.

80　*"a* coming *new faith"*　DLND, 25 April 1919.

　　later published versions　See the version that appears in Wingler, *Bauhaus*, p. 31.

81　*"bourgeois philistinism"*　WG, "Baukunst im freien Volksstaadt."

　　"we must all return to the crafts!"　AAA, W&IG, 2275; also in Conrads, *Programs and manifestoes*, p. 49, and Wingler, *The Bauhaus*, p. 31.

82　*beyond the classroom*　in Wingler, *The Bauhaus*, p. 32.

83　*not doing "anything by force"*　Address, WG to Bauhaus students, June 1919. Unsigned, handwritten, THAW/B, 132/5–10.

　　just another art academy　WG to Ferdinand Kramer, 15 October 1919, in Droste, *Bauhaus*, p. 50.

83–84　*dreamers and poets . . . brutal war*　Hüter, *Das Bauhaus*, p. 22.

84　*"rigidity and authoritarianism"*　WG to Herr Mahlberg, 3 May 1919, THAW/B, 1/65.

　　lack of constraints　Baird, "Bauhaus Conflicts."

　　"little Raphaels"　To the working committees of the Bauhaus Working Group, 18 May 1919, memorandum, THAW/B, 131/9.

85　*cropped their hair*　Alfred Arndt, "Life at the Bauhaus and Its Festivals," *50 Years Bauhaus*, p. 311.

"totally out of control"   LF to JF, May 1919, LFHU, 19/9.

"stuffed full of the military"   Ibid., 19/16.

86   *who he was to advise*   "n", "The Future of the Fine Arts in
Weimar," *DLND*, 18 May 1919.

a formal complaint   *DLND*, 20 May 1919.

moved to oust Gropius   LF to JF, May 1919, LFHU, 19/10.

"a hornets' nest"   LF to JF, 21 May 1919, LFHU, 19/4.

the Bauhaus's first budget   "Budget estimate of current and
unique expenses for Bauhaus for fiscal year October
1919/1920," 22 May 1919, THAW, C 14688-VBM/1+RS.

87   *a struggle with knives*   LF to JF, May 1919, LFHU, 19/10.
Feininger did not mention whether it was the shock of the
enlarged budget that had exasperated the Assembly or the
controversy swirling about the school.

a "frightful moment"   Kessler, *Diaries*, 9 July 1919
(Berlin), p. 105.

Scheidemann   Craig, *Germany*, p. 425.

unable to write   Kessler, *Diaries*, 12 June 1919 (Berlin), p. 100.

88   *"such products of madness"*   Dr. Hanns Kahle, "Einiges über
Expessionismus, Bolschewismus und Geisteskrankheit, *DLND*,
20 May 1919. Dr. Kahle was a Weimar neurologist.

A brochure   LF to JF, 19 May 1919, LFHU, 19/2.

unilaterally opposed   Craig, *Germany*, p. 426.

"the entire sap of life"   Kessler, *Diaries*, 22 June 1919 (Berlin), p.
102.

89   *agonizing pressure*   LF to JF, June 1919, LFHU, 19/29.

"incredibly confused state"   Address, WG to Bauhaus students,
June 1919.

the students' incomprehension   Ibid., 19/31.

"sharply and uncompromisingly"   LF to JF, June 1919, LFHU,
19/29. Wingler dates this letter 22 June 1919 (Wingler, *The
Bauhaus*, p. 34).

90   *afford to pay*   The Bauhaus tuition was subsidized by the state of
Thuringia. (166)

"a mystery, a nucleus of faith"   Address, WG to Bauhaus students, June 1919.

fair and equitable . . . at the expense of technique   LF to JF, June
1919, LFHU, 19/31.

"tremulous" Ibid., 19/41.

visiting Weimar Van de Velde, *Meines Lebens*, p. 505.

90 *on the brink of collapse* LF to JF, June 1919, LFHU, 19/29.

6. "A PLAGUE BACILLUS":
THE POLITICAL IMPLICATIONS OF THE BAUHAUS, IMAGINED AND REAL

91 *a "socially fermenting time"* "Sitzungsberichte der verfassungs-
    gebenden Preussischen Landesversammlung, Tagung
    1919/1921, vol. 6 (Berlin, 1921), p. 90. Session, 4 December
    1919, col. 7314, in Weinstein, *The End of Expressionism*, p. 92.

"decadent" internationalism Ibid.

"smash social conventions" Curt Glaser, "Kunstaustellung Berlin
    1919," review, *Kunstchronik und Kunstmarkt* 30, no. 45 (5
    September 1919): 962.

92 *"reckless fellow-travelers"* Walter Ley, *DK* 3 (1919): 320.

"politically crazy times" Fritz Stahl, "Kunstausstellung Berlin
    1919," review, *BTB*, 24 July 1919.

dishonor the fatherland "Bilderstürmer im Glaspalast," *BZM* (5
    September 1919), in Weinstein, *The End of Expressionism*, p. 91.

"bizarre madness" Fritz Stahl, "Kunstausstellung Berlin 1919."

degeneracy A. von Montbe, "Berliner Bilder," *DN* 63, (14
    September 1919), 254.

self-respect nearly demanded condemnation Craig, *Germany*, p.
    421.

93 *their attitude toward Expressionism* See Weinstein, *The End of
    Expressionism*, pp. 92–94.

opposition to the status quo . . . working class "Sitzungsberichte
    der verfassungsgebenden Preussischen Landesversammlung," in
    Weinstein, *The End of Expressionism*, p. 92.

"slanderous" T. Lux Feininger, personal conversation with
    author, Cambridge, Mass., 24 Oct. 1991.

94 *"art for political battle"* "Notizen," *Kunstchronik und
    Kunstmarkt* 30, no. 47 (19 September 1919): 1002.

Bauen See WG (Berlin) to Adolf Behne, 6 March 1919, BA/B;
    and BT to Osthaus, 24 April 1919, in Whyte, *Taut*, p. 146.

the school . . . distributed the group's brochures Ch. Luke (AfK-

Berlin) to WG (Bauhaus, Weimar), 21 May 1919, postcard, BA/B.

94 *"Spartacist propaganda leaflet"* WG response to charges, *DLND*, 29 January 1920, BA/B, F/1.

95 *"Call to Socialism"* "Aufruf zum Sozialismus," *An Alle Künstler!* (Berlin, 1919), p. 4.

"There Can Be No More Exploiters and Exploited" Ludwig Meidner, "An alle Künstler, Dichter, Musiker," *An Alle Künstler!*, pp. 7–8.

"What We Want" Max Pechstein, "Was Wir Wollen," *An Alle Künstler!* (Berlin, 1919), pp. 20–22, reprinted, *FREI*, 20 March 1919.

Friedrich Ernst Friedrich, "Etwas über Expressionismus," *FJ* 1, no. 5 (1919): 2.

other radical groups WG (Berlin) to Ewald Dülberg (Oberhambach), 3 April 1919, BA/B.

"international connections" Report ("Sehr geehrter Herr") to members of the AfK, sig. A. Behne, 17 June 1919, copy received by WG, BA/B.

"revolutionary world-renewal" Behne [sig.], AfK document undated (probably October 1919), BA/B.

He also sought support WG to MSG, undated (believed to be the last week in May 1919), AAA, RI.

96 *various local arts and craft groups* Hüter, *Das Bauhaus*, p. 20.

"extraordinary meeting" *DLND*, 10 December 1919, BA/B, F/1. (177)

met with applause Leonhard Schrickel, *DLND*, 14 December 1919, BA/B, F/1.

the code for Jews Unsigned editorial, *TLZ*, 23 December 1919, BA/B, F/1.

true German "fellows" Hüter, *Das Bauhaus*, p. 20.

"greet the new art cautiously" *TT*, 13 December 1919, BA/B, F/1.

anticipated being asked to join WG to Frl. von Rohden (Loheland b. Fulda), 15 January 1920, THAW/B, F/28, 14.

"true German values" *TT*, 13 December 1919, BA/B, F/1.

97 *present at the meeting* Ibid.

"poisonous propaganda" WG to MW (Frankfurt a/M), 15 January 1920, THAW/B, 6/170–72.

"narrow-minded dilettantes" WG to LH (Weimar), 13 December

1919, AAA, RI.

97 *"resident mummies"* WG to MW, 15 January 1920, AAA, RJ.
    correct the situation Schrickel, *DLND*, 14 December 1919.

98 *"leftist [threats]"* unsigned editorial, *TLZ*, 23 December 1919,
        BA/B, F/1.
    a "German" Bauhaus *DLND*, 19 December 1919.
    "will continue to scream" WG to LH (Weimar), undated
        (believed to be 19 December 1919 or 30 December 1919),
        AAA, RI.
    from the Bauhaus's own faculty Hüter, *Das Bauhaus*, p. 21.

99 *"a serious conflict"* HA, undated, marked in archive as mid-
        January 1920, BA/B, F/1.
    "The Struggle for the Staatliches Bauhaus" BAA, 27 December
        1919 and *VZ*, 1 January 1920, BA/B, F/1.
    a "smear campaign" *VRTS*, 5 January 1920, BA/B, F/1.
    "decline and loss" Letter from "a Craftsman," *DLND*, 7 January
        1920, BA/B, F/1.
    "Weimar's best artists" *DLND*, 1 January 1920.
    They accused . . . the conditions prevailing Ibid.
    too late Beginning with his June reproach to the students, the
        Bauhaus faculty would constantly complain about Gropius's
        delayed response to problems and his tendency to overreact
        when he finally moved. See Feininger's comment in his letter of
        July 1919 to his wife. Referring to Gropius, he wrote, "it takes
        him too long, it takes him too long!" (LF to JF, July 1919,
        LFHU, 19/50).

100 *"no political overtones"* WG to A. Behne (Berlin), 15 January
        1920, THAW/B, 6/22.
    "getting mixed up in politics" WG to MW (Frankfurt am Main),
        15 January 1920, AAA, RJ.
    "a German phenomenon" Ibid.
    "the terrible vortex" WG to LH (Weimar), 1 February 1920,
        AAA, RI.
    "I am proud of this fight" WG to MSG, December 1919, AAA, RI.
    "shock troops" WG to Redslob (Erfurt), 9 December 1919,
        THAW, B, 6/209.
    "must be fought" WG to Hans Poelzig (Dresden), 21 January
        1920, THAW/B, 6/198.

Workers' Art Exhibition With Gropius's Weimar difficulties undoubtedly taking up much of his attention, he probably turned over the management of the exhibition to Behne and perhaps also Taut.

101 *a successful lawsuit* "Berichte der Geschäftsführung," 31 March 1920, BA/B, Briefe AfK 1919/1921.

a battle of a new sort RUND, 13 January 1920, BA/B, F/1.

"something alien" DLND, 23 January 1920, BA/B, F/1.

7. THE PARADOX OF BAUHAUS POLITICS, 1920: DENIAL AND PURSUIT

102 *Gropius was deeply moved* Recollections of this event and Gropius's reaction from Alma Mahler-Werfel, *Mein Leben* (Frankfurt am Main: S. Fischer Verlag, 1960), p. 145.

103 *not get "mixed up in politics"* Ibid.

chastise those from the Bauhaus Bruno Adler, in Baird, "Bauhaus Conflicts."

raid on the school Nerdinger, *Gropius*, p. 46.

failed attempt Discussion of the Kapp Putsch and its ramifications on the Weimar Republic in Craig, *Germany*, pp. 424–33.

104 *history or farce* Kessler, *Diaries*, 13 March 1920 (Caux), p. 119.

closed . . . the Bauhaus workshops WG to KMW, 17 March 1920, THAW/B, 76.

a particularly bloody course This account of the Kapp Putsch in Weimar from Günther, *Geschichte*, pp. 534–36.

105 *an essential dilemma* In a letter to Behne on 26 June 1920, Gropius declared himself opposed to anything that reeked of "contemporary politics." Asserting that "politics must eventually be destroyed, because it is so removed from the spiritual realm," he lamented the use of culture for party-political purposes and declared himself to be turning his back on all such matters (WG [Weimar] to Behne ["Ekart," Berlin], 26 June 1920, BA/B). Speaking before the Thuringian State Assembly on July 9, 1920, Gropius declared that the Bauhaus "has nothing to do with party politics" (Landtag von Thüringen, 83. Stenographenprotokoll vom 9 Juli 1920, THAW, C1468/69–84).

Engelmann Richard Engelmann, a former professor of the Art

Academy, was a member of the Bauhaus faculty, until October 27, 1920, when he moved to the new College of Fine Arts. It is unclear whether or not Engelmann was a member of the Bauhaus faculty at the time he participated in this competition (*DLND*, 1920?, date illegible, BA/B, F/1).

105 *a Weimar "tradition"*   *DLND*, 1920(?), date illegible, BA/B, F/1.

106 *"Two artistic approaches"*   Ibid.

"victorious proletariat"   *DV*, 1 April 1921, BA/B, F/1.

financial support   Ibid.

a "'center' of socialist art"   *TT*, 20 April 1922, BA/B, F/1.

a political "plaything"   WG (Weimar) to "Ekart" [Behne] (Berlin), 26 June 1920, BA/B.

Until the issue was resolved   Hüter, *Das Bauhaus*, p. 31.

107 *"I can no longer be responsible"*   WG to KMW, 31 March 1920, handwritten, THAW, C1468/45.

neither "big enough [nor] rich enough"   *DLND*, 23 January 1920, BA/B, F/1.

a brochure   Emil Herfurth, *Weimar und das Staatliches Bauhaus* (Weimar: Hermann Böhlaus Nachfolgern, 1920), pp. 3–15, THAW/B, 5/22–29.

real grievances   Similar to many of the students and faculty members' reaction to Gropius's speech before the students in June 1919, Feininger had questioned the Bauhaus director's advocacy of a single Expressionist style for a school of 150 students (LF to JF, June 1919, LFHU, 19/35. LF to JF, June 1919, LFHU, 19/35. Wingler dates this letter 27 June 1919 [Wingler, *The Bauhaus*, p. 34]).

108 *the same conclusion*   It is unclear who first thought of the idea for the Bauhaus to seek national funding. In his letter to Poelzig of 21 January 1920, Gropius mentioned the question of the national government taking over the school as being "broached in the Berlin press and elsewhere. The more we think about this, the more important and better it seems as a solution" (WG to Poelzig [Dresden], 21 January 1920, THAW/B, 6/198). Gropius's letter to Behne of January 31 mentioned an individual by the name of Stehl, writing in the [Berliner?] *Tageblatt*, as having suggested the same. But Gropius commented that he "had taken steps along the same lines before Stehl" (WG to

Behne, 31 January 1920, THAW/B, 6/27–28).

108 *national importance* WG to Dr. Redslob, 13 January 1920,
    THAW/B, 6/205–6.

"Mr. Gropius's Bauhaus" "The Bauhaus Idea in Germany," 28
    November 1919, reported in *DLND*, 17 January 1920, BA/B, F/1.

109 *"at the forefront"* Ibid.

a series of meetings WG to Georg Tappert, 28 August 1919
    (Kunstarchiv), in Weinstein, *The End of Expressionism*, p. 86.

110 *called to Berlin* Campbell, *Werkbund*, p. 116.

"keep the ranters quiet" WG to Dr. Redslob, 13 January 1920,
    THAW/B, 6/205–206.

Bartning WG to Otto Bartning (Berlin), 29 January 1920,
    THAW/B, 6/4–5.

111 *"mobilized . . . in this direction"* WG to Behne, 31 January 1920,
    THAW/B, 6/27–28.

"benevolent cultural dictator" Paul Westheim,
    "Reichskunstwart," *FZ*, 14 January 1920.

look at paintings Max Thedy to WG, 1 September 1920, in
    Franciscono, *Gropius*, p. 167.

"an end in itself" Ibid.

"unbridgeable" WG to Hans Poelzig (Dresden), 21 January
    1920, THAW/B, 6/198.

112 *Old Weimar Painting School* Ibid.

"our new way" WG to Otto Bartning (Berlin), 29 January 1920,
    THAW/B, 6/4–5.

"the wishes of many Weimar artists" WG to KMW, 27 January
    1920, THAW/B, 12/29.

his strength was "growing" WG (Weimar) to MSG, 19 January
    1920, AAA, RI.

never give up WG to Dr. Redslob, 13 January 1920, THAW/B,
    6/205–6.

"outpost of art" WG to MW (Frankfurt am Main), 24 January
    1920, THAW/B, 6/176.

113 *"an unbelievable public demonstration"* WG to Otto Bartning
    (Berlin), 29 January 1920, THAW/B, 6/4–5.

pushed Professor Thedy "Professor Thedy has been so hurt by
    the article that he has gone over to the other side, which under
    the current circumstances is unfortunate" (WG to Behne, 31

January 1920, THAW/B, 6/27–28).

113 *"political overtones"* WG to A. Behne (Berlin), 15 January 1920, THAW/B, 6/22.

"every [political] party is dirt" WG to Behne, 31 January 1920, THAW/B, 6/27–28.

8. WHAT HAPPENED TO NOVEMBER?
THE END OF THE REVOLUTION AND ITS IMPLICATIONS FOR THE BAUHAUS

114 *"An act. An act."* English translation of Tucholsky's poem "Danton's Death" appears in John Willett, *Art and Politics in the Weimar Period: The New Sobriety, 1917–1933* (New York: Pantheon Books, 1978), p. 57.

a little astonished Andor Weininger, "Weininger spricht über das Bauhaus," *Andor Weininger: Vom Bauhaus zur konzeptuellen Kunst*, ed. Jiri Svestka, Katherine Jánszky Michaelsen, and Stefan Kraus (Düsseldorf: Kunstverein für die Rheinlande und Westfalen, 1990), pp. 26–27.

115 *"a high priest"* Ibid.

"half pastor" Paul Klee to Lily Klee, 16 January 1921, in Paul Klee, *Briefe an die Familie, 1893–1940*, 2 vols. Felix Klee, ed. (Cologne: DuMont Buchverlag, 1979), p. 970.

Citroen Paul Citroen, "Mazdaznan at the Bauhaus," response to Bauhaus students questionnaire prepared by RI, 1965, AAA, RI.

"highest-ranking officer" OS to OM, 7 August 1920, Schlemmer, *Tagebuch*.

leading personality Adams, "Memories," p. 192.

"brilliantly" OS to OM, 4 November 1920, Schlemmer, *Letters and Diaries*, p. 90.

dominated Gropius OS to OM, 4 November 1920, Schlemmer, *Tagebuch*. This sentence omitted in above letter in Schlemmer, *Letters and Diaries*.

succeed or fail OS to OM, 7 August 1920, Schlemmer, *Tagebuch*.

"brotherly" Alma Mahler-Werfel, *Mein Leben*, p. 31.

"at Frau Mahler's" Itten diary entry, 6 July 1918, Eva Badura-Triska, *Johannes Itten: Tagebücher, 1913–1916, 1916–1919 Wien*. 2 vols. (Stuttgart: Löcker Verlag, 1990), vol. 1, p. 280.

"We spoke about melody"   Ibid., 3 November 1918, p. 281.

116 *invite Itten*   Ibid., p. 33.

not understand Itten's abstract art   Ibid.

116 *no craft*   See Franciscono, *Gropius*, p. 216.

Itten had been trying to achieve   Johannes Itten, *Mein Vorkurs am Bauhaus: Gestaltungs—und Formenlehre* (Ravensburg: Otto Maier Verlag, 1963), p. 9.

freeing oneself   See Franciscono, *Gropius*, pp. 180–92.

principles he had applied in his Vienna classes   Itten, *Mein Vorkurs*, p. 9.

"dead convention"   Ibid., p. 10.

"a wild whirl"   Citroen, "Mazdaznan," AAA, RI.

"one had to discover oneself"   Weininger, "Weininger spricht," p. 30.

heads massaged   Herbert Bayer, interview with Arthur Cohen, Montecito, Cal., 3 and 7 November 1981, 8 October and 8–10 March 1982, AAA, Oral History Program.

117 *Schlemmer . . . slamming the door*   OS to OM, 16 May 1921, Schlemmer, *Letters and Diaries*, pp. 105–6.

Klee too was fascinated   Paul Klee to Lily Klee, 16 January 1921, Klee, *Briefe*, p. 970.

118 *traumatic experience*   Weininger, "Weininger spricht," p. 27.

"inner-directed thinking"   Itten, *Mein Vorkurs*, p. 11.

"monks"   OS to OM, 14 July 1921, Schlemmer, *Letters and Diaries*, p. 111.

"meditation and ritual"   OS to OM, 7 December 1921, ibid., p. 114.

"[a] saint"   Weininger, "Weininger spricht," p. 27.

"a mystery"   WG to Bauhaus students, Address, June 1919.

119 *"incredibly convincing"*   Weininger, "Weininger spricht," p. 30.

black shirt, and white tie   Werner Graeff, "Bemerkungen eines Bauhäuslers," in Werner Graeff, *Ein Pionier der Zwangziger Jahre* (Skulpturenmuseum der Stadt Karl Marx [exh. cat.], 1979), p. 7.

"Jesus"   Weininger, "Weininger spricht," p. 32.

"lucid tidiness"   H. L. C. Jaffé, *De Stijl: 1917–1931; The Dutch Contribution to Modern Art* (Cambridge, Mass. and London, Harvard University Press, Belknap Press, 1986), p. 5.

"an old and a new" Conrads, *Programs and Manifestoes*, p. 39.

120 *"work for the world"* Weininger, "Weininger spricht," p. 30.

"I live in the future" Ibid.

120 *gospel of the square* Mildred Friedman, ed., *De Stijl: 1917–1931; Visions of Utopia* (Minneapolis and New York: Walker Art Center, Abbeville Press, 1982), p. 90.

"poison" Van Doesburg to A. Kok, 7 January 1921, in Jaffé, *De Stijl*, p. 20.

121 *"salon Spartacists"* Ph. Leuthold, "Arbeiterkunstausstellung: Entgegnung," *Beilage der freien wissenschaftlichen sozialistischen Agrar-Korrespondenz* (April 1920).

"The Expressionist academy" Paul Westheim, "Das 'Ende des Expressionismus,'" *DK* 4 (June 1920): 188; in Whyte, *Bruno Taut*, p. 216.

"crooked dance halls" Adolf Behne, "Die Zukunft unserer Architektur," *SOZMON* 27, no. 56 (31 January 1921): 92, and A. Behne to WG, 9 December 1920, BA/B, GN 10/7/1561.

"leftward drift" Kessler, *Diaries*, 19 March 1920 (Lugano), p. 121.

122 *"right-wing putsch"* Ibid., 25 May 1920 (Hamburg), p. 126.

disbanded The group, however, managed to hang together until May 1921.

loss of its political support Gropius made his remarks at the AfK's final meeting on 20 May 1921, when the group formally disbanded. See Hüter, *Das Bauhaus*, p. 83.

"Chaotic" MC, 13 October 1920, THAW/B, 12/66–69.

"mixed-up mess" OS to TS, 3 March 1921, Schlemmer, *Letters and Diaries*, p. 103.

just another modern art school OS to OM, 21 December 1920, ibid., p. 96.

"lack of achievements" MC, 20 September 1920.

123 *"endangering public morals"* Privy Councilor Rudolph to WG, 4 September 1920, THAW/B, 130/6.

another uproar WG to KMW, 18 May 1920, THAW/B, 80/3–4.

"strange or just funny" Herbert Bayer, interview with Arthur Cohen.

"A fearless band" OS to OM, 3 February 1921, Schlemmer, *Letters and Diaries*, p. 98.

What few rules there were Lou Scheper, *BAUW* 43/44 (1968):

1340–41, AAA, W&IG, 2281.

"unwholesome place"   LF to JF, May 1920, LFHU, 20/12.

too "utopian" . . . state subsidy   OS to unknown recipient, 2
   March 1921, Schlemmer, *Letters and Diaries*, p. 100.

124 *forced to intervene*   WZB, 5 November 1920, BA/B, F/1.

Similar articles   See also *SSR*, 4 November 1920; *LNN*, 5
   November 1920; *MZ*, 4 November 1920; also newspapers in
   Munich, Leipzig, and Berlin, BA/B, F/1.

"a corrective"   GB, 1 January 1921, BA/B, F/1.

"the formerly well-known"   DLND, 6 June 1920.

"peace and order"   Ibid., 14 June 1920.

125 *ebulliently claimed victory*   Gropius based his claim of victory on
   the simultaneous approval by the Thuringian Finance Ministry
   of the budgets of both the Bauhaus and the new painting academy, which he interpreted as confirming the state's recognition
   of the Bauhaus's "radical character" (MC, 20 September 1920,
   THAW/B, 12/57–60).

"out of danger"   Schlemmer's conveyance of Gropius's understanding in his letter of 7 August 1920 to OM—more than a
   month before the formal recognition of the new school—indicates that the terms of this agreement were known to Gropius
   in advance (OS to OM, 7 August 1920, Schlemmer, *Letters and
   Diaries*, p. 86).

"slowly crumbling"   OS to OM, 4 November 1920, ibid., p. 89.

heat   KMW to WG (Direktion Staat. Bauhaus), 12 January 1921,
   THAW/B, 18/007.

light   State Senator Rudolph to cashier, HFBKW, 9 December
   1922, THAW/B, 18/132.

library   HFBKW to Bauhaus, 5 March 1921, THAW/B, 18/16.

canteen   THAW/B, 18/121.

art materials   Engelmann to Bauhaus, 4 May 1921, THAW/B,
   18/32.

"cat and mouse games"   WG to MW, 8 June 1921, THAW/B,
   6/180.

"The State College of Fine Arts . . . has reopened"   DV,
   12 April 1921.

"a slap in the face"   OS to Tut Schlemmer, 3 March 1921,
   Schlemmer, *Letters and Diaries*, p. 103.

"a monstrous reactionary creation" WG to MW (Frankfurt am Main), 8 June 1921, THAW/B, 6/180.

126 *"the ideal art school"* Program for the new school, THAW/HFBKW, 45/80–83 (RS), undated (1921?).

126 *"no longer what he was"* OS to unknown recipient, 2 March 1921, Schlemmer, *Letters and Diaries*, p. 100.

architectural practice In 1920 Gropius was working on the Sommerfeld Residence in Berlin-Steglitz; plans for a projected office building for the Sommerfeld Company in Berlin (Asternplatz); and row houses for employees of the Sommerfeld Company on Kamillenstrasse in Berlin.

"torn in pieces" WG to Maria Benemann, 16 April 1920, AAA, RI.

"a thousand things" WG (Weimar) to MSG, undated (believed to be summer 1920), AAA, RI.

126–127 *"cosmopolite"* . . . *"visibly bored"* LF to JF, 21 May 1919, LFHU, 19/4.

127 *"absolute power"* WG (Weimar) to MSG, undated (believed to be summer 1920), AAA, RI.

"Beloved" WG to AM/g, 12 July 1919, AAA, RI.

"a never-ending passion" WG (Weimar) to Maria Benemann, undated (postmarked 19 April 1920), in Isaacs, *Walter Gropius: Der Mensch*, p. 241.

"another stage" WG to LH, undated (believed to be mid-May 1920), AAA, RI.

"only half a man" WG to LH, undated (believed to be after departure of AM/g and their daughter in May 1920), AAA, RI.

"tears me to pieces" WG (Weimar) to MSG, undated (believed to be summer 1920), AAA, RI.

"stiff upper lip" WG to LH, undated (believed to be 19–20 December 1920), AAA, RI.

"[unable to] find . . . peace" WG to LH, undated (believed to be winter 1920), AAA, RI.

end of his rope WG to LH, undated (believed to be 30 December 1920), AAA, RI.

128 *beg Alma* IG to AM/g-Werfel, November 1926, photocopy, BA/B.

disciplined action MC, 13 October 1920, THAW/B, 12/66–69.

"the student chaos" OS to OM, 3 February 1921, Schlemmer, *Letters and Diaries*, p. 99.

"Expressionist hysteria" In Rose-Carol Washton Long, "Expressionism, Abstraction, and the Search for Utopia in Germany," in *The Spiritual in Art: Abstract Painting 1890–1985* (Los Angeles and New York: Los Angeles County Museum of Art and Abbeville Press, 1986), p. 213.

128 *"most vocal opponents"* OS to OM, end March 1922, Schlemmer, *Letters and Diaries*, p. 117.

widely attended Weininger, "Weininger spricht," p. 30.

129 *degraded the Bauhaus* OS to unknown recipient, 2 March 1921, Schlemmer, *Letters and Diaries*, p. 100.

"[T]hings look bad" OS to TS, 3 March 1921, ibid., p. 103.

"a no-holds-barred struggle" Schlemmer recounted Itten's comment (OS to unknown recipient, 2 March 1921, ibid., p. 100).

"collapse" . . . "secret putschist" Ibid., p. 101.

Gropius could no longer lead AAA, RI, notes.

nervous collapse AAA, RI, notes.

130 *"enslaved to a vision"* WG, MC, 13 October 1920, THAW/B, 12/66–69.

"not . . . promote any dogmas" In Franciscono, *Gropius*, p. 244.

9. FROM GEIST TO GADGETS: THE BAUHAUS ATTEMPTS TO CHANGE

132 *"proletarian policies"* DAZ, 8 November 1921.

a Communist adviser In Hüter, *Das Bauhaus*, p. 32.

the nation's most radical plan Ibid., p. 99.

memorandum to the faculty WG to Bauhaus Masters, 3 February 1922, memorandum, THAW/B, 3/18–26.

133 *Bauhaus's mushrooming problems* OS to TS, 3 March 1921, Schlemmer, *Letters and Diaries*, p. 103.

a craft school's need Wingler, *The Bauhaus*, p. 51.

architectural . . . preoccupations In 1921 Gropius's architectural practice boomed. That year his office worked on the design of an office building, a combination exhibition hall and warehouse, two private residences in Berlin, a major renovation of a theater, a Bauhaus housing settlement, and the Chicago Tribune competition, as well as participated in several exhibitions.

Gropius, like everyone else Gropius accused Itten and his coterie of "trying to seize the whole Bauhaus" (WG to LH, undated [perhaps 30 December 1920], AAA, RI).

134 *"at the helm"* OS to OM, June 1922, Schlemmer, *Tagebuch*.

134 *At Master's Council Meeting* WG, "The Necessity of Commissioned Work for the Bauhaus," 9 December 1921, notes, in Wingler, *The Bauhaus*, p. 51.

"where he belongs" OS to OM, 7 December 1921, Schlemmer, *Letters and Diaries*, p. 114.

"Itten's monopoly" OS to OM, ibid., p. 113.

artistic "stars" WG to Ernst Hardt (Berlin?), 14 April 1919, AAA, RI.

playing referee OS to OM, 7 December 1921, Schlemmer, *Letters and Diaries*, p. 114.

"in combat with Itten" WG to LH, undated (believed to be late winter 1922/1923), AAA, RI.

"the battle's tempo and vigor" WG to Bauhaus Masters, 3 February 1922, memorandum.

135 *old Werkbund industrial aesthetic* WG, "Der Stilbildende Wert," 1914, AAA, W&IG, 2275.

"[h]eadquarters" OS, diary, March 1922, Schlemmer, *Letters and Diaries*, p. 116.

"mechanical gadgets" WG to Bauhaus masters, 3 February 1922, memorandum.

136 *allusions to catastrophe* See WG address to students June 1919.

"technically . . . competent man" Wingler, *The Bauhaus*, p. 342.

From his suggestions "Recommendations regarding the proposed reorganization of the Bauhaus," sig. Otto Dorfner, March (1922?), THAW/B, 3/27–31.

137 *"new waves"* OS to OM, 13 March 1922, Schlemmer, *Letters and Diaries*, p. 116.

"handmaiden of the workshop" WG, "Idee und Entwicklung des Staatlichen Bauhauses zu Weimar," *Amtsblatt des Thüringischen Ministeriums für Volksbildung* (7–12 January 1923), AAA, W&IG, 2275.

"eventual unrest" MC, 26 May 1922, THAW/B, 12/134–35.

"palpable danger" WG to Form Masters, 13 May 1922, memorandum, THAW/B, 2/69.

simply "unacceptable" WG to G. Marcks (Dornburg/Saale), 21

May 1922, THAW/B, 2/48.

"to soothe souls"   Ibid.

138 *resounding reformulation*   "Change in Statutes," sig. Bauhaus masters, 4 May 1922, memorandum, THAW/B, 2/61.

138 *not yet ready*   MC, 24 March 1922, THAW/B, 12/114.

several reasons for his request   WG to TVB, 6 May 1922, THAW/B, 31/19.

a long-awaited loan   Droste, *Bauhaus*, p. 58.

"the outside world"   Weininger, "Weininger spricht," p. 29.

139 *"turn[ing] its back"*   OS, diary, June 1922, Schlemmer, *Letters and Diaries*, p 124.

"dreadful" . . . *appalled*   OS to OM, 21 October 1923, Schlemmer, *Tagebuch*.

engineers did better   OS, diary, mid-November 1922, Schlemmer, *Letters and Diaries*, p. 134.

"raped" the inner experience   Report, faculty meeting with workshop representatives and students about change of Bauhaus program, 6 October 1922, THAW/B, 12/198–99.

short sighted expediency   LF to JF, October 1922, LFHU, 22/41; extracts (and date of 5 October 1922) in Wingler, *The Bauhaus*, p. 56.

what painting had to do with machinery   OS to OM, end of March 1922, Schlemmer, *Letters and Diaries*, p. 118.

"deifying the machine"   Report, faculty meeting with workshop representatives and students about change of Bauhaus program, 6 October 1922.

Marcks   Gerhard Marcks to WG, 23 March 1923, THAW/B, 60.

metal teapot   George Adams in Baird, "Bauhaus Conflicts."

140 *contentious individualism*   Report, Bauhaus Syndikat (Lange), 9 December 1922, THAW/B, 12/266–69.

Schlemmer worried   OS, diary, mid-November 1922, Schlemmer, *Letters and Diaries*, p 134; see also minutes, meeting of entire Bauhaus faculty, 3 October 1922, THAW/B, 12/189–92.

Kandinsky urged   Minutes, ibid.

"totally unrealistic"   Report, faculty meeting with workshop representatives and students about change of Bauhaus program, 6 October 1922.

"[A] question of survival"   OS to OM, 19 December 1922,

Schlemmer, *Letters and Diaries*, p. 136.

all the work itself   MC, 20 October 1922, THAW/B, 12/237–40.

141 *looked down on them*   Ibid., 20 October 1922, and Hans Beyer to TVB, 20 October 1922, formal complaint, THAW/C, 1471/1–6.

141 *"nothing to do with us"*   MC, 14 October 1922, THAW/B, 12/218–27.

Whispered complaints   This issue about the use of Gropius's office had already been raised earlier in the year. Only when it was appropriated by the workshop masters, however, did it become a public issue. WG to G. Marcks (Dornburg/Saale), 21 May 1922, THAW/B, 2/48.

finalized new statutes   WG to TVB, statutes, THAW/TVB, C/1474, 1922.

"to create prototypes"   MC, 2 October 1922, THAW/B, 12/185–86.

openly questioned   MC, 5 October 1922, THAW/B, 12/194–99.

a personal attack   WG to LH, undated (believed to be October 1922), AAA, RI.

142 *"deplorable"*   MC, 5 October 1922, THAW/B, 12/194–99.

dismissed the charges   Report, Bauhaus committee investigating charges against WG, 13 October 1922, THAW/B, 12/213–16.

"short work of it"   WG to LH, undated (believed to be October 1922), AAA, RI.

142 *voted to fire*   MC, 14 October 1922, THAW/B, 12/218–27.

addressed formal complaints   Carl Schlemmer to TVB (handwritten), 16 October 1922, formal complaint, THAW, C1471/1–6.

the "Bauhaus's corporate head"   H. Beyer to TVB, 3 November 1922, memorandum, THAW, C1471/61–63.

an audit   MC, 14 October 1922, THAW/B, 12/218–27.

expressed his reservations   MC, 20 October 1922, THAW/B, 12/237–40.

143 *he too filed a formal complaint*   H. Beyer to TVB, 20 October 1922, formal complaint, THAW, C1471/1–6.

"[Beyer] can no longer . . . set foot"   WG to TVB, 28 October 1922, THAW, C1471/54–56.

considerable professional credentials   H. Beyer to TVB, 30

October 1922, memorandum, THAW, C1471/54–56.

thirty-eight . . . questions   Ibid.

salaries from the state   Ibid., THAW, C1471/11–26.

worse moment   WG to Dr. Neubauer, 10 November 1922,
THAW/B, 41/6–7.

loss of millions more   H. Beyer to TVB, 3 November 1922, memorandum, THAW, C1471/61–63.

"the grave importance"   C. Schlemmer and Zachmann to State
Minister Max Greil (TVB), 8 November 1922, THAW,
C1471/119–20.

only seven apprentices   H. Beyer to TVB, 13 December 1922,
memorandum, THAW, C1472/5–6.

144 *"a crime against the state"*   Vilmos Huszar, "Das Staatliche
Bauhaus in Weimar," *De Stijl 5*, no. 9 (September 1922).

a government investigation   DLND, 20 December 1922,
THAW/, B, 9/4.

an interpellation   Emil Herfurth, affidavit, Beyer vs. Thuringia,
31 October 1923, THAW/C1476/45–46.

no statutes or funding requests   WG, MC, 11 December 1922,
THAW/B, 12/259–64.

the lawsuit would titillate   Although Gropius would declare himself victorious, the accusations against him were ultimately dis-
charged by the court due to the statute of limitations.

remained unconvinced   Report, Bauhaus Syndikat (Lange),
9 December 1922.

145 *10 million marks*   Estimated budget, 1923 Bauhaus exhibition, 18
December 1922, THAW/B, 32/3.

"[T]hings look black to me"   OS to OM, 11 November 1922,
Schlemmer, *Tagebuch*.

"over the cliff"   DAZ, 17 October 1922.

feared civil war   WG to LH, September 1922, AAA, RI.

Moholy-Nagy   Although Gropius met Moholy-Nagy in 1922 and
asked of his interest in coming to the Bauhaus, there were no
faculty positions open at the time. The single opening had been
taken by Kandinsky. It was only with Itten's departure in 1923
that Moholy-Nagy was able to come (See WG to Bauhaus
Masters, 14 March 1923, memorandum requesting the
Masters' opinions regarding the appointment of Moholy-Nagy

to fill the faculty position opened by Itten's departure, THAW/B, 13/102).

"incomprehensible" RWZE, 5 August 1922, BA/B, F/1.

146 *"Red appearance"* WG to all Bauhaus masters, 23 February 1922, memorandum, THAW/B, 111/51.

keep the matter private Kandinsky's appointment was approved by the Thuringian government on 1 July 1922 (WG to all Masters, 1 July 1922, circulating memorandum, THAW/B, 13/99).

147 *According to his wife* Nina Kandinsky, *Kandinsky et moi* (originally published in German as *Kandinsky und Ich*), trans. J. M. Gaillard-Paquet (Paris: Flammarion, 1978), pp. 101–3.

"the socialism of vision" In Willett, *Art and Politics*, p. 76.

Lange as new Syndikus WG to TVB, 24 October 1922, THAW, C1471/11–26.

politically useful MC, 2 October 1922, THAW/B, 12/185–86.

148 *the Bauhaus's socialistic character* In Hüter, *Das Bauhaus*, pp. 150–51.

Finance Minister Hartmann Syndikus Lange to SPD, 17 November 1922, in Hüter, *Das Bauhaus*, p. 150.

Lange introduced Gropius to . . . Neubauer Ibid, p. 100.

"our party's . . . support" Syndikus Bauhaus (Lange) to SPD Party Chief Knauer (Thuringian State Assembly), 29 January 1923, THAW/B, 9/12.

anticlerical DAZ, 3 December 1921.

"the Christian segments" Ibid., 30 November 1921.

the vote as a "rape" Ibid., 10 December 1921.

more lay behind Ibid., 8 November 1921.

149 *"Gropius's artistic Bolshevism"* Rudolf Kayser, *BTB*, 26 November 1922, BA/B, F/7.

Bauhaus's socialist credentials Lange, for the most part, worked with the leftist members of the State Assembly and Gropius with Minister Greil's (and Redslob's) offices.

cited the similarities WG, "Idee und Entwicklung," AAA, W&IG, 2275.

"considerable advantages" WG to Bauhaus masters, 2 May 1923, memorandum, THAW/B, 14/318.

support of the Bauhaus In Hüter, *Das Bauhaus*, p. 99.

the Communists also strongly supported Landtag von Thüringen, 1923, stenographischer Bericht, "Beantwortung der Interpellation der Deutschnationalen, Organisation und Betriebsführung des Bauhauses betreffend," 16 März 1923, THAW/B, 9/20.

149 *the Bauhaus's workshop program as a model* In Hüter, *Das Bauhaus*, pp. 96–102.

150 *mismanagement of state funds* Weimar Craft Guild (sig. Karl Linkmann)] to the Thuringian State Government, 26 January 1923, THAW, C1472/30.

"pointless establishment" Finance Minister Hartmann to WG, 30 January 1923, THAW/B, 197/3–7.

the Right's ultimate goal—DV, 20 March 1923, BA/B, F/7.

a "cathedral of socialism" Typescript, undated, THAW/B, 30/3–5.

"the 'Living-machine'" OS, diary, June 1922, Schlemmer, *Letters and Diaries*, p. 124

151 *sent the Bauhaus's publicity program* Bauhaus and exhibition programs, 6 March 1923, THAW/B, 9/12–15.

Marx VSTM, 9 May 1923, BA/B, F/7.

conservative Munich newspaper MNN, 8 March 1923, BA/B, F/8.

"heaven-storming socialists" DZ, 24 April 1923, BA/B, F/8.

10. VICTORY OR TOTAL DESTRUCTION: THE END OF THE WEIMAR BAUHAUS

152 *"help me out again"* WG to Redslob, 2 January 1923, THAW/B, 33/12.

Gropius received his loan Gropius seemed to have received the bank loan on the basis of Redslob's personal assurance, for his actual letter was not sent until April 1. Redslob to WG, 1 April 1923, THAW/B, 33/15.

153 *inappropriateness* WG to Redslob, 8 January 1923, THAW/B, 33/16.

"You ask him yourself" Redslob to WG, 10 January 1923, THAW/B, 33/17–18.

still opposed Feininger, for one, claimed that he "hated" the implications of the school's new slogan (*"eine mir verhasste Anschauung"*) "Art and Technology: The New Unity." LF to JF,

July 1923, LFHU, 23/5.

153 *financial free fall*   Such as raising taxes or utilizing the gold
    reserve, or both. See Craig, *Germany*, pp. 444–48.

154 *the beleaguered Ebert*   WG to President Ebert, 20 January 1923,
    THAW/B, 33/20–23. Ebert offered instead a contribution of
    two hundred thousand marks. Finance Ministry, Office of
    Reichspresident (Ebert) to the Director of the Bauhaus (WG),
    22 March 1923, THAW/B, 33/27.

    dollar kings   in Christian Schädlich, "Die Beziehungen des
    Bauhauses zu den USA 1919–1933: Eine Dokumentation,"
    WZHAB 35, no. 2 (1989): 60.

    "Stuttgartners are not interested"   Direktor Löwenstein, Roth &
    Paschkis Aktien-Gesellschaft (Stuttgart) to WG, 9 February
    1923, THAW/B, 32/16.

155 *the Right's long complaints*   Landtag von Thüringen 1923,
    Stenographische Berichte, p. 156, 16 March 1923 session,
    p. 436, THAW/B, 1014/1244.

    the Bauhaus was indeed vulnerable   Lange testimony, Bauhaus
    response to report of Thuringian accounting office, 9
    September 1924, THAW, C1478/17–19.

156 *"the ideal aspects of things"*   W. F. Necker, "Bauhaus:
    '23–'24," *Architectural Review* (September, 1963): 159,
    AAA, W&IG, 2278.

    "tricky business"   Ibid.

    loose sheets of paper   Lange testimony, 9 September 1924,
    THAW, C1478/17–19.

    "a hundred thousand marks"   Kessler, *Diaries*, 7 April 1923
    (Berlin), p. 228.

    an advance of 2.5 million marks   OS to TS, 4 September 1923,
    Schlemmer, *Letters and Diaries*, p. 143.

157 *Breadlines grew*   Craig, *Germany*, p. 455.

    El Lissitzky   Sophie Lissitzky-Küppers, *El Lissitzky: Life, Letters,
    Texts* (Greenwich, Conn.: New York Graphic Society Ltd.,
    [1967] 1968), p. 35.

    Benscheidt   WG to C. Benscheidt Jr. (Alfeld a.d.L.),
    19 January 1923, THAW/B, 32/11; see also C. Benscheidt Jr.
    (Alfeld a.d.L.) to WG, 6 April 1923, THAW/B, 32/55.

    Lange   Vereinigte Seidenwebereinen A.G. H. (Krefeld) to WG, 6

July 1923, THAW/B, 32/60; see also THAW/B, 32 and 81.

advance that Gropius secured   MC, 16 May 1923, THAW/B,
12/312–13.

157 *"disastrous"*   WG to Dr. Fr. Rauth (Berlin), 21 June 1923,
THAW/B, 32/48–49.

157 *what had already been started*   WG to Dr. Fr. Rauth (Berlin), 6
July 1923, THAW/B, 32/53–57.

158 *including much of the Reichswehr*   Kessler, *Diaries*, 7 April 1923
(Berlin), p. 229.

158 *"national Bolshevism"*   Willett, *Art and Politics*, p. 72.

158 *"awful"*   LF to JF, July 1923, LFHU, 23/5.

158 *workers again demanded to be armed*   Günther, *Geschichte*, p. 540.

158 *savage political murder*   After a USPD and KPD rally, demonstrators, who forced passers-by to participate in their march,
moved on to the home of the city's public prosecutor, whom
they killed with his own gun after he attempted to defend himself. Heavy police forces were subsequently needed to keep the
city under control (*DAZ*, 24 July 1923).

158 *bloody rioting*   Ibid., 29 July 1923.

158 *a former monarchist*   Craig, *Germany*, p. 457.

158 *the Communists launched strikes*   "To make things worse, three
days before the opening of the exhibit a general strike broke
out." WG to Rudolph, 1 November 1923, THAW/B,
31/112–14.

159 *a desperate plea*   WG to Neubauer, 14 August 1923, marked
"Urgent!" THAW/B, 41/63.

159 *people had difficulty*   WG to Rudolph, 1 November 1923,
THAW/B, 31/112–14.

159 *brilliantly designed posters*   created by the young Herbert Bayer
and Josef Maltan.

160 *stripped-down, machine-planed product*   WG to Bauhaus masters,
3 February 1922, memorandum.

160 *"Misleading"*   Walter Passarge, "The Bauhaus Exhibition in
Weimar," review, *DK* 8 (1923): 309.

160 *"crude and not well thought-through"*   Ibid.

160 *even Gropius had to admit*   LF to JF, 1 August 1923, LFHU, 23/6.

161 *the exhibition's . . . "real heart"*   Passarge, "The Bauhaus
Exhibition," p. 309.

161 *faculty disapproval*   OS to OM, 13 February 1924, Schlemmer, *Letters and Diaries*, p. 151.

161 *Ise, would comment*   IG, 2 September 1924, AAA, IG/d.

161 *hope of making money*   WG to Rudolph, 1 November 1923, THAW/B, 31/112–14.

162 *seven billion marks*   WG to TVB, 30 September 1923, memorandum, THAW/B, 31/105.

Beyer lost no time   Deposition, Beyer, *Beyer v. Thuringia*, 19 September 1923, THAW, C1476/21–37.

not-to-be-missed opportunity   Craig, *Germany*, pp. 461–64.

Stalin   DRF, 10 October 1923, cited by Craig, *Germany*, p. 464.

164 *on Feininger's doorstep*   T. Lux Feininger, interview.

outraged the former officer   WG, Letter of complaint to Lieutenant-General Hasse, military commandant in Thuringia, 24 November 1923, in Wingler, *The Bauhaus*, p. 76.

"unverified, malicious and irresponsible"   Ibid.

"close to the Communist Party"   Exchange of letters between WG and the military commandant in Thuringia, in Hüter, *Das Bauhaus*, pp. 43 and 258 (docu. 72).

Second thoughts prevailed   in Hüter, *Das Bauhaus*, p. 43.

165 *Kandinsky*   WG to L. Justi, 26 September 1927, SMB/ZA.

Moholy-Nagy   Eva Weininger (former Bauhaus student), personal conversation with author, New York City, 5 February 1991.

the matter was dropped   in Hüter, *Das Bauhaus*, p. 43.

prominent Thuringian businessman   DAZ, 4 December 1923.

dispersed by armed force   Ibid., 7 December 1923.

"Think of the Bauhaus"   In Hüter, *Das Bauhaus*, p. 44.

166 *"wall of mud"*   WG to Franz May (Munich), 23 November 1923, THAW/B, 197/22–24.

Feininger . . . wanted to leave   WG to LF, September 1924, LFHU, 24/38.

exhausted and depressed   OS to OM, 20 May 1924, Schlemmer, *Letters and Diaries*, pp. 153–54.

Thuringian State Treasury   Thuringian Accounting Office to TVB, 6 August 1924, THAW/TVB, C1478/4–10 (1924–1927). A highly edited version of this report issued by the Thuringian Accounting Office appears in Wingler, *Bauhaus*, p. 87.

faculty contracts would not be renewed   TVB, 18 September 1924 (copy received by LF), LFHU, 24/38.

Gropius . . . announced the dissolution of the Weimar Bauhaus
IG, see diary entries 23, 24, and 27 December 1924, AAA, IG/d.

11. "THOSE HAPPIER SHORES": YOUNG AMERICANS MEET EUROPE

167 *"Dollarlande"* Eduard Fuchs (Berlin) to JBN (New York), 2
October 1927, JBN, MOMA.
"a pot of gold" J. B. Neumann, "Confessions of an Art Dealer,"
n.d., photocopy, JBN, MOMA.

168 *"Forget Europe"* Georg Muche to WG, 12 April 1924, in Georg
Muche, *Das künstlerische Werk, 1912–1927* (Berlin: Bauhaus-
Archiv, 1980), p. 67.
German books . . . for his course AHB (Cambridge) to JBN
(New York), 12 October 1926, AAA, JBN, microfilm, NJBN-1.

169 *"morbid hallucination"* Frank Jewett Mather, "Newest
Tendencies in Art," *Independent* (6 March 1913).
"a crazy galoot" F. W. Coburn, "In the World of Art," *The
Boston Herald*, 7 November 1926.
Claribel Cone See Alice Goldfarb Marquis, *Alfred H. Barr Jr.:
Missionary for the Modern* (Chicago: Contemporary Books,
Inc., 1989), p. 19.
An anonymously written brochure See Russell Lynes, *Good Old
Modern: An Intimate Portrait of the Museum of Modern Art*
(New York: Atheneum, 1973), p. 43.

170 *"left-wing painters"* Alfred H. Barr Jr., *German Painting and
Sculpture* (New York: MOMA, 1931), p. 7.
missionary interests In Marquis, *Barr*, p. 16.
eldest of the family's two sons Gropius, whose brother died at the
age of seventeen, had two older sisters.
a Castle Barr Rona Roob, comp. and ed., "Alfred H. Barr Jr.: A
Chronicle of the Years 1902–1929," *The New Criterion* 1, no.
19 (summer 1987), 1.
almost incestuous world Sir Isaiah Berlin, introduction to
Childhood, Youth and Exile, part 1 of *My Past and Thoughts*
by Alexander Herzen, (New York: Oxford University Press,
1980), pp. xiv–xv.

171 *This categorizing trait* In Roob, "Barr," p. 2.

major achievements In Marquis, *Barr*, pp. 13–14.

"five verses [and] four lines" In Roob, "Barr," p. 1.

military history in Marquis, *Barr*, p. 13.

"a form of religion" AHB to Katherine Gauss, February 1922,
date illegible, Katherine Gauss (Jackson) Papers, AAA, 115.

"[making] my throat feel queer" AHB to JBN, 15 November
1926, AAA, JBN, NJBN-1.

Barr went off to Princeton In Marquis, *Barr*, p. 20.

"timeless and placeless" scholarly world Malcolm Cowley, *Exile's
Return: A Literary Odyssey of the 1920s* (New York: Penguin
Books, [1951] 1976), p. 29.

situational context Henry-Russell Hitchcock, "Modern
Architecture—A Memoir," *Journal of the Society of
Architectural Historians* 27, no. 4 (December 1968): 230.

172 *"one carefully cracked pane"* AHB, preface to *Bauhaus:
1919–1928*, by Herbert Bayer, p. 5.

Hitchcock HRH, "Modern Architecture—A Memoir," p. 230.

Barr took several courses with him In Roob, "Barr," p. 4.

173 *famed museum course* P/i Scrapbook, General C, MOMA Archive.

after lunch Jere Abbott to Mrs. Barr, 10 July 1981, AAA,
AHB, 3262.

a candidate for the museum's directorship A. Conger Goodyear,
"10th Anniversary—Opening of the New Museum Building,"
The Bulletin of the Museum of Modern Art 6 (May–June
1939): 6–7, Goodyear Collection, vol. 52, MOMA Archive.

174 *its Christian spirit* Charles Rufus Morey, *Mediaeval Art* (New
York: W. W. Norton & Company, 1942), p. 391.

this family tradition In Marquis, *Barr*, p. 10.

"great beyond" AHB to Katherine Gauss, February 1922, date
illegible, Katherine Gauss (Jackson) Papers, AAA.

Barr was sharply critical AHB, Report to Board of Trustees,
MOMA, AAA, AHB, n.d. (undated report is attached to a let-
ter from A. Conger Goodyear, president of board of trustees,
MOMA, 11 October 1933), 3266.

"van Gogh and Matisse" AHB, preface to *Bauhaus: 1919–1928*,
by Herbert Bayer, p. 5.

piqued Barr's interest AHB, report to board of trustees.

"Old gray beard laughed"   In Roob, "Barr," p. 4.

175 *Isadora Duncan*   Ibid.

"their hospitality toward modern art"   AHB, report to board
    of trustees.

similar to what Morey had done   In Marquis, *Barr*, p. 30.

175 *a dual course*   AHB, report to board of trustees.

a variety of avant-garde art magazines   In Roob, "Barr," p. 4.

176 *he as yet knew nothing*   HRH, "Modern Architecture—
    A Memoir," p. 229.

traditional grand tour   In Marquis, *Barr*, p. 33.

unacquainted with the continent's spirit   In Roob, "Barr,"
    pp. 8–9.

he contacted Neumann   AHB (Princeton) to JBN (New York), 19
    July 1926, AAA, JBN, NJBN 1.

177 *"What Is the Bauhaus?"*   Subsequently republished in *Vanity Fair*
    (August 1927) as "A Modern Art Questionnaire," AHB, report
    to board of trustees.

a "publicly supported institution"   In Irving Sandler and Amy
    Newman, eds., *Defining Modern Art: Selected Writings of
    Alfred H. Barr, Jr.* (New York: Harry N. Abrams, 1986), p. 56.

178 *learned nothing useful*   HRH, "Modern Architecture—A
    Memoir," p. 228–29.

little attention to modern architecture   Ibid.

a part-time tutor   Ibid.

179 *the simple factory*   HRH, "The Decline of Architecture," *The
    Hound and Horn* 1, no. 1 (September 1927): 28–35.

Hitchcock moderated his insistence on pure function   HRH, "The
    Architectural Work of J. J. P. Oud," *The Arts* 13, no. 2
    (February 1928): 97–103.

influence of Le Corbusier   HRH, "Modern Architecture—
    A Memoir," p. 229.

"a machine for living in"   Le Corbusier, *Towards a New
    Architecture*, trans. Frederick Etchells (New York: Praeger
    Publishers, 1927), p. 89.

the importance of formal harmonies   Ibid., p. 37.

rather than American architects   Ibid., p. 42.

factories   AHB, report to board of trustees.

first article on architecture now appeared   AHB, "The Necco

Factory," *The Arts* 13, no. 5 (May 1928): 292–95.

"about recent architecture" HRH, "Modern Architecture—
A Memoir," p. 229.

the day's "unrest" Le Corbusier, *Towards a New Architecture*,
pp. 14 and 250.

179 *"Architecture or revolution"* Ibid., pp. 268–69.

180 *as Kingsley Porter had written* Porter, *Medieval Architecture*,
vol. 2, p. 253.

"various abstract currents" AHB, *Cubism and Abstract Art*
(New York: The Museum of Modern Art, 1936), p. 153.

"those happier shores" HRH (Vassar College) to AHB,
5 December 1927, AHB Archive, HRH file, MOMA.

12. "DESSAU IMPOSSIBLE"

181 *most Dessauers had never heard of it* Hesse, *Residenz*, p. 208.

"not so hot" LF to JF, February 1925, LFHU, 25/16.

Klee never got used to living there Felix Klee, comp. and ed., *Die
Tagebücher von Paul Klee, 1898–1918* (Cologne: M. Du Mont
Verlag, 1979), p. 421.

Feininger thought that even Weimar looked good LF to JF,
March 1925, LFHU, 25/30.

182 *Frankfurt or Munich* OS to OM, 17 February 1925, Schlemmer,
Letters and Diaries, p. 161.

"Dessau Impossible" FH, interview by RI, January 1965, AAA, RI.

ruined houses and streets Ulla Jablonowski, *Dessau—So wie es
war* (Dusseldorf: Droste Verlag, 1991), p. 59.

Franz von Hoesslin . . . Kurt Weil Ibid., p. 88.

quickly remedy the situation FH, VZ, 26 January 1922.

divided the town Walter Allner, personal conversation with
author, New York City, 15 January 1991.

bringing the Bauhaus to Dessau Hesse, *Residenz*, pp. 196–97.

183 *jumped at the idea* Ibid.

a liberal, socialistic reputation LF to JF, February 1925,
LFHU, 25/3.

184 *a generous offer* Ibid., 25/16.

Feininger . . . was particularly touched Ibid., 25/18.

city's proximity to Berlin OS to OM, 17 February 1925,
Schlemmer, *Letters and Diaries,* p. 161.

"They want us and need us" LF to JF, February 1925,
LFHU, 25/18.

Marcks . . . had never masked his opposition Gerhard Marcks to
WG, 23 March 1923, THAW/B, 60.

184–185 *"Thank God"* Gerhard Marcks to LF, summer 1925, LFHU,
25/53.

185 *thinking of doing the same* LF to JF, March 1925, LFHU,
25/23 and 29.

Feininger was being wooed . . . Schlemmer . . . and Klee Ibid.,
February 1925, 25/18.

Moholy . . . wanted to accept the offer Ibid., 25/13.

He was not there Hesse, *Residenz,* p. 197.

Gropius return to Weimar IG to MSG, 8 March 1925, AAA,
W&IG, 2270.

a month's rest Hesse, *Residenz,* p. 198.

"[G]ood Gropi isn't here" LF to JF, February 1925, LFHU, 25/3.

with or without their leader Ibid., 25/17.

blamed Gropius OS to OM, 3 November 1925, Schlemmer,
Tagebuch; see also LF to JF, April 1925, LFHU, 25/32.

the school's new direction OS to OM, April 1925, Schlemmer,
Letters and Diaries, p. 164.

186 *lamented Feininger* LF to JF, March 1925, LFHU, 25/24.

Gropius still could not bring himself to accept Ibid., 25/23.

"They seriously want to have us" Ibid., February 1925, 25/17.

the city's "main attraction" IG, 4 March 1925, AAA, IG/d.

"we will get quite a lot to do" IG to MSG, 8 March 1925, ibid.

187 *"Again only a private office"* OS to TS, 21 June 1925,
Schlemmer, *Tagebuch.*

hailed Grote AA, 10 March 1925.

his "pet idea" Hesse, *Residenz,* p. 200.

188 *figured little in the mayor's invitation* Ibid., p. 218.

Gropius courted him assiduously IG, 14 March 1925, AAA, IG/d.

the "second edition" LF to JF, February 1925, LFHU, 25/17.

Feininger almost feared the move Ibid., March 1925, 25/23.

"a pawn of political infighting" Hesse, *Residenz,* p. 202.

hostile brochures Ibid.

"Battle Around the Bauhaus" "The Battle Around the Bauhaus,"
ARD, 16 March 1925, BA/B, F/4.

Could Dessau afford . . . to support this school Ibid.

small number of students Ibid; also in Wingler, *The Bauhaus*, p.
87. According to the school's register, the Bauhaus opened in
Dessau with fifty students, rising to an unimpressive sixty-
three by the winter semester of 1925–1926 ("Register of
Bauhaus Students by City of Residence, Bauhaus, Dessau,"
SDA).

189 *questioned the school's claim* AA, 15 March 1925.

another sensitive issue Reply, Dr. Seiss to Dr. Koenig (of 18
March), ARD, 19 March 1925, BA/B, F/4.

"The Bauhaus Hoopla" Hesse, *Residenz*, p. 206.

Believing then that the issues . . . were spurious IG, 11 March
1925, AAA, IG/d.

190 *"the only way out"* Hesse, *Residenz*, p. 207.

ready to vote Ibid.

The proposition was simple SDA/vol. 51/Gemein, 23 March 1925.

A master parliamentarian Hesse, *Residenz*, p. 208.

tumultuous LF to JF, May 1925, LFHU, 25/34.

"boiling" state IG, 26 June 1925, AAA, IG/d.

191 *For someone like Kandinsky* Wassily Kandinsky, "The Work of
the Wall-Painting Workshop of the Staatliches Bauhaus," in
Wingler, *Bauhaus*, p. 80.

depleting their creative energy OS to TS, 21 June 1925,
Schlemmer, *Tagebuch*.

"Everywhere the same complaint" IG, 25 June 1925, AAA, IG/d.

Breuer . . . complained Ibid., 4 November 1925.

so too had Carl Fieger IG to MSG, May 1925, ibid. , [2270.]

"an excellent worker" Ibid.

192 *he too left Gropius's office* OS to TS, 22 March 1926,
Schlemmer, *Letters and Diaries*, p. 191; see also Nerdinger,
Gropius, p. 70.

a volcano IG, 15 October 1925, AAA, IG/d.

"he can't do it all" IG to MSG, May 1925, ibid. , [2270.]

"G. has to do all the work himself" IG, 30 April 1925, AAA, IG/d.

working himself to death Ibid., 20 November 1925.

"a palace revolt" Ibid., 5 June 1925.

assume these jobs himself   Ibid., 30 April 1925.

de facto director   Kandinsky, *Kandinsky*, p. 158.

Gropius also knew that Kandinsky had taken to propagating
IG, 10 July 1925, AAA, IG/d.

193 *Gropius blamed Kandinsky*   Ibid., 11 July 1925.

193 *"a quiet understanding"*   Ibid., 4 November 1925.

they disputed it forcefully   Reference to June City Council meeting
in SDA/vol. 51/Gemein, 5 November 1925.

threatened to air their complaints   IG, 27 June 1925, AAA, IG/d.

194 *a severe housing shortage*   Ulla Machlitt, "Das Bauhaus vor dem
Hintergrund sozialökonomischer Strukturen und politischer
Kräftegruppierungen in Dessau 1925 bis 1930," *WZHB* 23,
nos. 5/6 (Weimar, 1976): 478.

Gropius himself seemed startled   IG, between July and early
September 1925, AAA, IG/d.

Schlemmer . . . was also "shocked"   OS to TS, 8 October 1925,
Schlemmer, *Letters and Diaries*, pp. 180-81.

protect his privacy   Kandinsky, *Kandinsky*, p. 132.

angry workers   Wolfgang Thöner, personal conversation with
author, Bauhaus, Dessau, 28 September 1990.

repeatedly smashed   IG, 26 May 1926, AAA, IG/d.

nearly electrocuted   T. Lux Feininger, interview.

their tax money   Hesse, *Residenz*, pp. 204–5.

"Where was the City Council?"   Ibid., p. 215.

"[I]ncredible agitation"   IG, 12 October 1925, AAA, IG/d.

"Just keep quiet"   OS to TS, 8 October 1925, Schlemmer,
Letters and Diaries, p. 180.

impeach the mayor   Ibid.

a gloomy state   IG, 12 October 1925, AAA, IG/d.

a "storm in a teapot"   Ibid.

195 *whether or not a new school was even needed*   AA, 23
October 1925.

"the final straw"   Ibid., 31 October 1925.

demanding the immediate cessation   SDA/vol. 51/Gemein,
5 November 1925.

able to defeat the motion   OS to TS, 15 December 1925,
Schlemmer, *Letters and Diaries*, p. 187.

"out of control"   AA, 24 October 1925.

196 *"the philistines are delighted"*   Kessler, *Diaries*, 15 May 1925
(Weimar), p. 267.

"Hindenburg, alas!"   IG, 26 April 1925, AAA, IG/d.

Schlemmer was awed   OS to TS, 5 November 1925, Schlemmer,
Letters and Diaries, p. 182.

196 *waive 10 percent of their salaries*   IG, 30 November 1925,
AAA, IG/d.

"terrified"   AA, 1 January 1926.

the family's bills   IG, 15 January 1926, AAA, IG/d.

"[g]reat financial worries"   Ibid., 3 February 1926.

"dangerous"   AA, 1 May 1926.

197 *beer glasses and broken chairs*   Ibid., 10 June 1926.

protruding nails, and kitchen knives   Ibid., 20 June 1926.

students' political sympathies   Philipp Tolziner, "Mit Hannes
Meyer am Bauhaus und in der Sowjetunion (1927–1936),"
hannes meyer 1889–1954 architekt urbanist lehrer (Berlin:
Wilhelm Ernst und Sohn, 1989), p. 245

Kandinsky . . . would report to the mayor   IG, 20 November
1926, AAA, IG/d.

published their complaints   Ibid., 20 June 1926.

the anti-Bauhaus attacks   OS to OM, 7 July 1926, Schlemmer,
Tagebuch.

"wan and tired"   IG, 20 June 1926, AAA, IG/d.

"G. is worn out"   Ibid., 14 May 1926.

198 *Kurt Elster*   Kurt Elster, "A Response to the Bauhaus Reply,"
AA, 24 June 1926.

none other than Heinrich Peus   Ibid., 26 June 1926.

199 *For all Gropius's writings*   Included among Gropius's writings on
this subject were "Plan for the Construction of a Housing
Factory ("Plan zur Errichtung einer Wohnhausfabrik"), unpub-
lished manuscript, Dessau 1925 (Isaacs, *An Illustrated
Biography*, p. 124); "Forward, The Teachings of Uniformity in
the Construction Industry" ("Vorwort: Einheitslehre im
Baugewerbe"), *Technische Erziehung: Baufachliche
Einheitslehre und Spezialisierung* 5, no. 8 (1926–1927), AAA,
W&IG, 2275; "Glass Buildings" ("Glasbau"), *Die Bauzeitung*
23, no. 20 (25 May 1926): 159–62, AAA, W&IG, 2275.

200 *the mayor . . . wanted the students to participate*   IG, 26 April

1926, AAA, IG/d.

no legal basis Ibid.

Gropius had similarly denied Muche and Breuer's request Ibid., 28 April 1925.

a few interior furnishings Ibid., 7 December 1926.

200 *an alarming rate* Ibid., 22 March 1926.

lunch twice a week Ibid., 10 February 1926.

"a very productive period" Ibid., 12 February 1926.

200–201 *Kandinsky . . . accused Gropius of not working hard enough* Ibid., 29 May 1926.

201 *Muche . . . announced his departure* Ibid., 2 November 1926.

brooked no nonsense T. Lux Feininger, interview with Robert Brown, Cambridge, Mass., 19 May 1987, AAA, Oral History Program.

Gropius was aware IG, 20 November 1926, AAA, IG/d.

he could hardly speak Ibid., 4 December 1926.

improving society In Hesse, *Residenz*, p. 222.

"unwavering determination" In Wingler, *The Bauhaus*, p. 125.

13. DESSAU 1927:   A CRITICAL ELECTION

203 *"hell's doors"* IG, 6 December 1926, AAA, IG/d.

"[T]ired . . . run down . . . depressed" Ibid., 14 and 26 January and 3 and 28 February 1927.

unaccountably grumpy Ibid., 8 January 1927, AAA, IG/d.

204 *an astonishing overrun* in Isaacs, *An Illustrated Biography*, p. 126.

Hesse's political fate Hesse, *Residenz*, p. 227.

spawning the stunning growth Ibid.

Dorothy Thompson Dorothy Thompson's article appeared in *New York Evening Post* in August 1927. Quoted in Hesse, ibid., p. 225.

"beside himself" IG, 7 January 1927, AAA, IG/d.

Ernst Neufert Although Neufert's appointment in Weimar began on 1 April 1926, he had remained in Dessau until September. AAA, RI.

attributed them to overwork IG, 7 January 1927, AAA, IG/d.

such "miscalculations"   Ibid.

205 *inattentiveness to detail*   See Nerdinger, *Gropius*, p. 29.
search for basic artistic principles   IG, 2 February 1927, AAA, IG/d.
"unrealistic expectations"   Report, Bauhaus Syndikat (Lange), 9
December 1922, THAW/B, 12/266–69.

206 *"There is just not enough money"*   IG, 8 January 1927, AAA, IG/d.
temporarily eliminated   Ibid., 14 January 1927.
The resistance   Ibid., 8 January 1927.
an audience of one thousand   AA, 30 June 1927.
"Yellow Brochure"   IG, 11 March 1925, AAA, IG/d.
"a thief, an intriguer, and a coward"   AA, 30 June 1927.
criminal charges   "Lawsuit *Gropius* v. *Büchlein*," ibid.

207 *throughout the country*   "Report on the Meeting of the Citizens'
Association," ibid., 1 April 1927.
"a laughingstock"   Konrad N. Nonn, "The State Garbage
Supplies: The Staatliches Bauhaus in Weimar," *DZ*, 24 April 1924.
"Update on the Bauhaus"   Konrad N. Nonn,
"Zusammenfassendes über das Weimarer und Dessauer
'Bauhaus,'" *ZBW* 47, no. 10 (9 March 1927).

208 *paid for reprints*   "Report on the Meeting of the Citizens'
Association," *AA*, 1 April 1927.
"German interests"   Ibid., 16 June 1927.
condemned as "lies"   Ibid., 18 June 1927.
"Times are bad for modernism"   OS to W. Baumeister,
14 February 1925, Schlemmer, *Tagebuch*.
"momentous . . . rejection of . . . abstraction in art"   OS to OM,
17 February 1925, Schlemmer, *Letters and Diaries*, p. 162.
"Every German seems to despise"   LF to JF, August 1926,
LFHU, 26/12.

209 *the "new world" and "modern life"*   In Wingler, *The Bauhaus*,
p. 125.
varying complaints   Nerdinger, *Gropius*, p. 82; also Eva
Weininger, conversation.

210 *A committee from the RfG*   IG, 3 February 1927, AAA, IG/d.
Büchlein sent reprints   Ibid., 22 March 1927.
on his way out   Ibid., 25 March 1927.
Nonn's demotion has "already been signed"   Ibid., 28 March
1927.

On March 28 he wrote to a minister   Ibid.
gave Gropius the go-ahead   Ibid., 2 April 1927.
"The effect here in Dessau"   Ise erroneously mentions a
   three-hundred-thousand-mark subsidy. Ibid., 24 May 1927.
210–11 successful "coup"   Ibid., 13 July 1927.
petitioned the RfG   Hesse, Residenz, p. 230.
"only a question of time"   IG, 26 August 1927, AAA, IG/d.
Reports to the contrary   AA, 1 September 1927.
simply had no idea   IG, 3 February 1927, AAA, IG/d.
"confused"   WG (Dessau Bauhaus) to HM (Basel), 18 January
   1927, GC/HM.
211 "the core of [its] real work"   IG, 3 February 1927, AAA, IG/d.
212 allowing the students to participate   Hesse, Residenz, p. 221.
"the most radical"   Richard Pommer and Christian F. Otto,
   Weissenhof 1927 and the Modern Movement in Architecture
   (Chicago: University of Chicago Press, 1991), p. 48.
"Lissitzky's Dutch disciple"   See Donald Drew Egbert, Social
   Radicalism and the Arts: Western Europe (New York: Alfred A.
   Knopf, 1970), p. 654.
213 replace "the handcrafted"   ABC: Beiträge zum Bauen 1,
   no. 2 (1924).
not interested in teaching   IG, 5 December 1926, AAA, IG/d.
Stam once again turned down Gropius's offer   IG, Ibid.
"After having met you here"   WG to HM, 18 December 1926,
   GC/HM.
identified his views   HM to WG, 16 February 1927, GC/HM.
In this article   HM, "Die Neue Welt," Das Werk 13, no. 7
   (1926): 220.
214 Gropius's socialistic goals   Peter Hahn, personal conversation
   with author, Bauhaus-Archiv, Berlin, 26 September 1990.
"the longer breadth"   IG, 20 May 1925, AAA, IG/d.
prided himself on his patience   Ibid., 26 January 1928.
"the stubborn mule"   Ibid., 20 May 1925.
"cheap," and also be "beautiful"   WG, "The Aims of the Bauhaus
   at Dessau," 1927 (in English), pp. 187–90, BA/B, F/6.
215 the school's "aestheticism"   OS to W. Baumeister, 21 December
   1926, Schlemmer, Letters and Diaries, p. 198.
"mere superficialities"   HM (Basel) to WG (Dessau), 3 January

1927, GC/HM.

informing the faculty   IG, 14 January 1927, AAA, IG/d.

dismissed Kandinsky's concerns   Ibid.

cringing under Meyer's accusation   Ibid., 20 January 1927.

215   *After another visit*   Ibid., 2 February 1927.

"Thank God!"   Ibid., 10 February 1927.

a curriculum vitae   WG (Dessau Bauhaus) to HM (Basel), 18
    January 1927, GC/HM; see also HM (Basel) to WG (Dessau
    Bauhaus), 16 February 1927, GC/HM.

no political affiliation   HM, curriculum vitae, 15 February 1927,
    GC/HM.

216   *political turn*   in Magdalena Droste, "Unterrichtsstruktur und
    Werkstattarbeit am Bauhaus unter Hannes Meyer," in *Hannes
    Meyer 1889–1954*, p. 166.

Hesse approved Meyer's appointment   FH to HM, 21 February
    1927, DAM/HM.

included a copy   HM (Basel) to FH (Dessau), 9 March 1927,
    GC/HM.

Meyer arrived in Dessau   IG, 1 April 1927, AAA, IG/d.

shocked and humiliated Gropius   Ibid., 21 October 1927.

counting on the Törten commission financially   Ibid., 23 September
    1927.

Hesse and Gropius's continuing appeals   Ibid., 16 November and
    3 December 1927.

"buckets of dirt"   Ibid., 16 November 1927.

no money   AA, 5 November 1927.

217   *he described as "normal"*   Ibid.

"Exactly how much does the Bauhaus cost"   Ibid., 1 November
    1927.

there would have been no fees   Werner Eisenberg, "Response to
    FH," AA, 16 November 1927.

attributed the accusation to Peus   IG, 15 January 1928, AAA, IG/d.

What exactly has the Bauhaus achieved   AA, 5 November 1927.

"[T]hings are going to be hot"   OS to TS, 10 November 1927,
    Schlemmer, *Letters and Diaries*, p. 216.

So defensive was Hesse   FH, "The Bauhaus Battle," AA,
    15 November 1927.

218   *"a bourgeois result"*   Ibid., 29 November 1927.

"hardly bearable" IG, 5 December 1927, AAA, IG/d.

happy to see him go Ibid.

a grim mood OS to TS, 1 December 1927, Schlemmer, *Letters and Diaries*, pp. 216–17.

218 *the "wonderful time"* AHB to JBN, 12 December 1927, AAA, JBN, NJBN-1.

children of misery AA, 11 August 1929.

"irresponsibility [and professional] failure" Ibid., 19 January 1928.

legal action Dessau did take legal action against Gropius and won, the arbitration tribunal fining Gropius 4,294 marks plus interest as of 9 August 1928, plus two-thirds of the legal fees. SDA/vol. 51/Gemein II, 5 December 1929, p. 14.

he could not possibly remain IG, 13 January 1928, AAA, IG/d.

announce his decision Ibid. , 3 February 1928.

219 *the school's new director* DESZEIT, 6 February 1928, BA/B, F/5.

long been recognized See, for example, Marcel Franciscono, *Gropius*, p. 16.

"in flux" WG to Ferdinand Kramer, 15 October 1919, in Droste, *Bauhaus,* p.50.

a "serenity" Josef Albers, in Baird, "Bauhaus Conflicts."

a "creative vacuum" Anni Albers, interview by Neil Welliver, journal and date unknown, AAA, Anni Albers File, N69-140.

the "richness of invention" Anni Albers, in Baird, "Bauhaus Conflicts."

"iron willpower" IG, 20 May 1925, AAA, IG/d.

220 *"a shooting star"* WG to Maria Benemann, undated (postmarked 19 April 1920), in Reginald R. Isaacs, *Walter Gropius: Der Mensch*, p. 241.

"a thousand threads" LF to JF, June 1919, LFHU, 19/18.

"on the front line" WG (Weimar) to MSG, 19 January 1920, AAA, RI.

"between the past and the future" Klaus Karbe (Gropius's nephew) (Berlin) to RI, 29 June 1965, translation typescript, AAA, RI.

a "man in the middle" Julius Posener, *Berlin; auf dem Wege zu einer neuen Architektur. Das Zeitalter Wilhelms II* (Munich: Prestel-Verlag, 1979), p. 576.

223 *"murdering" workers*   AA, 7 May 1929.

223 *huge red signs*   Ibid., 24 November 1929.

up to 60 percent of the student population   Michael Siebenbrodt, "Zur Rolle der Kommunisten und anderer forschrittlicher Kräfte am Bauhaus," *WZHAB* 23, nos. 5/6 (1976): 482.

Only nine students   Folke Dietzsch, "Die Studierenden am Bauhaus: Eine analytische Betrachtung zur Struktur der Studentenschaft, zur Ausbildung und zum Leben der Studierenden am Bauhaus sowie zu ihrem späteren wirken," Ph.D. diss., WHAB, 1990, p. 40.

contacts made   Siebenbrodt, "Zu Rolle," p. 481.

The Bauhaus's first KPD cell   Ibid.

224 *an acknowledged cell*   IG, 13 January 1928, AAA, IG/d. (402)

supported the cell's activities   Siebenbrodt, "Zu Rolle," p. 481.

"propagandize"   HM to Adolf Behne, 30 April 1928, photocopy, BA/B.

Max Bill . . . Lotte Burckhardt   Max Bill, Lotte Burckhardt, interviews by "Editors," "bauen und leben," *Bauhaus* 2, nos. 2/3 (1928): 25–26, BA/B.

commemorated the anniversaries   Siebenbrodt, "Zu Rolle," p. 482.

kostufra operated covertly   Tolziner, "Mit Hannes Meyer," p. 249.

took place outside   Siebenbrodt, "Zu Rolle," p. 481.

225 *at Hannes Meyer's home*   Tolziner, "Mit Hannes Meyer," p. 249.

the normal vehicle   Ibid.

in Tolziner's apartment   Ibid. , p. 245.

"of course" refused   Ibid., p. 249.

rescind the invitation   WG to Heinrich Vogeler (Worpswede), 19 September 1921, THAW/B, 25/50.

"his own obliging attitude"   IG, 20 November 1926, AAA, IG/d.

226 *"a harmonious form of society"*   HM, "Bauhaus und Gesellschaft," *Bauhaus* 3, no. 1 (January 1929): 2, BA/B.

reorganized workshops   In Droste, *Bauhaus*, p. 174.

226–27 *"the needs of the . . . proletariat"*   Ibid., p. 175.

227 *little to complain about*   Hesse, *Residenz*, p. 235.

"as good as unknown"   Ibid., p. 239.

"productive pedagogy"   AA, 26 May 1929.

the delicacy of a hammer   IG, 10 November 1927, AAA, IG/d.

"a personality of extremes"   Konrad Püschel, personal conversation
with author (Weimar), 2 October 1990.

228 *"in a perpetual trance"*   OS to OM, 17 April 1927, Schlemmer,
Letters and Diaries, p. 202.

"astonishing"   IG, 27 January 1928, AAA, IG/d.

"trapped in formalism"   In Droste, *Bauhaus,* p. 200.

"We search for . . . ignorance of life"   HM, "Bauhaus und
Gesellschaft," *Bauhaus* 3, no. 1 (January 1929): 2.

Meyer had not been the artists' choice   IG, 13 January 1928,
AAA, IG/d.

dogmatic and inflexible   Ibid., 11 January 1928.

Joost Schmidt   Ibid., 3 February 1928.

Moholy-Nagy, no longer able to stand   OS to TS, 27 January
1928, Schlemmer, *Letters and Diaries,* p. 222.

Albers thought   IG, 1 March 1928, AAA, IG/d.

precipitate the school's downfall   OS to TS, 5 February 1928,
Schlemmer, *Letters and Diaries,* p. 225.

229 *So obviously unwanted*   T. Lux Feininger, "Notes on the
Pictures," *T. Lux Feininger: Photographs of the Twenties and
Thirties* (New York: Prakapas Gallery, 1980).

"honest indifference"   T. Lux Feininger, interview.

"merely tolerated"   OS to OM, 23 January 1928, Schlemmer,
Letters and Diaries, p. 221.

hostility toward abstract art   T. Lux Feininger, "Notes."

The battle . . . emerged into the open   OS to OM, 8 September
1929, Schlemmer, *Letters and Diaries,* p. 248.

artistic neuroses   In Droste, "Unterrichtsstruktur," p. 140.

"a new world order"   IG, 13 November 1927, AAA, IG/d.

condemned as "irrelevant"   OS to OM, 8 September 1929,
Schlemmer, *Letters and Diaries,* p. 248.

politicize the school's theater   In Droste, *Bauhaus,* p. 186.

"a soviet republic of the Bauhaus"   OS to OM, 9 June 1929,
Schlemmer, *Letters and Diaries,* p. 244.

"serious" students   In Droste, "Unterrichtsstruktur," p. 140.

230 *By the end of his speech*   AA, 7 March 1929.

231 *had to be canceled*   Ibid., 8 August 1929.

"[T]he moment had come"   Wolfgang Tümpel, response to

Bauhaus students questionnaire prepared by RI, 1965, AAA, RI.

what the Nazis meant   Fritz Sauckel, *Kampf und Sieg in Thüringen* (Weimar: Verlag der Thüringischen Staatszeitung, 1934), p. 21.

231 *now gathered within*   Siebenbrodt, "Zu Rolle," p. 482.

thirty-six-member KPD cell   In Droste, *Bauhaus*, p. 199.

the majority of students   Howard Dearstyne, in Baird, "Bauhaus Conflicts."

most decisive and intellectually dominant internal group Siebenbrodt, "Zu Rolle," p. 481.

collected funds   Ibid. , p. 482.

canvassed all new students   In Droste, "Unterrichtsstruktur," p. 161.

further radicalize   Ibid., p. 160.

Some kostufra members   Tolziner, "Mit Hannes Meyer," p. 245.

232 *easier and more socially acceptable*   In Droste, "Unterrichtsstruktur," p. 161.

eliminate the painters   Ibid., p. 137.

"much in demand"   *AA*, 3 March 1930.

Polish lullabies first   Konrad Püschel to Lieselotte Floss, undated, Briefe Konrad Püschels an Lieselotte Floss, 1928–1930, BA/D Collection.

Guests watched in dismay   Ibid.

Kandinsky complained to Grote   Hesse, *Residenz*, p. 243.

233 *"in no way politically engaged"*   Ibid.

various Marxist "working teams"   HM to Karol Teige, 29 August 1930, BA/B.

234 *flat roofs*   The Roofers' Newsletter (*Dachdecker Zeitung*) 37, no. 13 (March 1930).

the Bauhaus Communists unveiled their program   Siebenbrodt, "Zu Rolle," p. 483.

235 *"a reactionary Bauhaus spirit"*   *AA*, 7 May 1930.

The Right's reaction   *AA*, 7 May 1930.

Meyer admitted his commitment   HM (Berlin) to Karol Teige (Prague), 4 September 1930, DAM/HM, 82/1 (17).

"a Marxist theory of design"   Ibid.

236 *"a Communist-led Bauhaus"*   Hesse, *Residenz*, p. 243.

the impossibility of his position   Ibid., p. 244.

in a real bind   In Droste, "Unterrichtsstruktur," p. 162.

six months' notice   Agreement between HM and Dessau (signed
by HM and FH), 5 December 1928, DAM/HM, 82/1/399.

236 *a covert and complex scheme*   In Craig, *Germany*, pp. 531–32.

called upon . . . Heinrich Brüning   See Eberhard Kolb, *The
Weimar Republic*, P. S. Falla, trans. (London: Unwin Hyman,
[1984] 1988), p. 111, and Craig, *Germany*, pp. 535–36.

237 *ignored his threat*   Craig, *Germany*, p. 539.

firing at their fellow countrymen   *AA*, 16 June 1930.

called on all workers   Ibid.

little more than a subterfuge   Siebenbrodt, "Zur Rolle," p. 483.

solicited donations   Ibid.

A student delegation   Ibid.

still trying to mount a case   Josef Albers to Ludwig Grote, 20
June 1930, in Droste, "Unterrichtsstruktur," p. 143.

the leftist Magdeburger Tribüne: *AA*, 8 July 1930.

238 *an additional Bauhaus contribution*   Ibid., 14 July 1930.

"egocentric, inbred, and elitist"   HM, "Bauhaus und
Gesellschaft," p. 2.

His initial choice   WG to L. Grote, 16 May 1930, in Droste,
"Unterrichtsstruktur," p. 165.

Gropius come back   L. Grote to FH, 10 July 1930, in Droste, ibid.

the Reichstag ignored Brüning's threats   In Craig, *Germany*, p. 539.

"pale Red brother"   *AA*, 16 June 1930.

"[r]each out fraternally"   Ibid., 3 September 1930.

239 *"It seems strange"*   Wilhelm Karius, "The Twilight of the Bauhaus,"
AA, 9 August 1920.

"Unless you take it over"   Mies van der Rohe, "Talk with Mies,"
North Carolina State University College of Agriculture and
Engineering School of Design, Student Publication 3, no. 3
(spring 1953): 16.

"Pay them more money!"   Recounted by Philip Johnson, in John
W. Cook and Heinrich Klotz, *Conversations with Architects*
(New York: Praeger Publishers, 1973), p. 35.

240 *"pretentious" . . . the name "Bauhaus"*   In Elaine S. Hochman,
Architects of Fortune: Mies van der Rohe and the Third Reich
(New York: Weidenfeld & Nicolson, 1989; reprint, New York:
Fromm International Publishing Corp., 1990), p. 103.

241 *to demand his resignation*   Hesse, *Residenz*, p. 244.

   Meyer claimed the mayor came alone   HM to Katherine Teige, 4
      September 1930, DAM/HM, 82/1 (17).

241 *a venerable Bauhaus tradition*   Hesse, *Residenz*, p. 245.

242 *Hesse sought faculty support*   Ibid.

   announcing Meyer's resignation   AA, 1 August 1930.

   an immediate inquiry   HM to Dr. Redslob, 11 November 1930, in
      Droste, "Unterrichtsstruktur," pp. 173–74.

   "I just want to tell you briefly"   HM to Katherine Teige,
      31 July 1930, BA/B.

   "Grotesque"   Josef Gantner to HM, 1 August 1930, GC/HM.

   "Unbelievable"   A. Altherr, Direktion der Gewerbeschule und des
      Kunstgewerbemuseums der Stadt Zürich to HM, 26 August
      1930, GC/HM.

   "lust for murder"   HM to Dr. Josef Gantner, 6 August 1930,
      GC/HM.

   a "stab in the back"   HM to Gabriel Guevrekian (Architect,
      Paris), 26 August 1930, GC/HM.

   "fascistization"   HM (Berlin) to Josef Franck (Vienna), 3 October
      1930, GC/HM.

   "a warehouse of relics" . . . "terribly saddened"   Hermann
      Finsterlin to HM, 27 August 1930, GC/HM.

243 *"expansion of Gropius's ideas"*   J. Gartner (sig.), typescript of arti-
      cle about HM, 12 August 1930, DAM/HM, 82/1/765(1–3).

   "Germany's increasing cultural reactionism"   "Bauhaus Dessau,
      Bauhochschule Weimar—Cultural Reactionism and Architecture,"
      DRF, undated (August 1930?), Bildarchiv, WHAB.

   Hesse shifted his stance   Protokoll des Schiedsgerichts, Sitzung
      12 August 1930 im Büro des Reichskunstwarts, Bundesarchiv
      Koblenz, Reichskunstwart, R.32/141.

   out of the courts   Report of the arbitration panel in the case of
      HM v. City of Dessau, 5 November 1930, DAM/HM, 82/1/403.

   inspired by an upcoming trip   "The Case of Hannes Meyer and
      Ernst May," *DRF*, undated (August 1930?), Bildarchiv, WHAB.

244 *"the half-heartedness of my life"*   HM to El Lissitzky (Moscow),
      23 August 1930, DAM/HM, 82/1/789.

   "the best of the 'Marxist' Bauhaus"   HM to *Sowremennaya
      Architektura* (through architect M. Ginsberg), 2 September

1930, GC/HM.

"[H]err kandinsky" Bauhaus 3 (1930), in Wingler,
The Bauhaus, p. 169.

245 *"by no means"* AA, 1 August 1930.

"Hannes Meyer . . . should be honored" "Cultural Reactionism
and Architecture."

"Down with cultural reaction" AA, 11 August 1930.

little more than a subterfuge Karius, "The Twilight of
the Bauhaus."

246 *"a purely Communist institution"* AA, 21 August 1930.

judge his "suitability" Dearstyne, in Neumann, Bauhaus, p. 214.

the immediate closing Konrad Püschel to Lieselotte Floss, 11
September 1930, 1928–1930, BA/D Collection, F/1.

"keep their mouths shut" Ibid.

Vorkurs *was restored* "Cultural Reactionism and Architecture."

told "never to return" "Nochmals der Fall Bauhaus," Stein,
Holz, Eisen 44, no. 19 (6 October 1930): 417.

"to wipe Meyer's spirit" "Cultural Reactionism and Architecture."

from Left to Right OS to Gunta Stölzl, 2 September 1930,
Schlemmer, Letters and Diaries, p. 267.

"saddest chapter" Konrad Püschel to Lieselotte Floss, 11
September 1930, 1928–1930, BA/D Collection, F/1.

247 *never materialized* In Craig, Germany, p. 542.

Nazi thugs Kessler, Diaries, 13 October 1930 (Berlin), pp. 399–400.

deport other foreign students AA, 16 October 1930.

"headed for new shores" OS to Ludwig Grote, 4 December
1930, Schlemmer, Tagebuch.

15. DEATH AND TRANSFIGURATION

248 *as Schlemmer worried* OS to OM, 1 December 1930, Schlemmer,
Letters and Diaries, p. 275.

249 *no particular heed* PJ, in Cook, Conversations, p. 27.

"'Political' didn't mean anything" PJ, conversation with author,
New York City, 16 October 1990.

a "Saul-Paul" conversion PJ, Preface, in Helen Searing, ed., In
Search of Modern Architecture: A Tribute to Henry-Russell

Hitchcock (New York: The Architectural History Foundation, 1982), p. vii.

249 *a similar conversion* "I have changed from Saulus to Paulus through all the suffering during the war. . . . I have transformed my innermost being" (WG [Berlin] to MSG, 17 March 1919, AAA, RI).

a "vision" In Marquis, *Barr*, p. 30.

250 *an inspirational spark* AHB, "Modern Architecture," *The Hound and Horn* 3, no. 3 (April–June 1930): 431–35.

a more popular tone PJ to Mrs. Homer H. Johnson, 20 June 1920, Philip Johnson Papers, in Terence Riley, *The International Style: Exhibition 15 and The Museum of Modern Art* (New York: Rizzoli International Publications, 1922), p. 13.

Johnson would go by himself Ibid. , p. 18.

met Barr in Hamburg PJ to Mrs. Homer H. Johnson, 7 July 1930, ibid. , p. 14.

251 *turned down their proposal* Ibid.

a "purer" aesthetic conscience HRH, "America-Europe," *i 10* 4, no. 20 (April 1929): 150.

"make propaganda" PJ to J. J. P. Oud (published in Dutch) in *Americana* (catalog of exhibition 1975 at Kröller-Müller Museum, Otterlo): 102. Original presumably written in English, trans. from Dutch by Helen Searing, in Searing, "International Style: The Crimson Connection," *Progressive Architecture* (February 1982): 88.

more open to architecture as art HRH, "America-Europe."

Europe overemphasized technology HRH, *Modern Architecture: Romanticism and Reintegration* (New York: Hacker Art Books, [1929] 1970), p. 210.

Barr emphasized style . . . modernism's paradigm *Wellesley College News*, 23 May 1929, AAA, AHB.

252 *base the museum's organization* AHB to WG, 12 March 1962, BA/B.

"a new form of life" Professor von Meyenburg of Basel referred to this in a lecture he delivered at the Bauhaus. *AA*, 8 June 1929.

await the school's new director PJ, conversation.

"thrilled" to see the building PJ (Dessau) to AHB, 16 October

1929, in Roob, "Barr," p. 18.

did not visit the workshops   PJ, conversation.

253   *"Sometimes I'm so angry"*   Konrad Püschel to Lieselotte Floss,
    17 September 1930, Briefe Konrad Püschel an Lieselotte Floss,
    1928–1930, BA/D Collection, F/1.

Johnson wrote to Oud   PJ to J. J. P. Oud, 17 September 1930,
    Johnson Papers, in Riley, *The International Style*, p. 36.

"all the best, dear Hannes Meyer"   J. J. P. Oud to HM, 21 August
    1930, postcard, GC/HM.

254   *Memorial for the War Dead*   "Bauhaus Dessau, Bauhochschule
    Weimar—Cultural Reactionism and Architecture."

linked Mies with Gropius   "The Case of Hannes Meyer and Ernst
    May," *DRF*, undated (August 1930?), Bildarchiv, WHAB.

the same rightist cultural tendencies   "Bauhaus Dessau,
    Bauhochschule Weimar—Cultural Reactionism and Architecture."

the school's rightward turn   OS to Gunta Stölzl, 2 September
    1930, Schlemmer, *Letters and Diaries*, p. 268.

the spirit of the times   Mies, "Baukunst und Zeitwille," *Der
    Querschnitt* 4, no. 1 (spring 1924): 31.

"Anything less than perfection"   Mies, "Only the Patient Counts:
    Some Radical Ideas on Hospital Design," *Modern Hospital* 64,
    no. 3 (1945): 65.

"The new age is a fact"   Mies, address given on 1 August 1930,
    published as "The New Age," *Die Form* 15 (1930): 406.

255   *a "self-centered person"*   *Bauhaus* 3, no. 3 (1930), in Wingler,
    The Bauhaus, p. 170.

"nearly a million marks"   PJ to J. J. P. Oud, 17 September 1930,
    Johnson Papers in Riley, *The International Style*, p. 36.

"Cheap, cheap, cheap"   PJ, conversation.

Mies was "far past the stage"   PJ, "Berlin Building Exhibition of
    1931," *New York Times*, 9 August 1931.

256   *"a violent Mies man"*   PJ, conversation.

sought commissions for him   In Riley, *The International Style*, p. 39.

Johnson's contribution   HRH, *Modern Architecture:
    Romanticism*, p. 190.

daily occurrences   In Craig, *Germany*, p. 557.

257   *Bauhaus's subsidies*   In Droste, *Bauhaus*, p. 206.

"a starving nation"   NSDAP election poster, in Bauhaus-Archiv,

Berlin, comp. and ed., *Bauhaus Berlin: Auflösung Dessau 1932; Schliessung Berlin, 1933; Bauhäusler und Drittes Reich* (Berlin: Kunstverlag Weingarten, GmbH, und Bauhaus-Archiv, Berlin, 1985), p. 41.

257 *removed from a school exhibition* Howard Dearstyne, *Inside the Bauhaus*, David Spaeth, ed., (New York: Rizzoli International Publications, 1986), p. 231.

travel permits *Bauhaus Berlin*, p. 43.

Hans Freyer In Droste, *Bauhaus*, p. 209.

His actions assuaged See new student Hans Kessler's comments in ibid., p. 208.

258 *The liberal coalition . . . was finished* Machlitt, "Das Bauhaus," pp. 479–80.

more dependent than ever *Bauhaus Berlin*, pp. 47–49.

the Nazis demanded SDA/vol. 51/Gemein II, 21 January 1932.

the proposal was defeated Ibid. The magistrate members—all of whom were involved in all Bauhaus decisions—consisted of four council members (the mayor, two councilors, and one planning officer) in addition to the thirty-six representatives on Dessau's City Council (Machlitt, "Das Bauhaus," p. 479).

259 *"permanently endangered"* OS to Gunta Stölzl, 8 February 1932, Schlemmer, *Tagebuch*.

defied Mies's ban Siebenbrodt, "Zur Rolle," p. 483.

the number 4 Ibid.

a foolish scheme In Craig, *Germany*, pp. 557–58.

a "protective hand" Hesse, *Residenz*, p. 251.

"violently politicized" OS to OM, 21 March 1932, Schlemmer, *Letters and Diaries*, p. 290.

260 *a long-standing dispute* in Droste, *Bauhaus*, p. 207.

expelled from the school Ibid., p. 466. This chronology of Mies's calling in the police differs slightly from the account that appeared in my previous discussion of this event in *Architects of Fortune*, which was based on recollections of Bauhaus students who over the years had apparently confused the two events.

the Bauhaus's "absolute end" T. Lux Feininger, interview.

260–61 *The main gallery . . . average home in 1931* Riley, *The International Style*, p. 72.

261 *"adoration of power"* WG, "Die überwindung."

a secondary area   Brendan Gill, "The Sky Line: 1932," *The New Yorker* (27 April 1992), p. 96.

261 *"safe for millionaires"*   Catherine Bauer to Lewis Mumford, 29 January 1932, Mumford Papers, University of Pennsylvania.
the public's tepid response   Riley, *The International Style*, p. 85.
"Miss van der Rohe"   The Worcester, Mass., *Sunday Telegram*, in ibid., p. 86.

262 *"enlighten" the Nazis*   L. Grote to Dr. Hans Prinzhorn, 23 May 1932, in Droste, *Bauhaus*, p. 228.

263 *sickened Hesse*   LF to JF, July 1932, LFHU, 32/20.
a pointless sham   See Hochman, *Architects*, p. 101.
a thick slice of ham   Dearstyne, *Inside*, p. 233.
"a fascist" and "German architect"   L. Grote to Hugo Bruckmann, 3 August 1932, in Droste, *Bauhaus*, p. 230.
a different name   L. Grote to W. A. Fahrenholtz, 16 August 1932, in ibid.
Gerd Balzer   Gerd Balzer (Bauhaus Berlin-Steglitz) to Reinhold Rössig, November 1932, BA/D, Briefe Reinhold Rössig.

264 *Hubert Hoffmann*   Hoffmann complained that the expelled students were simply demanding what he considered to be their student rights (Hubert Hoffmann [Berlin-Steglitz] to Reinhold Rössig, 15 December 1932, typescript, BA/D, Briefe Hubert Hoffmann).
"past sins"   OS to Christof Hertel, 28 July 1932, Schlemmer, *Letters and Diaries*, p. 297.

EPILOGUE: THE BAUHAUS IN AMERICA

266 *fairly well documented*   See, for example, William H. Jordy, "The Aftermath of the Bauhaus in America," in *The Intellectual Migrations: Europe and America, 1930–1960*, vol. 2, of *Perspectives in American History*, eds. Donald Fleming and Bernard Bailyn (Cambridge, Mass., 1968); Tom Wolfe, *From Bauhaus to Our House* (New York: Farrar Straus Giroux, 1981); Klaus Herdeg, *The Decorated Diagram: Harvard Architecture and the Failure of the Bauhaus Legacy* (Cambridge, Mass., 1983); and Wingler, *The Bauhaus*.

267 *"a communist way of life"* MN, *Akasztott Ember* 3, no. 4 (1922): 3; in Krisztina Passuth, *Moholy-Nagy* (New York: Thames and Hudson, 1985), p. 288.

267 *"translate revolution"* MN (Weimar), letter to the editor, *DK* (1 July 1924); in ibid., p. 395.

emulate the Bauhaus curriculum The school's ambitions far exceeded its means, and it endured a tortured history. The New Bauhaus collapsed in 1938 and was subsequently reopened in January 1939 as the School of Design. Moholy-Nagy died of leukemia at the age of fifty-one in 1946.

one year after his emigration MN, "New Approach to Fundamentals of Design," *More Business* 3, no. 11 (November 1938), in Wingler, *Bauhaus*, p. 196.

268 *He returned to* Harvard PJ, conversation.

269 *Today nearly one in three . . . "the American experience"* The *Economist* (10 August 1996): 37–38.

270 *Hannes Meyer's name* Meyer is mentioned only as Gropius's successor, whose subsequent "conflict with the municipal authorities led to his resignation" (Bayer, *Bauhaus: 1919–1928*, p. 204).

"Art Barred by Nazis" New Haven (Conn.) *Register* (4 December 1938), MOMA Archive, album 38 (December 1938–February 1940), p. 55.

271 *Reyner Banham* IG to Reyner Banham (Toronto), 1 February 1970, AAA, W&IG, 2271.

Mies, who continued to try to sell modernism For more information, see Hochman, *Architects of Fortune*

273 *"Bauhaus blue"* Ada Louise Huxtable, "Mackintosh: Revolution and the Scent of Heliotrope," in *Will They Ever Finish Bruckner Boulevard?* (New York: Macmillan, 1970), p. 251; first published in *New York Times*, 17 November 1968.

neo-Nazi political party Influenced by Huey Long and claiming a membership of about one hundred people, Johnson's party possessed an awkward slogan ("The need is for One Party") and an emblem of a flying wedge, but neither platform nor program. Referring to this strange absence, the *New York Herald Tribune* reported that the two young men planned "to pick one up as they go" (*New York Herald Tribune*, 18 December 1934, MOMA Archive, Goodyear, vol. 31).

"those dear, dead days"   Philip Johnson, "Where Are We At?"
Architectural Review 127 (September 1960): 173–75; in Philip
Johnson: *Writings* (New York: Oxford University Press, 1979),
pp. 102–3.

273 *fifty-year flirtation*   Considering that building in postwar America
did not really get started until the early 1950s, the style may be
said to have lasted barely thirty years in its adopted homeland.

"velvet darkness"   Julie V. Iovine, the *New York Times*, 12 March
1995.

274 *flocking to Europe*   Patricia Leigh Brown, the *New York Times*,
13 July 1995.

now being criticized   A. Drexler, "Engineer's Architecture: Truth
and Its Consequences," *The Architecture of the École des
Beaux-Arts*, ed. A. Drexler (New York, 1977), pp. 43, 51, 53.

Bibliography

SELECTED WRITINGS BY WALTER GROPIUS

"Sind beim Bau von Industriegebäuden künstlerische Gesichtspunkte mit praktischen und wirtschaflichen vereinbar?" *Der Industriebau* 1 (1912).

"Die Entwicklung moderner Industriebaukunst." *Jahrbuch des Deutschen Werkbundes* (1913).

"Der Stilbildende Wert Industrieller Bauformen." *Jahrbuch des Deutschen Werkbundes* (1914).

"Baukunst im freien Volksstaat." *Deutscher Revolutions—Almanach für das Jahr 1919* (1919).

"'Sparsamer Hausrat' und Falsche Dürftigkeit." *Die Volkswohnung* 8 (1919).

"Was ist Baukunst?" *Weimarer Blätter* 1 (1 May 1919).

"Neues bauen." *Der Holzbau* 2 (1920).

"Idee und Entwicklung des Staatlichen Bauhauses zu Weimar." *Amtsblatt des Thüringischen Ministeriums für Volksbildung* (January 1923).

"Der Baugeist der neuen Volksgemeinde." *Die Glocke* 10 (1924).

"Glasbau." *Die Bauzeitung* 23 (25 May 1926).

"Grundsätze der Bauhausproduktion." *Vivos voco: Zeitschrift für neues Deutschtum* 5 (August 1926).

"Das Manifest der neuen Architektur." *Stein Holz Eisen* 40 (5 August 1926).

"Vorwort: Einheitslehre im Baugewerbe." *Technische Erziehung: Baufachliche Einheitslehre und Spezialisierung* (1926/1927).

"Geistige und technische Grundlagen des Wohnhauses." *Stein Holz Eisen:* 41 (14 April 1927).

"Bauhaussiedlung: Dessau-Törten; Wie bauen wir billigere, bessere, schönere Wohnungen?" *Deutschland* 1 (1928).

"die soziologischen grundlagen der minimalwohnung." *bauhaus* 3 (October–December 1929).

With Herbert Bayer and Ise Gropius, eds. *Bauhaus: 1919–1928*. New York: The Museum of Modern Art, 1938. Reprint, 1975.

SELECTED LECTURES AND SPEECHES

"Monumentale Kunst und Industriebau." Hagen lecture, 29 January 1911. In *Walter Gropius und das Faguswerk* by Helmut Weber. Munich: Baumeister-Bücher, 3, 1911. Reprint, 1961.

"A Speech Before a Meeting of the Membership of the Arbeitsrat für Kunst on 22 March 1919." Reprinted in *Arbeitsrat für Kunst, 1918–1921*. Berlin: Akademie der Künste, 1980.

"Die Wirtschaftlichkeit neuer Baumethoden." Dessau address, 27 May 1927, at the Conference of the Organization of Community Building Commisioners of Northwest Germany. *Südwestdeutsche Bauzeitung* 2 (15 September 1927).

SELECTED WRITINGS ON OR RELEVANT TO THE BAUHAUS AND BAUHAUS PEOPLE

1919–1969 Bauhaus. Exhibition catalogue. Musée national d'art moderne de la ville de Paris, 2 Avril–22 Juin 1969.

50 Jahre Bauhausnachfolge: New Bauhaus in Chicago. Exhibition catalogue. Bauhaus-Archiv, Museum für Gestaltung, Berlin. 7 November 1987 to 10 January 1988. Berlin: Argon Verlag GmbH, 1987.

50 Years Bauhaus. Prepared with the Bauhaus-Archiv. Stuttgart: Württembergischer Kunstverein, 1968.

Adams, George. "Memories of a Bauhaus Student." *Architectural Review* 144 (September 1968).

Badura-Triska, Eva. *Johannes Itten; Tagebücher, 1913–1916 Stuttgart; 1916–1919 Wien.* 2 vols. Vienna: Löcker Verlag, 1990.

Bauhaus-Archiv, Berlin, comp. and ed. *Bauhaus Berlin: Auflösung Dessau 1932; Schliessung Berlin, 1933; Bauhäusler und Drittes Reich.* Compiled by Peter Hahn. Compiled and edited by Christian Wolsdorff. Berlin: Kunstverlag Weingarten, GmbH, 1985.

Dearstyne, Howard. *Inside the Bauhaus.* David Spaeth, ed. New York: Rizzoli International Publications, 1986.

Droste, Magdalena. *Bauhaus: 1919–1933.* Translated by Karen Williams. Bauhaus-Archiv Museum für Gestaltung. Berlin: Benedikt Taschen Verlag GmbH & Co. KG, 1990.

Feininger, T. Lux. *Autobiography.* Unpublished manuscript.

———. "The Bauhaus: Evolution of an Idea." *Criticism* (published for the Wayne State English Department by Wayne State University Press) II (summer 1960).

———. "Notes on the Pictures." In *T. Lux Feininger: Photographs of the Twenties and Thirties.* Exhibition catalogue. New York, 11 November–13 December 1980. New York: Prakapas Gallery, 1980.

Franciscono, Marcel. *Walter Gropius and the Creation of the Bauhaus in Weimar: The Ideals and Artistic Theories of Its Founding Years.* Chicago: University of Chicago Press, 1971.

Gay, Peter. "Gropius: The Imperatives of Craft." In *Art and Act.* New York: Harper & Row, 1980.

Greenberg, Allan C. *Artists and Revolution: Dada and the Bauhaus.* Studies in the Fine Arts: The Avant-Garde. Ann Arbor, Mich.: UMI Research Press, 1979.

Hahl-Koch, Jelena. "Kandinsky's Role in the Avant-Garde." In *The Avant-Garde in Russia, 1910–1930: New Perspectives*, Stephanie Barron and Maurice Tuchman, organizers. Los Angeles: Los Angeles County Museum of Art, 1980. Reprint, 1986.

Hahn, Peter, Clark V. Poling, Magdalena Droste, and Charles W. Haxthausen. *Kandinsky: Russische Zeit und Bauhausjahre, 1915–1933.* Exhibition catalogue. Bauhaus-Archiv, Museum für Gestaltung, Berlin, 9 August–23 September 1984. Berlin: Bauhaus-Archiv, 1984.

Hannes Meyer 1889–1954 architekt urbanist lehrer. Berlin: Wilhelm Ernst und Sohn, 1989.

Hesse, Fritz. *Aus den Jahren 1925 bis 1950 Erinnerungen an Dessau.* Bad Pyrmont: privately printed, 1963. Reprint, 1990.

———. *Von der Residenz zur Bauhausstadt.* Bad Pyrmont: privately printed, 1963.

Hüter, Karl-Heinz. *Das Bauhaus in Weimar.* Berlin: Akademie-Verlag, 1976.

Isaacs, Reginald. *Gropius: An Illustrated Biography of the Creator of the Bauhaus.* Boston: Little, Brown, and Company, 1983. Reprint, 1990.

———. *Walter Gropius: Der Mensch und Sein Werk.* 2 vols. Berlin: Gebr. Mann Verlag, 1983.

Itten, Johannes. *Mein Vorkurs am Bauhaus: Gestaltungs und Formenlehre.* Ravensburg: Otto Maier Verlag, 1963.

———. "Utopia: Dokumente der Wirklichkeit." In *Analysis of Old Masters.* Bruno Adler, ed. Weimar: Utopia Verlag, 1921.

Julien, Charles-André. "Une interview de Kandinsky en 1921." *Revue de l'Art 5* (1969).

Kállai, Ernst (signed "e. k."). "bauen und leben." *bauhaus 3* (January 1929).

Kandinsky, Nina. *Kandinsky et moi.* (Originally published as *Kandinsky und Ich,* 1976.) Translated by J. M. Gaillard-Paquet. Paris: Flammarion, 1978.

Kandinsky, Wassily. *Concerning the Spiritual in Art.* 1911. Reprint, with introduction and translation by M. T. H. Sadler. New York: Dover Publications, 1977.

Klee, Paul. *Briefe an die Familie, 1893–1940.* Felix Klee, ed. 2 vols. Cologne: DuMont Buchverlag, 1979.

Konrad Püschel Studienarbeiten am Bauhaus Dessau 1926–1930. With an introduction by Wolfgang Paul. Dessau: Bauhaus-Archiv (Dessau), 1981 (March).

Lang, Lothar. *Das Bauhaus 1919–1933: Idee und Wirklichkeit.* Berlin: Zentralinstitut für Formgestaltung, 1965.

Machlitt, Ulla. "Das Bauhaus vor dem Hintergrund sozialökonomischer Strukturen und politischer Kräftegruppierungen in Dessau 1925 bis 1930." Wissenschaftliches Kolloquium in Weimar 27 bis 29 Oktober 1976. *Wissenschaftliche Zeitschrift der Hochschule für Architektur und Bauwesen, Weimar; 50 Jahre Bauhaus Dessau 23,* nos. 5/6 (1976).

Märten, Lu. "historischer materialismus und neue gestaltung." *bauhaus* 3 (January 1929).

Mengel, Willi. "Jugendstil und Bauhausidee." *Der Polygraph* 19 (1968).

Meyer, Hannes. "bauhaus und gesellschaft." *bauhaus* 3 (January 1929).

Necker, W. F. "Bauhaus: '23–'24." *Architectural Review* (September 1963).

Nerdinger, Winfried. *Walter Gropius*. The Architect Walter Gropius. Drawings, Prints and Photographs, Complete Project Catalogue. Exhibition catalogue. The Busch-Reisinger Museum, Harvard University Art Museums, Cambridge, Mass., and the Bauhaus-Archiv, Berlin. Berlin: Gebr. Mann Verlag, 1985.

Neumann, Eckhard, ed. *Bauhaus and Bauhaus People: Personal Opinions and Recollections of Former Bauhaus Members and Their Contemporaries*. New York: Van Nostrand Reinhold, 1970.

Passuth, Krisztina. *Moholy-Nagy*. New York: Thames and Hudson, 1985.

Pevsner, Nikolaus. "Any Old Bauhaus?" *The Listener*, 24 January 1963.

———. "Gropius and Van de Velde." *Architectural Review* (March 1963).

Posener, Julius. "From Schinkel to the Bauhaus: Five Lectures on the Growth of Modern German Architecture." *Architectural Association Paper 5* (1972). London: Lund Humphries for the Architectural Association.

Schädlich, Christian. "Die Beziehungen des Bauhauses zu den USA 1919–1933; Eine Dokumentation." *Wissenschaftliche Zeitschrift der Hochschule für Architektur und Bauwesen Weimar* 35, no. 2 (1989).

———. "Walter Gropius und seine Stellung in der Architektur des 20. Jahrhunderts." In *Walter Gropius*. Compiled and edited by Harmut Probst and Christian Schädlich. In vol. 1 of 3 vols. Verlag für Architektur und technische Wissenschaften. Berlin: Wilhelm Ernst und Sohn, 1987.

Schlemmer, Oskar. "Oskar Schlemmer: Tagebuch, 1907–1918, 1919–1923, 1924–1927." Unabridged diaries. Typed manuscript. Bauhaus-Archiv, Berlin. Donated by Tut Schlemmer.

Schlemmer, Tut, ed. *The Letters and Diaries of Oskar Schlemmer*. Translated by Krishna Winston. 1972. Reprint, Evanston, Ill.: Northwestern University Press, 1990.

Schnaidt, Claude. *Hannes Meyer: Buildings, Projects and Writings*. Stuttgart: Verlag Gerd Hatje, 1965.

Siebenbrodt, Michael. "Zur Rolle der Kommunisten und anderer forschrittlicher Kräfte am Bauhaus." Wissenschaftliches Kolloquium in Weimar 27 bis 29 Oktober 1976. *Wissenschaftliche Zeitschrift der Hochschule für Architektur und Bauwesen Weimar* 23, nos. 5/6 (1976).

Staatliches Bauhaus Weimar 1919–1923. Collection. Walter Gropius, Gertrud Grunow, Paul Klee, Wassily Kandinsky, and others. Weimar-Munich: Bauhausverlag, 1923.

Svestka, Jiri, ed. *Andor Weininger: Vom Bauhaus zur konzeptuellen Kunst*. Katherine Jánsky and Stefan Kraus, eds. Düsseldorf: Kunstverein für die Rheinlande und Westfalen, 1990.

von Erffa, Helmut. "The Bauhaus Before 1922." *College Art Journal* 3 (November 1943).

———. "Bauhaus: First Phase." *Architectural Review* 122 (August 1957).

Whitford, Frank. *Bauhaus*. London: Thames and Hudson, 1984.

Wingler, Hans M. *The Bauhaus: Weimar, Dessau, Berlin, Chicago*. Translated by Wolfgang Jabs and Basil Gilbert. Joseph Stein, ed. Cambridge, Mass.: The MIT Press, 1969.

SELECTED BACKGROUND MATERIAL

Angress, Werner T. *Stillborn Revolution: The Communist Bid for Power in Germany, 1921–1923*. Princeton, N.J.: Princeton University Press, 1963.

Arbeitsrat für Kunst 1918–1921. Published in connection with an exhibition organized by the Akademie der Künste, Berlin. 29 June–3 August 1980. Berlin: Akademie der Künste, 1980.

Barron, Stephanie, ed. *German Expressionism, 1915–1925: The Second Generation*. Published in connection with an exhibition "German Expressionism, 1915–1922," Los Angeles County Museum of Art, 9 October–31 December 1988. Munich: Prestel-Verlag, 1988.

Bletter, Rosemarie Haag. "Paul Scheerbart's Architectural Fantasies." *Journal of the Society of Architectural Historians* 34 (May 1975).

Buddensieg, Tilmann. *Industriekultur: Peter Behrens and the AEG*. In collaboration with Henning Rogge. Translated by Iain Boyd Whyte. Cambridge, Mass.: The MIT Press, 1984.

Campbell, Joan. *The German Werkbund: The Politics of Reform in the Applied Arts*. Princeton, N.J.: Princeton University Press, 1978.

Conrads, Ulrich, ed. *Programs and Manifestoes on 20th-Century Architecture*. Translated by Michael Bullock. Cambridge, Mass.: The MIT Press, 1970.

————, and Sperlich, Hans G. *The Architecture of Fantasy: Utopian Building and Planning in Modern Times*. New York: Frederick A. Praeger, 1962.

Craig, Gordon A. *Germany, 1866–1945*. New York: Oxford University Press, 1978.

Friedman, Mildred, ed. *De Stijl: 1917–1931; Visions of Utopia*. Walker Art Center, Minneapolis. New York: Abbeville Press, 1982.

Gay, Peter. *Weimar Culture: The Outsider as Insider*. New York: Harper & Row, 1968.

Hanson, Anne Coffin. *Manet and the Modern Tradition*. New Haven: Yale University Press, 1979.

Jaffé, H. L. C. *De Stijl: 1917–1931; The Dutch Contribution to Modern Art*. Cambridge, Mass.: Harvard University Press (Belknap), 1986.

Kessler, Count Harry. *The Diaries of a Cosmopolitan: 1918–1937*. With an introduction by Otto Friedrich. London: Weidenfeld and Nicolson, 1971.

Kirsch, Karin. *The Weissenhofsiedlung: Experimental Housing Built for the Deutscher Werkbund, Stuttgart, 1927*. New York: Rizzoli International Publications, 1989.

Kolb, Eberhard. *The Weimar Republic*. Translated by P. S. Falla. London: Unwin Hyman, 1988.

Kopp, Anatole. *Constructivist Architecture in the USSR*. London and New York: Academy Editions; St. Martins Press, 1985.

Laqueur, Walter. *Weimar: A Cultural History, 1918–1933*. New York: G. P. Putnam's Sons, 1974.

Lissitzky-Küppers, Sophie. *El Lissitzky: Life, Letters, Texts*. With an introduction by Herbert Read. Greenwich, Conn.: New York Graphic Society, 1968.

El Lissitzky, 1890–1941. With a foreword by Peter Nisbet. Th. Schäfer Druckerei GmbH, Hanover: Harvard University Art Museums, 1987.

Lodder, Christina. *Russian Constructivism*. New Haven: Yale University Press, 1983.

Miesel, Victor H., ed. and trans. *Voices of German Expressionism*.

Englewood Cliffs, N.J.: Prentice-Hall, 1970.

Miller Lane, Barbara. *Architecture and Politics in Germany, 1918–1945*. Cambridge, Mass.: Harvard University Press, 1968. Reprint, 1985.

Muthesius, Eckart, and Julius Posener. *Hermann Muthesius: 1861–1927*. Exhibit at the Architectural Assocation in London, 1979. London: The Architectural Association, 1979.

Neumann, J. B. *Confessions of an Art Dealer*. Unpublished manuscript, n.d. Special Collections, J. B. Neumann Collection, The Museum of Modern Art, New York.

Paret, Peter. *The Berlin Secession: Modernism and Its Enemies in Imperial Germany*. Cambridge Mass.: Harvard University Press (Belknap), 1980.

Pevsner, Nikolaus. *Pioneers of Modern Design: From William Morris to Walter Gropius*. 1940. Reprint, Baltimore, Md.: Penguin Books, 1964.

Pommer, Richard, and Christian F. Otto. *Weissenhof 1927 and the Modern Movement in Architecture*. Chicago: The University of Chicago Press, 1991.

Posener, Julius. *Anfänge des Funktionalismus: Von Arts und Crafts Zum Deutschen Werkbund*. Frankfurt am Main: Ullstein, 1964.

————. *Berlin; auf dem Wege zu einer neuen Architektur. Das Zeitalter Wilhelms II*. Munich: Prestel-Verlag, 1979.

————. "Der Deutsche Werkbund." *Werk und Zeit 5* (May 1970).

————. *Fast so alt wie das Jahrhundert*. Berlin: Wolf Jobst Siedler Verlag GmbH, 1990.

————. "Multhesius as Architect." *Lotus 9* (February 1975).

Schneede, Uwe M., ed. *Die Zwanziger Jahre: Manifeste und Dokumente Deutscher Künstler*. DuMont Dokumente. Cologne: DuMont Buchverlag, 1979.

Spengler, Oswald. *The Decline of the West*. 2 vols. 1918 and 1922. Reprint, (2 vols. in 1) translated by Charles Francis Atkinson, New York: Oxford University Press, 1991.

Stites, Richard. *Revolutionary Dreams: Utopian Vision and Experimental Life in the Russian Revolution*. New York: Oxford University Press, 1989.

Taylor, Seth. *Left-Wing Nietzscheans: The Politics of German Expressionism, 1910–1920*. Monographien und Texte zur Nietzsche-Forschung. Berlin: Walter de Gruyter und Co., 1990.

Toller, Ernst. *I Was a German: The Political Turmoil in Germany*

During and After World War I; The Autobiography of a Revolutionary. Translated by Edward Crankshaw. 1933. Reprint, New York: Paragon House, 1991.

Tucholsky, Kurt. *The Kurt Tucholsky Reader: Germany? Germany!* Harry Zohn, ed. Manchester, England: Carcanet Press, 1990.

Van de Velde, Henry. *Geschichte Meines Lebens.* 1959. Reprint, Munich: R. Piper GmbH und Co., K.G., 1986.

von Eckardt, Wolf, and Sander L. Gilman. *Bertolt Brecht's Berlin: A Scrapbook of the Twenties.* Garden City, N.Y.: Anchor Press/Doubleday, 1975.

Washton Long, Rose-Carol, ed. *German Expressionism: Documents from the End of the Wilhelmine Empire to the Rise of National Socialism.* Berkeley: University of California Press, 1993.

Weinstein, Joan. *The End of Expressionism: Art and the November Revolution in Germany, 1918–19.* Chicago: University of Chicago Press, 1990.

Whyte, Iain Boyd. *Bruno Taut and the Architecture of Activism.* Cambridge Urban and Architectural Studies. Cambridge, England: Cambridge University Press, 1982.

Willett, John. *Art and Politics in the Weimar Period: The New Sobriety, 1917–1933.* New York: Pantheon Books, 1978.

Zammito, John H. *The Great Debate: "Bolshevism" and the Literary Left in Germany, 1917–1930.* American University Studies, History. New York: Peter Lang, 1984.

SELECTED WRITINGS ON OR RELEVANT TO AMERICA
AND ITS INTERPRETERS OF THE BAUHAUS

The Armory Show: International Exhibition of Modern Art 1913. 3 vols. Arno Series of Contemporary Art. New York: Arno Press, 1972.

Barr, Alfred H. "Dutch Letter." *The Arts* 13 (January 1928).

————. *Cubism and Abstract Art.* Exhibition catalogue. The Museum of Modern Art, New York. New York: The Museum of Modern Art, 1936. Reprint, 1986.

————. "Modern Architecture." Review of "Modern Architecture" by Henry-Russell Hitchcock Jr. (New York: Payson and Clarke, Ltd., 1929.) *Hound and Horn* 3 (spring 1930).

————. "Russian Diary, 1927–28." *October* 7 (winter 1978).

Barr, Margaret Scolari. "'Our Campaigns,' Alfred H. Barr, Jr., and the Museum of Modern Art: A Biographical Chronicle of the Years 1930–1944." *The New Criterion* special issue (summer 1987).

Brown, Milton W. *The Story of the Armory Show.* 2d ed. New York: Abbeville Press, 1988.

Cook, John W., and Heinrich Klotz. *Conversations with Architects.* New York: Praeger Publishers, 1973.

Egbert, Donald Drew. *Social Radicalism and the Arts: Western Europe.* New York: Alfred A. Knopf, 1970.

————, and Stow Persons, eds. *Socialism and American Life.* Bibliographer T. D. Seymour Bassett. Princeton Studies in American Civilization. Princeton, N.J.: Princeton University Press, 1952.

Goodyear, A. Conger. *The Museum of Modern Art: The First Ten Years.* New York: privately printed, 1943.

Hitchcock, Henry-Russell. "Modern Architecture—A Memoir." *Journal of the Society of Architectural Historians* 27 (December 1968).

————, Philip Johnson, and Lewis Mumford. "Modern Architecture: International Exhibition." In exhibition catalogue, The Museum of Modern Art, New York, 10 February to 23 March 1932. New York: The Museum of Modern Art, 1932.

————. *Modern Architecture: Romanticism and Reintegration.* 1929. Reprint, New York: Hacker Art Books, 1970.

————. "The Decline of Architecture." *The Hound and Horn: A Harvard Miscellany* advance issue (1927).

————."The International Style: Twenty Years After." *Architectural Record* 110 (August 1951).

Johnson, Philip. "Machine Art." In exhibition catalogue, The Museum of Modern Art, 6 March to 30 April 1934. New York: The Museum of Modern Art, 1934.

Lynes, Russell. *Good Old Modern: An Intimate Portrait of the Museum of Modern Art*. New York: Atheneum, 1973.

Marquis, Alice Goldfarb. *Alfred H. Barr Jr.: Missionary for the Modern*. Chicago: Contemporary Books, 1989.

Riley, Terence. *The International Style: Exhibition 15 and The Museum of Modern Art*. Columbia Books of Architecture, Catalogue 3. New York: Rizzoli International Publications, 1992.

Roob, Rona, compiler and editor. "Alfred H. Barr, Jr.: A Chronicle of the Years 1902–1929." *The New Criterion* (summer 1987).

Sandler, Irving, and Amy Newman, eds. *Defining Modern Art: Selected Writings of Alfred H. Barr, Jr.* New York: Harry N. Abrams, 1986.

Schulz, Franz. *Philip Johnson: Life and Work*. New York: Alfred A. Knopf, 1994.

Searing, Helen. "International Style: The Crimson Connection." *Progressive Architecture* 2 (February 1982).

Wilson, Richard Guy. "International Style: The MoMA Exhibition." *Progressive Architecture* 2 (February 1982).

Index